D0919867

Victors Divided

Victors Divided

America and the Allies in Germany, 1918-1923

KEITH L. NELSON

UNIVERSITY OF CALIFORNIA PRESS
Berkeley   Los Angeles   London
1975

University of California Press
Berkeley and Los Angeles, California
University of California Press, Ltd.
London, England

ISBN: 0-520-02315-3
Library of Congress Catalog Card Number: 72-87203
Copyright © 1975 by The Regents of the University of California

Printed in the United States of America

*For my mother and father,
in affection
and friendship*

Contents

Contents

Preface

The history of American foreign policy following World War I appears commonly to have suffered from a certain narrowness of perspective. Indeed, to a surprising degree, scholars of this subject seem to have focused their attention either on America's rejection of the League of Nations or on the postwar expansion of American business and finance. As a result, discussions too often revolve around such simplifications as "the retreat from internationalism" or "the growth of economic imperialism." And though an awareness of widespread postwar concern regarding bolshevism has recently developed, historians threaten to overdo this insight as well.

It seems sounder to conceive of American policies during this period in a more general way, centering them in the attempt of the American leadership to cope effectively with the impact of war. This effort to recreate and bolster the "natural," that is, liberal, order took a number of forms—multilateral and unilateral, political and economic, public and private. From our present vantage point, perhaps not much was undertaken, largely because most Americans ("liberals" as well as "conservatives") were slow to recognize that World War I had undermined rather than strengthened the relationships they considered natural. But such proposals as the French Security Treaty (1919) and the American mandate over Armenia (1920) indicate that Woodrow Wilson did ultimately do more to counteract "instability" than simply to preach self-determination and to champion a league of nations. And after the Republicans refused to ratify the president's more ambitious projects, thereby severely complicating the cause of peace, they too began to develop stabilizing strategies. In fact, the Harding-Coolidge administration was inspired at times to innovate with considerable vigor, as demonstrated by the program of the Washington Conference (1921) and the establishment of the Dawes Plan (1924). If international "normalcy" was a long time in coming, refusing to make its appearance at least until 1925, Americans did play a crucial role in shaping it and in timing its arrival.

The central problem, of course, was the reintegration of Germany into the family of nations, a task that involved supervising that nation suitably, reinforcing its new government, and, in general, helping the country to relate to its neighbors. Unlike the victor states after World War II, Britain, France, and the United States did not on this occasion feel compelled to attempt a thoroughgoing and long-term intervention within the fabric of German society.* Nevertheless, because the French (and to some degree, the Belgians) possessed much more extensive notions than did their allies about the "managing" of Germany, British and American statesmen were confronted with a difficult challenge in creating a peace that they could endorse. Again and again, at the peace conference and later, they found themselves opposing French proposals and supporting more lenient territorial, military, and/or finan-

---

* This is not to say that there were not parallels. The "first" Amercian occupation of Germany was considered similar enough to the "second" in 1944–45, for example, that in the preparation of personnel for the latter, "Colonel I. L. Hunt's report on military government in the Rhineland became a sort of 'bible,' and had it been carefully heeded in practice, at least some of the later mistakes in Germany might have been avoided" (Harold Zink, *The United States in Germany, 1944–1955* [Princeton, 1957], p. 12). See also United States, Army, Office of Military Government, *Hunt Report Digest: American Military Government of Occupied Germany, 1918–1920* (United States Zone of Germany, 1946); Hajo Holborn, *American Military Government: Its Origins and Policies* (Washington, 1947), pp. 2–3; and Carl J. Friedrich et al., *American Experiences in Military Government in World War II* (New York, 1948), pp. 24–25.

cial arrangements for the defeated enemy. Moreover, following the Senate's rejection of the Treaty of Versailles, as Anglo-American coordination faltered, they found their efforts meeting with less and less success.

The American occupation in Germany from 1918 to 1923 presents a long-neglected opportunity for a study of developing American attitudes and contributions in this situation. Established without prior intent, prolonged through compromise and accident, perpetuated as much to restrain an ally as to impress a former foe, the American part of the Rhineland occupation mirrored in revealing fashion the way in which Americans came slowly to realize what they confronted in fostering peace. It also constituted the most direct and important means, aside from policies on trade and war debts, by which the United States influenced European affairs.

In the beginning, to be sure, most Americans could only view this occupation as a kind of unnecessary necessity. Their conceptions of the European world scarcely justified such an activity. They had acquired little desire to punish the Hun or forcibly to transform him. They found almost incomprehensible French fears of German power or French hopes that the Rhineland might be induced to leave the Reich. As a result, once Americans had agreed to participate (first under the armistice, later under the treaty), most of them wanted to be finished with the occupation as quickly as possible.

Yet Wilson, Harding, and many others ultimately saw good reasons for continuing to maintain the American establishment on the Rhine. Even before peace was signed, it was generally agreed that the army had become an example of considerable significance in moderating the occupation. In later months Americans discovered that their troops had also become a balance wheel in a precarious regional equilibrium, and that no one dared to dispense with them for fear of triggering a European explosion. Meanwhile, the existence of an American zone had obviously been a useful tool for the United States in such negotiations as those regarding the separate peace or the repayment of the occupation costs. And, if the American public did not always understand what its military people were doing at Coblenz, American representation there was nevertheless recognized in the United States as important in reestablishing foreign markets.

All in all, the American occupation was widely acknowledged as performing a constructive international function. The tragedy was that, until the advent of the Ruhr crisis in 1922–1923, American leaders failed to take its accomplishment as a spur to a more vigorous attack upon the basic problems left unresolved since the war.

May I take this opportunity to express my appreciation to some of the many persons who have aided me with this project. To begin with, I am deeply indebted to the librarians and archivists of the universities and depositaries that are listed in my bibliography. Among the individuals who assisted me I am particularly grateful to Hans Stephan Brather in Potsdam, Mme. Desmed-Thielemans in Brussells, Colonel Pierre Le Goyet at the Service Historique de l'Armée in Paris, Laura Cooper of the Cabinet Office in London, Colonel W. B. R. Neave Hill of the Ministry of Defence Library in London, Kenneth Duckett of the Ohio Historical Society, and Irene Kozlov and Agnes Peterson of the Hoover Institute at Stanford.

My debts to the late Wallace Day, the former American Deputy High Commissioner in the Rhineland, who became a true friend and who guided me with interviews and with countless letters, are incalculable. But others who participated in the occupation drama have helped me as well, including Walter Lippmann, Generals William B. Ruggles and Troy Middleton of the United States Army, Comte Raoul de Liedekerke, the former Belgian Deputy High Commissioner, Lady Maie Casey (sister of Colonel Rupert Ryan), Mme. André Isambert (wife of the French legal adviser in the Rhineland), and Mme. la Générale Charles Mangin. I have also been greatly assisted by relatives of the individuals in my story, especially by Constance Noyes Robertson, Sinclair Weeks, Amory Houghton, Lord Kilmarnock, Major Donald Robertson (son of Sir Malcolm Robertson), Lord Scarsdale (nephew of the Marquess of Curzon), Lord Robertson of Oakridge (son of Field Marshal Sir William Robertson), and Mme. Becourt-Foch.

Let me add to this my thanks to research committees of the University of California and University of Texas for grants that helped to defray the cost of travel and of photocopying, and to scholars at other universities who have provided useful advice, information, and/or encouragement: George Giacomini, David Levering, Charles Burdick, William Fletcher, Peter Stern, Stephen Shuker, Thomas A. Bailey, Seth Tillman, Larry Gelfand, David Trask, Frank Vandiver, H. Wayne Morgan, Paul Seabury, Hans Kohn, Herbert Strauss, Hajo Holborn, Arthur Link, and Arno Mayer.

Lastly, let me include a special word of appreciation to those who have labored with me on the manuscript itself—my typists (and "part-time" editors), Cathy Smith, Natalie Korp, Charlotte Diament, and Barbara Ellerbrock, my "Doktor Vater," Armin Rappaport, my teacher and counsellor, Raymond J. Sontag, my former colleagues but continuing friends, Loyd Swenson and William Braisted, and my present colleagues at UCI, Henry Cord Meyer, Arthur Marder, Jon Jacobson, and Spencer C. Olin, Jr.

K. L. N.

1

AN ARMISTICE OCCUPATION

> You will observe that the views expressed by the
> military men as to conditions of so-called armistice
> are quite as much political as they are military and
> probably foreshadow peace demands . . .
>
> General Tasker Bliss to
> Secretary of War New-
> ton Baker, October 23,
> 1918.

As the guns finally stopped firing on November 11, 1918,
probably most Americans would not have believed that it
would be four more years before the last of their expeditionary forces returned from Germany. With no desire to involve
their nation permanently in Europe and with little awareness
of what was in fact occurring there, they could hardly have
anticipated, much less appreciated, the events that would require their army to remain so long abroad. Granted, after the
French had insisted on writing a military occupation into the
armistice, Americans had willingly accepted a role in the endeavor, largely because they assumed that the enemy deserved
to experience the taste of war and because they knew that a
cease-fire was no guarantee of peace. Yet undoubtedly the
New York Times had spoken on behalf of the entire nation
the previous September when it described any suggestion of
"holding German cities and forts" as completely "beyond the
pale of reason."[1] By late October President Woodrow Wilson
and others had begun to doubt the wisdom of even a tempo-

1

rary occupation, fearing, from the increasing evidence at hand, that France possessed ulterior motives in pursuing such a venture.

A people at war seldom thinks carefully of peace, but why did Americans of 1917–1918 so completely disregard or overlook the possibility of a postwar military occupation in Germany? Certainly it was not because the nation was unfamiliar with such a phenomenon or, for that matter, with the aftereffects of a devastating conflict. In the South following the Civil War, and more recently in the Philippines and in Central America, United States armed forces had been faced with various types of reconstruction and police work.

The explanation, apparently, is that Americans were simply not ready to think of themselves as part of the European world. The vast majority of people in this era remained quite isolationist in spirit, at least so far as Europe was concerned. Though they had been brought to a fighting anger by the German submarine and caught up in a crusade against the Kaiser, they saw no reason why the World War, any more than Thomas Jefferson's war against the Barbary pirates, should force America to abandon traditional policies.[2] President Monroe's doctrine of mutual noninvolvement still made good sense to those who assumed as they did that Europe was both distant and almost consciously perverse.[3] They tended to believe that, as soon as the fighting ended, their own task would be "over, over there."[4]

Those individuals who did realize how rapidly the world was shrinking fell largely into two groups, both of which, for different reasons, ignored the problem of postwar Germany as much as did the isolationists. The more conservative internationalists (frequently wealthy, Eastern Republicans) revealed a strong Darwinian perspective, tending to think of the war as part of each nation's continuing struggle for power and survival.[5] These "unilateralists" saw the outcome in terms of a weaker Germany, but not of a very different one.[6] Theodore Roosevelt, their leading representative, was so pessimistic about real change abroad that he could support an international league only "as an addition to, and never a substitute for, the policy of preparing our own strength for our own defense."[7]

Other internationalists, reflecting the more benign side of nineteenth-century liberalism, maintained a greater faith in man's essential goodness and ability to redeem himself. Such Americans (generally those of the liberal Left) looked for the early appearance of a system of rationally motivated, self-governing nations, including Germany.[8] They also assumed that the experience of war and defeat would be sufficient to discredit the Kaiser and his clique in the eyes of a fundamentally democratic people.[9] As the *Chicago Daily News* proclaimed, "Our task is to bring the Germans to the point of themselves spewing forth all Hohenzollerns and all Junkers . . ."[10]

Thus neither isolationists nor internationalists of either variety saw a need to give much thought to the future of Germany. To them, victory in battle was all that was necessary. Indeed, Americans were almost totally lacking in a realistic attitude toward the peace, that is to say, the disposition to employ their power to achieve limited modifications in the structure of the defeated nation.[11] Few were even aware that the aftereffects of war or the policies of allies might complicate the postwar relationship of the United States and Germany.

Nevertheless, despite the lack of obvious interest in an occupation, mounting war fever had fostered a widespread desire to deliver the knockout blow against the enemy within the Reich.[12] Conservative publicists like George Harvey had become particularly insistent that it was not possible "to whip

3

the Germans outside of Germany,"[13] while even the moderate *New York Tribune* contended that the foe must be defeated on his "own soil."[14] By October President Wilson was "alarmed at the temper of some of our people..., [who] want us to devastate Germany as Germany has devastated other countries."[15] Yet officials like Secretary of the Treasury William Gibbs McAdoo were urging citizens to "keep hitting hard and smashing harder.... That is the way to eliminate the Rhine [*sic*]; that is the way to open an American parade on Unter den Linden."[16]

Perhaps sentiments like these would not have generated widespread approval for an occupation if Germany had surrendered unconditionally. But because the armistice neither completely disarmed the enemy nor compelled his ultimate capitulation, it seemed obvious that military sanctions must be obtained in order to preserve the Allied advantage. In this way the desire for a smashing triumph and the need for an armistice guarantee worked together to make good sense of a march to the Rhine. When President Wilson read the armistice to an assembled Congress on November 11, his references to the occupation twice resulted in sustained applause.[17] The *New York Times* concluded shortly that such a requirement was "just as necessary as fighting itself."[18]

Wilson himself, however, was not as pleased as might have been expected regarding this particular armistice provision. Indifferent earlier to the possibility of an occupation in Germany, he had recently become uneasy about the enthusiasm for the idea displayed by the French. During the last few days he had gone so far as to discourage his spokesmen at the armistice negotiations from agreeing that Allied troops should be sent to the Rhine.

An optimist in the sense that he hoped for a radical transformation of international affairs, this former professor and college president was realistic enough throughout the conflict to have remained very skeptical of Allied objectives. While he was certain that "when the war is over we can force them [the Allies] to our way of thinking,"[19] Wilson had never been willing to leave the peace conference entirely to the future. Beginning with his January 1918 speech on the Fourteen Points, he had striven to reinforce and coordinate the voices of international reform and national moderation in both the Allied and enemy camps.[20] Even earlier, in September 1917, the president had asked his confidant and friend, "Colonel" Edward M. House, to assemble a body of experts to "prepare our case with a full knowledge of the position of all the litigants" and to ascertain "what influences we can use."[21] It was three members of the colonel's "Inquiry" group who had put together the detailed war aims memoranda on which the president relied in formulating his Fourteen Points.[22]

Nowhere in these memoranda, though, nor in the later work of the Inquiry before the armistice, is there evidence that the prospect of postwar military intervention in Germany had been studied.[23] This fact is particularly astonishing when one considers that in November 1917 the Bolsheviks had published a French-Tsarist agreement that envisaged the creation of an independent Rhineland occupied by Allied armies until after Berlin had fulfilled all terms of peace.[24] In spite of this disclosure and the president's skepticism of Allied diplomacy, American experts found it as difficult as the public to foresee an occupation.

Wilson's speeches and papers indicate that until the month before the armistice he gave little attention to the schemes suggested by the Franco-Russian understanding. True, in the eighth of his Fourteen Points he refused to endorse "the demand for complete return" of Alsace-Lorraine to France,[25] but, according to Walter Lippmann of the Inquiry, in doing this he was motivated largely by a desire to exclude French claims to the Saar.[26] None of the other Fourteen Points, with the exception of the one requiring Polish independence, in any way affected Germany specifically and directly. In the president's succeeding addresses of 1918 the closest he came to discussing German affairs was to demand "destruction of every arbitrary power" and "territorial settlements for the benefit of the people immediately concerned."[27] His private correspondence was equally devoid of references.

If Americans and their president had better discerned what war had done to France, however, they would have given much more thought to French intentions regarding Germany. The relative silence of the French public regarding the peace masked what was in reality an intense and even obsessive concern. Lack of discussion of the subject was due primarily to the press censorship with which the government sought to counteract a growth of pacifism, especially strong among parties of the Left.[28]

Invasion and years of fighting had bequeathed the French not only hatred and insecurity, but also leaders who reflected the fears of the nation in their conviction that peace must bring, above all else, a reduction in Germany's physical strength. Though there were several means to this end, conservatives and military men had long contended that the most effective would be to take the Rhine region from the Reich, both because of that area's historical ties to France and because of its strategic location.[29] By late 1916 the government of Aristide Briand had made this policy its own, and in February of the following year it had entered into the secret agreement with the tsar mentioned above.[30] Developments at the end of the war and later indicate that the government of Georges Clemenceau continued to pursue the objective of separating, or at least neutralizing and occupying, the German Rhineland.[31]

The British had been much less cooperative than the Russians regarding French proposals. Though Briand had directed his ambassador to sound out London in January 1917 concerning a Rhenish buffer state, and though the latter had waited several months for the right moment to do so, in the end the British foreign secretary, Lord Balfour, had given him no encouragement at all for what Balfour privately considered a "rather wild project." Almost half a year later Balfour explained to Parliament that he could not believe such an idea represented any fixed part of French foreign policy. He had not even bothered to inform the prime minister, David Lloyd George, of the ambassador's inquiries.[32]

After the Franco-Russian agreement had been revealed to the world, the British were forced to take French designs more seriously, but aside from their francophile ambassador in Paris almost no one found convincing reasons to endorse them. British conservatives were as power-conscious as the French, but they regarded a "German threat" more in terms of ships and navies than of geography or population. The British people as a whole were less fearful of a resurgent Germany than were their Continental neighbors.[33]

At the beginning of January 1918, when revolution in Russia and growing pacifism at home compelled Lloyd George (as the Liberal leader of a Conservative-Liberal-Labour Coalition) to speak out on war aims, he proclaimed a program in many ways similar to the one President Wilson would shortly enunciate. Though the prime minister committed himself to returning Alsace-Lorraine to France, he was even more explicit than Wilson would be about the importance of self-determination in the territorial settlement. In fact, his assertion that Britain had "never aimed at the break-up of the German people" indicated a greater cognizance of and opposition to extremist currents in France than was to be found in Washington at the time.[34]

The crucial factors, then, were these. Neither the American nor the British public demanded that Germany be occupied by Allied armies after the war. Neither the American nor the British government evinced special interest in performing such a task. Only the French desired an occupation of the Rhineland, and only the French wanted to see a separation of that region from the Reich.

How, in that case, did the Allies come to occupy the left bank of the Rhine under the armistice agreement? Why could not the French be brought to accept some other form of safeguard, at least for the time being? How was one nation able to secure its peculiar interests in the face of unsympathetic allies?

The answer, of course, is that French negotiators in the prearmistice talks insisted upon an armistice occupation and refused to be satisfied without it. They knew that their countrymen expected a measure of revenge for the military incursions of 1871 and 1914–1918. They also realized that, unless the German army were removed to German soil, France would suffer renewed destruction if the armistice collapsed and fighting broke out again. Above all, they sensed that this was an unparalleled opportunity to put the French army into the very area that they hoped the peace conference would allow them to control. An Allied military presence in the Rhineland would make it much easier for the peacemakers to establish permanent arrangements there that were satisfactory to France.

Faced with French initiative and intransigence, American and British representatives found themselves relatively helpless. Their powers of resistance had been undermined by their own eagerness for peace and by their antagonism toward the enemy. Their negotiating positions had been weakened by the absence of previous commitments from France and by their lack of an agreed-upon alternative for guaranteeing the armistice.

Most of all, American and British statesmen had been handicapped by their failure to recognize the extent to which the French were attempting to bypass the Fourteen Points. On the American side, only the president and a few others had even begun to sense the truth, while Colonel House, Wilson's envoy at the final meetings, had been so determined to secure the acceptance of the President's formulas that he disregarded almost everything else. Among the British, Lloyd George had at one time clearly understood what the French were doing, but as the days passed he apparently had lost sight of it in his growing desire to end the war.

The story of the negotiations begins in Paris on October 5, 1918, following Germany's unexpected armistice appeal to Woodrow Wilson. Premiers Lloyd George, Clemenceau, and Vittorio Orlando of Italy were meeting on that date to discuss military strategy, but the sudden announcement of the German note forced them to undertake a major revision of agenda. Since they were certain that Germany was trying to lead the American president into compromising his allies, it behooved them to explore at once what kind of an agreement with Berlin would be desirable.[35]

Among other things, the three men talked much now of the need for military advice, partially because they hoped to hasten the transfer of negotiations from Washington to Paris. Indeed, after Wilson had informed the Germans on October 8 that he could not endorse an armistice without provision for withdrawal from invaded territory, Lloyd George expressed keen disappointment that such a matter had not been left up to the generals.[36] Within hours the Allied leaders had dispatched a cable to the president to emphasize their belief that terms must be dependent upon the estimates of the military professionals.[37]

Yet the margin and kind of armistice superiority necessary

to a victor is also dependent upon political factors (e.g., the type of treaty that is intended) and the Allied premiers were clearly aware of this fact. In referring the armistice question to the military representatives of the Supreme War Council,[38] for example, they revealed in their instructions a definite concern for certain of their minimum political objectives. In this instance they specified that the terms must at least require (1) the evacuation of all Allied countries, (2) a withdrawal from Alsace-Lorraine, and (3) the retirement of the German army to the far side of the Rhine.[39]

The military representatives convened on October 8, and quickly followed the lead of the premiers. In truth, the generals seemed as much aware of political considerations as were their chiefs. In addition to the withdrawal of German forces behind the Rhine, they urged an almost complete disarmament of the enemy, as well as Allied occupation of certain fortresses in northern France and Alsace-Lorraine.[40]

The American military representative, General Tasker Bliss, had been absent from the discussions because of illness, but his reactions to the recommendations provide a vivid insight into what had occurred. In letters to Secretary of War Newton Baker at this time, Bliss bewailed Allied "militarism," or the tendency of the military people to make decisions that should be left to the peace conference:

> It is an absolute surrender we must have. But in order to get that surrender the conditions which are to follow it should be determined in advance and made known. All of the military proposals I have seen plainly embody or point to the political conditions which will exist after the so-called armistice is agreed to. . . . These political conditions imposed by military men may be such as to keep the whole world in turmoil for many years to come.[41]

When Bliss penned these lines he was referring not only to the ideas of the military representatives, but also to those put forward by Marshal Ferdinand Foch. This renowned officer, commander-in-chief of the Allied armies, had been asked by Clemenceau as early as October 5 to make a study of possible armistice conditions.[42] Three days later, apparently without reference to the considerations of the military representatives, Foch had addressed a message to the premiers in which he summarized the terms that he considered essential. The heads of government had then invited him to expound his views before them at Quai d'Orsay.

What Foch suggested on these occasions amounted to the first open proposal for an Allied occupation of the Rhineland. Briefly, he demanded (1) that the German army evacuate Allied territory and Alsace-Lorraine within an early time limit, (2) that Allied armies occupy bridgeheads on the east bank of the Rhine with radii of thirty kilometers from Rastatt, Strassburg, and Neu Breisach, and (3) that the Allies occupy the left bank of the Rhine as a security for the payment of reparations. The bridgeheads, he contended, were especially important as a "suitable military base of departure" in case the enemy should renew the war.[43]

Despite the best efforts of Foch and the generals, however, the civilian leaders at the Paris sessions tended to think that the proposals of all the military men were too extreme to be acceptable. As of October 9 the situation in Germany was still largely unknown, and the premiers were afraid that by asking too much they might scare off the enemy.[44] Rather than endorse a specific plan, they preferred to adjourn their conference and await events.

As it happened, the negotiations between Berlin and Washington grew steadily more promising for the Allies. The German chancellor's reply to Wilson of October 12 announced his government's readiness to discuss actual details and thus provided the first proof that the enemy was serious about making peace. Moreover, the president now felt

11

impelled by recent submarine sinkings as well as by developments in Paris to take a tougher line against the Germans. In his communication of October 14 he even stipulated to Berlin that the requirements of the armistice must be left to the judgment and advice of the military advisors.[45]

This second American note went a considerable distance toward relieving Allied anxiety about Wilson's diplomacy, but much distrust still remained beneath the surface in both the British and French capitals. The early endeavors of Lloyd George and Clemenceau to ensure Allied war aims by writing certain political stipulations into their projected armistice have been described. Now, with Germany obviously reeling toward defeat, Lloyd George became pointedly explicit about the wisdom of obtaining clauses in the armistice approximating those that Britain would demand of the future treaty. As a result, British naval authorities completely redrafted their moderate proposals of October 8 to provide for the surrender of the entire German fleet.[46]

It was not as easy to apply Lloyd George's dictum to affairs of the army. In War Cabinet discussions Lord Balfour and others tended to support the view of the chief of the Imperial Staff, General Sir Henry Wilson, who argued that an armistice should stipulate "real guarantees, i.e., occupation of Boche territory," or terms similar to those suggested by Marshal Foch in Paris on October 8. The prime minister and certain colleagues, on the other hand, were more impressed with the ideas of the army commander, Marshal Sir Douglas Haig, who contended that the situation warranted asking only for what the victors would permanently hold. To Haig, this meant German evacuation of France, Belgium, and Alsace-Lorraine, as well as Allied occupation of Metz and Strassburg. He expressed opposition to allowing the French to enter Germany "to pay off old scores."[47]

Meanwhile, Premier Clemenceau found his principal commander increasingly concerned that there be no "slip-up" regarding the Rhineland.[48] In a letter to Clemenceau of October 16, Foch had reaffirmed his contention that German evacuations and Allied bridgeheads on the Rhine were military essentials, adding that the occupation of the left bank was an indispensable guarantee for "obtaining reparations." By implication he also pointed up his own potential usefulness in the negotiations, complaining that President Wilson's use of the words "military advisors" was ambiguous and asserting that only the commanders-in-chief of the armies (not the military representatives of the Supreme War Council), were qualified to deal with a definition of military superiority. Verging on presumption, the marshal asked to be kept fully informed about decisions of the government and even touched upon the most sensitive questions of all: "After reparations have been paid, what is to be the fate of those [Rhenish] territories? Are we going to annex a part of the country, or to favor the creation of neutral, autonomous, or independent states . . .?"[49]

Though Clemenceau's response to this letter was to rebuke Foch severely for mixing in politics, the premier was basically not unsympathetic to his marshal.[50] There can be little doubt that Clemenceau was fully convinced at this point of the desirability of radical and permanent changes on the eastern frontier. Furthermore, he was not adverse to using his military "experts" to do exactly what Lloyd George was doing, that is, to move as far as possible in the armistice negotiations toward his ultimate objectives. This fact must have become clear to the French High Command on October 24, after President Wilson had finally turned over his "separate" negotiations to the Allies and after Clemenceau had called Foch and General Philippe Petain (the French army commander) to the Ministry of War to receive new instructions.[51] The marshal was now directed to convene the commanders-in-chief of the Allied armies in order to obtain their views on the nature of an armistice.[52] He was also told that the French premier expected to find the occupation of the left bank of the Rhine among the final armistice provisions.[53]

As a result of these orders, a conference of Foch, Petain, Haig, and John J. Pershing took place on October 25 at French headquarters in Senlis. It was a rather brief and formal meeting. Marshal Haig spoke first, contending that since the German army was not yet broken, terms of a cease-fire must be moderate if they were to be acceptable to the foe. His position was essentially the same as he had taken at the sessions of the British war cabinet several days before. He maintained that in the event hostilities were renewed, it would be better to have the Germans astride the Rhine than entrenched upon the other side.

General Petain emphasized that an armistice should grant the victors both guarantees for its continued existence and the assurance that the enemy would resume fighting only at a disadvantage. He argued that an occupation of the left bank and bridgeheads on the far side would fully meet these requirements. In addition, however, he demanded the surrender of considerable railroad stock and, in order to deprive the enemy of precious material, rigid time limits on the German retreat. He also inadvertently disclosed what some Frenchmen hoped to do with reparations "guarantees" by speaking of an indemnity so large that Germany would never be able to pay it.

General Pershing's recommendations were apparently made in total ignorance of the hidden side of the debate. Two days before, Haig had received the distinct impression that Pershing agreed with his analysis of the situation.[54] Now the American seemed in almost complete accord with Petain, except that he preferred to occupy only the Rhine bridgeheads and also wanted a prohibition on German submarine warfare.[55] The truth was that though Pershing felt as Haig did that the enemy was still unbeaten, he was willing to concede that

French armistice terms were severe enough to guarantee Allied predominance.[56]

Marshal Foch did not attempt the formulation of a combined report at Senlis, but instead took advantage of his position as Allied commander to proceed to Paris with a new draft of his own. He explored this with Clemenceau on the evening of October 25, and submitted it as his recommendation to the premier on the following day. As one might have expected, his armistice ideas were similar to those that Petain had presented. The principal difference was that the marshal's provided for a neutral zone on the right bank forty kilometers wide.[57] This stipulation was probably included to counter Haig's argument that the enemy's army would be stronger on the other side of the river than at the German border.

In Washington, informed of the results of the Senlis conference, President Wilson reacted swiftly against Pershing's tendency to go along with French suggestions. Under the impact of such information as Bliss was sending,[58] the president was becoming increasingly skeptical of Allied intentions. In a conversation of October 16, for example, he had voiced the conviction that Germany must return Alsace-Lorraine, neither more nor less, to France,[59] and by the time he met his cabinet on October 22, Wilson could remark that the victors were "getting to a point where they were reaching out for more than they should have in justice."[60] Not surprisingly, then, on October 27, Secretary of War Baker cabled General Pershing that

> [the President] raises . . . [a] question as to whether it is necessary for an Allied or American army to occupy Alsace and Lorraine when evacuated under [the] Armistice. . . . [He also] doubts . . . the advisability of requiring Allied or American occupation on the eastern side of the Rhine, as that is practically an invasion of German soil under the Armistice.[61]

It was not to be the president, the secretary, or the general, however, who would finally establish American policy regarding these matters, but the honorary Texas colonel who arrived in Paris on October 26 as Woodrow Wilson's special envoy. This was Colonel House's fourth diplomatic assignment in Europe, where he had represented the president in 1913, 1916, and 1917. By no stretch of the imagination could he be called ignorant of European politics or conditions,[62] and indeed, in September 1918, he had warned the president that the time had come to commit the "reactionaries in authority in Europe to as much of the American peace program as possible."[63] Before leaving Washington on October 14, he had had lengthy discussions with Wilson, afterward noting in his diary that "neither the President nor I desire a vengeful peace. [Nor does] he desire to have the Allied armies ravage Germany. . . ."[64] Nonetheless, it is significant that House had left the United States while Wilson was still thinking in terms of avoiding the humiliation of the enemy rather than of frustrating the ambitions of the Allies.

Upon the colonel's arrival in the French capital, General Bliss quickly cautioned him against "[armistice] conditions which . . . foreshadow . . . certain of the peace terms,"[65] but the general's advice did not have lasting impact. House did at first evince dismay at Foch's demands[66] as well as considerable interest in Bliss's alternative proposal for a thoroughgoing disarmament of the enemy.[67] Yet soon, apparently, he came to see the controversy as a difference of opinion among technicians, and he implied as much in sending a request to Pershing "to get in touch with Marshals Foch and Haig and see if their views could be reconciled."[68] By October 28, House was even willing to accept at face value Foch's assertion that the Germans would not consent to complete disarmament;[69] this, even though he had heard Clemenceau affirm as his own and Foch's opinion that "Germany was so thoroughly beaten she would accept any terms offered. . . ."[70]

The counsel that House received from other Americans was

none too helpful in revealing the basic issues. Admiral William S. Benson expressed some concern about the Allied Naval Council's acceptance of the British naval terms (confiscating the enemy fleet), but rather than pressing for reconsideration of the decision, he desired only to obtain a pledge that in the peace treaty the ships would not be distributed among the victors.[71] General Pershing forwarded the message from Washington in which the president had criticized his commander's Senlis proposals, but at the same time Pershing reaffirmed his belief that if there actually were an armistice "the conditions laid down by Marshal Foch seem to be such as would protect very completely the interests of the Allies. . . ."[72]

Even the transatlantic cable seemed to conspire against House, to rob him of the president's growing insight. On October 29, the very day the colonel began his formal meetings with the premiers, Wilson sent him a message that went considerably beyond the instructions he had earlier dispatched to Pershing. The communication, as House received it, read in part as follows: "Too much *severity* on the part of the Allies will make a genuine peace settlement exceedingly difficult, if not impossible." Actually, the wire was badly garbled in transmission and completely altered in tone. The President had originally stated that he was becoming certain that "too much *success* or *security* on the part of the Allies will make a genuine peace settlement exceedingly difficult."[73]

House's interest in the military terms of the armistice was undoubtedly further diminished by his overriding desire to win formal approval for Wilson's program. "It seems to me of the utmost importance to have the Allies accept the Fourteen Points and the subsequent terms of the President," he noted on October 28, adding that "if this is done, the basis of a peace will already have been made."[74] With such an attitude on his part it is little wonder that the inter-Allied discussions quickly came to center upon the American prescription.

The colonel soon discovered, however, that Germany's impending defeat had made the Allies less eager than ever to follow Wilson. The first session with Lloyd George, Clemenceau, and Baron Sonnino, the Italian foreign minister, made little apparent progress in ratifying the Fourteen Points. Clemenceau claimed to be disturbed about the provisions for "open covenants," Lloyd George raised his long-standing objections to "freedom of the seas," and Sonnino suggested that Wilson be informed that his terms were simply not acceptable. House found it necessary to threaten that if the Allies persisted on this course, the president might consider the advisability of a separate peace with Germany and Austria. At length, Lloyd George suggested attempting a draft of reservations to the original propositions, and after considerable French and Italian grumbling, this proposal was adopted.[75]

Deeply worried, House left the conference casting about for a solution to the avalanche of objections he expected at the next meeting. His diary of the following day records what happened to him later:

> This morning around three o'clock, I was awakened by the motor-cycles of our messengers leaving the house with dispatches. . . . I fell to thinking about the dilemma I was in with the three Prime Ministers. It then occurred to me there was a way out of the difficulty. I would tell them that if they did not accept the President's Fourteen Points . . . , I would advise the President to go before Congress and lay the facts before it . . . and ask . . . [its] advice. . . . I turned over and went to sleep, knowing I had found a solution of a very troublesome problem.[76]

As it developed, October 30 was indeed the crucial day. At the start of the morning discussion, Lloyd George presented House with a proposed answer to the president establishing reservations on "freedom of the seas" and "reparations." Then, when it became clear that Clemenceau was having an elaborate brief prepared setting forth added stipulations, House decided to release his "bombshell." According to him, it was all that was needed: "Clemenceau at once abandoned his idea . . . and apparently accepted the proposed answer drafted by the British." Writing the next evening, the colonel felt that, as a result, "everything is changed for the better since yesterday."

Several facts, however, compel the historian to ask if House correctly understood the motivations of his colleagues. First, House had earlier made an almost identical threat with his reference to a separate peace, but at that time the reaction of his fellow conferees had not been out of the ordinary. Second, General Mordacq, an adviser to Clemenceau, writing at a later date, reported that the French premier had also had trouble sleeping the night before, but that, unlike the colonel, *he* had been worrying about the Rhineland.[77] Last, at the end of this session (on the morning of October 30), which had lasted a total of forty-five minutes, House reported to the president that the group had also talked about other matters:

> [Lloyd] George stated that he thought it might be unwise to insist on the occupation . . . of the Rhine. Clemenceau stated that he could not maintain himself in the Chamber of Deputies unless this was made a part of the armistice . . . , and that the French army would also insist on this as their due . . . ; but he gave us his word of honor that France would withdraw after the peace conditions had been fulfilled. I am inclined to sympathize with the position taken by Clemenceau.[78]

It thus seems highly probable that the thirtieth was a turning point for reasons other than those House believed.

Still, is it not possible that the colonel had subtly offered Clemenceau a *quid pro quo*, recognizing the need to reassure the Frenchman regarding the Rhine before the latter committed himself to the realms of Wilsonian idealism? This is certainly conceivable, and House may have so acted almost without realizing it, but the evidence indicates otherwise. For one thing, the colonel continued to speak of the military advisers without any apparent suspicion of their motives. As he later confessed to Sir Eric Geddes, "I would [in any case] have followed England in the naval terms as I had followed Marshal Foch in the military terms."[79] Even more noteworthy was House's failure to grasp the extent to which, at the time of the peace conference, the military situation would restrict the alternatives before the president. "I can assure you," he cabled Wilson the day after endorsing the occupation of the Rhineland, "that nothing will be done to embarrass you or to compromise any of your peace principles. You will have as free a hand after the Armistice is signed as you now have."[80] Beyond much doubt, House had been "held up" in the negotiations and did not realize it.

In the meantime, the occupation project had not remained inviolable. Mounting British pressures had compelled Foch to eliminate the Strassburg bridgehead, for example,[81] and to narrow the neutral strip on the right bank from forty kilometers to thirty kilometers south from Mannheim. He had also limited the occupying army's right to requisition from the public, though he had specified that the upkeep of the troops would be paid for by the Germans.[82]

Even so, Lloyd George still had to be convinced when the heads of government and Colonel House met Marshal Foch on November 1. Only after considerable debate with the marshal did the prime minister finally accept an occupation, and even then he insisted upon putting Haig's military terms into the record. If the armistice were so "stiff" that Germany continued to fight, he said, the Allied chiefs must be known to have examined all available alternatives.[83]

But why did Lloyd George agree to Foch's arrangements? Perhaps the lack of support from Colonel House had convinced him that he had little choice. He may also have feared that French approval of British naval terms would not otherwise be forthcoming.[84] And he may have been reassured somewhat about the future of the Rhineland by Clemenceau's promise of ultimate troop withdrawal.[85] Probably, however, the deciding factor for Lloyd George was Foch's confidence that the enemy would accept an occupation.

Indeed, the course of the discussion reveals that the prime minister, in his eagerness to make the armistice palatable to Germany, had come to forget or minimize the political implications of the various military proposals. Though Lloyd George knew of Bliss's suggested procedure (i.e., controlled German disarmament) and why it had been propounded, neither he nor House had defended it against Foch's assertion that such a requirement could only lead to an occupation of the entire Reich. Moreover, though the British leader had originally preferred Haig's terms (i.e., evacuation of France, Belgium, and Alsace-Lorraine) for the very reason that they were intended to foreshadow a moderate treaty, he had obviously been thinking only of tactical factors when he conceded that Haig did not mean the Allies would *not* be better off if they could get the bridgeheads.[86] Lloyd George's attitude toward the conceptions of both Bliss and Haig indicates that his desire to end the fighting had dulled his comprehension of why the French really wanted an armistice occupation.[87]

Hence by November 1 the Allies had made their decision to hold the Rhineland during the writing of the treaty. French initiative and doggedness had won their point. To a much greater extent than Colonel House or Lloyd George had realized or than later historians have recognized, Foch and Clemenceau had taken a giant step toward the achievement of French objectives at the peace conference.[88]

It was not long before the Germans were summoned. On November 5, the president informed the enemy that the Allies were ready to stop the fighting and to promise peace upon the basis of the Fourteen Points. Berlin was instructed to present a delegation on the western front to receive the armistice terms from Marshal Foch.[89]

With the situation in the Reich rapidly reaching crisis

proportions, the government wasted no time in reacting. The distracted chancellor, Prince Max of Baden, quickly chose Matthias Erzberger (the author of the 1917 Reichstag peace resolution) to represent his government on a predominantly military armistice delegation.[90] Within twenty-four hours, Erzberger was at army headquarters in Spa, Belgium, where in discussions with the High Command he agreed that the Allies might be more lenient if he, as a civilian, were to head the mission. By the morning of November 8, Erzberger and several German officers were sitting opposite Marshal Foch and other Allied representatives in a railway car near Compiègne, France.[91]

Of all the armistice conditions read off that day, that relating to the occupation on the Rhine was probably the most painful to the Germans. Erzberger later remembered that this provision had been especially galling to him.[92] A French participant in the meetings recalled that Captain Vanselow, the German naval representative, had wept openly as he had learned of the plans the Allies had for western Germany.[93]

Nevertheless, since it was imperative for the Germans to focus on those provisions where change appeared both possible and immediately important, only two of five counterproposals were concerned with the occupation. The first of these was a request for an extension of the early deadlines for German military evacuations. The second was a plea for the elimination of the Rhine bridgeheads and the demilitarized zone on the right bank of the river. Erzberger defended these suggestions not only as technically desirable but also as politically necessary to the German fight against bolshevism.

Foch's delegation was sufficiently impressed with these arguments to agree to a number of concessions. The time limit on evacuations was raised from twenty-five to thirty-one days to assist in preserving the discipline of the retreating army. The neutral zone was reduced in width from thirty and forty to ten kilometers to discourage civil unrest, particularly in the industrial Ruhr. It was also promised that German administrative ties between the left and right banks of the Rhine would be protected. Industrialists would not be prosecuted because they had accepted machines from German-occupied France or Belgium during the war. No measures would be taken to appropriate local factories or to reduce the number of employees.[94]

Yet the Allied representatives also showed their harder side. Foch, for instance, flatly rebuffed a German appeal to limit the size of the army of occupation, announcing that he intended to concentrate as many as fifty divisions in the area of the left bank.[95] And when Erzberger asked what the victors hoped to accomplish in the Rhineland, the marshal replied by saying, disingenuously, that he did not know and that, anyway, it was none of his (Foch's) business.[96]

Finally, at five in the morning on November 11, 1918, Erzberger's group, acting now as representatives of a two-day-old German republic, agreed to the armistice. Efforts to obtain further modifications had been seriously compromised on the previous evening by an open dispatch from Berlin accepting the original Allied draft.[97] Little had remained for those meeting at Compiègne but to formalize the understanding.

If the vanquished had been able to alter the schedule of occupation somewhat, the victors were responsible for its form and content. Indeed, the Rhineland was to be occupied primarily because Foch and Clemenceau had defined it as the critical area for French security and because the American representative in the armistice negotiations had not perceived that its possession might help the French to circumvent the Fourteen Points. In later months when Woodrow Wilson felt constrained to countenance and participate in a peacetime occupation at least he clearly saw the price he paid for peace, but the same cannot be said of Colonel House and the armistice occupation. To be sure, there had been other factors in the situation, not the least of them being the British prime minister's inability to make use of his earlier insight into French behavior. Yet none of the explanations can proceed too far from the attitudes of House and his inaccessibility to the president when the crucial meetings came. Perhaps such considerations were important to Wilson when he made up his mind to be present in person at the forthcoming peace talks.

2

AMERICANS, FRENCH, AND RHINELANDERS

> Relations with the Americans remain difficult. [Their new army] does not have that feeling of the battle which still drives the rest of us, and they allow themselves to be taken in by the flatteries of the Germans.
>
> General Charles Mangin,
> Commander of the Tenth
> French Army, in Mainz,
> December 30, 1918

The attitudes so apparent in the armistice bargaining now worked themselves out in the occupation itself. French anxiety, British disinterest, American naïveté, German fear and hope—all played a role in shaping the occupation and fashioning its reception. In the process there were a number of surprises for all the parties concerned.

On the surface, the American part of the occupation seemed to be an obvious and straightforward matter. The Americans were on the Rhine simply to remind themselves and the Germans that the Allies had won the war. They had no ulterior motives. They had no desire to change things. The regulations they enforced were designed primarily to protect themselves.

Yet the full story and meaning of the endeavor cannot be understood apart from the international arena in which it developed. The American occupation's very "differentness" from its neighbors, for example, assisted the Americans in working out unexpectedly successful relations with the local

25

population. The occupation's very independence of French designs drew its leaders into a series of complicated wrangles with Foch and the French army. At the same time, its successes and its failures were visibly affected by German images and expectations regarding America in general and President Wilson in particular. Moreover, the American occupation's own activities influenced the foreign policies of governments and the maneuverings of statesmen.

Approximately 12,000 square miles of Germany, an area about the size of Maryland and Delaware, had been marked out for the armistice occupation. This territory, the left bank and the three bridgeheads, constituted only 6.5 percent of the Reich in 1918, but it supported 7 million inhabitants, or almost 11 percent of the nation's population. The region included the great city of Cologne, and it bordered on both Frankfurt and Düsseldorf as well as the industrial complex of the Ruhr basin. Though the Rhine itself had been one of the most important commercial arteries of northern Europe for centuries, its left bank had remained devoted to small farming.

Politically, the territory included sections of four German states. More than two-thirds of it was part of Prussia. About 90 percent of this lay within the so-called Rhine Province and the rest in the Province of Hesse-Nassau. The remaining one-third of the left bank, the southernmost part, included the Bavarian Palatinate, a segment of Hesse-Darmstadt, and the enclave of Birkenfeld (State of Oldenburg).

Boundaries and governments had remained remarkably stable since 1815, when the Congress of Vienna had first drawn Prussia into the region as a bulwark against French expansion. Napoleon had welded the traditionally fragmented area into one administrative unit, originally as the Confederation of the Rhine, and later as a part of France. In later years the Prussian and Bavarian governments had preserved a centralized organization of their Rhenish lands.

The governmental structure of the Prussian Rhine Province was in many ways typical of the entire occupied territory. The basic administrative unit was the *Regierungsbezirk*, geographically about the size of a large American county. A *Bezirk* in turn was subdivided into *Kreise*, either urban and indivisible (*Stadtkreise*), or rural and further subdivided (*Landkreise*). Prussian provinces were administered by *Oberpräsidenten*, *Bezirk* by *Regierungspräsidenten*, and *Stadt-* and *Landkreise* respectively by *Oberbürgermeister* and *Landrate*. Of these officials, only the *Oberbürgermeister* was an exception to the rule that all directing officials were chosen by administrative superiors. Elected legislative bodies existed, notably on the provincial and Kreis levels, but their work was largely supplementary to the directives from Berlin.[1]

The people of the Rhineland were widely acknowledged to be a breed apart. They were parochial and conservative, good-natured yet skeptical. Predominantly Catholic, they constituted the backbone of both the Prussian and German Center (or Catholic) parties. Though they had developed great respect for the efficient bureaucrats from Berlin and Munich who administered their region, they had never become fully reconciled to governments whose officials were foreign in spirit and in temperament and often of a different religion as well. In fact, the Rhineland was one of several regions in Germany where the effects of the war had combined with longstanding dislike of distant government to produce a sizable if amorphous separatist movement. This phenomenon was particularly important because it encouraged French hopes of paring off the left bank from the right.[2]

The respective location of the Allied zones of occupation within the Rhineland was apparently dictated by both tactical and political considerations. When the fighting ended on November 11, the western armies stretched from Switzerland to

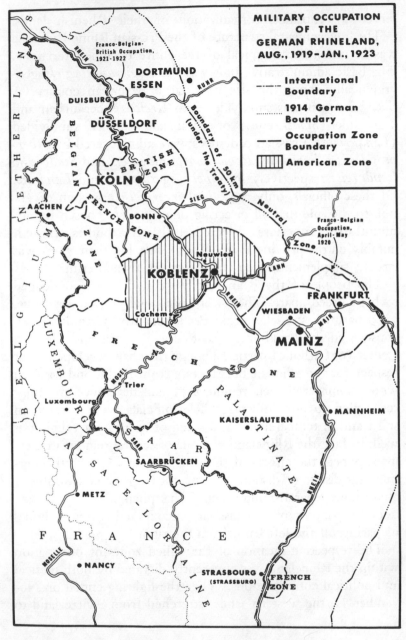

MILITARY OCCUPATION
OF THE
GERMAN RHINELAND,
AUG., 1919–JAN., 1923

International Boundary

1914 German Boundary

Occupation Zone Boundary

American Zone

the Dutch border, with French, American, French (again), British and Belgian forces on a line from south to north. It might have been anticipated that these groups would retain their relative positions in moving forward to the Rhine, but, as it turned out, the French troops that had fought between the British and American armies did not advance beyond the German border. Instead, Marshal Foch pushed the Americans northeastward, uniting French forces in the south in order to assign them the Saar, Palatinate, and Mainz regions—that is, the area of the Rhineland that bordered on France. Such an allocation of territory could well have been justified on administrative grounds (after all, the French were occupying the neighboring region of Alsace-Lorraine), but considering the territorial claims later advanced, it seems clear that the marshal had not forgotten French political objectives in making his decisions. It is interesting that American, British, and Belgian officers voiced no complaint regarding the location of the French zone. They were clearly much more concerned about the relative size of their own sectors and about Foch's announced plan to garrison the three bridgeheads with inter-Allied forces.

The United States zone during most of the first year of occupation was an area of approximately 2,500 square miles, extending from Luxemburg on the west along both sides of the Moselle River and into the Coblenz bridgehead on the east. The territory lay entirely in Prussia, and only a small part (one Kreis) of the bridgehead itself was not within the Rhine Province. The American zone was a region of steep hills and lovely scenery, with a relatively sparse population—893,000 in 1919. The only real cities were Coblenz (65,434) and Trier (55,190), both residential and governmental towns, without large industries. The land was extensively cultivated, especially in the Moselle Valley, which produced respectable crops of grain and celebrated wines. Just outside of Coblenz, in the

Neuwied basin, there were several good-sized steel and chemical factories.[3]

The British and the Belgian zones both lay to the north. The British area was the immediate neighbor of the American and included metropolitan Cologne, as well as the bridgehead opposite that city. The Belgian sector ranged north of the British to the point where the Rhine enters Dutch territory. It alone of the four Allied zones did not possess a bridgehead.

One must be careful not to exaggerate the number of Americans involved in the occupation. Whereas on November 11, 1918 there were over 2 million soldiers in the American Expeditionary Force (AEF) and half that number engaged in combat (primarily in the Meuse-Argonne), only about 240,000, or slightly less than one-eighth, participated in the advance into Germany. Since the entire Rhineland army, at its greatest extent, numbered in the vicinity of 750,000, this means that American troops comprised somewhat less than one-third of the Allied forces that were stationed on German soil.[4]

To take charge of the occupation, General Pershing on November 7 had established the United States Third Army, entrusting it to Major General Joseph T. Dickman, a cavalryman who had commanded the Third Division and later the Fourth and First Corps. The actual assignment of troops was held up for several days pending Foch's decisions about the advance. As finally constituted, the Third Army included five Regular Army divisions (First, Second, Third, Fourth, and Fifth), two National Guard divisions (32nd and 42nd), and two National Army divisions (89th and 90th).[5]

It was widely thought at the time that these units were being rewarded for the length and quality of their combat service,[6] but other considerations must have been equally important in the selection. Hardened troops could be counted on to treat the Germans with proper severity during the occupation. Experienced divisions were needed in the forward zones in case the armistice were broken off. A balance among the types of units included was desirable because National Army divisions were required by law to disband in the United States within four months after peace was signed.

Most of the men of the designated organizations were greatly pleased at the prospect of marching into Germany, for they saw this as the long-awaited chance to get even with the foe. Units cheered when informed they were to participate, and soldiers talked with eagerness of the "party."[7] That some of them also had more serious thoughts is indicated by the orders distributed in the Fourth Division. This directive asserted that, in occupying Germany, "We are to help build a new government to take the place of the one we have destroyed; we must feed those whom we have overcome; and we must do all this with infinite tact and patience, and a keen appreciation of the smart that still lies in the open wound of their pride."[8]

It was 5:30 on the morning of November 17 when, in accordance with the armistice, the Allied armies abandoned the line of their advanced trenches and began to move forward along the entire front. Ahead of them the enemy was retiring in orderly fashion, although for a few days previously there had been considerable unrest among German reserve units.[9] The Germans were required to evacuate Belgium, France, Luxemburg, and Alsace-Lorraine in three stages totalling fifteen days, while four additional stages of sixteen days had been designated for the retirement from the Rhine district. Originally, Allied armies were to be allowed to cross the various phase lines only after the expiration of the stipulated time limits, but during postarmistice negotiations the German High Command had agreed that its retreating forces might be followed at an interval of about six miles.[10]

For the Americans the next three weeks meant a punishing hike, 100 to 200 miles in length, along roads made almost impassable by rains and heavy German traffic. Though morale remained high, this was hardly attributable to the quality of the soldiers' equipment and supplies. Footwear presented a particular problem as old shoes wore out and new ones left feet raw and bloody.[11] A participant later described his unit as "clad in old and tattered uniforms, their shoes virtually a thing of memory, and the ration at this stage was nothing to boast of. In fact, they lacked everything but a heavy load of useless ammunition."[12]

At first the excitement and happiness of liberated French and Belgian villages helped to relieve the weariness of the march. As one of the doughboys remembered it, "In Belgium we were warmly welcomed in a way such as you would expect from such a noble little country. Little children would run out with cries, 'Vive la Americaine,' etc., and the village and town streets were decorated with many flags of the Allies. They did not have many flags of America, so, many of these were made with their own hands. Many were of amusing shapes with varying stripes, and stars of various shapes pinned on."[13]

When they entered the Duchy of Luxemburg on November 20, the Americans found almost as much enthusiasm. Within twenty-four hours the 32nd Division was parading through crowds in the capital city accompanied by local musicians, Boy Scouts, and civic functionaries. The soldiers were surprised to discover that the inhabitants spoke a German dialect, but no one seemed to encounter difficulty in conveying friendly feelings. Inasmuch as Luxemburg had protested Germany's invasion in the first days of the war, the Allies had no intention of treating the duchy as an enemy. General Pershing issued a proclamation promising the people that their institutions, persons, and property would be fully respected by the army.[14]

Though Luxemburg later figured prominently as an administrative center (and as a matter of controversy) for the Allied occupation, the area did not come under the jurisdiction of the United States Third Army for any length of time. American reserve units were stationed in the country as late as the summer of 1919, but the forces assigned to General Dickman remained there only a matter of days. By December 1, 1918, their schedule called for them to proceed beyond the bridges and barriers that marked the border of the enemy homeland.

Almost all the accounts of the march into the Reich focus upon the "astonishing" attitudes of the civilian population. Father Duffy of the "Fighting 69th" (a New York regiment, technically the 165th Infantry) relates that the first Germans his unit encountered were an elderly couple who came out to offer them a glass of schnapps.[15] Other reports tell of farmers who gave directions about the roads, villagers who heated water for the soldiers' feet, and little girls who threw flowers in the path of the troops.[16] If skepticism or restraint was more typical of adults during the first few days, nothing could inhibit the friendly curiosity of the children along the route of the march.[17]

It was difficult in such a situation for the troops to comprehend the enemy's frame of mind. They had come expecting to find open hatred, but there seemed to be none. They had anticipated meeting a spirit of nationalism, but such feelings apparently had vanished. In truth, Americans could little appreciate the confusion in German loyalties that four years of warfare had engendered. They were unfamiliar with the development of Rhenish separatism. They but vaguely sensed the citizenry's feeling of relief at escaping the "bolshevist danger." They were not even aware of the extent to which Wilson's Fourteen Points had persuaded Germans that the United States was the least brutal of their foes.[18]

Understandably, the Americans' earliest reaction was one of

dislike and suspicion. When a civilian tried to be polite, the soliders' tendency was to think him "servile" or "obsequious."[19] When a Bürgermeister attempted to accommodate the marchers, he frequently earned nothing but contempt.[20] Lack of visible physical destruction made it seem that the enemy had "gotten off easy." "For God's sake," exclaimed one doughboy, "not even a shell hole around here to throw things in!"[21] Rumors spread that the retreating Reichswehr had instructed the inhabitants to be gracious to the Americans in order to create dissension among the Allies and to impress President Wilson.[22] "We wouldn't act this way if the enemy had come to our country!" was a fairly typical response.[23]

Nevertheless, the occupation of the cities proceeded with no special problems. Trier was somewhat gray and apprehensive when the first American units appeared on December 2, but an army band enlivened the day with the strains of "Dixie," and the Bürgermeister and local soldier-worker (i.e. revolutionary) councils quickly allowed their "civic guards" to be disarmed.[24] Respectable Germans were so favorably impressed that within a week an infantry battalion was on its way by rail to Coblenz, invited by "authorities" there to serve in the guise of local police. Until December 11, when the American schedule of advance brought the bulk of Dickman's army to the Rhine, this unit was the guest of the Coblenz city fathers.[25]

Admittedly, the farther east the Third Army moved, the more it experienced occasional difficulties with the populace. Certain shopkeepers began to raise their prices. Town officials tried more frequently to quarter troops in poorer billets.[26] Such incidents, however, were in a sense indicative of the growing public confidence in American goodwill and discipline. They also helped the soldiers to recognize that the vast majority of Germans were genuinely ready to be friendly. On the whole, occupiers and the occupied had begun to develop a remarkably good relationship even before the First, Second, and 32nd divisions had reached the perimeter of the Coblenz bridgehead on December 17.[27]

What was the framework of structures within which these events occurred? How was the occupation of the Third Army being organized? How were the Rhinelanders to be governed? To answer these questions we must examine the development of Allied and American administrative policy after the armistice. We must also trace the interaction of the armies and the growth of disagreement among Foch, Pershing, and Dickman that contrasted strangely with improving German-American ties.

Marshal Foch's basic communication to his commanders regarding military government was dated November 15. In it, he proclaimed his desire to reestablish normal conditions of life for the civilian population as soon as possible. Foch also made clear, however, that he considered the occupation to be legally "belligerent," meaning that (under the rules of the Hague Convention) he would recognize existing German laws only when they did not contravene the security (or the orders) of the armies.[28] The marshal enumerated a list of principles for the guidance of officers charged with the administration of civil affairs. He also forwarded models of specific regulations, at the same time conceding that factors of circumstance and national tradition would necessitate modifications in each of the Allied zones.[29] That he was wise to make this concession is indicated by the considerable grumbling about his instructions. One of General Haig's staff officers is reported to have remarked that "the only possible way for a German to avoid contravening one or other of [Foch's] ... many by-laws will be to stay in bed," and even then "he will only escape provided he does not snore."[30]

Parenthetically, it is noteworthy that Foch's directives

completely disregarded the newly formed soldier-worker councils within the Rhineland. In later years some critics have seen this as a shortsighted, antidemocratic policy, which could only contribute to stunting the German revolution.[31] Nevertheless, there is good evidence that at least in the American area the Catholic and conservative temper of the population rendered those councils that did exist fully cooperative with established authorities.[32] In judging Foch, it is worth remembering that, in effect, the decision to deal with previously existing government had been made as early as the armistice negotiations at Compiègne. Moreover, Allied leadership was under unmistakable pressure from Berlin to condemn and reject the councils as a threat to public order.[33]

To implement the policies of the High Command, a welter of commissions and committees was rapidly established. The earliest of these was the Permanent Inter-Allied Armistice Commission (PIAC), which sat in continuous session with German representatives at Spa (later at Cologne) and remained in existence until the Versailles treaty came into effect in January 1920. The PIAC operated directly under Marshal Foch and was charged with general supervision of the armistice conditions as well as transmission of formal communications to and from the enemy government.[34]

More directly concerned with the Rhineland were two other organizations, both appointed by Foch within a week after the armistice and commonly identified as the Commission Inter-Alliée des Territoires Rhénans (CITR) and the Service des Territoires Rhénans (STR). The CITR was a supervisory agency that quickly relinquished the majority of its powers to fourteen independent subcommissions. It remained important only because its chairman, General Jean Payot, served as an adviser to Marshal Foch with regard to the orders that the latter promulgated on behalf of the subcommissions.[35]

Despite Payot's position and power, however, the STR soon

became at least as influential as he was. This organization was made up largely of civilian experts and was under the direction of Paul Tirard, a former French commissioner in Morocco. In constituency more French than Allied, the STR grew rapidly in size as it worked to coordinate zonal policies, especially at the lower staff levels. A measure of its success was the reorganization that occurred on December 22, 1918, bringing Tirard direct access to Foch and the title of comptroleur generale.[36] For Tirard, it was only the beginning of a long and increasingly significant association with the occupation in Germany.[37]

American policymakers, meanwhile, were attempting to conform to Marshal Foch's expressed desire for order and normality in the Rhineland. This became evident as early as November 28, when Pershing's (AEF) headquarters issued General Orders No. 218, reminding Third Army troops that they had not come to the defeated nation "as despoilers or oppressors, but simply as the instruments of a strong free government whose purposes toward the people of Germany are beneficent."[38] The same spirit was reflected in the Third Army's Memorandum No. 4, which systematized the procedures of subordinate commanders:

> In stopping in a town . . . the commanding officer will send for the Burgomaster [*sic*], Chief of Police and other prominent officials. . . . He will direct the Burgomaster to inform his people to avoid assembling in crowds and to go quietly about their ordinary affairs. . . . He will direct the Burgomaster to prohibit the sale of liquors . . . , to forbid the sale or carrying of deadly weapons . . . , [and] to furnish billets. . . . Food will not be requisitioned.[39]

These two directives were shortly coupled with the so-called antifraternization order, which directed personnel to limit their relations with the Germans to an attitude of "courteous tolerance."[40]

The Germans themselves were instructed by two additional American pronouncements, both published by AEF Headquarters at Chaumont (France). The first of these was a brief statement from General Pershing distributed by the advancing forces and warning the citizenry that "the American Army, on . . . its part, will adhere strictly to the laws of nations. The population, on their part, must offer no signs of enmity."[41]

The second American publication was dated December 9 and quickly became known by its German name as the *Anordnungen* ("regulations"). These were orders governing civilian daily life and were originally supposed to have been issued when the occupying army arrived in a town. They took Foch's model ordinances as guide and were intended to be somewhat provisional, pending the accumulation of experience in enforcement.

Many of the Anordnungen, especially those dealing with circulation and with alcoholic beverages, struck deeply at the customs of the people. Indeed, the fact that fully half of the early prosecutions by authorities were for "crimes" involving personal habits indicates that the rules should have been more carefully prepared.[42] Originally they required identity cards for every person over twelve and outlawed all travel without permission. They forbade the sale or giving of alcoholic drinks except wine and beer, and they narrowly restricted the hours of sale for those two beverages. There was to be no assemblage of persons without the approval of the local commander, except in schools, churches, courts, and municipal councils. Newspapers that published comment derogatory to the military were liable to suppression. Mail was to be censored, and the telegraph and long-distance telephone carefully controlled.[43]

To enforce such regulations, a military government was necessary, and the Americans quickly laid a foundation for the structure. On December 19, General Orders No. 225

appointed Brigadier General H. A. Smith officer in charge of civil affairs (OCCA) and established him at the new Advance General Headquarters in Trier.[44] As Pershing's immediate representative and the ultimate civil authority within the American zone, Smith in turn enunciated two basic principles of administration: (1) The OCCA, Advance General Headquarters, would promulgate and supervise all instructions regarding public matters; (2) The tactical formations of the Third Army would be used as units of governmental control.[45]

In succeeding months both of these rules proved somewhat unrealistic. The existence of a supervisory agency in Trier greatly weakened the authority of the commanding general, Third Army, at Coblenz, who was the officer responsible for public order and troop security within the zone. What is more, the failure to build the military government around the German administrative hierarchy (the provinces, Regierungsbezirke, and Kreise) resulted in a good deal of unnecessary confusion, particularly in the spring and summer of 1919, when army divisions began to be withdrawn from Germany to return to the United States.[46] These organizational errors, which neither the British nor the French armies committed, were not rectified for almost a year. Fortunately General Smith minimized difficulties by allowing the OCCA, Third Army, to oversee the political work of unit commanders and to serve as a direct contact with the Oberpräsident of the Rhine Province.[47]

The great irony of the occupation was that rather than draw the Allies together, it drove them apart. Behind the façade of Allied unity in the Rhineland significant tensions were developing, particularly between the French and American armies. Even during the war there had been considerable discord between representatives of these two nations, well

attested by the fact that as late as October 21, 1918, Clemenceau had written to Foch proposing that Pershing be removed
from his command.[48] Still, postwar friction on the Rhine was
more than a continuation of the old struggle between American desire for recognition and French pride in their own accomplishments. It was also a confrontation of American
confidence and French pessimism with regard to the future
of the defeated foe.

Pershing and Foch fell into a quarrel concerning one of the
very first orders that the latter promulgated. The specific issue was the marshal's decision on November 16 to "interna-
tionalize" the three bridgeheads and the territory north of
Cologne by assigning French divisions to the British, Belgian,
and American fronts while stationing one American division
opposite Mainz.[49] Though Foch's real purpose in such a plan
remains obscure, it is probable that he hoped to acquire a
greater voice in the administration of the northern areas and
to guard against any Allied abandonment of the bridgeheads.[50]

At any rate, whereas the British and Belgians quickly and
simply refused to accept French troops (with the result that
some of these units were given a small zone of their own, opposite Düsseldorf), the Americans were less prompt and less
candid in responding. It was not until November 28 that
Pershing protested the arrangement, contending that a shared
bridgehead would seriously complicate matters of supply and
civil affairs. By this time, the marshal possessed a perfect excuse to avoid debate, simply asserting that it was too late to
change the order.[51]

Pershing, however, insisted on having his way. He was more
than ever convinced that it was "time that the American
forces for once act independently of the French."[52] He may
also have feared that French colonial troops, who bulked
large among Foch's occupying forces, would create problems
within the Third Army zone.[53] By declining to execute the

marshal's commands and by exerting considerable pressure on Clemenceau through Colonel House in Paris, Pershing ultimately forced the marshal to back down.[54]

It was a Pyrrhic victory. On December 8, the Allied commander-in-chief removed the southern one-third of the Coblenz bridgehead from American control, assigning it to the same French forces originally scheduled for the integrated duty. Foch also ordered a French unit to replace the American division that had been selected for Mainz.[55] As a result of these two changes, particularly the first, considerable counter-marching was required of troops moving into Germany.[56]

Pershing was deeply angered and immediately requested a readjustment of the situation. When it was not forthcoming, he fumed for weeks about the "slight" to American arms implicit in the diminution of the Third Army front.[57] As late as April he could still tell Haig, in direct reference to the bridgehead affair, that it would be impossible for any officer or man in the United States Army ever to forget the treatment that they had received at the hands of the French.[58]

One effect of this incident, undoubtedly, was to fortify Pershing's resolve to proceed with the reduction of American forces in Europe. Though Secretary of War Baker had refused Foch's request that the AEF assist in the reconstruction of northern France, Baker had also expressed his willingness that the United States do more than its "strictly numerical share" in manning the Rhineland army.[59] Yet Pershing chose during these weeks to disregard the secretary's commitment in order to comply with an earlier War Department directive to return his troops as soon as possible.

This schedule of American troop withdrawal led to considerable feuding with Foch, since the marshal was determined to keep Allied forces at twice German strength throughout the peace conference and to retain at least thirty-two divisions (including six American divisions) on the Rhine indefinitely.[60]

In the end, although the controversy was carried to the Supreme War Council more than once, Pershing sustained a shipping schedule that reduced his army from thirty combat divisions on December 1, 1918, to ten on May 1, 1919.[61] He also made public his belief that it was inadvisable for the United States to leave so small a force as six divisions behind in Europe.[62] French concern about Pershing's attitudes became so great that in December, when Foch misunderstood something Pershing had said about the expiration of enlistments, Clemenceau quickly demanded a clarification from Colonel House in Paris.[63]

In the meantime, the occupation of Luxemburg had become another source of discord between Foch and Pershing. Here the problem involved French inability to let well enough alone in a somewhat delicate situation. Originally Foch must have been pleased to entrust the duchy to the Americans, for doing so had allowed him to deny a request from Belgium that its own troops participate, and he knew that Brussels was intent on foiling any French efforts to annex the country.[64] Soon, however, the marshal began to press the Americans for a larger French role in Luxemburg's affairs, first by moving his headquarters to the capital city, then by bringing in a French division to serve as an "appropriate" escort, and finally by insisting on a joint Franco-American proclamation integrating the little country into the larger occupation. Pershing resisted each of these actions, urging upon Foch both the necessity of respecting Luxemburg's independence and the advantage of having only one nationality in the occupying force.[65]

At length, in mid-January, an aborted coup d'etat in Luxemburg involving several French officers led the Allies to a confrontation and a solution. Within a few days Pershing visited the marshal personally and told him that if the French did not withdraw from Luxemburg immediately, the Americans would.[66] Faced with these alternatives and the unhappy prospect of defending a French occupation to the Belgians, Foch had had little choice but to capitulate. On January 25, he agreed that the duchy should become an American zone throughout. His only stipulation was that he retain his headquarters in the city of Luxemburg.[67]

Such disagreements as these had impact far beyond and below the higher levels of command. On the American side they stimulated a widespread if latent resentment against the French for what was remembered as their "greed," "cowardice," and "lack of cleanliness" during the war.[68] Among Foch's troops they gave rise to a variety of rumors; for example, that the Americans were going easy on the Germans,[69] or that General Dickman was of German descent and therefore anti-French.[70] By late December hostility along the Rhine had reached the point where Pershing felt compelled to ask the Third Army commander to caution his men against criticism of the Allies and "pro-German" feeling. Though Dickman quickly initiated "restraining action,"[71] French officers in the Rhineland continued to worry about antagonistic attitudes in the Third Army.[72]

It is worth emphasizing, however, that more than isolated incidents were involved in the alienation of French and Americans. There was also a visible divergence on basic policy between the two commands, a disagreement so severe that by January Pershing himself had complained to Colonel House about French efforts to use Foch's position to dominate the occupied area.[73] This difference of opinion was particularly obtrusive in the realm of economic affairs. Not without reason, it was also in this area that organizations were developed that eventually transformed the occupation.

Throughout this period the condition of the German economy remained precarious. Not only was the Allied blockade of the country still in effect, but, with the end of the war, the market for much of German industry had collapsed. Machinery for reconversion was almost unavailable, and the nation's transportation system had been gravely weakened by the surrender of 5,000 locomotives and 150,000 railroad cars to the Allies. Coal had long been scarce, and now the Ruhr mines were required to export considerable quantities to France. Hundreds of thousands of former soldiers swarmed the cities, unable to find jobs.

For a while at least the Rhenish situation was even worse than that in unoccupied Germany. The Allied armies had brought an extra blockade with them, meaning that the region was sealed off from trade both on the east and on the west. Industry was largely shut down, and commerce was at a minimum. Though food shortages never became as acute as the German Armistice Commission claimed, they were severe enough to require rationing of meats, dairy products, and fats.

To help to stabilize the Rhineland, the Allies were forced to permit a number of exceptions to the blockade. On December 16 and 28, for example, the High Command agreed to allow the passage of certain manufactured articles as well as simple foods and raw materials from the right bank to the left. In January the High Command lifted the prohibition on shipments in the opposite direction for a specific number of Rhenish factories.[74]

Even so, the situation was made to order for reorienting the area commercially toward France (as well as revivifying French industry), and Marshal Foch's correspondence with his government shows that he had no intention of overlooking this chance to strengthen his nation.[75] Thus, at the marshal's request, on December 13, the French Blockade Ministry proposed to British and American representatives that in matters of trade the Allies begin to treat the Rhineland as they had previously treated neutral countries. In other words, the

French were suggesting that western imports into the area should not be rationed and that there be only three legal requirements for the establishment of commerce: (1) that the material could be spared by the Allies; (2) that transportation was available; and (3) that concerns desiring to import were not competitors of similar Allied companies. The French also recommended the creation of an inter-Allied administrative committee (later designated the Committee for the Left Bank of the Rhine) to deal with general policy on trade and a second inter-Allied committee (later designated the Luxemburg Commission) to handle licensing for the parent body on the scene.[76]

In Washington the State Department and War Trade Board gave only perfunctory attention to this proposition, approving it in early January. Their experts knew that geography would prevent American businessmen from getting an equal break in Rhenish markets, but they hoped that the agreement was at least a start on the much-desired lifting of the German blockade.[77] They could hardly have anticipated to what extent French traders were already prepared to move in upon the Rhineland.

Indeed, such was Foch's enthusiasm for trade that even before the Allied governments had accepted his plan he had been able to persuade the armies themselves to establish the licensing organization. On January 12, 1919, at a meeting in Luxemburg, Allied civil affairs officers had agreed to implement his proposal despite the well-attested irritation of General H. A. Smith at having to deal with yet another committee. The only concession Smith could obtain on this occasion was the understanding that, as far as the American zone was concerned, the organization would be only "advisory."[78]

Once in existence, however, the Luxemburg Commission allowed France to build up an impressive trade relationship with the entire occupied territory. Though the commission delegated its specific licensing powers to *sections économiques* under each army,[79] the absence of interzonal trade barriers meant that the French could award licenses in Mainz for business throughout the left bank. The result was that from February to the end of May 1919 they sold more than 600 million francs worth of goods in the Rhineland, including an array of luxury items and surplus governmental stocks.[80] By the end of March French businessmen were arriving in the occupied territory in unprecedented numbers.[81]

American officers became increasingly apprehensive at such aggressiveness, particularly when it was combined with French refusal to enforce German customs regulations in the west and French insistence on maintaining the blockade of unoccupied Germany.[82] By February the fears of the Third Army were of sufficient magnitude to be influential in persuading the Big Four in Paris to create an economic coordinating agency within the peace conference.[83] By March the level of concern was enough to convince this Supreme Economic Council that it should itself investigate the activities of Marshal Foch and the Luxemburg Commission.

Friction between the Americans and French contrasted sharply with improving relations between the Third Army and the civilians of its zone. At Coblenz, fear and suspicion had given way by mid-December to tolerance and relaxation. This new mood was to be maintained and strengthened for a period of several months.[84]

Important to this achievement were the efforts made by the army in the issuing of new directives. Though it had been necessary to supplement the original Anordnungen with rules regarding the press, theater, health laws, and public utilities, military authorities increasingly tried to avoid needless regulation of civilians.[85] They also forbade troops to billet in churches, schools, or hospitals, and they prohibited them from requisitioning food or forage.[86] Since Allied procedures for purchasing supplies had provided that only receipts could be given to Germans, General Dickman prevailed upon Foch to modify this policy and remove a potential source of friction.[87] Cash payments were made possible by funds from Berlin, supplied to the Allied armies under Article IX of the armistice.[88]

As the weeks went by, many of the Anordnungen were liberalized to meet the needs and customs of the people. Telegraph and telephone communications were freed from control in early January,[89] and a few days later the closing hours of cafes and restaurants were extended from 8:00 P.M. to 10:00 P.M.[90] At the end of the month the ban on political activity was relaxed for both the Prussian and the national elections.[91]

Relations with the various levels of German government were satisfactory, if none too efficient. As noted previously, the responsibility for these contacts had devolved upon the officer in charge of civil affairs, Third Army, and the OCCAs of divisions, brigades and smaller units. This meant that the OCCA, Third Army, was accountable for (1) transmitting and receiving all communications that passed between the military government and the Oberpräsident of the Rhine Province, (2) reporting any failure to comply with American orders, (3) inspecting German governmental correspondence for propaganda against the occupying forces, and (4) examining new Prussian and German laws to discover possible conflicts with army policy. The OCCAs of tactical units were supposed to perform similar duties for Bezirke, Kreise, and so forth.[92]

According to the final report of Colonel I. L. Hunt, who remained the Third Army OCCA during this entire period, American military government, particularly at the lower levels, was rather ineffective. Not only was it handicapped by a rapid turnover in personnel and by a lack of coincidence between German and American administrative boundaries, but it also commonly suffered from the absence of the American officers responsible for it. Since OCCAs were staff advisers to their respective unit commanders, they could be and frequently were deprived of the time required for their occupation duties.[93]

Little was done to remedy this situation, apparently because the gain to be won seemed fairly marginal. The German bureaucracy was cooperating conscientiously—Rhenish officeholders were largely sympathetic to the foremost concern of the American army, its own physical security—and this cooperation must have appeared too important to risk for the chance of perfection. The relative satisfaction of the Americans is revealed by the fact that whereas during 1919 they were involved in disciplinary action against twenty German officials, with the majority paying moderate fines, the French during the same year punished more than twice as many local functionaries, usually by deportation.[94] It is true that Berlin was forbidden to make changes among officeholders without Third Army approval, but this was largely a precautionary move.

Meanwhile, despite the Rhineland's growing trade with France, it continued to suffer from inadequate food supplies. Many items remained scarcer in the occupied region than in the rest of the Reich, though, oddly enough, this condition was due not so much to Foch's separation of the left bank from the right as to Berlin's intentional retention of stocks in unoccupied territory in order to feed the population there.[95] By February 25 the Rhenish situation had become so bad, particularly in the British zone, that the Supreme Economic Council decided to make special arrangements for the provisioning of the area. An inter-Allied military committee was appointed to organize relief supplies, and the armies were freed of previous restrictions on selling foodstuffs to the populace.[96] At the end of March the British command began to make distributions from its reserve stores and within a few days the French and American headquarters followed suit.[97]

Of course, the occupation also worked in certain ways to the economic advantage of the inhabitants. Trade with France often meant profits for retailers and manufacturers, while Allied efforts to prevent strikes frequently resulted in highly successful labor settlements.[98] Even more important, the expenditures of the armies brought large sums of money into the area. Third Army reimbursement to civilians for billets and requisitions was well supplemented by the spending of the ordinary soldier. Merchants did a land-office business in insignia, service strips, English and American books, and souvenirs. "Gott mit uns" belt buckles were extraordinarily popular, and more iron crosses were sold than the Kaiser could possibly have awarded. The doughboys were so souvenir-happy that they assaulted German policemen to get their spiked helmets.[99]

General Dickman and his aides strove valiantly to keep their men constructively employed. During January and February the troops were given intensive maneuvers, training, drill, and range practice.[100] Later, athletic and educational programs were organized. Trade schools taught vocational skills, and grammar schools began to attack the 4 percent illiteracy rate. Leave was awarded to 150 men to attend English and French universities, while 6,000 studied at the AEF University in Beaunne, France. Military units of all sizes began to publish newspapers, and in April an independent daily, the *Amaroc News*, was established for the entire army.[101]

Even so, such activities could not prevent the American forces from rapidly becoming what one wit tagged an "army of no occupation."[102] Uncertain of the future, two years overseas, and largely isolated from the civilians around them, many of the troops became acutely bored and homesick.[103]

The 100 enforced marriages in the spring of 1919 and a climbing rate of venereal disease pointed to some slippage of morale. A soldier's poem caught the spirit of the occasion:

> Rumors are flying about fast and furious,
> Some good, some bad and all of them curious;
> We're leaving next Christmas, or maybe this
>   evening.
> Or any damn day of the time intervening.[104]

Antifraternization orders remained unmodified, although they became more and more difficult to enforce. To the amazement of the British and French, American military police continued to do their best to prevent all conversation between soldiers and civilians. Since large numbers of Americans were billeted with German families, however, friendships developed, even in Coblenz. MPs discovered that it was necessary to check on nurses being escorted about town to see if they were *Fräuleins* in borrowed uniforms. A much discussed question was whether an officer listening to a record of Beethoven in a German drawing room had committed a breach of regulations.[105]

Unfortunately, many Germans misunderstood American antifraternization, believing it the result of an attitude of superiority on the part of the occupying army. Only after closely studying the situation was an editor of the *Berliner Tageblatt* ready to conclude that the policy "originates not from any hostile feeling toward us, but from a peculiarity in the American way of thinking."[106] Antifraternization may have served some useful purpose in avoiding friction, but the isolation of the army also injured German pride and whetted German suspicions.

Everything considered, the winter and early spring went relatively well. Newspapers in the Coblenz area, while forbidden to criticize the United States or the Allies, nevertheless provided a notable measure of praise for the actions of the

Third Army. The *Bitburger Zeitung*, for example, asserted, "It is just to acknowledge that the American military authorities are efficient without harshness, and the behavior of the American troops is wonderfully good. Not only officers but soldiers are considerate and seem obliging."[107]

Third Army censorship reports indicate that the grievances of the citizenry against Americans were minor and inconsequential. The most severe criticism involved the extensive billeting demands. There was also some feeling that military regulations were too strict and military courts too rigorous, but, at the same time, doughboys were described as "friendly," "good business," and "better than bolshevism."[108]

These months of good German-American relations gave way in mid-April to about ten weeks of tension and mutual antagonism. Disappointment at the peace terms and irritation at continuing food and fuel shortages now encouraged insubordination among the Germans. The newly anxious troops reacted violently. Drunkenness, street brawling, and the trading of insults became common among the rougher elements of the populace and the army.[109] Harmony did not return until after the signing of the treaty in June.

American troops who had advanced to the Rhine had surprised, and had been surprised, by those they encountered. Both the French and the Rhinelanders were somewhat shocked at their behavior, the former at their lack of sympathy for an ally, the latter at their tolerance for the vanquished. Americans, in turn, not only found themselves amazingly well received by the inhabitants but also discovered that their relations with the French had become a constant disillusionment. Indeed, the recurring disputes between Pershing and Foch both restricted French achievement in the occupied area and embittered Allied ties. For a time at least this struggle was also to have important effects upon the Germans across the Rhine.

3

UNOCCUPIED GERMANY AND THE OCCUPATION

The American Army is our firmest ally. It has had enough of the French.

General Wilhelm Groener,
German Cabinet Meeting,
January 21, 1919.

The Americans are the ones most sympathetic to us, then the English, then the French, and then the Belgians . . .

Matthias Erzberger,
German Cabinet Meeting,
January 21, 1919.

To grasp the significance of the American occupation for the rest of Germany it is necessary to put it in the context of the more general situation in that country. The American presence, for example, must be seen in connection with the difficulties under which the Berlin government labored. It must also be viewed in relation to the campaign of protest that was mounted to oppose Marshal Foch's activities upon the Rhine.

From this perspective, it becomes apparent that the Americans at Coblenz played two successive, and quite different roles for unoccupied Germany. For a time, during December and January, both the German government and the German people felt encouraged by their presence and clearly saw them as potential allies. As weeks passed, however, and the defeated nation examined the realities, the ease with which the French obtained their way led to a progressive disillusionment with "Wilson's army." Berlin continued to denounce what it considered to be infractions of the armistice, but with less and less hope of immediate American (or British) assistance. By March the government had begun to focus its attention on preparing the demands to be presented at the peace conference. The German public, in the interim, had begun to regard the Third Army as somewhat of a "false friend."

The first months after the cessation of hostilities found the provisional government in Berlin struggling to preserve itself and to reorganize the nation. Defeat and revolution had unleashed a myriad of forces, many of which were bidding vigorously to overturn the young regime. "Majority" Socialist leaders had proclaimed the new republic, but it was an open question as to whether they could build it or preserve it.

An attempt by the Majority Socialists to govern in combination with smaller and more radical Independent Socialist Party proved to be short-lived. By early December the Independent Socialists could no longer tolerate the government's recognition of the old officer corps, its antagonism to the soldier-worker councils, or its tough treatment of insurrectionary outbreaks in Berlin. The left wing of the Independents (which often made common cause with the Spartacists, or Communist League) also objected to Chancellor Frederich Ebert's insistence on the calling of a constitutional assembly.

Largely as a result of the Independents' withdrawal, radical agitation continued to plague the Ebert regime. At the beginning of January a Spartacist revolt within the capital was suppressed only with difficulty. Later in the month strikes and much disorder accompanied the elections to the National Assembly. In February the assassination of the Bavarian premier led to several weeks of civil war in Munich.

Such difficulties, together with economic crises and international tension, rendered the Majority Socialists extremely cautious. Thus, Ebert and his colleagues found it necessary to assume that political experimentation and socialization must await industrial recovery, constitutional government, and peace. Their only real "reform" of the autumn and winter was to sponsor a voluntary agreement between capital and labor establishing the right of collective bargaining and the eight-hour day.[1]

Nevertheless, when more than 30 million Germans went to the polls in January, the Majority Socialists seemed to have won a strong endorsement for their policies. Ebert's party obtained 11.5 million votes, or a surprising 38 percent of the total, while the Center (Catholic) Party, an advocate of federalism and moderate social reform, received almost 6 million ballots, or about 20 percent. About 5 million chose the Democratic Party, organized the previous November and backed by industrialists as well as professional and academic leaders. The Nationalists (the prewar Conservative Party) and the Independent Socialists each polled fewer than 3 million votes, and the newly established, business-oriented People's Party obtained about 1.6 million.[2]

Parenthetically, it is interesting to note that the percentages in the American zone were quite different from those in the nation at large. There, the Center Party achieved an overwhelming victory, while the Majority Socialists and parties of the Left and Right were given relatively weak support:

Center	277,800	71.5%
Majority Socialist	58,300	15.0%
Democratic	46,200	12.0%
Nationalist	2,800	.7%
Other	3,200	.8%

SOURCE: United States, Army, *American Military Government of Occupied Germany, 1918–1920* (Washington, D.C., 1943), p. 271.

These returns reveal convincingly how much more Catholic and traditional was the Coblenz region than was the rest of Germany.[3]

The National Assembly convened in Weimar on February 6, 1919 and quickly moved to take control. A fundamental law was enacted and Ebert was elected president of the Reich. He, in turn, appointed his party colleague Philipp Scheidemann to form a government of Majority Socialists, Centrists, and Democrats—the parties of the so-called Weimar coalition. The new chancellor announced a relatively noncontroversial program, including peace on the basis of the Fourteen Points, complusory international arbitration, multilateral disarmament, a democratic army, and education for all Germans. Clearly, Scheidemann was looking toward the peace conference and the peace.[4]

The government faced immediate problems, however, and, among them, the occupation in the west continued to be, as it had been from November, of prime importance. The great danger, of course, was that France might create a situation on the left bank that would permit or cause that region to be alienated from the Reich. It was this development that Berlin had been determined to prevent from the beginning.

In fact, no sooner had French troops isolated Alsace-Lorraine in November 1918, than Foreign Minister Wilhelm Solf had begun subtly to pressure the Americans and British to help the Germans protect the Rhineland. In messages relayed through Washington on November 18 and 21, he had attempted to obtain from the Allies a promise that they would not interfere with normal commercial traffic across the Rhine.[5] Solf had also urged the victors to forego the establishment of bridgeheads on the river in the interest of preserving the region's economy.[6]

The foreign minister, however, did not long remain the German spokesman on such subjects. The dual foreign and

domestic nature of the occupation, the heavily Catholic population of the left bank, the absence of formal diplomatic
relations with the enemy—these among other considerations
soon impelled Matthias Erzberger, the Centrist minister who
directed the German armistice commission, to assume virtually complete responsibility for Rhenish affairs. Despite certain
jurisdictional disputes with Solf's successor, Count Ulrich von
Brockdorff-Rantzau, Erzberger was able to retain this control
throughout the winter and the spring of 1919. In February he
and Brockdorff-Rantzau even signed a formal agreement that
relieved the Foreign Ministry of all obligations in the Rhineland situation.[7]

Erzberger, like Solf, had quickly revealed a deep concern
about what was going on in western Germany. The day after
participating in the original armistice negotiations at Compiègne he had warned Berlin that the enemy planned intensive
"Frenchifying" of the Rhineland in order to claim the region
under the principle of self-determination.[8] Back in the capital,
he had striven throughout November to expedite the signing
of preliminary peace with the Allies in hopes of saving the left
bank from occupation under the armistice.[9]

In December, obviously with the Americans and British in
mind, Erzberger's armistice commission instituted a drumfire
of protest against Foch's occupation policies.[10] At the December armistice renewal, for example, Erzberger not only spoke
out against the marshal's assertion of right to occupy the neutral
zone north of Cologne, but also vigorously attacked the way
in which the Rhineland was being "separated" from Germany
economically.[11] In January he reemphasized his objections to
the interruption of Rhenish commerce and denounced, as a
violation of the armistice, Foch's decision to retrieve the Strassburg (Kehl) bridgehead, a provision the French had abandoned under British pressure before the original armstice.[12]

In the intervals between negotiations additional protests

were transmitted via the armistice representatives at Spa. During December, for instance, the Germans objected several times to Allied restrictions on traffic in foodstuffs across the Rhine.[13] In January they called attention to the disregard for German "trade regulations" along the western border.[14] In February they complained about Allied arrests of Rhenish citizens charged with the possession of confiscated French and Belgian property.[15]

Meanwhile, Erzberger and others were also working behind the scenes to encourage American and British opposition to French designs. At one point Erzberger himself asked General Pershing to play a larger role on the Allied armistice commission,[16] and General Wilhelm Groener, second in command of the German army, did even more. "In the next months (December, January, and February)," Groener later recalled, "I was in constant touch with the mayors of Coblenz and Cologne for the purpose of influencing American and British occupation authorities [to thwart French separatist ambitions]."[17] The general was spurred on by an awareness of growing Allied tensions on the Rhine, and by his feeling that, as he put it, "the Americans are finished with the French and want to come together with Germany."[18]

Other German leaders demonstrated their public support of Erzberger as well as their determination to have the Rhineland remain within the Reich. President Ebert, in his opening speech to the National Assembly on February 6, sharply criticized the "harsh" implementation of armistice terms and bemoaned the fact that "the left bank of the Rhine is separated from the rest of Germany!"[19] Somewhat later Foreign Minister Brockdorff-Rantzau denounced the French and Belgians for supporting what he called "centrifugal forces" within the occupied regions.[20] In March Chancellor Scheidemann served notice on the Allies that his government would view any attempt to amputate the western area as a "deed of violence."[21]

Nonministerial members of the National Assembly also devoted a great deal of attention to the occupation, usually in an attempt to remedy specific local grievances.[22]

It is noteworthy, however, that representatives of the German government made no public appeal to American leaders regarding the Rhineland during these weeks. Indeed, in December when Cardinal Hartmann of Cologne had suggested inviting President Wilson to the region to see for himself how the populace felt about French activities, the cardinal had been promptly rebuffed by the Foreign Ministry in Berlin.[23] The reasons for the continuing silence are fairly clear. In the winter of 1918 the Germans had not only possessed considerable confidence in American power and intentions, but they had also realized that they would only make matters more difficult for Wilson and his compatriots by putting them in the position of supporting an "enemy" program.[24] By March and April, German confidence in the Americans was draining rapidly away, but at this point it had become clear that if the situation was not already lost, it was much too delicate to tamper with.[25]

Whatever the prospects, Erzberger and his commission continued to pursue their frustrating endeavor to find support by means of protests.[26] On occasion they won clear concessions, as for example, in March, when the German Ministry of Economics was allowed to appoint a special trade commissioner to deal with Rhineland economic sections.[27] More frequently, results were disappointing, as when the Allies ignored Erzberger's April warning that controls on securities, currency, and customs were endangering the viability of German food payments.[28]

Still, the Germans were indefatigable. They objected to, among other things, the harshness of military courts, the interference in Berlin's appointment of officeholders, and the exclusion of certain newspapers and periodicals from the occupied territory. They protested against the way that the press in the French area was compelled to publish propaganda articles. They also complained about the French practice of forcing the children in their zone to study the French language in school.[29]

German opinion regarding the occupation remained in approximate accord with the changing attitudes of the statesmen. In December, clearly, the average citizen had been somewhat dismayed by the enemy "invasion," though he had appreciated the fact that Allied troops had brought "order" with them.[30] In succeeding weeks he had found serious fault with the actions of the French army, but he had also been pleased to learn of a certain fairness among the Americans and British as well as of their antagonism to the French.[31] By January, if he had discussed the Rhineland with friends, he probably would have echoed the *Hamburger Nachrichten* in contending that "certainly the United States is to be regarded as among our enemies, but not as sharing the fanatical hatred."[32]

The German view of the American occupation was, of course, to a great extent dependent upon factors other than the Third Army's immediate policies or even those of the other Allied forces. As previously noted, at the beginning of the occupation a fund of goodwill toward Americans had already existed for months.[33] From December 1918 into February 1919, the Americans' reputation had profited from the German belief that President Wilson was fighting for their cause in Paris. In March 1919, however, when Wilson returned home without even having ended the blockade, the American army's popularity could hardly have avoided a sharp decline.[34]

Erich Wulff in the *Berliner Tageblatt* (a Democratic Party organ) was typical of the critics who appeared at the end of winter. On March 19 he told of a recent visit to Coblenz during which shortage of hotel space had forced him to stay at an inn without water or light. According to Wulff, three separate civilizations had developed in the city—American, French, and native. Legal distinctions were so severe that Third Army soldiers could not even share their surplus food with the civilians. Possession by Germans of an army cigarette could mean instant arrest, and the sale of alcohol was controlled through an "unbelievable" system of spying. To Wulff, the one redeeming feature of the occupation was the fact that American enlisted men refused to salute French officers.[35]

A month later the *Tägliche Rundschau* (People's Party) of Berlin published the impressions of another eye witness. This writer declared that there was hardly a house in the American zone that was not groaning under the load of billeting. Monks had even been expelled from monasteries to make room for troops. What is more, Rhinelanders were not being properly recompensed for requisitions; the citizenry was being harassed with petty ordinances; and German officials were being humiliated whenever possible.[36]

For a period in April the German mood improved, but by May 1919 the bitterness generated by the draft treaty, together with the deterioration of relations at Coblenz, prompted a new stream of accusations. The *Rheinisch-Westfälische Zeitung* (Nationalist) now described the American soldier as a "spendthrift," and declared that the way in which army cooks wasted fats and oils was "absolutely criminal."[37] A commentator in the Berlin *Lokal Anzeiger* (Nationalist) called Americans "cockroaches" and "knaves," and claimed that the Coblenz area was witnessing a complete breakdown of law and order. Instead of American "freedom," he said, the troops had brought "Wild West manners" and 50 percent illiteracy. Sobriety stopped at 7:00 P.M.; and soldiers roamed the streets demanding money and souvenirs, smashing windows, attacking elderly women, and indulging in paroxysms of spitting.[38]

Such accusations were hardly necessary to persuade the German government to commit itself to terminate or limit the occupation. As early as the previous February, Erzberger and others had spelled out this position in the instructions they were preparing for the future peace delegation. On March 21, this goal had been approved by the German cabinet in the following candid exchange:

ERZBERGER: We must demand first of all that the occupied territories be evacuated on the day the peace treaty is concluded. This demand should be backed up energetically by the press. The Allied soldiers, anxious to return home, are our natural allies on that score. Very well, let us insist on a referendum in Alsace-Lorraine, with the possibilities: autonomy, autonomy within France, autonomy within Germany (possible autonomy within a French or American protectorate). . . .

SCHEIDEMANN [chancellor]: Our demand that the occupied territories be evacuated before the referendum will be countered with our own conduct after Brest Litovsk in Lithuania, etc. . . .

JOHANNES BELL [minister for colonial affairs]: Even if evacuation of occupied territories cannot be obtained, the demand should be raised. At the very least, it will prevent the occupation from dragging on for years. . . .

BROCKDORFF-RANTZAU [foreign minister]: It would be very valuable if public opinion pressed for lifting the occupation before peace is concluded.

EDUARD DAVID [Reich minister]: Yes, propaganda for it should be started right now. But we won't get anywhere. The year 1871 will be referred to. [Therefore] conditions of occupation should be clarified: personal and economic communication; mail; precise guarantees for the safety of our people. English and American occupation troops. . . .

EBERT [president]: We want to urge immediate evacuation of the occupied territories, possible withdrawal of colored troops; the nature of the plebiscite should be determined and treaties on economic questions, especially potash and iron ore, drawn up.[39]

To be sure, the Germans had not waited for the period of the peace conference to wrestle with the problems of the postwar situation. A Bureau for Economic Peace Preparations had been established by the government in December 1917, and in the following October the former ambassador to the United States, Count Johann-Heinrich von Bernstorff, had been recalled from Turkey to refashion and to lead the organization. By February, 1919, Bernstorff's *Paxkonferenz* had come to number more than forty people and was deeply involved in its research assignment.[40]

Among the fruits of Paxkonferenz labors were fifty-one background papers, or *Drucksache*, prepared with special reference to the impending negotiations. These Drucksache covered a wide variety of topics, although the majority were economic in orientation and included, for example, studies of the commercial interrelationships among the Saar, Palatinate, Alsace-Lorraine, and Rhineland.[41] Though no specific analysis was made of Rhenish separatism, the demilitarized area, or the armistice occupation, the fact that ten of the fifty-one investigations dealt with problems related to the left bank of the Rhine indicates how much concern there was among informed Germans regarding the future of this region.

During May and June 1919 the Paxkonferenz was divided, with most of its members accompanying the plenipotentiaries to France, and the rest remaining at work in Germany. The larger group thus became, in effect, the functioning staff of the peace delegation. The smaller, also known as the Berlin *Geschäftstelle*, kept the Paris Germans informed of relevant publications, speeches, and governmental decisions, as well as its own opinions regarding aspects of the treaty. Whether or not the formulations of either group (much less those of the Drucksache) were influential is difficult to ascertain, but as we shall see, they do reveal something of what went on within the German delegation as it wrestled with Allied requirements.[42]

The German National Assembly's Committee for Peace Negotiations had also given thought to the forthcoming conference, but in this case there is even less evidence than with the Paxkonferenz to guide our judgment of its influence. The most complete reference to the Rhine among the committee's records is an impressively accurate intelligence estimate of April that predicted that the Allies would end by insisting on at least the permanent demilitarization of the entire left bank. According to this report, the French had been forced to abandon their plan for an autonomous Rhineland, but Clemenceau was still demanding a threefold frontier: political, including Alsace-Lorraine; economic, including the Saar; and military, including the left bank of the Rhine.[43]

Whatever the sources of German policy, however, when the 180 members of the official peace delegation left Berlin for Paris on April 28, they possessed detailed instructions from their government. They had been directed to contend that, as a result of the armistice, Woodrow Wilson's Fourteen Points had become binding on all parties. They had been told to demand reasonable reparations, a return of colonies, reciprocal disarmament, and immediate German admission to the League of Nations. Plebiscites were to be asked for those areas that conceivably could be lost to Germany: Posen, Schleswig, and Alsace-Lorraine. Unilateral war guilt was to be denied.

Concerning the Rhineland, the delegates had been instructed to concede only the destruction of military fortifications. German troops were not to be withdrawn permanently from the area unless France and Belgium established a corresponding neutral zone.[44] The separation of any part of the Rhineland from the Reich was to be rejected on principle. The customs frontier in the west was to be maintained at all costs.

Further, the representatives had been enjoined to insist that the military occupation come to an end as soon as peace became final. The victors must at all costs be persuaded that there were stronger guarantees against attack than the possession of the left bank. They must also be convinced that better gages could be obtained for the payment of Germany's financial obligations.

If, however, there was no escaping occupation, it was thought imperative that the legal powers and size of foreign armies be well defined. It should be clearly established that local German officials would have access to their superiors, and that all officeholders would be appointed and dismissed solely by the appropriate civil authority. It should also be agreed that Allied personnel would not interfere with political and economic conditions in the country, and that tariff regulations would be supervised by Germans. Finally, it should be stipulated that "colored troops" would not be made a part of the army of the occupation.[45]

The requirement regarding colored soldiers deserves an added comment. In future months, after the alleged outrages of French colonial troops in the Mainz region had suddenly become grist for an immense anti-French propaganda campaign, a question naturally arose as to the sincerity and the truthfulness of the German plaintiffs. The answer is far from obvious, but the existence of this instruction to the peace delegation and the fact that as early as November 7, 1918 Foreign Minister Solf had tried to forestall the use of colored units along the Rhine would seem to indicate that the charges were not simply a means to an end.[46]

In reality, the German people were both extremely curious about and intensely fearful of the non-Caucasian soldiers. Third Army newspapers reported that, in the early days of the occupation, crowds had assembled whenever American Negro troops appeared. Former German soldiers told that their commanders had offered rewards during the war for the capture of a Negro.[47] The officers themselves recalled with horror the "black waves" of Africans who had often "massacred, or worse, tortured our defenseless men."[48]

Nor were the Germans the only ones who had mixed emotions about the presence of African and Asian troops on European soil. President Wilson took up the matter with Clemenceau at the Paris Peace Conference,[49] and the French premier responded by declaring his intention "to retire [the Senegalese as soon as possible], for I believe as you do, it would be a grave error to occupy the left bank with blacks."[50] What later persuaded Paris to turn its back upon this "promise" has never been fully explained, but the decision unquestionably owes much to the fear and insecurity that developed in France after the United States refused to ratify the Treaty of Versailles.

Favorably viewed and considerably praised in unoccupied Germany, the American occupation had been an important political factor for the enemy nation from the beginning. In the first crucial weeks Third Army troops had helped to make a difficult position bearable for Germans by providing both an example of Allied moderation and an implicit promise of assistance. Simultaneously if unintentionally, they had also encouraged Berlin to mount a vigorous campaign of resistance against French encroachments in the west. Though German faith in American power had waned somewhat with the coming of spring, there can be no doubt that the Third Army's presence on the Rhine had long had a buoying effect on the nation's morale. The paradox is that, in April and in May, as American opposition to Foch's policies became less visible to Germany, it was on its way to becoming more effective at Coblenz.

4

THE GENESIS OF THE PEACETIME OCCUPATION

> The Rhine was the background of all manoeuvre [at
> the peace conference] for weeks and months. Wheth-
> er the subject matter was the League of Nations, the
> German fleet, or the status of Fiume, we knew that
> the real struggle would come over the Rhine.
>
> David Lloyd George,
> writing in December 1922

> In a word, the occupation is a lever that we have in
> our hand and with which we can call the tune.
>
> Marshal Ferdinand Foch,
> Notebook entry of April
> 28, 1919

Impelled by French concern with security, the Allied peace
conference from its inception in January 1919 had been
driven into controversies and decisions involving the Rhineland. Admittedly, the French had taken several weeks to make
their desire to separate and occupy the area completely
clear. Since they had assumed that Wilson and his program
would be the primary obstacles to such a policy, they had first
attempted not only to commit the American leadership to a
"broadened" agenda but also to work out a united front with
Lloyd George against the Americans. Only after they had
failed in these endeavors and after the president and prime
minister had left Paris in February did Clemenceau bring his
demands into the open, hoping to use the occasion to rush

them through the conference. As it developed, he almost accomplished his objective, for only a lack of coordination within French ranks, Wilson's precautionary cables from on board ship, and Lloyd George's objections to military occupation prevented Colonel House and Lord Balfour from agreeing to the establishment of a buffer state.

After the president returned on March 14, the struggle became more forthright and intense. Hoping to divert French attention from the Rhine, Lloyd George and Wilson now took the unprecedented step of offering Clemenceau a tripartite defensive alliance against Germany. Responding favorably, the premier abandoned his demand that the Rhineland be independent, but he also insisted that the pact itself be rendered foolproof and that it be supplemented by a thirty-year Allied occupation of the left bank. For the next two weeks, as pressures mounted on all sides and as conditions in Europe became increasingly chaotic, the conference remained in virtual deadlock. An understanding was not achieved until the first days of April, when Wilson's concessions regarding reparations, the Saar, and the treaty of alliance compelled Clemenceau to join in further compromise. In true *clemenciste* fashion, however, the premier waited until Lloyd George was absent in London before informing Wilson of his willingness to accept a fifteen-year term for the occupation. In obtaining the president's agreement to this arrangement he placed the British prime minister in the unhappy position of returning to face a *fait accompli*.

The American and British statesmen, then, had come to the Paris Conference with "German policies" very different from Clemenceau's. In the winter of 1918 Wilson's attitudes were not yet explicit, but his Fourteen Points and recent statements implied that, in his opinion, a peaceful Germany required national boundaries, freedom of trade, and membership in an international organization. Lloyd George would have endorsed a similar program, although his speeches in the December electoral campaign indicated that he was more interested than Wilson in punishing "war criminals" and obtaining reparations. Since the United States and Britain were safe behind their "watery moats" (and the German navy was destroyed), their leaders could afford to be sanguine about the German "democracy" and its potential military power.[1]

Clemenceau, of course, was precluded by geography and history from pursuing such "liberal" visions. Like the majority of his countrymen, he saw no alternative to obtaining stringent guarantees and heavy reparations from Germany, a combination that not only ran counter to most Anglo-American ideas, but verged on incompatibility. Still, the possibility that a reduction in Germany's physical strength might undermine the new republic or lessen its ability to pay did not appear to worry him. And since he seriously doubted that disarmament schemes or an international league could deprive the Reich of its relative advantage in terms of power, he had become extremely interested in other arrangements to redress the balance.

Granted, Clemenceau did play his cards close to his vest in matters touching French security. As the conference neared, he let almost no one in on his exact intentions, at the same time doing everything possible to maximize his freedom of action with the public. Though he could not prevent the Foreign Affairs Commission of the Chamber of Deputies from urging the government to seek the "detachment" of the Rhineland from Germany,[2] he could and did order the censorship services to prevent the subject of the left bank from being discussed openly in the French press.[3] His main preoccupation, he explained to the Chamber on December 29, was "not to give rise to extravagant hopes for fear of later arousing too many disappointments."[4]

Nevertheless, there is sufficient evidence for at least two important conclusions: (1) The French government at this time was fully committed to depriving Germany of its Rhineland base of operations for offensive action against France; (2) Clemenceau was quite convinced that his greatest problem in this regard would be the policies of Woodrow Wilson. Both of these assertions derive considerable support from an examination of the agenda that the French constructed for the conference. They are buttressed almost beyond doubt by a study of the overtures that Clemenceau and Foch made to the British government in November and December 1918.

The timing and nature of the agenda demonstrate that the French were very much concerned about what the armistice "contract" had done to their security. Indeed, the ink was hardly dry on the armistice terms when the French Foreign Office began to submit draft agenda to the Allies designed to supplant or supplement Wilsonian principles and to bring French war aims under an acceptable formula. Copies of the first and second drafts, dated November 15 and 21 and transmitted to Washington through Colonel House in Paris, contained references to, among other things, "territories neutralized for the purpose of protection" and "territorial occupations."[5] A revised and more official version of these papers, dated November 29, was received by the president in early December and listed similar topics for discussion.[6] Only the fourth and final French draft, prepared by André Tardieu and distributed on January 8, recognized the primary significance of the Fourteen Points, and even this spoke of the need for "guarantees against the revival of militarism" and the military "neutralization of certain regions."[7] None of these proposed agenda, it might be added, was given serious consideration by Wilson or his delegation.[8]

Meanwhile, in order to obtain insurance, the French approached the British behind the backs of their trans-Atlantic allies. As early as November 12, the French ambassador in London had hinted broadly to Lloyd George about the need for British support against the Americans,[9] and on November 15, Clemenceau himself had wired the prime minister, urging that they meet to draw up "preparatory memoranda" for the conference.[10] On November 26 had come the most clear-cut overture of all, in which the French proposed a bilateral agreement dealing with major changes in the German frontier (east and west), an occupation to guarantee the execution of the treaty, and a special military regime for the left bank of the Rhine. The hope, it seems, was that bargaining on such essentials could be accomplished quickly. The intent was that (in the words of the preamble) "the arrangement thus reached between the two countries will enable them both to appear with complete safety at the Conference which, immediately after the arrival of President Wilson, will be held at Versailles for the purpose of exchanging views and agreements among the greater allies."[11]

Whether or not the British replied to this proposition is not known, but Clemenceau was obviously still probing for support when British and French leaders met on December 1 in London (Colonel House had been invited but had remained in Paris, indisposed). On this occasion the premier permitted Marshal Foch to present a memorandum that the marshal had drawn up for the French government and that went considerably beyond the plans suggested by the Foreign Ministry. It was a proposal for the creation of an independent Rhineland that could combine with Britain, France, Belgium, and Luxemburg in defending western Europe.[12] As Lloyd George later noted, "the fact that this was the first topic raised by the French at the first conference held after the Armistice to discuss the Peace Settlement, shows the importance they attached to it."[13]

Since Clemenceau had absented himself from the conference table during Marshal Foch's presentation he was able to avoid taking a formal position on these matters, but the British government was in little doubt about what the French premier was doing. One indication of this was Lord Balfour's assertion to the Imperial War Cabinet on December 18 that "there was already a disagreeable tendency among some of our Allies to adopt the system of 'log-rolling.' "[14] Another bit of proof was Sir William Wiseman's remark to David Hunter Miller in March 1919 that "right after the Armistice the French had asked the British to mutually support each other in their demands about the Peace."[15]

Though apparently the British government made no promises, these Anglo-French exchanges of November and December did give rise to rumors of a secret agreement. Such stories may have been spawned in part because Clemenceau had made important concessions at the time regarding the situation in the Middle East (giving Britain control of both Palestine and the Mosul oil fields),[16] but there are other explanations too, not the least of which was the impression created by Lloyd George's surprisingly anti-German electoral campaign and his coalition's smashing triumph at the polls in December. Whatever the cause, Lord Esher, for example, soon reached the conclusion that "we have entered into a cabal with France and Italy in order to counter the policy of the United States."[17] Secretary of State Robert Lansing was also "convinced that the two principal governments, with which we are to deal, have come to a working understanding and will endeavor to frustrate any plan which will defeat their ambitions."[18] Even President Wilson developed a similar opinion. "As you know," he told newsmen during his voyage to Europe early in December, "Clemenceau, Lloyd George, and Orlando have held a meeting in London. Colonel House was unable to be there. . . . The men apparently got together on a programme which I have just received. . . . It is very obvious in reading between the lines of Colonel House's report to me that these representatives of France, Great Britain, and Italy are determined to get everything out of Germany that they can."[19]

The strangest thing was that the Americans were suspicious without being very knowledgeable. They were aware, naturally, of the content of the French agenda. In addition, they had received a copy of the French note (to the British) of November 26, passed on to them under rather peculiar circumstances by the French embassy in London. Yet they had not been allowed to see the incriminating preamble to the latter document,[20] nor had they been informed of Marshal Foch's pleadings before the British cabinet. Colonel House had obtained Allied reports on the London meeting, but these contained no reference to the fact that German borders had been discussed.[21]

In fact, it was only beginning with the next month that Americans focused any attention at all upon the Rhineland. It was December 5, for example, before Walter Lippmann (then an assistant to Colonel House) reported to the head of the Inquiry that the "frontiers of 1814" and "left bank of the Rhine" had now become pressing "territorial questions."[22] It was almost two weeks later before Charles Seymour (one of the Inquiry specialists) observed that "there is a strong movement [in France] for the annexation of the Saar coal district. . . . There is a movement, not so strong, for the annexation of the whole west bank of the Rhine. . . . "[23] It was Christmas Eve before Seymour and three other members of the Inquiry submitted a memorandum that included the assertion that "the loss of the whole Left Bank [to Germany] is highly questionable, though some provision for autonomy and disarmament might well be made."[24]

As late as the opening of the conference, General Bliss was deeply concerned about the readiness of the American commissioners (Wilson, Lansing, House, Henry White, and Bliss himself) to confront such issues as the Rhine. On December 26, Bliss had even written to Secretary Lansing requesting a clarification of policy in this regard. "Are we agreed on a principle with which we will meet a demand for a session of the entire left bank?" he asked. "How are we going to get the President's views or instructions on such questions?"[25] Two weeks later, in a letter to the War Department, Bliss was still complaining about the lack of "preparation."[26]

Fortunately for the Americans, such fears of confrontation were premature. The French continued throughout January to seek informal support for their objectives, particularly among the British. Marshal Foch now circulated a revision of his earlier memorandum in which he argued that it was necessary to establish a military barrier at the Rhine on behalf of the new League of Nations.[27] The marshal also took time to discuss the problem of the Rhine with members of the British delegation like Lord Robert Cecil.[28] Clemenceau held several meetings on the subject with Lloyd George and others.[29]

Still, by the first weeks of February there were a number of reasons why the French might well have wished to change their tactics. In the first place, the British were not responding to private overtures with anything like the enthusiasm that had been hoped for.[30] Then again, it had become clear that neither the Americans nor British were interested in fashioning a league of nations that would provide much real security for France.[31] Beyond this, Lloyd George had just come frightfully close to persuading the conference to require demobilization of the German army as part of the armistice renewal, thereby depriving Marshal Foch of one of his strongest arguments for continuing the occupation.[32] Finally, both Wilson and Lloyd George were scheduled to be absent from Paris after February 14 (the president, for a full month), thus opening up the possibility of French collaboration with other

American and British delegates, and especially with the compromise-minded Texan of whom Clemenceau was so fond.[33]

Whether or not these were the crucial considerations, the fact is that the American and British leaders had hardly left for home in February before the French began a vigorous campaign to win their objectives with regard to the Rhine. To be sure, this effort was not well-coordinated, waged as it was at a number of places, at a number of times, by a number of different individuals. Yet the existence of a common thrust was unmistakable.

Not surprisingly, Marshal Foch was the first to take the offensive, attempting to exploit recent political developments to force the conference to adopt an extensive preliminary treaty.[34] On February 18, he returned from the third armistice renewal to proclaim his belief that, if the Allies were to act quickly, they could dictate virtually any peace terms they desired. For this reason, he asserted, and because peace with Germany would free western hands to deal with the increasing menace of Russia, the conference leadership should resolve to set a lump sum reparations figure, establish limitations on the German armed forces, and determine boundaries for the Reich excluding the occupied Rhine territory. The marshal wanted to take the essentials now and leave the details to a final peace congress.[35]

Foch, however, reckoned without President Wilson. No sooner had Colonel House cabled the president about the marshal's proposal than the latter responded with a devastating rejection of the scheme. In a wire to House from mid-Atlantic, Wilson declared:

> It seems to me like an attempt to . . . hurry us into an acquiescence in their plans with regard to the Western bank of the Rhine. . . . I beg that you stand steady with regard to everything other than the strictly military and naval terms

74

until I return. Marshal Foch is acting in this matter I'm sure under exterior guidance of the most unsafe kind.[36]

The result was that, although the Council of Ten did decide to hurry committee work on territorial and economic questions, it was agreed that any decisions regarding a preliminary treaty would await the return of the prime minister and the president in March.[37] Foch was left to concentrate on the military terms.[38]

By this time Clemenceau had begun his own campaign to limit Germany to the Rhine. Not even the shoulder wound he had received from a would-be assassin on February 18 could dampen his sudden commitment to his cause, and in a bedside interview with Colonel House on February 22 he dwelt at length upon the desirability of a Rhineland republic. The premier was willing for the new state to be exempt from indemnity and without armed forces. He wished to do everything possible to make it prosperous and contented.[39]

It was André Tardieu, Clemenceau's second-in-command, however, who found the argument that overcame the qualms of House and Balfour. In discussions on February 23, Tardieu persuaded the two men that France had no intention of permanently barring a Rhine republic from political union with Germany. After five or more years, he said, when the League of Nations was working well, there would be no objection to the Rhineland relinquishing its independence if its people so desired. Thus, the right of self-determination for the area would be preserved.[40]

House and Balfour were visibly impressed. The Colonel noted in his diary that Tardieu's information "relieves that question of one of its most objectionable features,"[41] and Balfour was eager to conclude that the French "are ready to modify their schemes for neutralizing the left bank of the river so as to make them more tolerable to British and American opinion."[42] By February 27, both men had tentatively decided

75

to accept the French suggestion.[43] On March 2, Vance Mc-Cormick (a member of the American delegation) recorded in his journal that Tardieu and House had come to tea, where they had "agreed on [a] plan for [a] Rhenish republic" and discussed the means for obtaining Lloyd George's approval.[44]

Had Clemenceau backed up Tardieu fully and immediately, he probably could have achieved an understanding, but apparently he concluded that his subordinate had given away too much. At a meeting with Colonel House and Lloyd George on March 7, the premier made it very clear, with regard to the Rhineland, "that he did not believe in the principle of self-determination" and that "he would not consent to any limitation of time being placed upon the enforced separation of the Rhenish Republic from the rest of Germany."[45] The colonel was forced to cable President Wilson that "no tentative agreement was reached because of Clemenceau's very unreasonable attitude. He wants the Rhenish republics [sic] to be perpetually restrained from joining the German federation. Tardieu tells me he will urge him to modify this view."[46]

The president, however, was much more disturbed at House's compromising than at the position Clemenceau had taken. He had not expected things to go so far, particularly in such an important direction. He hastened, therefore, to make his earlier instructions more specific:

> [I am rendered] a little uneasy by what you say of the left bank of the Rhine. I hope you will not even provisionally consent to the separation of the Rhine provinces from Germany under any arrangement but will reserve the whole matter until my arrival.[47]

In effect, he was calling off the colonel's negotiations.

Lloyd George was also pulling in the reins, but for other reasons. As he had emphasized both to his cabinet in London (during his visit there) and at the peace conference on March 7,[48] what troubled him was not so much the idea of a buffer state as the thought of maintaining an army of occupation. He had visions of at least 300,000 men being required for the task. Although Clemenceau contended that 100,000 was more realistic and that two-thirds of these could be French, the prime minister remained quite skeptical of what an occupation would "really mean."[49] On March 10, he persuaded his colleagues to appoint a special ad hoc committee to reexamine the entire matter. As members, the Council selected André Tardieu, Phillip Kerr (Lloyd George's secretary), and Sidney Mezes (Colonel House's brother-in-law and the director of the American Inquiry).[50]

The deliberations of these three men, meeting on March 11 and 12, made it clear just how serious the disagreements had become. Tardieu, quite naturally, had somewhat revised his earlier emphasis. While reaffirming his willingness to see a Rhenish republic return to Germany in time, he now insisted very openly on a permanent occupation of the region by an inter-Allied army. Yet he emphasized that large contingents of British and American troops would not be needed, since even a token representation would have the desired moral effect. He also offered to relinquish the bridgeheads on the far bank in return for permission to conduct periodic inspections in Germany.

Kerr was not particularly sympathetic. A separated Rhineland, he contended, would constitute a grave irritation to German nationalists, far outweighing the advantages of a military frontier upon the Rhine. An occupation was also undesirable if only because a preponderance of the British people would object to the maintenance of even one British division upon the continent. To him the real peril was that the settlement might offend his nation's sense of fair play and alienate her from France.

Mezes, if somewhat inhibited by the president's instructions to Colonel House, was definitely more open-minded than

77

Kerr. Though he specified his belief that any occupation must be temporary, it was clearly an occupation of "German" soil that concerned him most. If the left bank was independent, he said, time limitations on the occupation might not be so crucial.[51]

Though hardly successful as an effort to resolve disagreement, the talks of the special committee did have an important impact on Lloyd George. The apparent rigidity of the stalemate left him aggravated at the French, irritated with Colonel House, and pushed to the point of radical innovation as a means of establishing a stronger position against Clemenceau.[52] By March 12, when he was visited by the colonel, the prime minister had begun to think in terms of a defensive guarantee by Britain to meet the demands of French security. He was looking forward anxiously to the chance to coordinate his strategy with that of President Wilson.[53]

The arriving president must have felt anxious too, not only at returning to a conference that seemed to be dangerously adrift, but also at leaving behind his increasingly apprehensive nation. During his two weeks at home he could hardly have avoided noticing how rapidly the postwar euphoria was dissipating. Nor could he have missed the extent to which the impression was growing (and being encouraged to partisan advantage) that it was *he* who was prolonging the conference and delaying the return of American armies. On March 4, thirty-nine Republican senators and senators-elect had published a round robin attacking the League Covenant "in the form now proposed" and urging that the peace conference address itself to making a treaty with Germany before it tackled long-range problems.[54] A few days later Senator Lodge had written to Henry White that "the demand for the complete return of our soldiers, which can only follow on the proclamation of the German peace, is constantly rising more loudly and strongly."[55]

78

For a while after the armistice Americans had loyally accepted their unexpected responsibilities around the globe. At the end of January, for instance, the *New York Times* had concluded that an army of occupation would continue to be necessary "until [the German has] proved his good faith by his works."[56] In February an Ohio newspaper cartoon had portrayed a doughboy forcing a fat Rhinelander and his dachshund to march in step while the caption read, "It hurts, but he's got to do it."[57] About the same time the *Seattle Post Intelligencer* had acknowledged that "it is probably a part of the war duty of the Americans to remain in Europe until the civilized world is safely started upon its peaceful reconstruction plans."[58]

Be that as it may, the length of the conference, the growing unrest in Europe, the unhappiness of the AEF, and the foreign appeals for economic and military assistance began to take their toll of American sympathy and patience. By February many citizens found it increasingly difficult to understand why American troops were needed in such far-away places as Russia, Italy, the Balkans, and Armenia.[59] Indeed, Secretary of War Baker's voluminous mail from families of servicemen soon convinced him that perhaps the president should use American forces only to "relieve Great Britain of some part of her duty . . . in France and Germany, for which the reasons would be obvious to our people."[60] By April 12, the *San Francisco Chronicle* was not so sure about the wisdom of even a European assignment. In its view, the nation was being held responsible for maintaining order in a situation of deliberately created confusion.[61]

All of these circumstances, then—Clemenceau's obstinacy, Lloyd George's anxiety, Europe's desperation, and America's impatience—must have intensified the president's desire to break the impasse and helped to render him receptive to Lloyd George's ideas regarding French security. In any event, Wilson had not been in Paris more than a few hours on March 14 before the two leaders had decided to offer Clemenceau a provisional tripartite alliance against German attack, coupling this with the assertion that, as far as the Rhineland was concerned, they could agree to no more than a demilitarized zone on the right bank as a provisional reparations guarantee.[62] It is some indication of the president's haste (and determination that he did not bother to consult the remainder of the American delegation in making this proposal. House, Lansing, Bliss, and White were not to discover what the president had done for almost two weeks.[63]

If the French themselves were surprised and intrigued by the Anglo-American suggestion, they were also considerably disconcerted. In fact, Clemenceau's delegation was compelled to retreat into two days of private discussions merely in order to agree upon a response.[64] In these encounters, apparently, André Tardieu and Foreign Minister Stephen Pichon took the harder line, skeptical of sacrificing the reality of an army on the Rhine in order to obtain a mere alliance. Clemenceau, on the other hand, was openly relieved at having an excuse for reducing France's military requirements. Unlike Tardieu, he was much more enthusiastic about a buffer state than about an occupation.

Even so, the premier was not unwilling to forego an independent Rhineland in return for the advantages he had been offered. He realized full well that if the tripartite agreement could be made to be effective, it would bring his nation far more strength than any territory could. Not only would it allow France to unburden herself of much of her immense military establishment, but it would also relieve her of the necessity to impose a crushing treaty upon Germany.[65]

Clemenceau seems to have foreseen but three problems in accepting such an arrangement. The first and greatest, of course, was that the tripartite pact would have to be formulated, presented, and even supplemented in such a way that the majority of the French people (and German) would be convinced of its validity. A second problem was that, even with the treaty in existence, France would have to retain enough means of defense that in case of war she would not be overrun by enemy forces before her maritime allies could mobilize to come to her assistance. A third difficulty was that the alliance would have to be arranged so that it could never be terminated or lapse before an adequate substitute could be found. Clemenceau had become particularly concerned regarding this point because on March 14 Wilson had referred to the American guarantee as a temporary and not permanent arrangement. The premier concluded, perhaps unjustifiably, that the president was thinking of an even briefer period of alliance than was Lloyd George.[66]

Faced with these eventualities, Clemenceau decided to negotiate on two different fronts. To begin with, he informed Wilson and Lloyd George that though he could renounce his demand for a separated Rhineland in return for a guarantee, he could not dispense with certain military safeguards. A lengthy occupation of the left bank would still be necessary, he said, and a fifty-kilometer demilitarized zone on the right bank would also be essential. France must have permission to occupy at least five Rhine bridgeheads if Germany violated the demilitarized zone or the military clauses of the treaty. France must also obtain the northeastern frontier of 1814, and the privilege of occupying the entire Saar.[67]

Meanwhile, on a second front, Clemenceau secretly approached Colonel House with a view of securing a more satisfactory American commitment regarding the span of time for the alliance. In doing so he seems to have convinced the colonel both that the president, on the fourteenth, had had in mind a very temporary obligation on the part of the United States and that the French point of view with regard to a more permanent alliance was worthy of House's own support. Clemenceau left this meeting with the colonel's promise to do what he could to persuade the president to endorse this kind of arrangement.[68]

Yet, despite his assurances to Clemenceau, House proved unable to carry out his mission. The reason was that after drafting a formula that received Clemenceau's approval, the colonel paused to show it to his fellow commissioners, and the reactions of Lansing, White, and Bliss were so extremely negative that they shook House from his original intentions.[69] By March 21 he had shifted his attention to the task of assisting the American experts in dissecting and rejecting the safeguards demanded in Clemenceau's note of March 17 (and Tardieu's glosses upon it).[70] By March 26, when House learned from the president of Wilson's readiness to duplicate Lloyd George's guarantee to France, the colonel had forgotten his promise to press the president beyond the latter's original (i.e., temporary) commitment.[71]

As a result, when Clemenceau on March 27 took it upon himself to emphasize to Wilson and Lloyd George the unacceptability of a temporary guarantee, the Frenchman was turned away quite empty-handed.[72] The president responded with what was essentially a restatement of his earlier offer, providing for (1) a demilitarized Rhineland to fifty kilometers east of the river, (2) a statement that violations of the demilitarization (i.e., *not* of the military clauses) would be considered "hostile acts" by treaty signatories, and (3) a pledge that Britain and the United States, until the League of Nations had proved itself of adequate security, would come to French assistance in case of an "unprovoked movement of aggression."[73] Lloyd George stood by a set of similar terms, summarized in a March 25 memorandum that he and his advisers had composed during a brief respite at Fontainebleau. In this communication the British leader had pleaded with the

French for moderation on issues including reparations, disarmament, and German boundaries. "I cannot conceive of any greater cause of future war," he had written regarding the latter, "than that the German people . . . should be surrounded by a number of small states . . . containing large masses of Germans clamouring for reunion with their native land."[74]

The French reply to these propositions was formulated quickly. Indeed, its first installment had been contained in the "general observations" that Clemenceau had handed to the British on March 26 and that he forwarded to Wilson on March 31. The premier argued indignantly that if a means of appeasing Germany were needed, it should be sought not on the Continent, but in such things as ships, colonies, and trade, that is, areas in which the maritime powers had already achieved their own interests and security. Otherwise, he asserted, those allies who could afford it least would be called upon to accept the most provisional guarantees. Moreover, taking needed territory from countries like Poland and Czechoslovakia (and France) in order to pacify the Germans would only serve to enrage *their* publics instead of Germany's.[75]

The second French note, referring specifically to the Rhineland and dated April 2, was equally intransigent. In addition to what had been asked before, the French now demanded a wider demilitarized zone and the right to organize a local police force in the region. Though they were willing to set aside the proposed commission of inspection, they stipulated that each signatory power must be given the right to notify the League of Nations whenever Germany had violated the clauses on disarmament or demilitarization. Even more significantly, they insisted that the tripartite treaty of guarantee should remain in operation until the contracting parties had agreed that the League of Nations offered a satisfactory substitute.[76]

Thus by the beginning of April the conference had slipped

back into a deadlock that, from the standpoint of much of Europe, had all the earmarks of disaster. March 19 had witnessed the advent of a bolshevist regime in Budapest; April 5 would bring a similar coup in Munich.[77] Ugly rumors in the British press had led members of the House of Commons to attack Lloyd George for "going soft on the enemy."[78] The "impatient ones" in the French Chamber demanded that Clemenceau obtain concessions at the conference or resign.[79]

It was an extremely trying period for all three statesmen. The president was exhausted and discouraged by French "stubbornness";[80] Lloyd George was frustrated and irritated with the lack of progress;[81] and Clemenceau was furious at the British and American rejection of his minimum requirements.[82] On March 28, when Wilson refused to approve a French proposal regarding the Saar, the premier exploded in anger, called him "pro-German," and stalked out of the room.[83] In like fashion, recriminations between Lloyd George and the French concerning Poland led to a complete breakdown in discussions on that subject.[84] On April 1, Wilson "flew into a rage" when an acquaintance suggested that the Allies might occupy the left bank for the entire reparations period as mandatories of the League.[85]

The matters of the Saar, reparations, and the Rhineland occupation were becoming more interrelated as time went on. Ostensibly the question of the Saar had always involved compensation to France for damage to coalfields, but at the end of March Clemenceau revealed that he now saw his objectives there largely in terms of reducing German power. In refusing to be satisfied with the use of the Saar mines (which both Wilson and Lloyd George were willing to concede) and in insisting on political control of the area, he was in effect forcing the president to fall back upon the principle of self-determination. The issue was becoming the same as that involved in the struggle over the Rhine, that is, the security of France versus the moral rights of Germany.

On the other hand, if reparations were less relevant to the Saar, they had become more significant to the Rhenish occupation. The latter, of course, had consistently been justified in terms of French security, and as late as March 31, Marshal Foch had been content to harangue the Council of Four about the indispensability of the occupation on that score. Yet from the moment the British and Americans had offered the security pact in March, the French had become increasingly willing to see the occupation treated as a guarantee of reparations. On March 24 the French minister of finance had gone so far as to urge before the reparations subcommittee that Germany be subjected to occupation of strategic points and to export-import controls until she had completely paid off her debt.[86]

Just when it appeared that the Paris Conference might end in rupture, the president made what turned out to be the crucial concession. Wilson did this in an indirect fashion, having first made overtures to the French through Colonel House and later deputized House to represent him after he had fallen ill on April 3. Everyone knew that the colonel was one of the few Americans in Paris who was in any mood to compromise, and this may have been the reason he was chosen.[87] But whatever Wilson's motives, when House, on April 5, overruled the American financial experts and abandoned their long-standing demand that reparations be limited to thirty years or less,[88] the president did not repudiate him.[89] On the contrary, after Wilson returned to the Council of Four on April 8, he ratified what House had done and pushed on to achieve a tentative settlement of the reparations issue.[90]

With momentum reestablished, the Saar question also moved to a solution. The president had endorsed French ownership of the region's mines on March 31, but he had subsequently resisted both the British proposals for an autonomous state and the French demands for political arrangements that would allow a Gallicization of the area. Then, on April 9, after Wilson had suggested that a neutral commission administer the Saar for a period of fifteen years, Lloyd George altered his position in order to support that of the president.[91] On April 10, Clemenceau joined them in accepting Wilson's idea, although it took two more days of negotiations before the detalis of the bargain were completed.[92]

Given the close ties among the issues, this kind of progress could not fail to have its impact on the Rhineland question. The agreement on an indeterminate period for reparations, for example, made it much less difficult for Clemenceau to accept a Rhenish occupation shorter than thirty years. The understanding on a fifteen-year administration of the Saar gave him a new criteria for judging the length of time he might reasonably seek to hold the Rhineland. Even prior to these agreements, on the day after House's first concession on reparations, the premier had asked his military adviser, General Mordacq, to study the possibility of evacuating an occupation in two successive phases, after five years and after ten. If Clemenceau was not rushing to show his hand, he was surely beginning to think of compromise.[93]

On April 12, President Wilson decided to be blunt about the left bank of the Rhine. He asked Colonel House therefore to convey a "very solemn warning" to the French that the tripartite guarantee treaty "was an extraordinary step for the United States to take," and that "there would be no hope of achieving its ratification if stipulations were added to it."[94] He also requested House to transmit a letter to Tardieu in which he (the president) rejected almost *in toto* the latter's note of April 2. Wilson accepted only one French demand: that the guarantee treaty remain in force until the contracting parties had agreed that the League provided an adequate substitute.[95]

Nonetheless, the president's yielding this point appears to have been just what Clemenceau was waiting for. As a result of this concession the existence of the League of Nations could not be used as a pretext to overturn the tripartite pact. As a result of this concession the Allied guarantee had become substantial. The time had come for him to split the difference with the president, especially if in so doing he could organize a common front against the prime minister, who was temporarily in London.

So it occurred that Clemenceau called upon House on the afternoon of April 14 for what the colonel described in his diary as a "love feast." Coming straight to the point, the premier announced his readiness to accept the president's terms for the protection of France. They were not exactly what he wanted, he said, but he thought them sufficient and asked only one amendment to them. Since "he would have to fight Foch and the other marshals" to get them through, it would make his task a great deal easier if "the President would agree to let the French occupy three stages of German territory, the first for five years, the second for ten, and the third for fifteen years. . . . If the President would consent to [this], he, Clemenceau could beat his marshals and the Chamber of Deputies and the Senate, and he would also take occasion to state the generous actions of the President toward France in the peace conference."[96]

Clemenceau was driving a hard bargain, but he was displaying an ability to compromise as well. In addition to offering a 50 percent reduction in the length of the occupation, he was proposing to dispense with his earlier demands for a widened demilitarized zone, a Rhenish gendarmerie, and special access to the League of Nations. He was also acceding in the president's wish to exclude the disarmament clauses of the treaty from relevance to the tripartite pact.

It took House less than twenty-four hours to gain Wilson's assent to the French proposal. "The President made a wry face over some of it, particularly the three five-year periods of occupation, but he agreed to do it all. I told him we had better do it with a *beau geste* rather than grudgingly."[97] The colonel then hastened over to inform Clemenceau, who was "delighted"[98]—so delighted, in fact, that after House left he quickly telephoned Tardieu to let him know that "I have obtained the fifteen years; I now consider the peace complete."[99]

Thus, on April 19, Lloyd George returned from England to find a whole "new world" in Paris. "The outlook had entirely changed," he later wrote. "I did my best to convince President Wilson of the mischievous possibilities of the occupation, but in vain."[100] Try as he would, he could not budge Wilson from his agreement with the French.

On April 22, the prime minister capitulated. The occasion was Clemenceau's presentation of articles on the Rhineland that he and Wilson had approved two days before and that for the first time described the occupation as a sanction for the execution of the treaty, not as a guarantee against attack.[101] The transcript of the meeting reveals both the tenacity of the negotiators and the way in which they interacted:

> LLOYD GEORGE: The occupation for fifteen years!
>
> CLEMENCEAU: I cannot reduce it. It is difficult to pass as is.
>
> LLOYD GEORGE: You ought not to expect we will leave British troops there fifteen years.
>
> CLEMENCEAU: It seems necessary to write "international." All I strictly ask is a battalion and a flag.
>
> LLOYD GEORGE: You know with what impatience Britain awaits the ending of compulsory military service?
>
> CLEMENCEAU: I do not know if the word "international" is in the President's copy.
>
> WILSON: Why not say territory will be occupied without other indication?
>
> CLEMENCEAU: Without your flag by mine, I will not be able to present this to parliament.
>
> LLOYD GEORGE: These fifteen years as an absolute limit? They will not vary with Germany's payments?
>
> CLEMENCEAU: No, unless Germany refuses to pay. If the League of Nations confirms that Germany does not keep its commitments, we can prolong or even remodel the occupation.
>
> LLOYD GEORGE: I accept.[102]

One might wonder, even so, why the prime minister gave in so easily. Considering his antipathy to the occupation and his fight of so many months against it, could he not have held out a little longer against the Wilson-Clemenceau alliance? Could he not have fought his way out of isolation, perhaps by offering the president British support on other matters?

A number of considerations may have influenced his decision. Since it had previously been agreed that the treaty would be presented to the Germans in a week to ten days, there was relatively little time left to maneuver for advantage. What is more, the prime minister had been under increasing pressure from home during April not to give the Germans an easy peace. The defeat of government forces in a by-election at Hull and a "get tough" telegram from 370 members of Parliament on April 8 had worried him so much that he found it necessary to make the special trip back to England from which he had returned.[103]

Clemenceau, too, had been under "get tough" pressure from his countrymen, much of it quite flagrant, and this consideration may also have been a factor in determining Lloyd George's attitude. President Poincaré had openly informed his premier of his disappointment regarding the Rhineland and was reported to be holding conferences on the subject with legislative leaders and with Foch.[104] The marshal had embarked upon a vigorous campaign of his own to overturn the compromise.[105] In a letter to Clemenceau of April 15, Foch had not only protested against the fifteen-year provision, but had also demanded to be heard in person by the council of ministers and the French delegation.[106] Two days later he went as far as intentional insubordination, delaying an instruction from the Allied leaders to the German armistice commission concerning the sending of the enemy's peace delegation.[107] Though such behavior almost brought Clemenceau to the point of dismissing the marshal from command, quick meetings between the two men eased the tension temporarily, and the premier promised Poincaré to allow Foch to address the cabinet.[108] The same week reverberations of the struggle had reached the French Senate, where Clemenceau's supporters were compelled to produce a resolution calling for the military guarantees "indispensable to France" in order to head off one that demanded the "guarantees recommended by the Inter-Allied High Command."[109]

Foch had his say before the French cabinet on April 25, but in the private session that followed, the premier won unanimous support for the policies he had pursued. Justifying himself on this occasion, Clemenceau explained that though his delegation had wanted a buffer state along the Rhine, it had simply had to recognize that there was irreducible American and British opposition to such an arrangement and even to an occupation of length. Because of this opposition, because of the Allied guarantee treaties, and because of the changing technology of war, he argued, a permanent occupation could not be made a *sine qua non*. He was satisfied to have had the Allies agree that if Germany defaulted on her debt, the Reparations Commission could extend the occupation almost indefinitely.[110]

Though Poincaré and Foch had been turned back, their continuing concern did have the effect of inducing Clemenceau to face up to the one remaining loophole in his arrangements: the possibility that the American Senate or the British Parliament might refuse to ratify the special alliance. The premier brought this problem to Wilson's attention on April 25—the very day of the French cabinet meeting—suggesting that as insurance the fifteen years of occupation be made to begin with the coming into force of the tripartite treaties.[111] Following their conversation he presented a formula to the Council of Four that he and Wilson had worked out. It stipulated that if the need arose to replace the alliance, Germany would consent "to accept such similar guarantees as [the Allies] might require."[112]

The prime minister was cooperative, but an understanding was not reached easily, for Lloyd George feared that such a proviso would be ammunition for his parliamentary opposition. It took six days and five exchanges of written proposals before all sides were satisfied. In the final version, approved April 30, the draft treaty was amended to read that "if at that date [in fifteen years] the guarantees against unprovoked aggression by Germany are not considered sufficient by the Allied and Associated governments, the evacuation of the occupying troops may be delayed to the extent regarded as necessary for the purpose of obtaining the required guarantees."[113] The passage was sufficiently vague to stimulate Tardieu and Poincaré to a lengthy public debate in 1921 as to just what rights it gave to France.[114]

In the meantime, Clemenceau moved to cement the council's unanimity on the Rhineland by turning the dissatisfaction of Poincaré and Foch against the Allies, obviously hoping to convince Wilson and Lloyd George of his own moderation. Thus, he privately informed Poincaré on April 28 that it might be "useful to make a new effort" to have the occupation prolonged, and when the latter responded with a letter proposing that the left bank be held until reparations were paid, he forwarded this to the British and Americans.[115] Similarly, on May 6, Clemenceau allowed Foch to register his objections to the Rhine compromise before the plenary session of the entire conference even though he knew that these would not be well received. Not unexpectedly, the marshal had altered his basic argument again. Instead of asking for the entire Rhineland, he now demanded only the river passage and the bridgeheads of the right bank. Instead of talking of security, he voiced his pleas for a longer occupation almost entirely in terms of a guarantee for reparations. Like Poincaré, he apparently saw a greater chance for success in playing down the earlier emphasis on the need for a "defensive barrier."[116]

The week before this Foch had found incidental support

from the British side when General Sir Henry Wilson had written to Lloyd George criticizing Clemenceau's plan for a three-stage, north-to-south reduction of the occupation. Though the prime minister had not endorsed Sir Henry's suggested alternative (a south-to-north progression), he did notify the Allied chiefs of his adviser's views. Foch, in turn, was delighted, probably not so much because he was in accord with the general as because he hoped that the criticism might undermine the whole idea of phased evacuation. In any case, Sir Henry's letter had little effect. It is important mainly because it was the first indication of what would ultimately become a rather widespread, if partly unjustified suspicion: that the French had arranged the shape and order of the withdrawal with political rather than military ends in view.[117]

Lloyd George, in the interim, had been making a last effort of his own to "improve" the occupation before the Germans received the treaty on May 7. Aware of the desperate shortage of financial resources in western Europe and reminded by his experts that occupation charges would come off the top of reparations,[118] the prime minister now tried to employ the costs of the armies as a means of restricting the occupation itself. On May 5 he told the Supreme Council that it was imperative to limit the number of occupying forces for the simple reason that the payment of their expenditures—currently running at £300,000,000 ($1,400,000,000) a year—would leave nothing over for the allies who were not participating. Yet despite the obvious strength of Lloyd George's case, the most he could obtain from the wily Clemenceau was an admission that a study of the problem was desirable. In the end, it was agreed to ask the permanent military representatives at Versailles to do the research.[119]

Partly in order to forestall such efforts as Lloyd George's and partly because it was to their immediate advantage to do so, the French had actually been trying to reduce the costs of the occupation throughout the previous winter and spring. It was not that they objected to Germany having to pay these bills, of course, nor that they had any qualms about the number of Allied soldiers stationed on German soil, but only that, under the arrangements that had been established, the higher the occupation costs, the more France lost financially. Under the armistice (as later, the treaty), occupation debts possessed priority over reparations, and although France would receive a maximum of 30 to 40 percent of the sums that Germany paid for the occupation (i.e., her percentage of the Allied troops on the Rhine), she expected to (and did, under international agreement) receive 55 to 65 percent of the money transferred as reparations. (Theoretically, once French troops exceeded 65 percent of those in the occupation, as they ultimately did, the French would begin to gain rather than lose from the priority, but this might be months or even years away. Moreover, due to the fact that armistice and peacetime debts were to be lumped together, the French reimbursement from occupation costs would probably never reach 65 percent.)

The result was a considerable amount of maneuvering on the part of the French, who were trying, quite understandably, to achieve the best of both worlds (a thoroughgoing occupation without losing money). Their most obvious effort to accomplish this had been their suggestion in the subcommittees of the conference that the treaty not follow the armistice in giving full priority to occupation costs—a proposal that had been virtually ignored by the British and Americans.[120] Less obvious, but equally important both for the present and the future, were French attempts at manipulating two basic tools of occupation cost accounting: (1) the meaning of the French word *entretien* ("maintenance"), as used in the armistice,[121] and (2) the average cost figure per soldier, as calculated by the participating armies. In neither case were they finally to have their way, in the first instance running up against combined

British and American resistance, and in the second against stubborn American opposition.

The conflict regarding "entretien" was of shorter duration than the other dispute. Originally, on January 9, an Allied armistice subcommission had unanimously recommended that "entretien" be interpreted to include the total costs of occupation.[122] Within a month, however, after it had become apparent that the armistice would not be brief, the German contention that, legally, "entretien" included only food, equipment, shelter, and transportation (i.e., it did not include wages) gave Marshal Foch the idea for a new and more advantageous interpretation.[123] In late February, with the support of Belgian officers,[124] he proposed that the compensation on the occupation be split into two parts: a narrowly defined "entretien," which would be paid by Germany to each Ally as first priority; and the remaining costs, which would be considered a part of the general war debt, with no priority. The British army at first approved and then, after considering the implications, objected to such an arrangement.[125] General Pershing, in a letter to Marshal Foch dated March 8, flatly rejected it.[126] At a meeting of the permanent military representatives at Versailles on April 22, General Bliss adhered to Pershing's position, contending that otherwise the United States would end by making a sizable financial contribution to the occupation.[127] It was not until the middle of May that the armies accepted a compromise definition of "entretien," closer to the American than to the French conception.[128]

The disagreement over the average cost figures was much more difficult to solve, probably because it was even more obviously a question involving America's special interest. This problem, like that of "entretien," grew out of the fact that it cost different countries dissimilar amounts to maintain a soldier in the Rhineland. There was a plausible explanation of this variation (for example, both salaries and transportation charges were far greater for the United States). Nevertheless, for reasons enumerated above, the French in particular objected to the Americans asking over twice as much reimbursement as they themselves claimed for the same assignment.[129] (This meant not only a larger sum for the occupation debt, with its priority over reparations, but also that Americans might be receiving as much as 40 to 50 percent of the payments on that debt.) The British, whose costs were much closer to the French than to the American and who were undoubtedly hoping to head off a compromise that would give the French more for each soldier than they actually spent, proposed in March that all armies take the French daily expenditure as a base. The Americans, however, objected vehemently to such an idea and showed no interest in bargaining.[130] The controversy dragged on throughout the spring, sowing in the process seeds of what would finally become a far greater dispute over the reimbursement of army charges.

The permanent military representatives, meanwhile, had made little progress toward a recommendation for the premiers on limiting the occupation's size and cost. Marshal Foch had submitted a memorandum proposing that the forty Allied divisions in Germany be reduced to thirty within two months after treaty signing, and ultimately to ten, of which one to two (i.e., 20,000 to 40,000 men) would be American.[131] Yet neither Bliss nor Pershing, who conferred regarding this plan at the president's request, was enthusiastic about agreement. In fact, the two men still believed that the entire American army should be withdrawn from Europe, and they presented Wilson with several arguments to support this view. They contended, among other things, (1) that taking the occupying contingent from an American Regular Army of only 212,000 men would seriously weaken home defenses; (2) that less than a division would be of no moral or physical value in the Rhineland and would only be absorbed into neighboring French units; and (3) that American soldiers in Europe desired almost universally to return home.[132]

It was with such convictions that Bliss postponed action by the permanent military representatives from day to day, first on the excuse of waiting for a meeting between Foch and Pershing on May 24, and then by pleading that the entire subject of the occupation was due to be considered again by the heads of government.[133] He realized that army strengths and costs were merging into a larger issue involving the very nature of the occupation itself. His secret hope was that from these new deliberations the United States could emerge without specific troop commitments in Europe.

If the conference had made momentous decisions regarding the Rhine, much remained to be settled. Such questions as the structure of the occupation, its size, its cost, and the relative contributions of the Allied nations—all were still pending as the treaty draft was given to the Germans in May. Not only was the resolution of these matters important in its own right, but it was also related directly to the success of the peace conference itself.

5

THE RHINELAND COMMISSION
AND RHINELAND AGREEMENT

> No matter how readily the United States may respond
> to a future call for help from France . . . , the ques-
> tion as to whether we might have to come again, and
> that in the near future, may depend materially on
> the wise and just and decent administration of the
> occupied territory.
>
> General Tasker Bliss,
> May 31, 1919

> Pressured by Wilson and Lloyd George, who in turn
> were guided by Pierrepont Noyes and Harold Stuart,
> Clemenceau was literally forced to sign . . . that
> convention for the administration of the Rhenish
> territories which, . . . has so greatly weakened the
> value of the moral sanction which was placed in
> our hands.
>
> Pertinax in *L'Echo de
> Paris*, June 2, 1921

The contest that now ensued regarding the structure of the permanent occupation was brief but significant. It was first precipitated in the middle of May, after Anglo-American unhappiness with projected military conventions had become increasingly severe. It came to a head again in early June, after French encouragement of separatist uprisings and German antagonism to the treaty had inspired Lloyd George to renew his attack upon the whole idea of occupation. On both occasions Clemenceau encountered what was potentially a strong

97

British-American front, but each time he was astute enough to profit from the fact that Lloyd George remained more basically dissatisfied than Wilson. Indeed, in a real sense, the French premier's endorsement of a civil high commission can be described as a successful effort on his part to isolate the prime minister by mollifying the president on a point of particular concern to Wilson.

Admittedly, the battle for civilian control had long since been underway within the armistice holding itself. Fully aware that precedents were being established for a postwar occupation, French military leaders had consistently fought to keep existing administrative machinery subordinate to Marshal Foch. The Americans and British, on the other hand, recognizing the special meaning the left bank possessed for France, had increasingly attempted to render the occupation responsible to inter-Allied councils. First with the Luxemburg Commission and then with the Rhineland Commission, they had striven to take the decisive economic and political power out of the hands of the French commander. They were still pursuing these efforts in May, at the time the peace conference began its work on permanent arrangements.

This earlier struggle had noteworthy consequences for the disagreement that developed over the peacetime occupation. In the first place, it helped to alert the British and Americans to the obsession of French concern regarding both security and reparations. Beyond this, it helped to set in motion Anglo-American proposals designed to prevent the French from converting the permanent occupation into the instrument of a single nation. It was thus in part responsible for generating that memorandum of Pierrepont Noyes (the American Rhineland commissioner) that became the Council of Four's directive to the committee created to "civilianize" the occupation.

In the end, the controversy regarding the occupation and the accomodation that emerged were to be of central importance to both the Rhineland and the peace conference. They were crucial, of course, in determining just how the citizens of the occupied regions would live their lives throughout the 1920s. Yet, on a more immediate front, they also proved essential in preserving the April understanding that had originally allowed Wilson, Lloyd George, and Clemenceau to unite upon a peacetime occupation. The new agreements held together a coalition that was threatening to come apart, thereby making it possible for the Allies to get on with the task of facing down the Germans.

The story, however, must start in January and February 1919, when the representatives of the Allied powers in the Rhineland had first begun to realize that their national interests and policies might not always coincide. The first battleground was the Luxemburg Commission.

Some of the concern that had arisen following the establishment of this commission to encourage trade between the Rhineland and the West was alluded to in Chapter 2. In theory, the organization had operated within the guidelines of the Superior Blockade Council and later under the supervision of the Supreme Economic Council. In actuality, however, the fact that the commission was still subordinate to the Allied High Command had allowed Foch to manipulate its decisions to French advantage. One effect had been a rapid growth of inter-Allied dissension. As early as January 17, the American military representatives on the new body had complained to General Pershing that the marshal's prestige was being used to force through self-serving legislation.[1] A month later, American compliance with the commission's regulations had become so sporadic that Foch himself was threatening to post guards around the American zone and seal it off from the surrounding region.[2]

Confronted with such discord, American and British leaders had attempted to call in the experts. On February 2, Colonel House had suggested to Lloyd George and Clemenceau that special governmental delegates be appointed to deal with Rhenish economic questions.[3] Subsequently, at the first meeting of the Committee for the Left Bank of the Rhine, the British themselves had proposed that Rhenish trade-licensing bodies should become "civil and expert."[4] Though no explicit agreement had resulted, the British had shortly thereafter placed a Foreign Office representative on the Luxemburg Commission and begun to substitute civilians for army men in the "sections economiques" of their own zone.[5] By March 6, officials of the United States War Trade Board in Paris had followed suit, sending Special Assistant Wallace Day to replace American officers on the commission.[6]

Still, while such experts could put more backbone into the Luxemburg body, they were handicapped by its lack of jurisdiction and of power. For weeks the American and British armies had tried to block Foch's endeavors by treating the organization as advisory, and Day and his colleagues now had little means at their disposal to change this attitude of disregard.[7] Furthermore, if the commission could not make American and British "sections" obey, there was little chance it could control the actions of the French equivalent. There was even less chance that it could supervise the economic affairs that Foch had assigned to the jurisdiction of completely independent agencies such as the Inter-Allied Military Food Committee in Mainz.[8]

As time passed, American and British authorities in Paris found their concern increasing with regard to the Rhineland. Existing Allied arrangements seemed unable to stem either the extraordinary French commercial expansion on the left bank or the rampant blockade-running between France and unoccupied Germany. Indigenous industry and business were in the doldrums. The region was not responding as it should if it were to be utilized as a means for priming German international trade and economic recovery.[9]

At length, E. F. Wise, a British representative on the Supreme Economic Council, decided to make an "on the ground" inspection of the situation that proved to be a turning point in the history of the occupation. Leaving Paris in late March, Wise went first to Cologne, where he interviewed the civil-affairs officers of the British army, and thence to Luxemburg where he had long discussions with the British and American representatives. In both places he sought to find out what was happening with regard to economic and financial matters.[10]

In his report to the Supreme Economic Council on April 5, Wise drew attention to the problems of jurisdiction and enforcement confronting the Luxemburg Commission and emphasized the need for a stronger civil body in its place, working more closely with the Supreme Economic Council and the peace conference in Paris. He proposed, therefore, that the Council of Foreign Ministers[11] be requested to establish a four-member Inter-Allied Rhineland Commission that would be given full control of political and economic matters on the left bank. To make the arrangement less obnoxious to the French, he suggested that Paul Tirard, Foch's comptroleur generale, be named the chairman of the new commission. He also recommended that the Supreme Economic Council create its own "subcommittee on Germany" to ensure that the occupied and unoccupied territories would be considered as an entity on the highest level. Such a subcommittee could act as the direct superior to the Rhineland Commission.[12]

The Wise proposals were accepted by the Supreme Economic Council on April 14 with less opposition that might have been anticipated.[13] The American representatives, quite naturally, were ready to lend their full support, requesting and obtaining only such modifications as that the new commission be located in Cologne (away from Foch) and that, if Tirard were named the chairman, he terminate his official connections with the marshal.[14] The French voted for the recommendations without enthusiasm, possibly with the thought in mind that they could later stymie them if they wished.

Yet the Council of Foreign Ministers lent its endorsement to the creation of the new organization, acting on April 21, one day after Clemenceau had received Wilson's endorsement of the draft articles on the occupation.[15] Perhaps this was part of an arrangement between the two men, or perhaps, by supporting the proposal, the premier was hoping to make it difficult for the president to renege on his commitment. It is even possible that the tensions between Foch and Clemenceau, which had now reached a new peak, were working to the advantage of those who disliked the military, as much in the French delegation as in the British and American.

Whatever the case, the Americans who were associated with the Supreme Economic Council wasted no time in designating an individual to represent them on the new commission. The men who were immediately responsible, Bernard Baruch and Alexander Legge, had originally planned to appoint an economist from Washington,[16] but when a mutual friend and well-known manufacturer, Pierrepont Noyes, took time out from a business trip to call on them, both Baruch and Legge recognized that he possessed exactly the courage and experience needed for the job.[17] An hour's discussion over lunch was enough to interest Noyes in the idea of a three-month stay in Germany. Twenty-four hours later (April 25) Baruch had the appointment informally approved.[18]

"We've smoked Clemenceau out and got a Rhineland Commission with teeth in it," Noyes was informed, but when it came to specific directions or advice he found himself surprisingly ill-supplied.[19] Even interviews with Herbert Hoover,

Vance McCormick, and the other Americans on the Supreme Economic Council were of little assistance, although McCormick did make what turned out to be a valuable suggestion: that Noyes invite Wallace Day (of the defunct Luxemburg Commission) to serve as deputy commissioner. The Americans in Paris wanted to ensure that the French played fair in the Rhineland, but how to accomplish this they could not say. As Baruch put it, "Hell, Noyes, if I knew what to do I would go there myself. Use your bean."[20]

The task was to be far from easy. In truth, for Noyes and his colleagues, the next forty days were hardly more than one long series of wrangles. That Noyes survived the experience at all, much less triumphed over it, is ample testimony to his toughness.

Just getting the new commission started demonstrated how far Foch was from giving up his Rhineland authority. Though Noyes and Sir Harold Stuart, the newly appointed British commissioner,[21] were both in Luxemburg ready for work by April 30, Tirard, their French counterpart, refused to schedule even a date of arrival.[22] He remained "temporarily" away, although he was not so distant that he was unable to raise additional obstacles to the functioning of the organization. For a week he claimed that he had not been officially appointed,[23] and then, on May 7, he argued by letter that the commission would not be needed. He urged Noyes and Stuart to return to Paris.[24]

Only when the two commissioners threatened to meet without their chairman did he finally appear, and even then he did not cooperate.[25] At the commission's organizing session on May 10, for example, Tirard proposed a set of procedures that would have given him the right to deal with business either as comptroleur generale or as president of the commission, as he saw fit. And although he finally abandoned this demand and agreed to follow rules of order devised by Stuart, the Frenchman simply could not be persuaded to resign the post he held with Foch.[26] It was rumored that Tirard was planning to keep the major portion of his staff at the marshal's headquarters in Luxemburg.[27]

There were other kinds of difficulties too, particularly with the subcommissions of the High Command. General Payot refused to relinquish any of the Inter-Allied Military Food Committee's powers, even after Noyes had threatened to attend without invitation a meeting of that organization in Mainz.[28] The chairman of the Inter-Allied Military Coal Committee was equally unresponsive to the Rhineland Commission.[29]

The Americans and British did not completely lack success during these weeks of debate. By cooperating closely on May 10, Noyes and Stuart did obtain agreement to transfer the seat of the commission from Luxemburg to Coblenz.[30] On May 13, they were able to thwart an attempt by Tirard to postpone the implementation of Paris decisions freeing the trade of the left bank with neutral countries.[31] Meanwhile, Wallace Day had made discoveries that were greatly to assist in reducing blockade-running into the Reich. As a result of private espionage, he had been able to send documented proof to Vance McCormick that within a ten-day period, over 300 carloads of "contraband" textiles had entered unoccupied territory from France carrying permits from the comptroleur generale's office. As Noyes noted in his diary, "The French have been taking big advantage of the blockade in this way and no wonder they oppose removing it. Vance says with such a list [as this] he can 'blow the blockade wide open immediately.' "[32]

Before the Rhineland Commission could really function, however, it was necessary that the issue of its authority be resolved. The opportunity came on May 16, precipitated in Paris by Legge, Baruch, and Wise. It was here, at a meeting of the Subcommittee on Germany to which the Rhineland commissioners had been invited, that Tirard finally became completely candid. Pointing out that Britain and the United States were about to withdraw the bulk of their troops from the occupation, he argued that France and Belgium, being most involved, should have the preponderant control. Since Foch "simply would not submit to civil management," Tirard asked that the subcommittee alter the arrangements in the Rhineland so that the High Command would once more have final authority.

Predictably, British and American reaction to this request was extremely negative. Emphasizing their belief that the responsibilities of partners in the occupation must be equal, Legge and Wise pointed out to the French to what extent the latter had been violating this particular principle as well as the spirit of a past agreement. They demanded of Tirard that he either cease to be comptroleur generale or step down from the commission. Then, when the exchange of views produced no agreement, they insisted that the dispute be forwarded by the subcommittee to its parent body.[33]

It was at a secret session of the Supreme Economic Council on May 19 that Foch's cause was conclusively lost. As in the subcommittee, the debate was both extended and intense, but at the end the French representative, Etienne Clémentel, declared himself open to compromise. Accordingly, it was agreed that if Foch would accept Tirard's resignation as comptroleur generale and recognize the commission as supreme in civil and economic matters, the procedures of control in the occupation could be defined in such a way that "the president of the High [i.e., Rhineland] Commission [would] transmit the decisions of the Commission in the name of the Supreme Economic Council by order of the Inter-Allied High Command."[34]

This formula, then, provided the modus vivendi by which the civil and the military in the Rhineland could coexist. Though Foch refused to countenance such a solution for a full week following the meeting, by May 27 he had reversed himself and expressed his willingness to accept it.[35] By that date the rapid passage of events had apparently convinced him that for the sake of more permanent concerns he would be well advised to put the lingering dispute behind him.

Nevertheless, the marshal had waited too long to be able to prevent the controversy from having a powerful effect on the contest now emerging over the peacetime occupation. Instead of accepting the new commission at the beginning of May and being credited with foresight or compromising with it two weeks later and being credited with good intentions, he had opposed it in a way that stirred up considerable antagonism. In the process, Foch had intimately involved its principal proponents in the more important decision-making that followed. He had gambled that he could keep the Rhineland Commission from coming to life until after a "military" convention had been adopted for the Rhineland and the commission itself had become a lame duck. He might have been wiser to have allowed the organization to go its own way.

To be sure, the Americans and British had known for some time that the French were thinking in terms of military control of the permanent occupation. In fact, at the end of April certain British officers in Cologne had participated with the French in drawing up a proposal that took as its original starting point the assignment of complete authority to an Allied commander-in-chief. This document was later examined and discussed by Generals Thwaites and Weygand, and a copy had been given to General Bliss on May 1.[36] It was submitted to the permanent military representatives at Versailles on May 8, the same day on which the premiers entrusted these advisers with the preliminary formulation of a basic law for the occupation.[37]

Though the British and French military representatives (Bliss was absent) had quickly approved a slate of articles resembling the Cologne project,[38] American officers had been less than pleased with such an arrangement. Pershing had informed Bliss that he preferred to see the national commanders in the Rhineland coordinate their work voluntarily.[39] Bliss himself had been concerned enough to make a special trip to the occupied areas to discuss the matter with Noyes and military men on the scene.[40]

Even so, if Noyes and Stuart had not come down to Paris to fight for the life of their own commission, American (and British) dislike of the Cologne plan (now called the Versailles plan) might never have taken positive form. The two commissioners, with their own official status in jeopardy, were the first to begin a sustained attack on what Noyes described as a "barbarous document" designed to "put the Rhineland under . . . harassing military domination."[41] Sir Harold Stuart, with Noyes's assistance, offered the first revision of the proposal, having worked an entire day to develop exceptions to military authority that could be assigned to a high commission.[42] The Stuart draft was apparently prepared for the consideration of the British delegation, but Noyes brought it to the attention of his own superiors as well, arguing that since the American people were committed to come to the aid of France, a "French-style" military occupation in Germany must at all costs be avoided.[43] During his three days in Paris (May 15–17) Noyes spoke in this vein to Baruch, McCormick, Hoover, House, and Norman Davis.[44]

These efforts, together with Foch's continuing obstinacy regarding the Rhineland Commission, seem to have inspired a considerable reassessment of the situation. By the seventeenth, Lord Robert Cecil, now a British member of the Supreme Economic Council, had arranged to have the "Versailles" convention temporarily withheld from the Supreme Council so that he could talk about it with British army representatives.[45] That same day the American section of the

Supreme Economic Council discussed the Rhineland for several hours, following which Baruch reported to President Wilson that the members had become convinced of the need for civilian governance in the area.[46] Subsequently General Bliss also advised the president of his conclusion that the occupying army "should be there under the same conditions that a military force exists in any country in time of peace, . . . prepared to quell disorder but to take no part whatever in the civil administration. In my judgment, a strong Inter-Allied civilian Commission should be formed."[47] By May 20, Wilson had been visibly impressed by such counsel as this, replying to Bliss that, "I entirely agree with you about the Rhine convention and shall try to obtain a radical modification of it."[48] On May 23 the president conferred with Pershing and Bliss in meetings covering various phases of these problems.[49]

Yet more advice was to follow, for by the twenty-sixth, with the military convention once again on the conference agenda, Pierrepont Noyes had returned to Paris with even more radical ideas than he had previously held. The French army had recently encouraged at least two separatist uprisings in the Rhineland, and as a result of these developments and lengthy talks with American officers, Noyes had now moved beyond the position represented by the Stuart draft. On arriving at the conference he submitted a memorandum to the Subcommittee on Germany urging that, in addition to establishing a civil commission, it was desirable to restrict occupying forces to certain stipulated areas, as had been done in China.[50] Then, on May 27, at the suggestion of his friend Felix Frankfurter,[51] Noyes wrote of his views directly to President Wilson, sketching the principles of a plan for a new and completely different convention:

I. As few troops as possible concentrated in barracks or reserve areas with no "billeting," except possibly for officers.

II. Complete self-government for the territory, with the exceptions below.
III. A Civil Commission with powers:
   a. to make regulations or change old ones whenever German law or actions
      1. Threaten the carrying out of Treaty terms.
      2. Threaten the comfort or security of troops.
   b. to authorize the army to take control under martial law, either in danger-spots or throughout the territory, whenever conditions seem to the commission to make this necessary.[52]

As soon became quite evident, this letter reached the chief executive at just the right "psychological moment."[53] Not only had Wilson developed considerable antipathy to the military convention, but he had also begun to suspect that an "amended" plan might not sufficiently limit Foch. Moreover, Lloyd George was ready to make a renewed assault upon the very idea of occupation, his fears having been aroused by French machinations with the separatists, by German objections to the treaty, and by increasing British criticism of the peace conference.

The result was a thorough airing of the subject when the Big Four met on May 29. Wilson himself began the session by reading parts of Noyes's letter and commenting upon the dangers of a "solution dictated by the military." The prime minister then broadened the discussion by adding that, in his opinion, the whole question of the occupation would have to be reconsidered and reargued. Nothing, he said, had done as much to popularize bolshevism in Russia as had foreign intervention. Furthermore, the expenses of the occupation would be exorbitant, since troops in a foreign country cost at least two or three times what they do at home.

Under this barrage, Clemenceau, as in earlier weeks, saw the necessity of attempting to divide his opponents. Therefore, while completely rejecting any change in what had earlier been decided regarding the Rhineland, he quickly accepted the president's suggestion that a committee be created to write a "political" convention. When Wilson in turn stood loyally by him on the larger issues, Lloyd George found himself forced to agree, grudgingly, to the appointment of four civilians and four military men to draft a project on the basis of Noyes's outline. The question of army strengths was also referred to this committee, since, as the president noted, the number of soldiers required for the operation depended upon the kind of occupation envisaged.[54]

Considering Wilson's original feelings regarding the occupation, it is difficult to explain why he did not take advantage of this opportunity to make common cause with the British. The answer, apparently, is that he had somehow persuaded himself of the soundness of the earlier compromise on this issue whereas the prime minister had remained unconvinced. Hence, when the crisis came, Wilson sought only more insurance that the previous agreement was valid, while Lloyd George sought to accomodate shifting pressures by altering the bargain itself. The differences in their approaches virtually ensured that it would be the prime minister, rather than the president, who would make still another foray against the occupation when separatist plottings and public dissatisfaction with the treaty had become even more obvious.

The so-called separatists had been active in the Rhineland since the beginning of the occupation, but not until the last few weeks had they received any encouragement or achieved any success. Diverse in perspective and severely handicapped by their lack of organization and leadership, they had been deeply frustrated during the early months of 1919 by having had almost no direct access to local Alllied authorities.[55] One of their better-known representatives, Hans Adam Dorten of Düsseldorf, had been denied an interview with General Dickman in March,[56] and it was not until April that he was permitted to talk to General Charles Mangin, the commander of the French Tenth Army, headquartered in Mainz.[57] The French were more sympathetic than the Americans to separatism, but lack of specific instructions from Foch and, above all, the lack of a need for organized agitation had made them slow to react.[58] General Augustin Gérard, the commander of the French Eighth Army at Ludwigshafen, had become interested in the movement only after it received new impetus as a result of the Commuist seizure of Munich in April.[59]

Developments regarding the peace settlement finally led the French generals actively to assist the separatists. Before mid-April they had tended to assume that their objectives in the Rhineland would be accomplished for them by the diplomats in Paris. Afterward, they realized that if the region were going to be successfully "separated," they would have to help along the process. They also recognized that, by acting promptly, they could offer a number of inducements to the separatists (e.g., reduced reparations, Saar territory) that they would no longer control once the peace treaty had been signed. In early May, therefore, Gérard and Mangin has begun to scheme with local citizens to present the peace conference with a *fait accompli*, though, odd as it may seem, they did little to coordinate their efforts. Thus, the plotters in the south struck first, posting proclamations on the night of May 20 to announce the creation of an independent Palatinate linked by customs union with the Saar. Unhappily for Gérard's followers, their most vigorous efforts were insufficient to give the new arrangement life.[60]

Meantime, however, General Mangin's activities had been gaining momentum. On May 19, after several talks with Dorten and other separatist leaders, he had approved a project of Dorten's to create a semi-independent republic comprising the entire left bank. Later, he had also agreed to a schedule accord-

111

ing to which the separatists would seize control of the region within the next few days.[61] Still later, because he knew that success depended upon the tolerance of the other Allied armies and because appearances demanded that the new nation be proclaimed outside his own zone, Mangin had acted to minimize the possibility of adverse reactions from his fellow commanding officers. On the night of May 21 he had dispatched couriers to the American, British, and Belgian areas to warn the generals in charge that the separatists would consumate their "revolution" in Coblenz on May 24.[62]

It was probably the worst mistake that Mangin could have made. Not only did General Hunter Liggett (Third Army commander since May 2) inform the courier that his instructions required him "to maintain in power the government with which we are treating, no matter who they may be who wish to replace it,"[63] but Liggett also reported the incident directly to Paris, where the news and a protest were relayed from Pershing to Wilson to Clemenceau.[64] In addition, the Americans gave detailed information about the conspiracy to Prussian officials in Coblenz, adding considerably to Dorten's discomfiture.[65]

Despite these setbacks and even an investigation from Paris, Mangin and Dorten refused to accept defeat.[66] For a moment they planned a proclamation in the Belgian zone on the twenty-ninth, but after German countermeasures had foreclosed this possibility and after Palatinate separatists had showed renewed signs of life, Dorten decided to proceed to Wiesbaden and to take action within the French zone. So it was that late on June 1 the French military wire announced to the world: "This morning the Rhine Republic was proclaimed in all cities without difficulty." In reality, the establishment of the new regime was marked by riots, strikes, and other public disorders. The German government protested vehemently in Paris and Spa, while American and British leaders expressed considerable antagonism.[67] Within a few hours Mangin had received emphatic directions from Clemenceau to "confine himself to his military duty" and within several days the republic had ignominiously collapsed. The French premier was understandably furious at the entire affair, which clearly had made it no easier for him to deal with Lloyd George and Wilson.[68]

Yet, as far as negotiations were concerned, an overzealous army on the Rhine was only one of Clemenceau's newer problems. Equally important, for its effect upon the Rhenish movement as well as for its impact on the peace conference, was the rising tide of German dissatisfaction with the treaty. Beginning on that "black" May 7 when the draft of the document had been published, this bitterness and defiance had increased to major proportions by the time the German delegation submitted its counterproposals to the Allies.

The occupation clauses of the treaty had played a substantial role in bringing on this wave of resentment. Judging from the speeches in the National Assembly, the presence of foreign troops ranked with reparations, "war guilt," and boundary settlements as the most objectionable features of the treaty.[69] Chancellor Scheidemann called the occupation "unjustifiable"; Walther Rathenau considered it "acceptable only if no customs barriers were erected to tempt French annexationists."[70] The conservative *Tägliche Rundschau* typified a growing fear in complaining that "we are to disappear from the map as a world power. . . . Witness the Rhineland occupation and the loss of northeast Prussia!"[71]

The German Foreign Ministry, of course, was more careful in the arguments it mustered. The Berlin Geschäftstelle, for example, in a confidential study for the Paris delegation, contended that the occupation envisaged by the Allies was both "out of date" and "out of place." It was out of date, the authors argued, because in an age of popular sovereignty, military control amounted to taking power from the people. It was out of place, and unnecessary, because the Allies already possessed many potential sanctions. In the event, however, that an occupation were unavoidable, the experts did suggest the following: (1) that it be purely military, (2) that it guarantee political freedom to the citizenry, (3) that it discontinue armistice ordinances, and (4) that it grant an amnesty to all Germans convicted previously by the Allies. Ironically, considering the battle Foch was waging at the peace conference, the Geschäftstelle urged that the commander-in-chief of the occupying forces be given sole authority to issue orders binding on civilians.[72]

The official German counterproposals of May 29 included an attack upon the occupation that blended the work of the Geschäftstelle with the cabinet's earlier instructions and a dozen delegation memoranda.[73] The covering letter made reference to perhaps the most basic German fear: that the occupying army would be "free to ... weaken the economic and moral ties between [the Rhineland] and the mother-land, and finally [to] warp the mind of the population." The text of the note emphasized the argument that an occupation was unnecessary, not only because there were better guarantees for the fulfillment of financial obligations, but also because German disarmament had made any threat to the Allies ridiculous. Certain treaty clauses were said to be particularly dangerous; for example, Article 212, which allowed the perpetuation of armistice provisions, and Article 270, which permitted the establishment of a customs regime within the Rhineland. If there had to be an occupation, the Germans proposed that it should be exclusively military in character; that commerce between the left and right banks of the Rhine should not be obstructed; that a German commissioner should remain in contact with military commanders to regulate administrative matters; and that the territory be evacuated no later than six months after the signing of the peace.[74]

It remains only to add that the German position was not as firm as it appeared and that Wilson, at least, had known this for some time. There were many within the government of the Reich who had begun to believe that it was more important to have peace than to haggle over details. Matthias Erzberger, for example, so feared the obduracy of Brockdorff-Rantzau's entourage that he had secretly conferred on May 19 with American army officers about the treaty, offering in return for a reduction of the occupation to six months a pledge to maintain no military forces within fifty kilometers of the Rhine and to pay reparations with receipts from customs and internal revenues. President Wilson had been informed of these proposals but had instructed the intermediaries to reply that there was no alternative to accepting the treaty. Indeed, his awareness of German "weakness" probably strengthened his determination to resist alterations in the text.[75]

Still, if Erzberger's ideas met with little American approval, the counterproposals of the German government did strike a responsive chord within the British delegation. This became especially evident at a meeting of the British Empire representatives convened by Lloyd George from May 30 to June 2, where many of those present spoke out against the failure to promise Germany early admission to the League of Nations, the reductions in her eastern frontiers, and the provision for an occupation. General Jan Smuts of South Africa was especially critical of the last point and received considerable support from Lord Balfour and from G. N. Barnes, the Labour Party member of the coalition government. As early as the beginning of May, Smuts had written to Lloyd George and Wilson to protest the "far too long period of fifteen years [for the occupation]" and the "undefined regime of martial law."[76]

115

Now he called the occupation "incompatible" with modern industrial conditions and urged, if the arrangement were unavoidable, that the army be limited in size and set down at certain specified points. Balfour dwelt upon the cost of the occupation to the British taxpayer and added that, in his view, the less the French army was allowed to manage German affairs, the better.[77]

Lloyd George, as we know, was basically in full agreement. As he subsequently noted, he had originally "opposed this provision [for an occupation] and [had] only accepted it under pressure from President Wilson." He also shared in the apprehension that "the Germans [would] refuse to sign the Treaty and that as a consequence we [would] have to march to Berlin." He could only have been delighted when the meeting resolved to require, among other alterations in the text, "a modification of the clauses dealing with the Army of Occupation in the direction of (a) reducing the numerical strength, ... and (b) making the period of occupation as short as possible."[78]

So it happened that repeated French indiscretions, German criticism of the treaty, and a new mood among the British brought Lloyd George to a second counteroffensive against the sterner features of the peace. At the meeting of the Big Four on June 2, he informed Clemenceau and Wilson that his cabinet simply would not authorize him to sign the treaty as it stood. He demanded substantial changes, including German admission to the League, boundary changes in the east, and reduction of the Rhineland occupation from fifteen to two years. Holding the left bank meant no advantage, he asserted, because the Germans would not be strong enough to become a menace again until precisely the years in which the occupation ended. An army on the Rhine could only be a drain on reparations and a continued source of international irritation.[79]

Clemenceau, in reply, was at his stubborn and weary best.

Openly confessing that no subject was more painful or difficult for him than the occupation, he conceded that certain "errors" had been committed by his generals on the Rhine. Even so, he saw no reason to change his mind about the previous understanding. In his view, the danger was not that Germany would attack France, but that she would sign the treaty intending to challenge it clause by clause. Therefore France must have the means to enforce the contract. His only possible concession, he said, was a limit on expenses designed to guarantee that everyone would receive his share of reparations.[80]

On this occasion, as during the week before, the American president was noticeably silent. Though Wilson was under great pressure form his countrymen to support the British,[81] he refused, in this moment of crisis, to go back upon his earlier agreements with Clemenceau. As he later revealed to the American delegation, he neither trusted Lloyd George's motivations nor believed it feasible to ignore the French desire for security:

> PRESIDENT: Well, I don't want to seem to be unreasonable, but my feeling is this: that we ought not, with the object of getting it signed, make changes in the Treaty, if we think it embodies what we were contending for; that the time to consider all these questions was when we were writing the treaty. . . . If I am right that it [the occupation] is not strictly a military question, and if it is a civil question, it is a question, involving many embarrassments, chiefly the embarrassment of French public opinion.
>
> BLISS: It is so likely to result in incidents that will bring about the very thing which we want, of course, to avoid, and that is a resumption of war. It has always seemed to me that it is almost a slap in the face of the League of Nations. . . .
>
> PRESIDENT: The great problem of the moment is the problem of agreement. . . . [Britain and France] ought to be held together, if it can reasonably be done, and that makes a problem like the problem of occupation almost look insoluble, because the British are at one extreme and the French refusal

to move is at the opposite extreme. *Personally, I think the thing will solve itself upon the admission of Germany into the League of Nations.* I think that all the powers feel that the right thing to do is to withdraw the army. But we cannot arrange the Treaty because we cannot fix the date at which Germany is to be admitted into the League.[82]

If the confrontation of the three Allied leaders on June 2 did not bring Lloyd George immediate satisfaction, it did "save" the committee that had been appointed to draft the occupation statute. The members of this group (Louis Loucheur and Marshal Foch for France, Lord Cecil and General Wilson for Britain, and John W. Davis and General Bliss for the United States)[83] had been holding sessions since May 31, and would continue to meet until June 9.[84] Though under explicit orders to base their work upon Noyes's principles, they almost certainly would have violated these instructions without the sort of pressure Lloyd George provided.

Marshal Foch did everything possible to undermine Noyes's plan, or, as John Davis later put it, to block "any interference whatever with absolute military supremacy."[85] Attacking in any way he could, Foch told the group on the one hand that a civil commission would inevitably become a meddling superstate, and on the other, that such a commission could not be constituted to act effectively in times of disorder. Instead of Noyes's proposed arrangement, Foch urged a regime like that the Germans had used in 1871, allowing military authorities to suspend local government whenever necessary.[86]

Lord Cecil was the only member of the committee who fell at all seriously under the marshal's spell. Loucheur wavered to an extent, but at the crucial junctures he remained cognizant of the need of France for American support. Hence there were sufficient votes to carry through a draft convention that did not deviate in essentials from what the president had wanted. It was supplemented by a memorandum defining the relations between the Allied military authorities and the Inter-Allied High Commission.[87]

Certain decisions of the group are particularly worthy of attention. For example, because everyone present felt that, within limits, the prerogatives of the High Commission should be so clear as to go unchallenged, it was agreed to permit the commission to issue ordinances not only for the protection of troops but also for the "execution of the treaty."[88] Moreover, because everyone knew that the occupying army would be predominantly French, it was decided that the commission's chairmanship and a tie-breaking vote should be assigned to the French member.[89] Foch had estimated that ten Allied divisions, or 150,000 men, would be required to garrison the Rhineland, and this was the figure that was recommended to the Supreme Council.[90] However, Bliss informed President Wilson privately that, as he saw it, this total could be cut in half.[91]

In the interim, while Lloyd George's pressure on Clemenceau was working to the advantage of the special committee, it was also beginning to achieve results at the meetings of the Council of Four. On June 10, after the prime minister had urged that the Allies decide immediately upon the future expenses of the occupation, the premier had responded most agreeably: "To you I will say all you would like, but not to the Germans."[92] Two days later, after Lloyd George had demanded Clemenceau's promise to reexamine the pending Rhineland convention as of a certain date, the premier had again proved acquiescent, remarking, "Something which you could cite [to Parliament] might be arranged."[93]

Probably because of such unwritten pledges, the council was able to examine its special committee's report on June 13 in relative accord. Clemenceau had complained at least twice in previous sessions about the "length" of the proposed convention,[94] but in the final discussion neither he nor Lloyd George advanced serious objections. There were only two major changes in the text, both of which were accepted upon the motion of President Wilson. In Article III, "execution of the treaty" was removed from the responsibilities of the High Commission on the ground that the focus of that body should remain upon the Rhineland. In Article V, safeguards for local German government were rendered even more explicit with a change that Wilson had drafted personally: "The civil administration of these areas shall continue under German law and under the authority of the central German government except insofar as it may be necessary for the Commission by ordinance . . . to accommodate . . . the needs and circumstances of military occupation."[95]

Before the convention (also called the Rhineland Agreement) was finally approved, however, there remained the business of Clemenceau's promised protocol, and dealing with this required considerable effort. In particular, the commitment to reconsider the occupation was difficult to agree upon, since, despite heated entreaties by Barnes and Andrew Bonar Law (Conservative leader and War Cabinet member), the French premier refused to set a specific date for such a study.[96] The British were finally forced to accept the relatively indefinite promise that occupying forces could be prematurely withdrawn if and when (1) Germany had fulfilled her obligations under the treaty, or (2) the Allies had agreed that Berlin had given substantial proof of goodwill. These two propositions were supplemented by an understanding that, once Germany was disarmed, the total cost of occupation would not be allowed to exceed 240 milllion gold marks annually. The entire package was incorporated in a declaration that was initialed by the Allied leaders on June 16.[97]

That same day the Rhineland Agreement was also accepted and made a part of the ultimatum that the Big Four now dispatched in answer to the German counterproposals.[98] As such, the agreement became one of the principal concessions of the

Allies in what was otherwise a relatively uncompromising response. The only other concessions of significance involved the granting of a plebiscite in Silesia and the adjustment of several disputed boundaries.

Of course, from the American and British point of view, what Wilson and Lloyd George had achieved with the Rhineland Agreement represented something of importance. Most American and British representatives took their traditions of civil supremacy very seriously, tending to assume that such institutional changes could be vastly significant in preventing the misuse of power. Furthermore, under the commission, the United States obtained a much more potent voice in Rhenish affairs than it otherwise would have possessed, and this fact helped to persuade Americans that a real improvement had been made.[99]

To the Germans, the achievement may have looked somewhat less impressive. Not only did they have a considerably different tradition of civil-military relations, but their historical experience had given them as little reason to trust French civilians as they had to trust French generals. They were angered (and had protested) at being asked to sign the Rhineland Agreement as an adjunct to the treaty without ever having discussed it with the Allies and when the treaty itself had specified that the agreement would be a "subsequent" convention.[100] They were also disappointed that (as far as they knew) the Allies had made no provision for limiting the occupation as to numbers or to costs and had not reduced its length.[101]

Despite all this, there is evidence that the Rhineland Agreement may have had some impact in persuading the Germans to look more favorably on the treaty. True, the German peace delegation soon reported to its government that the occupation regime was simply "the first step toward permanent political separation of the Rhineland."[102] Nonetheless, if the comments of the department chiefs in Erzberger's armistice commission are any indication, some Germans found the Allied project a positive improvement and appreciated the protection it gave to German laws and administration.[103] Their reactions were remarkably similar to those later published by John Maynard Keynes, who, despite his unhappiness with the treaty, could describe the Rhineland Agreement as having been "very fairly and reasonably drawn."[104]

Now came the denouement. On the one hand, the Allies concentrated and organized their forces for a possible advance from the Rhine bridgeheads into Germany. On the other, the Germans wrestled with the dilemma of whether or not to sign the treaty. For a few days, the scales for Germany were balanced between further occupation and surrender.

American troops participated in this mobilization, just as they had been participating in the steadily mounting tension. Though the strength of the Third Army had declined since April, well over 150,000 troops remained in the area, and these were put on a wartime footing.[105] At the same time the quality of relations between soldiers and civilians sank to an all-time low. Germans were resentful and insulting; the troops were angry because they were being prevented from going home.[106] Cases of assault upon civilians increased so markedly that precautionary orders were issued to the soldiers,[107] while the *Amaroc News* editorialized that "beating up . . . a defeated foe is not an American characteristic."[108]

Across the Rhine the German nation and its leadership were badly split. For several weeks the Socialists and Democrats had vigorously opposed accepting the Allied "Diktat," while the Center Party, especially sensitive to sentiment favorable to acceptance in western Germany,[109] had become more and more susceptible to compromise. Then, after the Allied ultimatum and the recommendation of the German peace delegation that the treaty be rejected, the Centrists demanded further bargaining while many Socialists changed their minds to side with them. The result was the resignation, on June 20, of the Scheidemann government and its replacement by a Socialist–Center Party coalition under the Majority Socialist Gustav Bauer.[110]

There followed three frantic days during which the new chancellor sought in vain to obtain modifications of the clauses regarding war guilt and war criminals. At the end, even the Center Party was prepared to reject the Allied demand for unqualified acceptance. Only the unwillingness of the Nationalists, People's Party, and Democrats to form a government of defiance made it possible for Bauer to send the final telegram of capitulation on June 23.[111]

The ceremony at Versailles on June 28 was mere formality.

So the war ended, and the occupation acquired a second life. Clemenceau and Foch, together and separately, had managed to win a considerable degree of postwar protection for their nation. At the same time, however, largely as a result of the marshal's activities, they had been forced to concede certain safeguards regarding the Rhineland to both the Germans and their own allies.

Lloyd George and Wilson had also played their roles in tandem, though not with as much cooperation or success as had the Frenchmen. Nonetheless, if the president had originally "given" Clemenceau the occupation without Lloyd George's approval, the prime minister had made it possible for Wilson's later suggestions to be used in an attempt to modify and transform the French creation. It now remained to be seen how well this French-Anglo-American compromise would work in practice.

6

THE OCCUPATION AND THE TREATY
STRUGGLE IN AMERICA, JUNE 1919–MAY 1920

> SENATOR JOHNSON: The idea in my mind was this:
> Will we be maintaining American
> troops upon the Rhine for the
> next fifteen years?
> PRESIDENT: That is entirely within our choice, Sena-
> tor; but I suppose we will.
>
> Interview of
> August 19, 1919.

During the next year the fate of the American occupation in
Germany was to be closely interwoven with the fate of the
Treaty of Versailles in the United States. As the debate over
the treaty developed and changed in character, so American
policies and attitudes regarding the occupation reflected and
occasionally influenced these shifts. Thus, in the period before
the Senate's first vote (November 1919), the American Mission in Paris permitted its representatives to share fully in the
preparations for the peacetime occupation. Later, during the
months the treaty was being reconsidered, the State Department insisted upon limiting this kind of activity despite several
developments in Europe that virtually compelled American
cooperation. Finally, after the Senate's second failure to ratify
(March 1920), the government reduced its role to an even
greater extent, going so far as to recall its Rhineland commissioner, at least in part because of the vigor with which he carried out his office.

On the congressional and popular level, the periods of greatest interest in (and involvement with) the occupation corresponded roughly to the months of most intense controversy regarding the treaty. During the debate-filled summer and fall of 1919, for example, the so-called Irreconcilables in the Senate focused considerable attention on American troops abroad as a means of dramatizing their belief that League membership would entail permanent involvement overseas. If their success in blurring distinctions among the obligations potentially imposed by treaty, League, and other relationships (e.g., the Siberian intervention) was not spectacular, this was probably because wartime emotions were still strong enough in most citizens to put the Rhineland in a special category. At any rate, after the treaty was defeated in November, the occupation dropped from public sight, emerging only in the spring of 1920 when the second treaty struggle together with the Kapp *Putsch* and Frankfurt occupation reminded Americans (including their president) that their troops remained in zones of danger. Sentiment developed at this time for the immediate recall of the Rhine contingent, but the European crisis also stimulated sympathies for France and Germany that inspired an opposing point of view.

Throughout the summer and early autumn of 1919, then, the American Mission in Paris (that remnant of the peace delegation comprising General Bliss, Henry White, and Undersecretary of State Frank Polk)[1] acted as the developer and coordinator of a surprisingly energetic policy regarding Germany. It was this body which endorsed the lifting of the Allied naval blockade in July, and it was Polk who helped to draft the Allies' September letter ordering the Germans to make certain alterations in their new constitution.[2] About the only important American policy affecting Germany that did not emanate from the mission during these weeks was the July

11 order from Washington revoking import-export restrictions with the Reich.[3]

Bliss, White, and Polk also involved themselves in occupation matters. (See chapter 7.) During July they devoted considerable attention to the permanent size and the costs of the Rhineland armies—two questions that had been left unresolved by the peace conference. That same month they sent a representative (John Foster Dulles) to participate in the discussions of the Rhineland Agreement. Simultaneously they directed Pierrepont Noyes to join in the Rhineland Commission's formulation of the ordinances that the High Commission would issue upon its establishment.[4]

Meanwhile, the American zone was being transformed by the departure of the AEF. On July 2, the day the Third Army had been reconstituted as American Forces in Germany (AFG) and entrusted to the command of Major General Henry T. Allen,[5] there had still been more than 110,000 troops in the American area of control.[6] By September the number was down to 11,000,[7] many of whom had recently been transferred from the United States.[8] A month earlier the geographic size of the zone had been reduced, through process of evacuation, to little more than Coblenz and its environs. By September, however, under pressure from Noyes and Allen and as a result of the scheduled arrival of 10,000 men awaiting duty in Silesia, Marshal Foch had agreed to define the American sector to include somewhat less than the eastern half of its original area.

In light of the rapid return of men to the United States, it is particularly ironic (if understandable) that it was during these very months that the political opposition to Congress became increasingly alarmed at the number of soldiers remaining overseas. As Secretary of War Newton Baker emphasized to the president on July 15, "every advantage is [being] taken by those opposed to the treaty of the presence of our troops in various parts of the world."[9] In short, many Republicans, particularly the Irreconcilables, had begun to point to the contingents in Germany, Russia, and elsewhere as proof not only that the treaty was harsh, but also that it obligated Americans (through the League) to fight other peoples' battles.

The critics were assisted in their campaign of misrepresentation by several tactical errors on the part of the administration. For example, Baker himself had publicly implied that immense new responsibilities were in the offing by demanding a peacetime army of 500,000 men (more than twice the number stipulated in the National Defense Act of 1916).[10] Appearing in June before the military affairs committees of the House and Senate, he had testified that, among other things, the requirements of the German occupation and the Mexican border patrol made it necessary to establish such a force.[11] Then, in July, after Congress had disregarded his advice and enacted a law stipulating a figure of 325,000, he had returned to the respective committees to repeat his earlier recommendations.[12] On June 16, as if to document Baker's case, the army had begun a drive to enlist 50,000 volunteers for extended duty in France and Germany.[13]

Oddly enough, such enlistments were being sought even before the public was informed of what its postwar obligations were to be. Though the draft of the Treaty of Versailles had made specific reference to an "inter-Allied force" of occupation, a *New York Times* correspondent had reported as late as May 12 that the United States would not participate.[14] On May 18, State Department officials were quoted as doubting the authenticity of a press dispatch from Paris that claimed that Wilson had agreed to keep troops in Germany at least five years.[15] It was not until June 18 that American newspapers stated definitively that one regiment was due to remain there semipermanently.[16]

The wildest of rumors were allowed to circulate. At the end

of June the *Boston Evening Transcript* reported that the First, Second and Third Divisions in Germany would soon need 40,000 replacements.[17] A month later, Secretary Baker told the House Military Affairs Committee that at one time it had been officially estimated the United States would have to maintain some 200,000 men in France and Germany.[18] He added that while he was now certain that America's share of the occupation would be less than one division, the exact number of troops would have to remain temporarily secret for reasons of security.

In the interim, President Wilson's handling of the agreements relating to the occupation appeared almost purposely designed to encourage congressional suspicion. Considering that the Senate was already irritated because it had been denied a copy of the treaty until July 8 and the text of the French security pact until July 17,[19] it would seem that the submission of the Rhineland convention and the declaration of June 16 might have helped to pacify the legislators by emphasizing the modesty of American involvement overseas (not to speak of the triumph of American principles these documents represented). Nevertheless, although Lloyd George had transmitted these documents to Parliament early in July,[20] Wilson did not send even the first of them to Capitol Hill until August 29.[21] By that time Senator Lodge had long since obtained them from British sources and made them available in the *Congressional Record*.[22]

Nor did the president, in his August 19 interview at the White House with the Senate Foreign Relations Committee, do much to put congressional minds at ease regarding the occupation:

SENATOR [HIRAM] JOHNSON [R–Calif.]: [Will] troops have to be maintained under the various treaties of peace until the ultimate consummation of the terms of those treaties?
PRESIDENT: Yes, Senator; but that is not long. In no case, as

I remember, does that exceed eighteen months.

SENATOR JOHNSON: I was rather under the impression that the occupation of Germany was to be for fifteen years.

PRESIDENT: Oh, I beg your pardon.

CHAIRMAN [Senator Lodge]: Along the Rhine.

PRESIDENT: Along the Rhine; yes. I was thinking of upper Silesia and other places where plebiscites are created. . . .

SENATOR JOHNSON: The idea in my mind was this: Will we be maintaining American troops upon the Rhine for the next fifteen years?

PRESIDENT: That is entirely within our choice, Senator; but I suppose we will.[23]

One is tempted to ask what had happened to Wilson's hopes of June 2, when he had suggested to the American delegation in Paris that the admission of Germany to the League might bring an early modification of the occupation. His change of attitude, of course, could be attributed to fatigue or strain. Such a hypothesis is buttressed by the fact that this interview was also the famous occasion on which the president falsely asserted that he had only learned of the Allies' secret treaties upon his arrival in Paris.[24] The more probable explanation is that Wilson was simply trying to affirm the widely accepted view of the occupation as the finishing phase of the war experience. To treat it as the first of a series of international police actions, even if of relatively short duration, would only have assisted his isolationist enemies.

Even so, as the autumn approached, Irreconcilables tended with mounting frequency to construe the maintenance of any troops abroad as creating a precedent for the League. Earlier, politicians requesting the return of soldiers had carefully excluded the forces required to fulfill treaty terms.[25] Now, however, congressmen did not hesitate to advocate the immediate recall of every American stationed on foreign soil.[26] In August, the imminent dispatch of troops from the United States to police the Silesian plebiscite led to vehement protests in both the House and Senate.[27] In September, when American Marines were landed from ships to restore order in a Dalmatian city, there was a barrage of hostile comment.[28] Senator Joseph Frelinghuysen (R-N.J.) reflected the spirit of criticism on the latter occasion when he declared that Americans were being asked to "involve ourselves and our people forever in all the European matters, to police the Rhine, to send troops to Armenia,[29] to send them God alone knows where."[30] And Senator Hiram Johnson of California made the same point at greater length:

> This morning's news visualized the League of Nations for all. . . . We read today of: American boys fighting an undeclared and undisclosed war in Siberia; American boys sent to Silesia; American boys alleged to have been cruelly treated in Dalmatia; American boys to remain on the Rhine for fifteen years. . . . The logic of events demonstrates what the League of Nations is for—to have America underwrite the peace treaty in which are interwoven the secret treaties disposing of the world among the allies.[31]

Though such outbursts were impressive, it is doubtful that the Irreconcilables succeeded in convincing the majority of congressmen that the Rhineland occupation should be linked up with the League. Regular (moderate and conservative) Republicans were generally too loyal to the Allied cause not to agree with Senator James Wadsworth (R-N.Y.) when he asserted that the existing occupation remained a creature of the armistice, not the treaty, and that the seizure of the Rhineland was a necessity of war.[32] The Democrats stood behind their president, apparently almost oblivious to any criticism of current policy.

Moreover, if the absence of editorial comment is any indication, the public at large seems to have been more favorable to the Rhineland army than were the Irreconcilables. Part of the reason for this "flexibility," quite clearly, lay in the continuing vigor of feelings generated by the war. According to the *Literary Digest*, the American press during the week of treaty signature had revealed an almost unanimous opinion that "Germany invites and necessitates compulsion."[33] In June even the liberal (New York) *Nation* had felt that the 144 American soldiers who had applied to marry German girls were well-deserving of court-martial.[34] As late as September an author in *The Atlantic* professed to be "aghast" at the nature of the "German soul."[35]

Another explanation of the popular mood was simply that demobilization, strikes, Wilson's illness (beginning September 25), and the prolonged debate on the League had crowded news from Europe out of the headlines. Information from Germany was scarce and often garbled, as for instance, when the *New York Times*, in its description of the arrival of Silesian plebiscite troops in Europe, announced that the units would remain on the Rhine pending "transfer to upper Siberia."[36] The American press made only occasional reference to the Rhineland Commission, reporting hardly more than that it was supervising commerce on the "Luxemburg line," preparing itself to become a "governing body,"[37] regulating the activities of the generals,[38] and ruling the Rhine area "like monarchs of old." The army in Coblenz was said to be keeping busy endeavoring to locate housing space for the growing bureaucracy.[39]

There was also a smattering of support for the occupation among the news items, and this almost certainly contributed something to the formation of public opinion. American authorities in Coblenz inspired several articles stressing the importance of their Rhenish "alliance" with the British,[40] and Noyes himself wrote a letter to the *New York World* concerning the significance of his work.[41] Concurrently, the American German-language press attempted to defend the AFG by explaining that, without it, France would long since have absorbed the German Rhineland.[42] The only danger in such an argument, of course, was that the extent it fell among German-ophobes, it weakened public willingness to have the troops stay on in Europe.

As the vote on the treaty neared, the Department of State remained cautious but not immobilized with regard to Germany. Though it reminded the American Mission in October that the United States must not be associated with the proclamation of the Rhineland High Commission prior to the Senate's action,[43] it did become concerned enough about American trade interests on the Rhine to dispatch consular representatives to Coblenz.[44] In addition, at the urging of the delegation in Paris, the department sent an "unofficial" American representative (Ellis Loring Dresel) to Berlin, largely for the purpose of assisting the German government during the critical winter ahead.[45]

The failure of ratification on November 19, however, inspired the beginnings of a general reorientation in Washington. On the following day, after a conversation with Senator Oscar Underwood (D-Ala.), Secretary Lansing reported to the president that Underwood "thought we ought to withdraw all our people from Europe who have anything to do with the Supreme War Council . . . only continuing those who are operating under the terms of the Armistice. I feel, myself, that this advice is good and will, if you approve, carry it out."[46] A few days later there was a brief reply from the invalid in the White House scribbled in the handwriting of Edith Bolling Wilson: "The President says he agrees with the Secretary."[47] Thus the new course of state was fixed.

Nevertheless, Lansing was to find the implementation of this policy far from simple. First, because of America's vast economic stake in Europe, he felt compelled to maintain an "unofficial" association with the reparations commissions.[48] Second, because the United States was still deeply involved

132

in armistice affairs, he thought it essential to retain his access to Allied political councils. As it developed, there were to be at least three incidents relating to the Rhine army—the crisis over the treaty "protocol," the struggle regarding a military council, and the establishment of the High Commission—in which it was imperative for him to proceed with great discretion.

The protocol affair occurred in early December and became a problem because it coincided with Lansing's attempt to bring the American Mission home from Paris. The original issue had arisen from the Allied demand that Germany obligate itself to pay for the armistice violation that resulted when the High Seas Fleet was scuttled at Scapa Flow. Berlin's refusal to accept this protocol to the treaty had created a considerable international crisis, leading to, among other things, an Anglo-French threat to occupy the Ruhr Valley.[49] In this situation, Lansing had been informed by Polk on December 6 that American withdrawal from the Supreme Council would appear to the French as "sheer desertion." The secretary was also faced with the fact that newspapers in the United States had reported American troops already committed to act as part of Foch's offensive force.[50]

Lansing was keenly opposed to the imposition of what he considered to be unnecessary terms, but he was also aware that American failure to join in such an armistice matter might be criticized severely by a German-hating public. On December 7, therefore, he wrote to the president suggesting that the administration make at least some effort to relieve French anxiety, either by allowing Ambassador Hugh Wallace to become an "observer" on the Supreme Council or by laying the whole problem before the Senate Foreign Relations Committee (of which Senator Lodge was chairman). He also asked for an immediate decision as to whether or not the American Rhineland army should cooperate in coercive action against Germany.[51]

It is not surprising that Wilson found Lansing's first alternative by far the more palatable. As for the military matter, he was willing to "leave that to General Bliss."[52] So it happened that on December 9, when the American commissioners took their leave of the Supreme Council, Ambassador Wallace began his own attendance there. However, the ambassador was without the aid of General Bliss, for the latter did not think it "practical" to accept military responsibility overseas and decided to return to the United States with Polk and White.[53] Considering the confusion in American ranks, it was fortunate for everyone that within a few days Germany capitulated and agreed to sign the protocol.[54]

The second incident in which Americans endeavored to maintain their distance pertained to the French proposal for a new inter-Allied military council at Versailles. As originally suggested by Marshal Foch in October, this body was to assume rather considerable powers after treaty ratification, including (1) direction of the "control commissions" (disarmament teams) within the former Central Powers, (2) command of the Allied occupation forces in the Rhineland and plebiscite areas, and (3) supervision of military affairs in eastern Europe.[55] Secretary Lansing had quickly rejected the possibility of American participation,[56] but the French government had refused to accept a negative response. As late as mid-December, Clemenceau, in a special message to the secretary, thought it "unimaginable" that the Senate would object to American membership in the council. He could "scarcely conceive" of the possibility, he said, that the AFG might be left without any future connection to the Allied armies. He pointed out that the council would in no case have final authority over the disposition of American troops.[57]

Though there were clear-cut arguments for military coordination, there were also sufficient reasons for officials in Washington to be somewhat wary of the French proposition.

For one thing, the suggested arrangements bore a striking resemblance to the schemes that the French had advanced at the Paris Peace Conference, proposals that Americans like Bliss had rejected as tantamount to international general staffs. For another, whatever policy Clemenceau now had in mind (and this is hard to determine), there had recently been unmistakable signs in Coblenz that the French military was renewing its efforts to nullify civilian control in the Rhineland. (See Chapter 7.) By the spring of 1920 there would be overwhelming evidence that the French High Command was determined to run the occupation.

Yet the State Department was more concerned on this occasion with getting the troops out of a direct command relationship to Foch than with preserving civil administration in the occupied region. Even General Bliss, in a discussion with Polk after their return to Washington, now centered his analysis of the situation upon the fact that "we cannot give supreme direction of American forces to Foch or any one else."[58] Decentralized military control (i.e., an independent American commander) appeared to be the best way to preserve both American freedom of action and a "moderate" occupation, at least in the Coblenz zone. But it was primarily with the objective of American freedom in mind that Washington officials finally decided to let General Allen sit on Foch's new council only in the role of an "observer."[59]

Meanwhile, a third dilemma of relationship had developed for the United States, this one with regard to the coming into force of the Treaty of Versailles on January 10, 1920. As of that date the AFG found itself in an unusually awkward position, legally and morally. Although Americans had played a major role in designing the Rhineland conventions and although the Coblenz zone was as much entitled to peace as any other area of the left bank, America technically remained at war. Her representatives could not be expected to abide by agreements that had been prepared for other situations.

Noyes, Allen, and their colleagues had long debated the advantages and disadvantages of the various possible accomodations. In November, the commissioner had apparently convinced the general that if ratification was accomplished before the Senate had acted, Allen should issue the ordinances of the High Commission on his own responsibility as military commander.[60] Six weeks later, however, Noyes had expressed considerable doubt to Allen about the wisdom of following such a course. Why the commissioner changed his mind is not apparent, but he may have been influenced by Allied attitudes or by the advice he was receiving from American legal officers. He may also have feared that he had been encouraging an arrangement that might well become permanent and thereby undermine civilian control.[61]

As it turned out, the two men never reached an understanding. General Allen ultimately recommended Noyes's earlier plan to the War Department as the only possible way to escape the impasse,[62] believing as he did so that he had persuaded Noyes to support him in a wire to the Department of State.[63] Unbeknownst to Allen, however, the commissioner had confidentially proposed to Lansing that the American army remain quiescent at Coblenz while the High Commission (with Noyes as un unofficial member) take control of all four Allied zones.[64]

The Secretary of State, in his decision, again attempted to preserve as much freedom of action as possible. He therefore rejected Noyes's suggestion and accepted Allen's, although he agreed that it would be desirable for Noyes to attend the meetings of the High Commission.[65] The amusing thing was that, as a result of telegraphic delay, Lansing's instructions did not reach Coblenz until January 13, by which time Allen, after considerable soul-searching, had already published the proclamation of the High Commission without comment and the first ordinances as his own orders.[66] Fortunately, it seems, the general had guessed right.

Thus Lansing, despite three awkward compromises in two months, was able once again to prevent the Rhineland from generating undue public concern. Congress had said little on the subject during the winter, and the press had published only scattered comment. To some periodicals the occupation continued to seem the "logical consequence" of Germany's defeat; to others it remained an unpleasant necessity pending the arrival of peace.[67] Francophobes, like the *New Yorker Staats-Zeitung*, claimed that the occupation was still the best way to prevent France from dominating the Rhine.[68] Francophiles, like the *New York Times*, noted that "the Army on the Rhine provides a means of pressure—the only pressure which can apparently be put on the Germans now—to make them live up to at least some of the provisions [of the treaty]."[69]

In the interim the struggle over treaty ratification had entered its second phase. Efforts to reach a compromise were well advanced in the Senate by January despite opposition from both the convalescing president and the Irreconcilables. The country was ready for a settlement, and Wilson's unceremonious firing of Secretary of State Lansing in February only enhanced the general impatience. On March 19, when the treaty again came up for decision, twenty-one Democrats crossed over to support Senator Lodge's position, convinced that peace with reservations was better than no peace at all. Unfortunately, a two-thirds majority was still beyond the Senate's reach, and the United States was condemned to continue in its state of drift.[70]

For an administration seeking an uneventful foreign policy, the most notable development of the Rhineland situation during this period was the refusal of the American commissioner in Coblenz to accept the status of a mere observer. Perhaps it was simply asking too much of a man who had been so intimately involved in devising civilian control for the occupation to expect him to stand by and watch the French dismantle this arrangement. In any event, throughout the spring Pierrepont Noyes strove continuously both to preserve the Rhineland Agreement and to compel the administration to take constructive action with regard to Franco-German relations. His success in restraining the French drive for domination will be evaluated in the next chapter, but in Washington his efforts presumably had at least two distinct effects: to strengthen the president's growing alienation from the Allies, and to increase the State Department's distrust for Noyes himself.

Beginning in February, the American commissioner had reported in detail to Washington of the struggle that was being "forced" upon him to prevent the French from virtually destroying the High Commission. Convinced as he was of France's "sinister purposes" and "illegitimate ends," Noyes submitted considerable evidence in biweekly letters to substantiate his growing belief that the United States must either come into Europe with "both feet" or pull out "before the crash." As things stood, he argued, the American occupation had become, at best, a needless financial burden to Germany and an irrelevant factor in the securing of reparations. At the worst, he said, it had become a cover for French activities aimed at separating the left bank of the Rhine or at seizing the Ruhr.[71]

While there is no documentary proof that President Wilson examined Noyes's reports, his actions indicate that he probably did see them and may well have been seriously influenced by them. In early March, for example, Wilson created a furor in Paris by asserting in a public letter to Senator Gilbert Hitchcock (D-Neb.) that France had lately come under the domination of its "militaristic party."[72] A week later, in response to Ambassador Jules Jusserand's protest at his remarks, the president instructed Polk to warn Jusserand that he would have to face "the constant opposition of the American government if his government continues to take advantage of every technical deficiency in the carrying out of the peace terms, to press for prolongation of the period of occupation or for some new military action against Germany."[73] A month after this, during the French occupation of Frankfurt, the president seemed to be even more confirmed in these attitudes, for he wrote to his new secretary of state, Bainbridge Colby,[74] in blistering tones:

> Frankly I have no confidence whatever in the French assurances. What has evidently happened is that Foch has at last gained his object. He showed while I was in Paris, a perfect obsession with regard to the Rhine Provinces. . . . He is not only stubborn but has a touch of insubordination about him. I have lost all confidence in him.[75]

Colby, in the meantime, had begun to test Noyes's "either-or" proposition upon other American representatives in Europe. In mid-March the State Department had called Noyes and Allen to Paris for an interview with Ambassador Wallace,[76] and a week later it had requested an opinion from the new and unofficial American envoy in Berlin, Ellis Loring Dresel.[77] As it happened, neither ambassador, general, nor minister agreed with Noyes's appraisal of the situation. Wallace and Allen possessed essentially moderate views. Both were convinced that the French would continue to insist upon the occupation and that the American commissioner and the American zone could continue to exercise a restraining influence on the French and Germans.[78] Dresel was less cautious, suggesting that Noyes's "one-sided" attitudes were widening the rift between the United States and France, and emphasizing his own belief that (1) separatist schemes could never be a source of serious trouble, (2) France could not invade the Ruhr against the united opposition of British and American representatives, and (3) French unreasonableness would be mitigated in time by Allied insistence upon conciliatory methods.[79]

If the State Department had begun to feel uneasy with Noyes in Coblenz, however, the French seizure of Frankfurt in early April put a temporary end to its misgivings. For the time being events appeared to have validated the commissioner's perception of European trends. Moreover, a crisis was decidedly not the occasion to change representatives. Indeed, the situation at one point seemed so critical to Secretary of War Baker that he recommended strengthening Allen's force or withdrawing it completely (ironically, just what Noyes had urged).[80] His proposal was not acted upon because the danger of a Franco-German clash receded quickly, but both Baker and Colby remained apprehensive about the Rhineland for several days.[81]

A month later, in May, Washington had developed a quite different perspective. A conference of the Allies had been held at San Remo in Italy; French troops had been withdrawn from Frankfurt; the moment of danger seemed safely past. Yet Noyes was as impatient as ever. With considerable bluntness he had begun to preach to the Department of State and to the press[82] that if Europe were to be saved from anarchy, the treaty must be ratified, "reservations, mild reservations, no reservations, League . . . or no League."[83] At length, when Dresel sent a detailed report of Noyes's "tactlessness" to the department (along with the suggestion that General Allen could perform Noyes's duties with less civilian help),[84] Frank Polk and William Castle (the chief of the Western European desk) decided that the time had come to replace the commissioner. Their decision was facilitated by the fact that the department was vigorously attempting to cut expenditures,[85] but, at least as far as Castle was concerned, the primary consideration was simply that Noyes was not "the man for the job."[86] On May 17, a telegram was dispatched to inform him that Allen had been appointed to take his place as observer on the High Commission.[87]

Congressional militancy may also have played a role in the decision to relieve Noyes. In the weeks following the Kapp *Putsch* and second treaty debate Congress had displayed renewed concern about the retention of American forces in Europe. On March 19, Congressman Julius Kahn (R-Calif.), chairman of the House Military Affairs Committee, had introduced a resolution inquiring of the president about the size and status of the Rhine army, and the House had passed this unanimously within a week.[88] Wilson had responded on April 2, informing Congress that there were 17,482 officers and men at Coblenz and that General Allen's command stood solely under the terms of the armistice, not recognizing the jurisdiction of either the High Commission or Marshal Foch.[89]

How well this message had reassured members of the House was evident a few days later when Congressman Kahn experienced great difficulty in preventing the introduction of an amendment to an appropriations bill that would have eliminated all pay for American soldiers overseas. Kahn opposed such a rider on constitutional grounds, but in the same breath he estimated the cumulative cost of the occupation at about $750 million (or more than three times the actual figure) and expressed grave doubts that the United States would ever be reimbursed. His statement prompted Congressman Martin Madden (R-Ill.) to wonder "whether we are going to continue on forever in this altruistic expenditure of the public money or whether we are ever going to be able to relieve the burden of taxation from the backs of the American people." Congressman Sam Rayburn (D-Tex.) was also skeptical, although he cautioned the House against the withdrawal of occupation forces without consulting France and Britain. Congressman Percy Quin (D-Miss.) suggested patience in collecting debts but saw no reason why the current cost should not be reduced.[90]

Though Congress undertook no further action regarding

the occupation, its eagerness for normal times was soon reiterated. On April 9, the House passed a joint resolution for the establishment of a separate peace with Germany.[91] On May 15, the Senate approved a similar resolution, which was quickly accepted by the House as a substitute for its own bill. The fact that the measure was promptly and successfully vetoed by President Wilson only served to render the majority more determined.[92]

All the while, public opinion about western Europe was becoming steadily more divided and confused. The secretary of war had noted in April that Americans remained suspicious of Germany and unwilling to see her fully rehabilitated, but he felt it important to warn General Allen that the citizenry would be "much shocked if you undertook actual hostilities [against the Reich]."[93] During the Frankfurt occupation the majority of the press had rallied to the French[94] (the *Los Angeles Times* had exulted that the Teuton was "no longer chuckling"),[95] but there was also much criticism of the seizure, especially from Democratic and liberal journals such as the *New York World* and the *Springfield Republican*.[96] The *Nation* asserted that France must be restrained from such actions in her own interest.[97] The *New Republic* sympathized with Premier Millerand but concluded that his policies were "too risky" and might force Germany to align herself with the Soviet Union.[98]

The interesting point is that this division in American attitudes did not work against a continuation of the occupation. Few citizens as yet were willing to turn their backs on Europe. And because conservatives were generally opposed to weakening their wartime allies (e.g., France) and liberals to oppressing the defeated (e.g., Germany), both could counteract their natural desire for troop recall with hope that the army at Coblenz was strengthening the European country with which they each identified.

Thus, despite the changing forms that the American occupation had been forced to take, it had continued to exert a traceable impact on the political scene within the United States. During its ostensibly more active phase, in later 1919, the occupation had been used by the Irreconcilables with modest success as an argument against the League of Nations. Six months later, during what should have been a somewhat passive stage, the occupation had almost surely become an important factor in drawing President Wilson's attention to those French activities that alienated him from the Allied cause. (This alienation helps to explain the president's complete refusal during this period to participate in Allied conferences or to listen to Allied advice.) American liberals seem to have shared in Wilson's reactions, although unlike him, many of them had developed a concern for Germany that permitted them to view the American occupation as desirable protection for the Reich. This was undoubtedly one of the reasons why there was less public demand for the return of troops than might have been anticipated, especially considering the new crisis in Europe that had accompanied the second defeat of the treaty. While conservatives (and probably most of the public) were still thinking in terms of restraining Germany (to preserve the victory and obtain a separate peace), liberals and German-Americans were hopeful that the AFG would have a sobering effect upon the French. Even Irreconcilables may finally have found some advantage in the American presence overseas, for they were quite aware that an election was soon to be held.

7

NOYES AND "PARTICIPATION," JUNE 1919–MAY 1920

> The High Commission guarantees to the Rhenish population the full execution, both in word and spirit, of the occupation statutes, the especially generous regime of which is unprecedented in history.
>
> Proclamation of the High Commission, January 10, 1920

> . . . the Rhineland Commission and its policy are suffering from pressure—hidden pressure and open pressure—directly from the French government.
>
> Pierrepont Noyes to the Acting Secretary of State, February 27, 1920

During the year following the signing of the treaty, Americans on the Rhine found themselves in the strangely anomalous position of fighting to hold others to international agreements that their own country was repudiating. There had been a brief "honeymoon," of course, but after the Senate had rejected the treaty in October and French policy had once again turned assertive, it had become more and more difficult for American representatives to avoid head-on clashes with their allies. It was especially difficult for Pierrepont Noyes, who, as one of the authors of the Rhineland Agreement, remained firmly convinced that to depart from that understanding would bring disaster to western Europe. Confronted as he was with a steadily mounting French attack upon "civilian control" of the left bank, Noyes fought doggedly throughout the winter to preserve the "original idea" of the occupation. Yet he waged these battles, unlike those of the previous May, with scant support from his superiors. Although his efforts met with some success, they ended abruptly after the treaty had gone down to final defeat in Washington at the end of March.

The summer of 1919, then, was an interval of relaxation and cooperation along the Rhine. The return of "peace" and the departure of thousands of Allied soldiers from the area made it possible, even necessary, to work out new and easier relationships. In the process, the troop strength of the permanent occupation was agreed upon and zonal boundaries redesigned. Restrictions on the civilian population were reduced and the structure of the occupation somewhat lightened.

The size of the peacetime garrison had been established by the Supreme Council on July 26, 1919, four weeks after Wilson and Lloyd George had finally left Paris. The figure selected was the same one that Foch and the Loucheur Committee had recommended at the beginning of June: 151,000 men and 6,500 officers.[1] The Big Four had discussed this recommendation on June 27, but Lloyd George had made a last attempt to secure a reduction by having the matter reconsidered by the military representatives at Versailles.[2] It was not until these officers (General Bliss abstaining) had refused to suggest modifications that the British delegation abandoned its opposition.[3]

Shortly before, it had been determined that the United States would furnish one regiment, or approximately 5 percent of the Allied representation on the Rhine. Marshal Foch had hoped that the American share would be at least three times this much,[4] but the president had been so intent on not exceeding the figure of 5,000 infantrymen that General Pershing and Bliss had had great difficulty in convincing him of the need for auxiliary services that would raise the total strength to

6,800 men. Wilson ultimately had left the arrangement to Pershing's "best judgment,"[5] and the general and Foch had reached agreement on details at a meeting on June 30. They decided that three United States divisions (i.e., 75,000 men) would remain in Germany until July 15, two divisions until August 15, and one division until three months following ratification of the treaty, at which point the last division would be reduced to an enlarged regiment.[6]

As we have noted, July 2, 1919 saw the official disappearance of the United States Third Army and its replacement by the newly created American Forces in Germany, an independent entity with its headquarters in Coblenz.[7] The man whom Pershing selected to head the AFG, Major General Henry T. Allen, was a West Point graduate who at one time had served as a military attaché in Germany and in Russia and had led the 90th ("Alamo") Division during the war.[8] Normally, a regiment such as the AFG would have been commanded by a colonel, but in this case it was felt that a general officer was essential in order to prevent the organization from being "handled," or manipulated, as the regiments in Italy and northern Russia were reported to have been.[9]

Because of its reduced size and the restructuring of the entire occupation, however, the AFG was soon obliged to face the necessity of changes in its territory. Indeed, by July 25, when Pershing first discussed the subject with Foch, he and Bliss had already concluded that they could no longer manage an American "zone," but only an American "spot."[10] Pershing therefore told the marshal that he was "open-minded" as to boundaries, although he emphasized that President Wilson had spoken of the desirability of the AFG retaining its headquarters in Coblenz.[11]

Even so, the negotiations were strenuous. Marshal Foch's representatives conferred with General Allen and his aides at the end of July, but the two groups made little progress

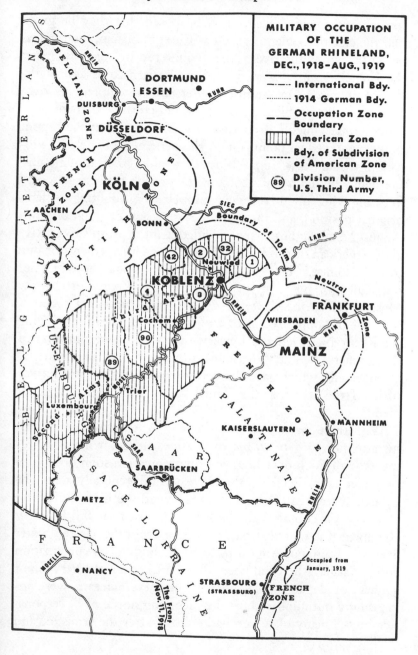

MILITARY OCCUPATION
OF THE
GERMAN RHINELAND,
DEC., 1918–AUG., 1919

—·—·— International Bdy.

·········· 1914 German Bdy.

— — — Occupation Zone
Boundary

▨▨▨ American Zone

········· Bdy. of Subdivision
of American Zone

(89) Division Number,
U.S. Third Army

toward agreement. The French proposed that they be given half the city of Coblenz as well as Ehrenbreitstein, the fortress landmark across the river. Allen countered by suggesting that the French occupy everything but the Landkreis and Stadtkreis Coblenz.[12] On August 7, Pershing attempted his own solution to the problem by promising Foch those parts of both these Kreise which lay north of the Moselle,[13] but Pierrepont Noyes hastened to point out to the general that such an allocation would leave him (Noyes) unable to deal with any German who did not also look to the French for instructions.[14] Pershing thereupon reversed himself by adopting Allen's original position, and the dispute with Foch dragged on until August 27, when the marshal decided that the prospective arrival of American troops for Silesia had made it expedient for him to compromise.[15] He was now willing to grant the AFG not only Coblenz and its environs, but also four Kreise north of the Moselle (Cochem, Mayen, Adenau, and Ahrweiler) together with the old upper sector of the Rhine bridgehead (including the Kreise Neuwied and Unterwesterwald, as well as parts of three others).[16] The Americans, in turn, gladly accepted this arrangement, which gave them approximately the eastern two-fifths of the area that the Third Army had originally occupied.[17]

With these matters settled, General Allen was able to turn his attention largely to his own zone, although his disagreements with Foch over lines of communication soon brought a reminder from Pershing that "we should generally meet the French at least half way."[18] In any event, the most immediate problem was coping with the raw recruits of the 8th Infantry Regiment, the unit that had been sent from the United States at the beginning of August to form the body of the occupation force. Earlier Allen had been allowed to retain the very finest soldiers of departing divisions,[19] but these veterans were increasingly outnumbered by the incoming horde of "irresponsible boys," many of whom had enlisted after the armistice and were only sixteen or seventeen years of age.[20] In September Allen informed Pershing that he had received "about 1,000 men . . . who, because of physical or mental defects, should not be representing the United States,"[21] and his dismay turned into genuine anguish in October when the Silesian brigade reported to Coblenz with an even greater proportion "below standard." His only recourse was to undertake intensive military and vocational training, but as late as Christmas he noted an excess of "court martials, AWOLS, and venereals" among his forces.[22] In November he had unofficially persuaded Undersecretary of State Frank Polk to cable Washington about the importance of improving military replacements, and in later months the War Department was more careful.[23]

In the meantime Allen had presided over a general easing of restrictions on the German population. Foch had acted in August to remove the prohibition on local elections,[24] and a subsequent agreement had made it possible for mail, telegrams, and telephone messages to return to regular routing with only intermittent censorship.[25] By September travel among the four zones was limited only by the requirement that one's identity card be stamped by his local zonal authority.[26]

In the American sector the Anordnungen were further modified. In July German customs guards were given permission to carry arms, and in August German cafés were granted an extension on their curfews. That same month control of public meetings was returned to the municipal government, and a few weeks later it was announced that press supervision would henceforth be confined to holding vendors responsible for what they sold.[27] On September 27, the antifraternization order was finally rescinded, apparently with the hope that the soldiers would now more frequently associate with German women other than camp followers. It is not clear why the Americans had waited several weeks longer than the French, British, or Belgians to remove this regulation.[28]

Though these changes did improve the local mood, by October a certain anxiety had returned, largely in anticipation of the winter of shortages that lay ahead. Falling monetary exchange rates and rumors of revolution in Berlin reflected the general concern. In Coblenz American authorities found it necessary to publish regulations outlawing the use of uniforms by civilians, prohibiting the exchange of "gifts" with servicemen, and barring discrimination against military personnel in shops and stores.[29]

Despite such "adjustments," however, most of the citizenry remained content under the American flag. Prices were often lower than across the river because of the occupied area's free trade with the West.[30] Merchants prospered as a result of American army spending,[31] and employers and employees alike expressed appreciation of American fairness in helping to adjust industrial disputes.[32] Local respect for the Military Police was so profound that Allen was afraid Rhinelanders were not developing the "democratic" habit of relying upon their municipal law officers.[33]

From the viewpoint of unoccupied Germany, the American occupation seemed to be the best of the lot,[34] although one Berlin newspaper claimed that the doughboys were always intoxicated with either love or alcohol.[35] Foreign Ministry officials were so favorable to the AFG that during the protocol dispute in December 1919 they considered excluding the Coblenz zone from a strike to be called in the event of military action.[36] By this time, understandably, American rejection of the treaty was raising brave hopes among the Germans about the possibility of permanently detaching the United States from the Allies.

Less in public view than army affairs during the summer of 1919, but perhaps of greater importance to the occupation, were the accomplishments of the Rhineland Commission. Though both commission and commissioners were now serving strictly on an interim basis, they remained extremely active in framing ordinances, building organizations, and coordinating the region's economy. Their actions acquired added significance from the fact that the longer the delay in ratifying the treaty the greater the chances that the Allied governments would choose to continue the incumbents as members of the High Commission. As it happened, both Tirard and Stuart were nominated for the new positions at the beginning of the autumn.[37] Noyes's nomination was held up by the president's illness, but on October 27 he was informed by Lansing that there was no reason why he should not be the eventual appointee.[38] The Belgian government was the only one to change its representative, deciding in November to select the legal adviser of its conference delegation, Baron Rolin-Jacquemyns, as its permanent commissioner.[39]

By then Noyes and his colleagues had long been at work to avoid a hiatus of power between regimes. Since the future commission, unlike its predecessor, required political and social as well as economic regulations, and since it was clearly desirable that these decrees be ready when the organization came into being, Tirard, Noyes, and Stuart had persuaded the subcommittee on Germany to authorize the Rhineland Commission to formulate them.[40] Polk in July had approved Noyes's full participation in the project, and by the beginning of August the commissioners and their legal committee were deeply involved in discussions.[41] The rough drafts of the first five ordinances were finished before September, but polishing and details postponed completion until mid-November. Noyes was well pleased with the results, and he noted in his diary that James Brown Scott, the legal counselor of the American Mission, found the ordinances "Bully! All!" and "in the American spirit."[42]

More difficult for Noyes were the tasks involved in building a civilian organization for the American occupation. There was no problem with the plan of operations itself, for Wallace Day had developed a workmanlike scheme involving a "cabinet" of several department chiefs and a field staff of seven "Kreis men."[43] The difficulty lay in obtaining and paying for the personnel who were qualified to do the jobs. It took Noyes several weeks to persuade the army to allow "retiring" civil affairs officers to be demobilized in Europe, where Noyes was in a position to employ them.[44] It took him even longer to convince the State Department that it must begin to pay these individuals once they had become civilians.[45] In October and again in December Noyes was virtually reduced to begging for appropriations to meet a $15,000 per month budget.[46] To make matters worse, at the end of the year he received a bill from General Allen in which the latter attempted to charge him $22,000 for the use of officers and enlisted men during the previous eight months.[47]

In defense of the State Department (and Allen), it should be pointed out that Noyes's money troubles were only part of a larger problem involving the means by which debts would ultimately be assessed against Germany. Not only was there considerable doubt at this time as to how the costs of the Rhineland Commission would be computed,[48] but prospects for Allied agreement on the apportionment of total armistice charges continued to appear dim. As we have seen in Chapter 4, the main difficulty was that if expenditures were paid in full, as the United States had been demanding since the spring, France, with a Rhine army more than double the size of the combined British and American forces, would receive the smallest reimbursement. The interim committee on reparations had wrestled with various ratios from October through December 1919, but none had been found that was acceptable to all the parties concerned.[49] On December 9, before the American Mission left Paris, the Supreme Council had pondered the dispute but had referred it back to the committee.[50]

Far graver challenges than this, however, loomed for western Europe and for the Rhineland as a result of the shifts that were occurring in French foreign policy. From July through September Clemenceau had pursued a relaxed course as he waited for the Allied parliaments to complete their approval of the work done at the peace conference. Yet, eventually, American failure to ratify the treaty, German slowness to comply with it, and a victory by the Right (*Bloc National*) in the French parliamentary elections prompted the premier to become more aggressive, or at least to tolerate more aggressiveness on the part of his subordinates. One of the first indications of the change came in late October when Commissioner Tirard spoke out publicly to advocate greater penetration of the "French spirit" into Rhenish schools and to assert that French administrative controls and sections economiques would not be withdrawn from the left bank under the treaty.[51] Somewhat later both Foch in Paris and Tirard in Coblenz proposed the establishment of a new inter-Allied military council, the marshal's to supervise the occupation from Versailles, and Tirard's to act as a buffer between the armies and the High Commission.[52] To Noyes it seemed clear that "Tirard has shown signs (a long time absent) of playing cat's paw for Payot and the military and nullifying civilian control . . ."[53]

The German government, already under intense pressure regarding the completion of disarmament, the fulfillment of coal deliveries, and the surrender of its "war criminals," was particularly incensed at the remarks of the French commissioner. Berlin had long been suspicious of French objectives in the occupation, and Tirard's open disregard for the Rhineland Agreement now led the German Foreign Ministry to mount an intensive attack upon French policy in both the domestic and foreign press.[54] At the same time, an all-party interpellation in the Prussian Landtag resulted in a formal condemnation by the Prussian government of the statements that Tirard had made.[55]

British leaders were also provoked by what the French

were saying and doing concerning the Rhine. At the beginning of December Lord Curzon, the new foreign secretary, expressed the hope that America's hesitancy regarding the tripartite security treaty might prod the French into improving what he described as an "unnecessarily exasperating" occupation.[56] A week or so earlier Lloyd George had confided to Frank Polk that he was afraid that French "abuses" on the left bank might drive the Germans into desperate actions.[57] Subsequently, during the period of the protocol crisis, the prime minister developed a severe case of the jitters at the prospect of finding his government involved in military action by Foch.[58]

On the Rhineland Commission, meanwhile, Noyes had become heavily engaged in combating the new French effort to dominate affairs. When Tirard had proposed the military council, for example, Noyes had sent a blunt warning to the Frenchman:

> I believe that this suggestion would be likely to establish . . . conditions of occupation virtually the same as those provided by [the plan of the military representatives in Versailles in May]. . . . You have specified as [the council's] functions . . . the concentration of information . . . , the control of representatives in the Kreise, and liaison with the high command. . . . [This would mean] for the commissioners, practically to surrender their function.[59]

This message had apparently led Tirard to withdraw the matter from the commission's agenda. "[He] is the most instinctive, perceptive man I ever met," Noyes commented in his diary. "He smells trouble from afar and comes in with modifications or compromises before there is time to join the issues."[60]

A few weeks later Noyes had had a similar run-in with the French over future control of communications and transportation. As he recounted it at the time, "Payot and his Wiesbaden crowd have submitted ordinances which would put the railways, telegraph and navigation entirely under control of the military (meaning Payot). If they succeed, all previous work for a decent occupation is wasted. His control of these commissions during the armistice has been a scandal. Through them, the economic life of the Rhineland is at the mercy of France."[61] Noyes's ensuing attack had led to a fierce struggle, but by standing firm (and prodding Stuart to do the same), he had once again been able to bring about a French retreat. When the ordinances were drafted, they provided that the armies could issue orders to the railways only for strictly military purposes.[62]

The American commissioner was less successful in winning French cooperation in his work to improve the Rhenish coal supply. As early as July he had noted that German coal production was running at only 60 percent of requirements, largely because much of it was allotted to reparations. "It looks damn bad [for the winter]," he had written Bernard Baruch at home, trying in vain to interest the Wilson administration in a movement of American coal to Europe.[63] In October, after the situation had finally reached the "serious stage," Noyes was appointed by Tirard to head a special coal subcommittee, but the most that his group could accomplish was to persuade the German government to raise prices and to allow a single agency in Cologne to supervise the distribution of coal from unoccupied Germany.[64] Noyes found, to his consternation, that the French were using the Essen Coal Committee of the Reparations Commission to block his efforts to relieve the local shortage. Paris was taking no chances on reducing the amount of coal that was moving from the Ruhr to France.[65]

Probably Noyes's greatest achievement of this period was his contribution to closing the so-called hole in the West. This phrase, which had come into common parlance in the autumn of 1919, referred to the French army's continuing interference with the collection of customs on the German frontier.[66] It signified that the French had been able to preserve a situation that was very much to their advantage—the Rhineland inundated with French merchandise, and an extensive quantity of goods moving duty free into the interior of Germany.[67] Indeed, the flow of French products had become so patently disadvantageous to the Reich that in September Noyes and Stuart had mounted a campaign to stop it.[68] Their efforts were immeasurably bolstered by the fact that the German government, in retaliation against the French, had begun to restrict foreign commerce between the occupied and unoccupied regions.[69]

Though several months were required, Anglo-American criticism of French policy and the effect of the German controls ultimately forced the French to abandon their attempt to have the best of war and peace. By October Tirard had intimated that German tariffs could be reestablished if Berlin would proceed to grant most-favored-nation status to each of the Allies.[70] By November he had agreed that German customs officials could take up their stations,[71] and by January his government had finally permitted them to assess rates in (nondepreciated) gold marks.[72] Despite this progress, the hole in the West was not fully closed until April 1920, when the French belatedly allowed the High Commission to ratify recent German commercial legislation.[73] Even then, as Chapter 9 will reveal, the closure was to be far from permanent.

Though the arrival of peace in January 1920 did not in any sense diminish Noyes's efforts to restrain the French, it did alter the nature of the occupation. The reader should bear in mind that when the treaty came into effect the entire institutional basis of the Allied presence was rearranged. During the armistice period the Rhineland Commission (as the one exception to the authority of the High Command) had supervised the economics of the left bank under the direction of the

156

Supreme Economic Council. Beginning with the new year, the High Commission assumed broader powers but a narrower responsibility: that of protecting the Allied armies as provided for in the Rhineland Agreement.

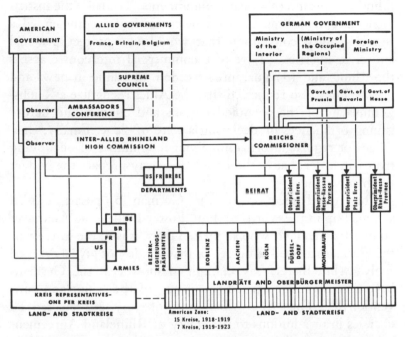

ADMINISTRATION OF THE OCCUPIED RHINELAND, JANUARY, 1920 – JANUARY, 1923

The process of interpreting the Rhineland Agreement had actually begun the preceding July, long before the preparation of the first public decrees (ordinances) of the High Commission. In accord with the informal understanding of June 27,[74] committees representing both the Allied and German governments had met in Paris for what the Allies called "explanatory discussions." What was said and written on this occasion set the tone for much that followed.

The Germans had been in no mood for "explanation." In meetings on July 11 and 12, they had expressed the conviction that the Rhineland Agreement, as it stood, took into account neither the necessities of a peacetime situation nor the dependence of Germany upon the occupied region in fulfilling various international commitments. To make the instrument acceptable, the German delegates had recommended a supplementary convention that would (1) protect personal and civic liberties, (2) restore commercial intercourse across the Rhine, and (3) guarantee freedom of traffic in news and goods. They also requested that the Allies recognize a Reichskommissar for the occupied regions and consult him before issuing ordinances or declaring a state of siege. Finally, they asked for regular information about the number of occupying troops in order that Berlin could efficiently prepare the budget for maintenance.[75]

The Allied reaction to the German proposals is well summed up in the words of John Foster Dulles, the American committee member, who suggested that "it is in the interest of the Germans as well as ourselves that we do not give a detailed reply . . . but merely say enough to show that the Germans have entirely misconstrued the spirit [of the Rhineland convention]."[76] Thus, the Allied note of July 29 rejected all changes in or additions to the treaty or Rhineland Agreement but took a conciliatory attitude in questions of interpretation. The Germans were assured that the Allies had never intended to interfere in such matters as economic affairs or public education. They were also promised that they would receive sufficient information on army strength for budgetary purposes.[77]

The Germans were not so easily placated, however. On August 7, 1919, they expressed their pleasure at the Allied commitment to "as light [an occupation] as possible," but went on to register complaints regarding the severe billeting requirements, interference with the customs frontier, and

158

French assistance to the separatist cause. They also announced their expectation that the supervisors of local administration (the Kreis men) would be withdrawn. The Germans must have been badly disappointed on October 14 when the Allies responded with replies that scarcely went beyond their previous statements.[78]

The Allied perspective on the Rhineland Agreement was further clarified in the five basic ordinances that the High Commission enacted upon its inception (January 10, 1920). The first of these defined the legislative rights of the regime, the second dealt with judicial relationships, and the third set down administrative rules for German publications and public meetings. The two additional ordinances (technically numbers five and six) were concerned with industrial disputes and the powers and duties of the Inter-Allied Railway Commission.[79] The government of the High Commission was to be characterized neither by separation of powers nor by responsibility to the people, although it was plainly limited by its own view of what it had promised to perform. The commission's activities were to be partly direct, through its powers to issue ordinances and to annul court decisions, and partly indirect, through its powers to issue instructions to German agencies and to exclude German laws.[80]

These first pronouncements of the new authority caused considerable unhappiness among the Germans. Reichskommissar Carl von Starck,[81] who had been shown the draft ordinances but had asked in vain for modifications, expressed his strong disapproval by refusing to participate in the inaugural ceremonies of the High Commission.[82] The German Foreign Ministry delivered its own formal protest to the Supreme Council on January 12, noting that there was no procedure to appeal the "legality" of the High Commission's actions, and asserting that the first ordinances had violated the Rhineland Agreement in at least three ways: (1) by requiring that the

High Commission approve German laws before they could come into effect, instead of considering them valid until vetoed, (2) by entrusting German violators of ordinances to Allied military courts instead of to the German judiciary, and (3) by appointing Kreis representatives with supervisory and executive duties instead of only liaison functions.[83] None of these contentions was accepted by the Allies, although the third did exert some influence upon the British and American commissioners.[84]

As noted in the preceding chapter, the relationship of the American zone and commissioner to the new government of the occupation was particularly difficult. Not only had the principles of the Rhineland Agreement originated to a great extent with Pierrepont Noyes, but he had also been deeply involved in drafting the ordinances of the High Commission. Yet because the United States Senate had not accepted the Treaty of Versailles, neither the American army nor its commissioner could be bound by the convention when the Allies deposited their ratifications on January 10.

This eventuality had concerned Allied diplomats as early as the previous October and had become the subject of considerable discussion. Tirard and Stuart (and ultimately the Supreme Council) had urged that the American government meet the problem by allowing the jurisdiction of the High Commission to extend into its zone.[85] But T. H. Urwick, an assistant to the British commissioner, had suggested what was to become the final if "unsatisfactory" solution to the dilemma: that the American army agree to issue the High Commission's ordinances in the Coblenz sector as military orders.[86] Noyes had recommended Urwick's idea to General Allen and to Undersecretary Polk (in Paris), and both of these men had apparently become persuaded of its merits.[87] The unexpected part, of course, was that by the end of the year Noyes himself had begun to prefer the Tirard-Stuart plan.

The modus vivendi that was finally achieved was largely General Allen's doing. Despite Noyes's new qualms and the obvious pressure from the Allies, the general had held fast to Noyes's original proposal and had endorsed it to the War Department on January 2. In so doing, he had given Washington a clear-cut alternative to the arrangement suggested by the Allies and secretly by Noyes.[88] He had made it possible for Secretary Lansing to choose a maximum of independence.

It took several days for Noyes and Allen to, as Noyes put it, "sweep up" the "rubbish of the negotiations."[89] It was January 17 before they had agreed that members of Noyes's staff, and not army Kreis officers, should be the local representatives of the High Commission.[90] It was almost February before they had approved a code of military regulations designed to conform to the ordinances of the High Commission.[91] Meanwhile, Noyes had been accepted on that council as liaison with Allen's military administration, and Tirard had been so pleased to retain American participation that he told Noyes that his opinion "should have the same weight as heretofore."[92] Though German agencies had been confused momentarily by the new situation, Berlin had refrained from protest for fear of endangering the American presence on the Rhine.[93]

Nevertheless, it is not surprising that the personal relationship of Noyes and Allen was considerably disturbed by the twist of fate that had left the American commissioner so completely dependent upon the commanding general. By temperament Noyes was a "battler" and Allen a "diplomat," and this fact together with the latter's new sense of responsibility now caused Allen to become extremely critical of Noyes's methods and unmindful of his frustrations. The two men had been on friendly terms as late as December 1919,[94] but by February 1920, Noyes had become convinced that the general was both "pro-French" and a "disbeliever in the High Commission."[95] Allen, on the other hand, had developed an open contempt for businessmen who meddled in international politics.[96] In the weeks that followed, the quarrel. was to be somewhat papered over, but it would return to haunt and undermine Noyes during the troubles of the later spring.

During the first five months of the new regime (January–May 1920) the now "unofficial" American commissioner continued and intensified his struggle to preserve the spirit of the Rhineland Agreement. As developments led France into a more and more aggressive policy, Noyes struck back with a courage and desperation that could only impress his French opponents as much as it unnerved his American colleagues in Europe and Washington. In his idealism and his honesty, not to mention his innocence, he was, in a very real sense, the last of the Wilsonians in Europe.

During the long winter of 1919–1920 France had become increasingly apprehensive about its own security. In January the Chamber of Deputies had responded to a widespread impatience for "results" by defeating Clemenceau in his bid for the French presidency and forcing him to resign the premiership. For several weeks afterward it had put a mounting pressure on his successor, Alexandre Millerand (like Clemenceau, a Republican and leader of the Bloc National), to guarantee a strict enforcement of the treaty.[97] In March, President Wilson's criticism of French "militarism" and America's second rejection of the treaty had driven the entire body politic into a real spasm of anxiety.[98] The assertions of former foreign minister Gabriel Hanotaux, who charged Clemenceau with incompetence for not having insisted in 1918 that the Allies advance to the Elbe, were symptomatic of the general dismay.[99]

The touchstone of French concern regarding Germany,

Noyes and "Participation"

Noyes came to realize, was invariably their Rhenish policy. The nervousness of the autumn had shown itself clearly in Tirard's activities, and the newest tension in Paris was reflected in Millerand's use of coal deficiencies to threaten Germany with "all kinds of force" and even a longer occupation.[100] The American noted in his diary that "French propaganda is [now] directed to persuade the Allies to occupy the Ruhr," and that Tirard had taken to asking him repeatedly if such a move were not desirable.[101] He also knew (because Sir Harold Stuart had told him) that Millerand had recently proposed this action to Lloyd George, and that the prime minister had put the Frenchman off only by recourse to a technicality of the treaty.[102]

For obvious reasons, then, Noyes and Stuart did their best to oppose what seemed to them "1001 encroachments" on "both the word and letter" of the Rhineland Agreement.[103] Their successes were frequently significant, as when they fended off the demands of the French High Command for control of river navigation[104] or when Noyes prevented the veto of a German law establishing workers' councils in Rhenish factories.[105] Their disappointments were also noteworthy, as, for example, when they failed to prevent the establishment of a "Kreis system" that functioned independently in the French and Belgian zones. To Noyes, this defeat was particularly distressing:

> The French area now comprises three-quarters of the occupied territory, so that the establishment of "Kreis control" by them covers most of the [Rhineland] without the trouble of fighting issues in the commission. The only knowledge we have as to how the local representation is organized is derived from Tirard's memo submitted three weeks ago (ca. January 20) and which I replied to very vigorously in a memo which is preserved. . . . No move has been made to coordinate the systems in the different zones and both the French and Belgians run theirs as though private property.[106]

Even more irritating was the counterpressure to which Noyes

and Stuart were subjected. On one occasion, after they had been able to show that a German tobacco-monopoly law had been voided by the French High Command, Tirard had warned them openly that if the French military were pushed too hard, both he and General Degoutte (the army commander) might well be replaced.[107]

Understandably, as Noyes watched Germany tottering toward economic ruin and France maneuvering to control the Rhineland and the Ruhr, he became more and more convinced that the occupation as it existed must not continue. As early as February 7 he had written Secretary of State Lansing that the situation was about "as bad as it could possibly be":

> France was always governed by mixed motives. Her desire for [the] ruin of Germany was periodically checked by hopes for reparations. I believe that check is now practically removed. Her hope of gain is secretly pinned to illegitimate ends, to be accomplished by illegitimate use of the powers of occupation.[108]

By February 27 Noyes's concern had become so intense that he was evidently on the verge of despair:

> . . . the Rhineland Commission and its policy are suffering from pressure—hidden pressure and open pressure—directly from the French Government. Mr. Tirard would, I think, personally be inclined to give fair trial to the plan laid down in the Rhineland agreement last June. He, however, spends more than half of his time in Paris where the pressure for a "strong policy" in the Rhineland is evidently kept before him with great emphasis. . . .
> Sir Harold and I agree that the recent attempts in the Commission to take food control in the Rhineland away from the Germans, to take the coal distribution away from the Germans, and many other of the annoying incidents, are part of a general policy to throw off moderate control and to move much more energetically in the matter of separating the Occupied territory from the rest of Germany.[109]

A week later his message had been even more drastic:

Having become convinced that any occupation of Germany beyond perhaps the period necessary to put into effect disarmament provisions will prove a blunder and [be] fraught with serious perils for all the world, I think [it would be] best to place my resignation in your hands so that you may, if you think best, replace me by a man who still has faith in this method of obtaining reparations. . . . I believe it is impossible that a military occupation of Germany conducted largely with French forces can be made such a tolerable burden as the President had hoped.[110]

As we have previously observed, Washington's reaction to these cries of distress had not been sympathetic. In the face of what Noyes had defined as an "either-or" situation, the State Department did not feel itself capable of following any course other than that suggested by General Allen, Ambassador Wallace (Paris), and Commissioner Dresel (Berlin). None of these men agreed with Noyes that the problem was so desperate as to necessitate American intervention or withdrawal. Noyes wanted either to enforce the Rhineland Agreement fully or to renounce responsibility (and perhaps clear the way for effective action later); his colleagues believed that continuing mitigation was both salutary and the best to be hoped for from America.

In this regard it is interesting that British diplomats, though on the whole quite favorable to Noyes, were also clearly of a mind to prefer half a loaf to none. In February Sir Harold Stuart had pleaded with Noyes, at all costs, not to "desert him," emphasizing that America's very presence in the occupation greatly reduced the danger of hostilities in Europe.[111] In March Lord Curzon revealed almost the same opinion in commenting on a report that General Allen had criticized Noyes to Stuart:

The system of inter-allied civilian government of the Rhineland is an American creation. It was put through at Paris last summer owing to the personal intervention of President

Wilson, and in opposition to all military opinion. Yet I am not at all sure that there is not a real possibility that the Americans will withdraw altogether. I have had several indications of this lately. If they do it will be a disaster. French influence, political, military, and commercial, will become paramount, and Sir Harold Stuart will be in a permanent minority. Mr. Noyes, his American colleague, is somewhat unskilled in affairs, but he is a sensible and downright [*sic*] man.[112]

In any case, the State Department's decision regarding Noyes's future did not come before he had played a noteworthy role in the series of crises that occurred in Germany in late March and early April. The Kapp *Putsch*, Ruhr rebellion, and Frankfurt occupation provided Noyes with an opportunity to experience and react to the very "disasters" that he had been predicting. They also, on at least one occasion, involved him openly in the struggle between the Germans and the French.

The critical events followed each other in rapid and bewildering succession. On March 13, 1920, military elements took advantage of German discontent with shortages, strikes, and inflation to seize Berlin and to institute a right-wing government under Wolfgang Kapp. Then, after most of the country had rallied to President Ebert and a general strike had discredited the *Putsch*,[113] the Spartacists in the Ruhr parlayed the strikes of that region into a full-scale communist revolt. Following this, because the Ruhr basin lay largely within the fifty-kilometer neutral zone, the Ebert government requested permission from the Allies to send Reichswehr troops into the area to put down the Communists.[114]

To the French the Spartacist uprising and the request from Ebert appeared in the guises of both danger and opportunity. The danger was that by allowing German soldiers into the neutral zone under the pretext of a "crisis," the Allies would be establishing a precedent for future treaty violations. The opportunity lay in the fact that the situation provided a plausible excuse for the Allies to secure an added sanction (i.e., the Ruhr) for observance of the treaty. The end result possessed a certain logic. For two weeks following March 17, Millerand had attempted in vain to persuade the British to advance with the French into the Ruhr, all the while stubbornly refusing Berlin's request that the limits of the neutral zone be temporarily waived.[115] By April 2, however, the Germans had become so fearful of Bolshevik success and/or intervention by the French or by the Allies that the Ebert government had dispatched military units into the Ruhr without Allied consent. Four days later, Millerand had retaliated by sending the French army into the city of Frankfurt in the neutral zone opposite Mainz.[116]

Meanwhile, through a surprising French miscalculation, Noyes was virtually compelled to put the United States on record as "not responsible" for what was happening in Frankfurt. To be sure, when Tirard on April 4 had informed the High Commission of the pending countermove and requested a declaration of martial law for the Mainz bridgehead, Noyes had quietly and informally declined to take a position.[117] Nor had Noyes been alone in this reaction, for though the British deputy commissioner, Malcolm Robertson,[118] had approved the French proposal, the Belgian commissioner had quickly followed the American's lead. Nevertheless, on April 6, after instructions from Brussels had directed Rolin-Jacquemyns to support the French,[119] Tirard had publicly announced that the High Commission's decision was now "unanimous." "This is the first time an action opposed by me had been called 'unanimous,' " Noyes fumed. "I immediately wrote a short, carefully worded statement [for the press, asserting] that I disassociated myself from the action."[120]

"This was the only positive evidence of the U.S. attitude [in the whole crisis]," Noyes recalled three weeks later,[121] and his announcement seems to have attracted considerable attention. In 1921 the German Reichskommissar remembered that Noyes had "ostentatiously separated himself" from the Frankfurt move, although von Starck also noted that the American had been unable to persuade his government openly to follow suit.[122] At the time, Malcolm Robertson, who was strongly pro-French, had been predictably furious at Noyes. Robertson reported to London that the commissioner's announcement had created a "painful impression" among his colleagues (meaning, probably, Allen as well as the others) and deplored the fact that Noyes had publicized a disagreement among the Allies.[123] In any event, Noyes's statement was the subject of much comment in the British, French, and German press, the French attacking his "desertion," and the Germans praising the commissioner's "forthrightness."[124]

For the French government, unfortunately, Noyes's assertion (published April 7) was but an early indication of the general if confidential protest that was to follow. Washington had already conveyed its deep concern to Paris in several communications, and on April 12 it dispatched a formal note to express its displeasure at what the French army had done.[125] By that date London had gone considerably farther. Curzon had threatened to withdraw British troops from the Rhine if France continued to act unilaterally,[126] and Lloyd George, after instituting a boycott of the Ambassadors' Conference, had sent Millerand a message in which he had branded the Frankfurt seizure as "incompatible with the entire spirit . . . [of] the alliance."[127]

The immediate effect of the incident was to relieve somewhat the tension. Millerand, having by his intervention reduced the pressure on himself from the French armed forces and the Right, was now in a better position to reach an accomodation with his foreign critics. Though he did not apologize for what he had done, he did assure the British privately on April 11 that in the future France would act vis à vis Germany only in cooperation with its allies.[128] He also agreed that the forthcoming conference at San Remo (Italy) should take up the question of achieving French withdrawal from the neutral zone.[129]

Following the Kapp *Putsch* and the Frankfurt affair, Noyes's official career in Europe came rapidly to an end. His position at home had been temporarily bolstered by the crisis on the Rhine, but circumstances and his own convictions now conspired to make his recall almost inevitable. On the High Commission he remained extremely vigorous, observing in his diary that "by luck or otherwise the agenda were full of French encroachments (deporting Landrats, etc.) so that I was obliged to oppose nearly every question."[130] At the same time Noyes decided that someone ought to tell the truth to Woodrow Wilson, and on April 22 he sent off his message urging ratification of the treaty "reservations, mild reservations, [or] no reservations."[131] It was Noyes's firm conviction that "the general direction of the now hopelessly mixed European settlement will be, with temporary ups and downs, steadily downward toward disaster until the U.S. ratifies and takes the lead."[132]

Given such actions and opinions on the part of the American commissioner, it is largely irrelevant whether it was the criticism of men like Dresel and Allen, congressional militancy, or the economy drive in the State Department that provided the immediate excuse for the decision to recall him. The underlying reason was that Noyes's aggressive participation in the affairs of his province was no longer in accord with the aloofness from Europe that the recent decisions of the Senate had decreed. It should have come as no surprise to him when, on May 20, 1920, he received a cable from the State Department directing him to "wind up the Commissionership and turn over to General Allen as much of [your] staff as he needs temporarily."[133]

In contrast to the affairs of the High Commission, the relations between American troops and the inhabitants of their zone in the period after January 1920 remained highly satisfactory. Rumors of possible American withdrawal brought anguished protests from a wide variety of citizens,[134] while adverse criticism of the occupation was confined to problems of billeting and the military court system.[135] The number of marriages of enlisted men to German women increased at such a rapid rate that General Allen finally decided to disapprove the applications of all soldiers below Grade 3 (corporal).[136] Other restrictive action was limited to placing certain German shops off limits, primarily in order to stop their proprietors from price gouging.[137]

The reasons for the good relations were fairly obvious. American unwillingness to accept the treaty and refusal to join in the occupation of Frankfurt had redounded strongly to the army's advantage. In addition General Allen and his forces had achieved a certain measure of success in their efforts to be unobtrusive yet helpful. Germans widely appreciated, for instance, that Allen had been willing to follow the High Commission in abandoning such military prerogatives as censorship and restrictions on circulation.[138] It was also appreciated that army authorities had insisted upon the arbitration of local strikes, worked with the Prussian administration in a campaign against profiteers and smugglers, and made supplies of food available to civilians during the winter and spring.[139]

The High Commission itself was not given much credit by citizens of Coblenz for what was healthy about their situation. Doubtless the significance of the "civilian" government was obscured by General Allen's unusual position in the American zone. Yet Rhinelanders were shrewd enough to sense that the manner in which ordinances were enforced depended ultimately upon who was enforcing them. The "man on the street," when interviewed, was surprisingly skeptical regarding the advantages allegedly being derived from the presence of the *Interallierte Rheinland Kommission* (IRKO).[140] One citizen told his questioners that the commission's ordinances reminded him of "Prussian police regulations." Another contended that, no matter who might be in charge, people would always feel that they were dealing with the military anyway.[141]

In unoccupied Germany attitudes toward the Americans on the Rhine both reflected and contributed to more basic feelings about the United States. Faith in the possibility of American political and economic assistance was still substantial in 1920,[142] and this optimism almost certainly helped to enhance the favorable view of the occupation. At the same time reports of decent relations in Coblenz must have fortified German hopes and expectations with regard to Washington's intentions.

On the popular level, the developing image of the doughboy tended to confirm a belief in America's power and impartiality. According to Erich Roehrer in the *Berliner Börsenzeitung*, for example, the American soldier was a "likable" "grown-up child" whose "fabulous wages" had made Coblenz into the "most expensive town in Germany." From time to time, Roehrer asserted, the doughboy had his "brutal" moods, but whatever he did, it was obvious that he never meant to harm anyone.[143]

A similar process of hopeful thinking was at work on the governmental level, where the achievements of both Noyes and Allen were usually taken to be proof of America's good intentions. This, assuredly, did not prevent German officials from admiring these men as individuals, and von Starck for one was honestly impressed with Noyes's accomplishments, making this report to his superiors:

171

The decision of the American government [to recall him] is very regrettable from the German standpoint, since American influence in the High Commission has always been directed both to secure a correct implementation of the Rhineland Agreement and to prevent an interference in German affairs above and beyond its stipulations. The personal influence of Mr. Noyes is largely responsible for this, for he has always taken the view that the war between Germany and the United States is over. . . .[144]

Even so, personal gratitude to such men as Noyes did not blind the Germans to the significance of the American point of view per se. As if to demonstrate this point, in June 1920 Reichskommissar von Starck and Regierungspräsident von Groening paid an official visit to General Allen to express the hope that American troops would remain on the Rhine as long as those of any foreign power.[145]

On the international scene, the weeks of May and June did seem to offer grounds for hope, France and Britain having reached a compromise at San Remo that not only reconstructed their alliance but also offered Germany a measure of cooperation. Quite predictably, Millerand had tried to link withdrawal from Frankfurt to an occupation of the Ruhr, but Lloyd George had rejected this and argued instead for an era of direct negotiations with the Germans. In the end, Millerand had agreed to the British suggestion on condition that the Allies formalize both the terms that they would present and the sanctions to be employed if understandings were later broken. Berlin was to be invited to send a delegation to a multinational conference at Spa in July.[146]

This news, together with the arrival of spring, helped the Germans to regain some sense of confidence. The mark, at sixty-nine to the dollar on April 1, increased in value steadily to twenty-nine on May 26, and although the nation's export trade suffered as a result, the economy as a whole responded vigorously.[147] The Reichstag elections of June 6 represented a severe defeat for the Majority Socialists and Democrats, but the extremist parties of Right and Left did not register decisive gains. As Konstantin Fehrenbach came to head a new Center-Right coalition, prospects were good for the continued existence of moderate and stable government in Germany.[148]

Commissioner Noyes's forebodings seemed to have been proven false. The American zone appeared serene, and on all sides the situation looked more promising. Though Noyes himself had been forced to abandon his fight on behalf of the Rhineland Agreement, France's precipitant action at Frankfurt had apparently opened up new possibilities for European accommodation.

The future would show, however, that the "tenderfoot" commissioner had not simply been imagining things. In 1920 Europe was experiencing only a brief respite on its turbulent path to an even greater international crisis. On the High Commission General Allen was shortly to find himself as deeply affected by the results of French fears as his predecessor had been. Perhaps it was only justice that, before his own return to America, Allen would be compelled to fight some of the same battles that Noyes had fought before him.

8

THE SOLEMN REFERENDUM, HARDING, AND THE OCCUPATION, JUNE 1920–JUNE 1922

> They [the American Forces in Germany] haven't any business there, and just as soon as we have formal peace we can be sure they will be coming home, as they ought to come.
>
> Warren G. Harding
> October 7, 1920

> [General Allen's letter] confirms many impressions which I have entertained right along and tends to add to the confidence I have so frequently expressed in General Allen. I very much fear that there would be a bad mess all the time in Europe if it were not for the mollifying and harmonizing influences which are wielded by spokesmen for this Republic.
>
> Warren G. Harding to
> Henry P. Fletcher,
> October 11, 1921

The Senate's rejection of the Treaty of Versailles may have relieved the United States of its legal obligations on the Rhine, but it also ushered in, and in part created, a succession of new and different reasons for maintaining American soldiers at Coblenz. First the presidential contest of 1920 necessitated the postponement of all important foreign policy decisions (although, significantly, it also put Warren Harding on record as in favor of bringing the boys home from overseas). Then, following the Republican electoral avalanche, President Wilson's attempts to cut back American ties to Europe ran up against the fact that the occupation was a valuable lever for future bargaining with the Germans. Finally, with Harding in the White House—a lingering loyalty to the Allies, the deliberations of the Washington Conference, the controversy regarding army costs, and a deepening crisis in European affairs—each rendered a withdrawal unpropitious. And while a strong drive for economy on the part of Congress repeatedly threatened to end the occupation, other domestic developments, such as renewed demands for overseas markets, worked to perpetuate it.

Though the campaign of 1920 had great significance for the occupation and was affected by it in turn, the electoral race could hardly have been other than an obstacle to American decision-making about the Rhineland. With foreign policy so central an issue in the election, the State Department was not about to do anything at Coblenz that could complicate the domestic political picture. Nor were the president or the candidates in any position to propose or accomplish alterations in basic occupation policy.

There is considerable evidence to show that the Wilson administration seriously neglected German (as well as other) affairs during the summer and fall of 1920. Secretary Colby was away from Washington a good deal, and the upper echelons of his staff were badly undermanned.[1] "The 'digestive' power of the Department is weak," Allen Dulles wrote to a friend, "and the power of taking action is almost gone as a result of politics."[2] Lithgow Osborne of the German desk complained that it was "impossible to have a logical foreign policy in the present state of political chaos."[3]

Meanwhile, the presidential candidates and their supporters were too much absorbed in general issues to examine such specific matters as the occupation. The Rhineland army was mentioned on only a few occasions, as for example when Pierrepont Noyes explained its existence in newspaper interviews designed to assist the Democratic cause.[4] By and large, Republicans referred to American troops overseas primarily to illustrate the results of Wilson's stubbornness with the Senate.[5] Democrats conveniently forgot to notice that there even was an AFG. Harding himself alluded to the occupation only once, and though the statement was of some importance, he had surely not intended that it be.

Weeks before, Boies Penrose, the Pennsylvania Republican boss, had advised his party colleagues from his sickbed in regard to the coming presidential canvass: "Keep Warren at home. Don't let him make any speeches. If he goes out on tour, somebody's sure to ask him questions, and Warren's just the sort of damned fool that will try to answer them."[6] As it turned out, Penrose could hardly have better predicted what would happen to his presidential candidate concerning both the League and the related issue of the German occupation. Had the heavily favored Harding been content to remain at home in Marion, Ohio, he might have continued indefinitely both to endorse an international association and at the same time condemn the "Wilson League." By the beginning of October, however, the extensive touring of his opponent (James Cox) had persuaded the Republican nominee to take the stump. Once he had done so, the demands of the Irreconcilables that he disavow all leagues frightened him into proclaiming his fervent nationalism.[7] In Des Moines, Iowa, on October 7, Harding was particularly extreme in berating those who sought to sacrifice American sovereignty, and afterwards he amplified his thoughts in an extemporaneous exchange with several individuals in the crowd. When one of them demanded to know his position regarding the "boys over in Germany yet," the nominee responded strongly: "They haven't any business there, and just as soon as we have formal peace we can be sure they will be coming home, as they ought to come." He added that, as far as he was concerned, a separate peace with Germany was by no means a necessity, or, in other words, that a Treaty of Versailles with reservations would be acceptable.[8]

Such a combination of comments received nation-wide attention, particularly from the opposition press. The (Democratic) *Springfield Republican* was ready to conclude that Harding was hardly serious about the treaty if he would nullify its provisions for an occupation.[9] The *New York Times* felt prompted to remind the candidate that France had been turned aside from annexing the Rhineland by a promise that she would not have to stand alone against Germany.[10] Republican internationalists were so troubled by the tone of the Harding's Des Moines assertions that thirty-one of them published a statement affirming their belief that a vote for their party was a vote for a properly modified League. That their appeal had serious impact on the candidate is indicated by the swiftness with which he retreated to the safety of ambiguous pronouncements.[11]

Nevertheless, Harding's remarks about the occupation did probably work to his advantage with many voters, including isolationists, German-Americans, and white Southerners. As the anti-Wilson candidate, he appealed to the first two groups in any case,[12] but by emphasizing his antagonism toward Europe he almost certainly stimulated isolationist enthusiasm for his cause. In addition, his remarks enabled him to profit from the fact that both German-Americans and white Southerners were at this moment being turned against the occupation by a wave of "black horror" propaganda.[13]

The so-called black horror on the Rhine (a series of atrocities that French colonial troops were alleged to be perpetrating in the occupied regions) had been the object of widespread public protest for several months. To be sure, in 1918 and 1919, when German diplomats had voiced complaints about the "colored" troops of the Allies, relatively few people had listened. After the Frankfurt occupation (April 1920), however, when the German press had begun to focus specific criticism upon the French colonial units, the response had been far different.[14] Soon a campaign had taken shape, mobilized in many countries and organized to convince world opinion that France had unleashed a horde of savages who were raping, molesting, and murdering at will.[15] The agitation was subsidized by German sources and built around the speeches and articles of the English reformer E. D. Morel.[16] In the United States the movement was concentrated in the Midwest and South.[17]

Despite French assurances that colonial troops in Germany numbered but a few thousand and in most cases were neither Negroid nor guilty of unusual crime,[18] the efforts of the campaign's instigators combined with a heightened postwar race consciousness to keep the American public aroused for many months. In October, for instance, Dudley Field Malone had written President Wilson on behalf of the Farmer Labor Party that "continued occupation of Germany in conjunction with these beasts in French uniform is equivalent to an approval by the United States of the inhuman policy."[19] A week before the election the *Christian Science Monitor* had leaped to the conclusion that the "French [had] gone even further than [an eye for an eye] and [had] outplayed Germany, at its very worst, in a way so terrible that it is impossible to indulge in details."[20] Two years later one citizen remembered that "I was in the midst of the presidential campaign in Connecticut, when the word went along that Mr. Harding should be voted for because he would do his best to get those niggers out of Germany."[21] Thus, individuals who believed the story of the black shame were apparently impressed by Harding's statements at Des Moines.

The effect of the presidential contest of 1920, then, was

mixed as far as the American occupation was concerned. If the campaign postponed the withdrawal of troops from Germany, it also produced a pledge by the ultimately victorious candidate to seek an early end to the endeavor. And if Harding's promise of action lost him internationalist support, it strengthened the Republican cause in both the South and the Midwest. In fact, the Des Moines remarks had had an impact on foreign chancelleries as well, for E.L. Dresel heard on good authority from Paris that Harding's promise had "bucked up the French military party considerably [about the prospects of entering the Ruhr]."[22]

In any event, the four-month postelection interregnum now made it clear that there were reasons beyond an indeterminate political situation for preserving the Rhineland occupation. Central to this development was the fact that Woodrow Wilson had resolved after November to draw the full implications of defeat and (by way of making a point) to end all special representation in Europe before he left office. William R. Castle of the State Department noted that the president was removing everyone possible no matter what the result, "as he puts it, to force the Republicans to act quickly when they come into power; as the ordinary man would put it, to make things for the Republicans just as difficult as he jolly well can."[23] Thus, by the beginning of 1921, the administration had recalled the American observer at the League of Nations, the representative on the Council of Allied Ambassadors, and the delegate to the Reparations Commission, the last in spite of considerable opposition from the State Department.[24] The only exceptions that Wilson allowed to this policy were the American Forces in Germany and the American observer on the Rhineland High Commission (General Allen). The president undoubtedly realized that this representation remained indispensable for the success of peace negotiations between the United States and Germany. He may have also concluded that by withdrawing the troops he would make it next to impossible for the incoming administration to secure an unamended ratification of the Treaty of Versailles (inasmuch as participating in the occupation was an implicit obligation of that treaty).[25]

Even so, the president's desire for withdrawal found its reflection in a decision of the War Department to reduce the AFG in size. Wilson and Pershing had originally decided to leave about 6,800 soldiers in Europe, or slightly more than one regiment. Because of the presence of the Silesian brigade and an extraordinarily high rate of reenlistment at Coblenz, however, the number of troops under General Allen's command had seldom fallen below 15,000.[26] The administration had made no changes in this situation throughout the long presidential campaign, but no sooner had the votes been tallied in November than the War Department established a schedule of return intended to diminish American forces to 8,200 men by May 31, 1921.[27]

This decision, which was first publicized in January, was well received by most Americans.[28] Popular concern about reducing the military establishment and cutting wartime taxes had become so pronounced by the winter congressional session that Senator William Borah (R-Idaho) and others were now calling for an international disarmament conference.[29] During these same weeks Congress had passed a resolution over presidential veto requiring the War Department to discontinue military enlistments until the army had been cut to 175,000.[30] Though there had been little criticism of the occupation per se, several congressmen had begun to ask quite pointed questions about the repayment of the Rhineland army costs.[31]

Not all citizens, however, gave disarmament and frugality such high priority. Hamilton Holt, editor of *The Independent*, returned from an autumn tour of Europe to plead with his countrymen to "keep the army there the next ten years . . .

as an example of America's friendship for the Allies and especially France."[32] Similarly, Maude Radford Warren, a correspondent of the *New York Times*, expounded with considerable pride in February upon the "delicate" work that doughboys were accomplishing on the Rhine.[33] In January, Senator Lodge attempted to counter renewed black-horror agitation (and two potential resolutions of protest) by arranging to have a recent speech by Marshal Foch printed as a Senate document.[34] In February he obtained the same privilege for a letter from the undersecretary of state that included reports exonerating the African troops by General Allen and Commissioner Dresel.[35] That very week the commander of the American Legion, Colonel F. W. Galbraith, achieved nation-wide prominence by publicly tongue-lashing a German-American leader who requested his support for a rally planned to denounce the French "colonials."[36]

March 4, 1921 brought Warren G. Harding to the White House, and with him both the pledge to end the occupation and, potentially, at least, new reasons not to do so. The root of such inconsistency, undoubtedly, lay in Harding's own ambivalence, symbolized so clearly by a continuing loyalty both to "normalcy" and to the wartime alliance.[37] Yet there were elements beyond his control, such as the need to preserve the occupation until a treaty was achieved. There were also partly determined factors, like the obligations that the president incurred in conjunction with his various programs. From Harding's point of view, these considerations never allowed him to deal with the Rhineland as a separate issue. From a later vantage point, they only contributed to a policy of indecisiveness and procrastination.

Nonetheless, for a while at least, it seemed as if things might be otherwise. Despite Harding's pledge regarding the occupation and his obvious disinclination to become involved with the

League of Nations, the new administration not only displayed much more attachment to the European allies than had the outgoing regime but was also much more willing than Wilson's government to allow this tie to affect its attitudes toward the occupation. The direct implication was that the United States might continue to play a role upon the Rhine.

That such a loyalty was even temporarily possible seems to have been the result of several factors. First, American conservatives generally possessed less traumatic memories of the war and retained more hostility toward the Germans than did their liberal counterparts.[38] Second, the recent success of the British and French in uniting upon "reasonable" reparations demands, together with a deceptively negative response on the part of the Germans, had rendered Allied policy more attractive to everyone than it had been previously. Third, the extremism of the black horror campaign had now begun to backfire badly among those Americans who kept abreast of European affairs. In March, after Secretary of State Charles Evans Hughes had rebuffed a German feeler concerning reparations with the statement that the United States "stood with the Allies,"[39] William R. Castle confided to an acquaintance that such a pronouncement would hardly have been possible before Germany had indulged herself in such "shameless propaganda" and "stupid" reparations proposals.[40]

Europe during this period was experiencing its first real crisis over reparations. In January prime ministers Lloyd George and Briand had attempted to define Germany's obligations by endorsing a reparations total of 226 billion marks over forty-two years, but in March the Germans had countered by offering only 50 billion marks over a five-year period. This response had so infuriated the Allied leaders that they had agreed upon the need for military and economic sanctions. On March 8, they had directed French troops to occupy Ruhrort, Duisberg, and Düsseldorf, and instructed the High

Commission in Coblenz both to collect tariffs in the Rhineland and to impose a special customs line on the eastern (interior) boundary of its territory. Later, on May 2, after the Reparations Commission had voted to set the German indemnity at 132 billion marks, the Allies dispatched an ultimatum to Berlin demanding acceptance of this newest total on penalty of an occupation of the Ruhr. This threat finally produced "agreement," for, though the Fehrenbach government resigned in protest, German resolve declined so rapidly that by May 10 Joseph Wirth (Center Party) was able to form a cabinet that promised fulfillment of reparations requirements.[41]

In the interim cooperating with the Allied sanctions on the Rhine was one of the ways in which the incoming Harding administration first made known its attitudes regarding Europe. Thus, on March 9, when Secretary of War John Weeks announced that the AFG would remain at Coblenz in order to avoid giving any impression of support for Germany, he was making it clear with which nations his loyalty lay.[42] Similarly, when Secretary of State Hughes quickly went out of his way to ensure that the new Allied trade regulations would not be nullified by the special status of the American zone, he spoke "volumes" of support for Britain and for France.[43] He did so once again at the beginning of May, when, after refusing a German request to serve as a reparations umpire,[44] he returned American observers to the Council of Allied Ambassadors and to the Reparations Commission.[45]

There were others besides members of the administration, however, for whom continued loyalty to the Allies provided a reason to maintain the occupation. The springtime debate in Congress on legislative peace resolutions had revealed that such convictions were once again (or still) present among certain Democrats as well. Indeed, some members of the opposition were not adverse to arguing that a unilateral declaration of peace, by relinquishing American rights in the Rhineland, amounted to a betrayal of our former comrades-in-arms:

> SENATOR KENNETH MCKELLAR (D–Tenn.): . . . if the
> Germans do not fulfill their treaty obligations with the Allies,
> and we should pass this [Joint Resolution] . . . and withdraw
> our troops . . . , and the Allies should invade Germany to force
> a compliance with the terms of the treaty, would it not be
> inevitable that we thereby ally ourselves with Germany . . . ?
> SENATOR OSCAR UNDERWOOD (D–Ala.): I cannot say that I
> would go as far [as that] . . . , but I agree thoroughly with
> [the senator] in the proposition he states, that it is a most in-
> opportune time [to pass this]. . . . We have a right to expect of
> [the Republicans] that they shall make peace along lines that
> will not only protect us and our rights, but that shall not be
> an abandonment of the men we fought with. . . .[46]

Though Regular Republicans tended to support the congressional peace resolutions, they generally chose not to answer
criticisms of this kind but to leave that task to the Irreconcilables. Caught like the administration between a deep regard for
the Allies and a desire to pacify the "bitter-enders," the Regulars undoubtedly preferred to conceal the divided state of their
own feelings. After all, the separate peace resolution was not,
in the fullest sense, an administration measure, but had been
forced upon Harding and Hughes by the isolationists of
Congress.[47] Moreover, since the Regulars knew that the resolution if enacted would necessarily be followed by a "Republican" treaty, they could afford to be unconcerned.

With the Irreconcilables it was completely different. To
men like Senator James Reed (D-Mo.) or Senator Frank
Brandegee (R-Conn.) the argument that a declaration of peace
was an abandonment of the Allies was like waving a red flag at
a bull. The vitriolic Reed thought that what some of his
colleagues were demanding was beyond all reason: "We held
our sword at the throat of Germany while [the Allies]
wrote the treaty they wanted. They abandoned us, and now
some say we should keep ourselves in a technical state of war

to help our former allies collect indemnities!"[48] Brandegee, when asked if passage of the proposal would require the return of troops, replied that, in his opinion, leaving them there afterward would constitute "a grave usurpation on the part of the President."[49]

In the light of Brandegee's remark, then, it is not surprising that it was after Harding's acceptance of the separate peace resolution on July 2, 1921 that the occupation first became a major issue in the United States. For this the Irreconcilables were responsible, and their motives were clear. Not only were they now convinced that there was no longer any legal basis for leaving an army overseas, but they were also very much concerned about the treaty negotiations that Hughes was initiating in Berlin. Because they feared that the secretary of state might reaffirm some of Wilson's promises to Europe, they seized upon the occupation as one of the areas of decision in which he should prove the purity of his intentions. Even before the treaty with Germany was signed in August,[50] their demands for troop withdrawal had set off a debate on the Rhineland army that was to continue until after the agreement was formally ratified in October.

Senators Hiram Johnson and William Borah led the parade of the impatient and the anxious. As early as July 5, Johnson had threatened to introduce a bill "requiring" the recall of all troops from Germany if Harding did not immediately return them.[51] A few days later Borah pushed through a resolution directing the secretary of war to publish the size, cost, and indebtedness of the forces on the Rhine.[52] Then, after Secretary Weeks had disclosed that Germany owed the United States about $240 million on this account, Johnson again took up the attack: "I want them brought home. I do not want to pay a million dollars a month . . . whether England wishes it, or France wishes it, whether the Entente desires it, or whether Germany now asks for it."[53]

Such statements as these found considerable echo from the public, particularly among reformist groups and ultrapatriots (the constituents of the Irreconcilables). The *Freeman* of New York, for example, contended that the War Department's reluctance to give up what it considered to be a "good thing" (i.e., a "soft life" for its soldiers on the Rhine) was no reason at all to maintain the occupation.[54] And William Randolph Hearst's *Wisconsin Times* saw only folly in allowing the cost of this "wholly useless" army to accumulate, no matter who finally paid for it. In the opinion of the *Times*, "the same papers which [had] printed the falsehoods about German cruelty" were the ones that were now reporting that American "troops don't want to come home."[55]

In late September, when the Senate received the Treaty of Berlin and discovered clauses preserving American "rights" under the Treaty of Versailles, the Irreconcilables only intensified their attack upon the occupation.[56] "We are drifting into the League," complained Senator Reed, who needed no answers when he asked, "Does the treaty take the troops off the Rhine? Has the President said one thing about bringing them home?"[57] Senator Tom Watson (D-Ga.) was equally disturbed, contending that under no circumstances should the United States army serve as a debt collector for any other nation, particularly not for France, with its "five million black troops on the Niger River."[58] Senators Robert LaFollette (R-Wisc) and William Borah were also outspoken, although, ironically, they now voiced criticisms of the treaty which, once it was ratified, would only weaken their own endeavors to end the Rhineland occupation. LaFollette maintained that the agreement would put American soldiers and money on draft to Europe for at least the next forty years.[59] Borah, the "lion of Idaho," suggested that ratification would permanently obligate the nation to assist the Allies:

I am not . . . in favor of claiming advantages and benefits under the Versailles treaty which the French troops are to execute. . . . If we are to have those advantages, then every sense of moral responsibility insists that we should do our part in the way of executing the treaty.[60]

Though it may have been an exaggeration to assert, as did a reporter for the *New York Times*, that the desire to bring the AFG home was "peculiar to the left wing of the Republican party,"[61] it is certainly true that the majority of Republicans and Democrats exhibited much more patience regarding the Rhineland army than did the Irreconcilables. Senator Lodge and the GOP Regulars not only recognized a certain responsibility on their part for the intricacies of the new treaty but also openly acknowledged the difficulties involved in abandoning the occupation. In the Senate, Lodge spoke out now to this effect while emphasizing that the administration had incurred no *new* legal or moral obligation to station soldiers along the Rhine.[62] The Republican *Washington Post* endorsed the majority leader's view, affirming that whereas the treaty facilitated recall, the United States might "decide not to withdraw . . . if it concludes that France is endangered or that Germany is not acting in good faith."[63] In a similar vein, the directors of the American Legion had wired both the president and the secretary of state that their organizations saw no reason to hurry with the return of troops.[64]

Democrats, except for such isolationists as Reed and Watson, seemed even more willing than the Republicans to accept the prolongation of the occupation. In fact, most of them wished to go beyond what the Treaty of Berlin allowed in redeeming President Wilson's commitments, though there was disagreement as to why this was desirable. Senators like John Sharp Williams (D-Miss.) and journals like the *New York Times* could still contend that the United States must play a role in guarding against a resurgent Germany.[65] By contrast, Senator Frank Walsh (D-Mont) and other liberal Democrats were convinced that America's real concern should be the protection of Germany from a France "possessed of unreasoning fear."[66] They were fortified in this perspective by the increasing stream of tourists and former servicemen who returned from Coblenz to tell of France's machinations in the Rhineland.[67]

A considerable number of domestic factors were also at work to influence opinion, and some of these served primarily to reduce support for the occupation. Public dissatisfaction with the expanded costs of government, for example, was producing a demand for economy that continually threatened to cut off funds for garrisons abroad. Though the National Defense Act of 1920 had specified an army of 297,000 men,[68] by June 1921 Congress was appropriating funds for only 150,000, and Senator Reed was informing his colleagues that the easiest way to save money was to recall the 15,000 troops in Germany.[69] Simultaneously, the economy drive was strengthening and being strengthened by a growing popular revulsion against the use of force in international relations, a feeling openly spurred by Senator Borah in hopes of achieving serious disarmament negotiations. In May and June 1921, a flood of peace petitions had persuaded the Senate and House to endorse Borah's objectives.[70] On July 7, the president had joined the movement by extending invitations to an international disarmament conference to meet in Washington.[71] This was the very week that the Irreconcilables had launched their first intensive attack upon the occupation.

Yet other developments on the American scene increased support for General Allen and his troops. The economic recession of 1920–1922, for instance, brought both businessmen and farmers a renewed appreciation of European markets and a renewed willingness to assist in stabilizing them.[72] Since the American occupation was widely recognized as a pacifying agent, it seemed to follow that, by continuing its existence, the nation was providing a boon to trade.[73] A special committee of the United States Chamber of Commerce, after visiting the Rhineland in the summer of 1921, submitted a report in which it strongly endorsed the American presence there as an encouragement to "normal" commerce.[74] And Senator William B. McKinley (R-Ill.), after touring widely in western Europe, reached somewhat the same conclusions. He told the Senate that Illinois corn that had cost fifty-eight cents to produce was selling for twenty-eight cents because Europe could not take its usual share: "If keeping 5,000 American soldiers on the Rhine will tend to restore the equilibrium in Europe and bring back a market for the excess products of the United States, it seems to me to be a good business investment."[75]

A second development that supported the continued existence of the occupation was the growth of public pride in the endeavor, even among pronounced isolationists. This phenomenon surely bore a direct relationship to the postwar wave of xenophobia in America, since an almost childish desire to "show" the Europeans seems to have been the obverse side of the coin that demanded isolation from them.[76] In any event, that pride in the AFG had become very real by 1921 is indicated by the pleasure with which Colonel Robert McCormick, publisher of the *Chicago Tribune*, viewed at Coblenz "the only tangible evidence of unalloyed Americanism in Europe."[77] This pride is also demonstrated by Harding's October 1921 remark, with reference to the occupation, that he feared "there would be a bad mess all the time in Europe if it were not for the mollifying and harmonizing influences which are wielded by spokesmen for this Republic."[78]

The rise of legislative-executive tension was a third development that strengthened the case for the occupation. By the autumn of 1921 both the president and his secretary of state had become extremely sensitive to the repeated incursions of those on Capitol Hill into affairs of foreign policy.[79] In October, for example, when a House resolution was introduced that "required" the recall of the American forces in Germany, Hughes chose to interpret it as a constitutional challenge that could not be ignored. In fact, the secretary persuaded Harding to discuss the matter with the chairman of the Foreign Affairs Committee in order to ensure that the bill would ultimately be sidetracked.[80] In the realm of military policy, the administration had no wish to follow a congressional lead.

Yet Harding's policy regarding the occupation was so unclear during the summer and fall of 1921 that both Paris and Coblenz were repeatedly alarmed by rumors of American withdrawal.[81] In September the confusion had been compounded by conflicting predictions on the part of administration spokesmen in the Congress. To begin with, Senator Harry New (R-Ind.), a close friend of the president, had announced that, according to his information, a full evacuation of troops would take place upon ratification of the treaty with Germany. Somewhat later Senator Lodge had reported that he had been told of plans for only a substantial withdrawal of forces.[82] Which of the two gentlemen was the more nearly correct was not made apparent to the public until October 22, 1921. On that day, with treaty approval in sight, Secretary Weeks finally informed the press that 5,600 American soldiers would remain in Germany on an indefinite basis. Eight thousand more were to be shuttled home on two transports during the next five months.[83]

The reasons for this decision are not completely known, but it is doubtful that either domestic considerations or allegiance to the Allies could have persuaded the president to continue the occupation if the Washington Conference had not now loomed upon the scene. Though he had been unenthusiastic about such a gathering until the previous summer, Harding had rapidly come to look upon it as the keystone of his foreign policy. With its scope enlarged under British and Canadian pressure to include problems of the Far East as well as disarmament matters,[84] the conclave had begun to seem an unprecedented opportunity to reclaim the moral leadership that the United States had forfeited at Versailles.[85]

Still, a serious obstacle to the success of the conference quite obviously lay in France's attitudes. This had become apparent even before the opening session on November 12 from Briand's insistence on the exclusion of land armaments from discussion.[86] It was to become even more evident by early December, after French representatives had claimed the right to build a navy twice as large as they currently possessed and after Hughes had had to appeal to Briand in Paris in order to secure French acceptance of a tonnage ratio for battleships.[87]

In such a situation, then, it behooved Harding and Hughes not to pursue a Rhineland policy that could give Paris any cause for concern.[88] Indeed, Roland Boyden, the American observer on the Reparations Commission, had seen the connection between American cooperation at Coblenz and French cooperation at the pending conference as early as September,[89] and the *New York Times* had recognized this tie in October.[90] That the president and secretary of state saw it and acted accordingly is indicated not only by their October decisions regarding the AFG, but also by the fact that the administration waited to make its next reduction in the Rhineland army until February 15, 1922,[91] the week in which the conference adjourned.

European affairs, in the meantime, had once more taken a turn toward greater discord and complexity. September 1921 had brought an end to Allied economic sanctions on the Rhine, but within a month the League of Nations' decision to partition Silesia had catapulted Germany into another round of turmoil and inflation.[92] Then, when the Cannes Conference of

January 1922 had promised not only some relief from reparations but a better Franco-British understanding, Briand had lost the support of his parliament and was superseded as premier by the much less moderate Raymond Poincaré. Almost immediately, French foreign policy had begun to display those characteristics that would lead within twelve months to the Ruhr crisis.[93]

As far as the occupation was concerned, however, the weeks following the Washington Conference were distinguished primarily by the outbreak of a bitter quarrel between the United States and the Allies regarding the reimbursement of American army costs. This conflict was, in a way, only a continuation of an earlier dispute, but this time it came within a hair's breadth of ending the occupation once and for all, though, paradoxically, it later provided another excuse for the United States to prolong it.

The origins of the quarrel were grounded in five considerations: (1) Under the Treaty of Versailles (Articles 248-251), the occupation expenditures of the armies held first priority for repayment from German reparations. (2) The United States, by continuing to insist on full reimbursement of its army costs (i.e., on considerably more money per soldier than its allies demanded) had amassed an unpaid credit of relatively large proportions, namely, 966 million gold marks, or $230 million, as of May 1, 1921.[94] (3) The United States, by failing to ratify the Treaty of Versailles, had thrown into question its legal right to collect its army expenses through the Reparations Commission.[95] (4) France, by embarking upon a costly program of reconstruction, had put itself in the position of needing early cash payments under the reparations account.[96] (5) Belgium, which had received a reparations priority of 2 billion marks at Versailles, had come to anticipate early cash payments under this account.[97]

The possible implications had been clear for some time. As

early as the Spa Conference of July 1920 Roland Boyden had become concerned that his country might ultimately not receive its army costs at all. "We are getting into a position," he had cabled the Department of State, "where whatever our rights, it will be difficult to get the money, perhaps because it is not there, or perhaps because we will be ashamed to be seen carrying it away."[98] It was Boyden's conviction that when the commission began to receive German funds, the Allies would be tempted by legal technicalities to postpone American payments and ultimately to ask Washington to take reimbursement from its own wartime Alien Property Fund. In his opinion, it was largely beside the point that the United States had repeatedly specified in Paris the validity of its rights to repayment.[99]

Boyden's success as prognosticator had become apparent during the summer and fall of 1921, after the Allies had obtained their first annual payment from Germany (1 billion gold marks) and after the Allied finance ministers had taken up the problem of distribution.[100] During this period the ministers acted on two different fronts with regard to occupation debts. First, they made arrangements to bring the future operating expenses of the armies (or at least the amounts due from Germany on these accounts) down to or below the 240 million gold marks per year envisaged by the statesmen at Versailles.[101] Second, and more important, the ministers worked out an apportionment of the money receipts that, although it compensated Britain, France, and Belgium for their respective army costs, made no provision for the United States.[102]

Originally, upon receipt of the first billion marks from Germany, the Reparations Commission had assigned 450 million to Britain for occupation costs and 550 million to Belgium under its priority, apparently accepting the contention of these countries that the Saar mines constituted payment for French army claims.[103] Subsequently, though Lloyd George and Briand had approved of this arrangement as late as August, the French had found themselves becoming more and more dissatisfied at not having shared the cash award.[104] As a result, in December, after German economic difficulties had brought the Allied premiers to London in order to reduce the Reich's 1922 obligations, a new and more elaborate bargain was struck. According to its provisions, Britain agreed to approve a recent Franco-German understanding for reparations in kind,[105] to accept a uniform scale for calculating army costs,[106] and to allow the French to take a portion of current moneys in lieu of the Saar mines. France in turn agreed to give Belgium and Britain the largest parts of the receipts and to debit the Saar mines to its army costs *after* 1922.[107] This agreement was formalized at the Cannes Conference in January 1922, although it was not ratified until March.[108] The final cash distribution of the European allies for the two years 1921 and 1922 assigned Belgium 1,000 million marks, Britain 580 million, and France 140 million.[109] The United States was to receive nothing.

Allied domestic needs, the size and the questionable legal status of the American claim, Washington's acquiescence in the provisional disbursement, and Germany's inability to accomplish its full payments had combined by 1922 to lead the finance ministers into the situation that Boyden had foreseen. Even so, it is worth emphasizing that there is no evidence indicating a desire on the part of the Allies to obscure what they were doing or to defraud the United States. Not only had American exclusion from the distribution of funds been public knowledge since August 1921,[110] but the Allies had repeatedly conceded, both before that month and after, that American rights to reimbursement were completely beyond questioning.[111]

The worst that could be said of them is that they had somewhat disingenuously connived to arrange the postponement and/or prorating of the payments due the United States. Furthermore, though there is some evidence that London wanted to use the issue to achieve other objectives too (e.g., full American participation in the Reparations Commission),[112] Foreign Office records reveal that there was genuine surprise in Whitehall at the severity of the American reaction.[113] Secretary Hughes's directive to Boyden of March 9, 1922 to notify the finance ministers convening in Paris that the United States expected to be paid in full before reparations were distributed had, in Lord Curzon's words "fallen like a bombshell" on the conference.[114] Even Boyden had been surprised at the "abruptness" of the secretary's action.[115]

The puzzling thing is that Hughes waited so long to notice what was happening in Europe. Perhaps he had been preoccupied with the Washington Conference, or possibly his attention had been diverted by the army-costs discussions that had taken place in Paris in October 1921 and that had prepared a report on current expenses for the Supreme Council.[116] Then again, he may simply have not been interested enough in debts or reparations generally. It may have taken Congress's establishment of the War Debt Commission in February 1922 to remind him of the importance of what was in effect America's first postwar debt settlement.[117]

Whatever the case, the way in which the secretary seized upon the army-costs dispute was bound to bring about repercussions in the United States. When as calm a man as Hughes complained, as he did to correspondents, that America was being "told to whistle for our money,"[118] it was obvious that the Congress, the public, and even the president would soon be very agitated. The congressional backlash was intense. In the Senate, Lodge, Borah, Underwood, and others took time off from crucial discussions of the Four Power Pacific Treaty to excoriate the cost decision of the Allies.[119] In the House, an emboldened Military Affairs Committee reported

an appropriations bill stipulating the withdrawal of all troops from Europe and Asia and drastically reducing the size of the entire military establishment.[120] When floor debate began on March 16, administration forces in the House found that their oft-heard constitutional arguments had suddenly become unpersuasive.[121]

The attitude of the press was also soured by the failure to obtain reimbursement. If some Democratic papers pointed out that the administration was in part to blame for what had occurred,[122] journalists in general agreed that the behavior of the Allies was inexcusable,[123] and conservative editors completely abandoned the Francophilia of orthodox Republicanism.[124] Democratic publications, usually sympathetic to the occupation, now remained silent or emulated the *New Orleans Times-Picayune*, which suggested that "as a means of meeting part of its expenses, Sam's army might pawn its watch on the Rhine."[125]

In this context, President Harding saw what he took to be the handwriting on the wall. Angry at European "ingratitude," impressed with American irritation, and concerned about both the survival of an effective army and the ratification of the Washington treaties, he concluded that the moment had come to honor his campaign pledge regarding the occupation. In consequence, between March 15 and 19, while he sojourned with John Weeks and other friends in St. Augustine, Florida, the president accepted the secretary of war's recommendation that all forces in Germany be brought home by the end of the fiscal year.[126] Weeks's public announcement of the decision on March 20 came precisely in time to persuade the House of Representatives to eliminate the "objectionable" specifications from the appropriations bill.[127] It also assisted the Senate in approving the Four Power Pacific Treaty.[128]

The president and his secretary of war had reckoned without the secretary of state, however. Though Hughes had never been an ardent advocate of the occupation, it now developed that he was not nearly as eager as they were to abandon it. Informed of Harding's Florida decision only as the War Department published the news, Hughes quickly turned the president's arguments around, pointing out that the AFG was much too valuable to relinquish while he was trying to

197

cope with "the unsettled matter of army costs."[129] By pressuring Harding vigorously he was able to obtain the promise that, behind the scenes, final policy on the occupation would be held open as late as June 1.[130]

Whether Hughes was being candid with the president about his objectives is debatable. In subsequent conversations with the Allies regarding army costs he never so much as mentioned the possibility of American withdrawal, but, then, the Allies had acted so quickly to assure him of their "reasonableness" that perhaps statements of this kind were simply unnecessary.[131] Or possibly the secretary had never intended to raise the point, being satisfied simply if he could avoid the irritation of recalling the troops while negotiations were going on. At any rate, during the next few weeks Hughes took it upon himself to see that Harding was fully informed of reasons other than financial why the army might be kept upon the Rhine. On March 27, for example, he forwarded to the White House a cable from General Allen in which the latter reported that "my Allied associates unanimously ask that the flag remain."[132] On March 30, he sent over a note received from Berlin in which Foreign Minister Walther Rathenau expressed his apprehension at the loss of an army "distinguished by its impartiality and detachment."[133] On April 26, he relayed a message from the new American ambassador in Germany, Alanson Houghton, disclosing that Houghton's inquiries in Coblenz and in Berlin had convinced him that Americans were doing ameliorative work in the Rhineland.[134]

If Harding had hoped that such pressures would grow less with time, he was badly disappointed. The prospects for peace in Europe declined steadily throughout April and May, and as they did, the proponents of the American occupation became more aroused and active.[135] The new undersecretary of state, William Phillips, had no sooner arrived from his former embassy in Belgium than he launched an energetic effort to win support for the AFG.[136] General James Harbord, deputy chief of staff, also campaigned for the occupation, even wiring Pershing (now chief of staff) from Paris that, as he had told Allen, "it would be a crime to send [the army] away now."[137] Moreover, such touring Americans as former Governor Frank Lowden of Illinois and Congressman John Tilson (R-Conn.) cabled home their belief that Allen's forces should remain to assist in heading off a new international crisis.[138]

The arguments of the "friends" of the occupation were summarized in a staff study prepared by William Phillips and submitted to Secretary Hughes at the end of May. According to this document, there were four principal justifications for perpetuating the endeavor: (1) Britain, France, Belgium, and Germany had all made direct or indirect requests to the United States for its continuation.[139] (2) Numerous (listed) examples attested to the moderating influence that American representatives had freqently exercised upon the High Commission. (3) French policy vis à vis Germany needed to be restrained if European stability were to be preserved. (4) American trade interests would suffer in the event there were any recourse to force in the Rhine area.[140] Despite Hughes's recent willingness to relate the maintenance of the occupation to reimbursement of army expenses, such short-range considerations were now largely forgotten. There was no longer any presidential campaign, unfinished peace treaty, Washington Conference, or occupation debts to cloud the issue. The question for the president had been distilled to its most basic form. Was the American occupation in Germany worth preserving if only for the sake of peace in Europe?

There could be little doubt how President Harding would respond. Long before the first of June he had given hints that he was not adverse to compromise. "The idea has begun to sprout," Phillips had written to his predecessor on May 9, "that a decision in a month's time to keep the remaining men—

about a thousand—may be appropriate."[141] Hence, when Harding finally met with his secretaries of state and war to make the policy determination, there was very little debate. General Allen and 1,000 troops would remain at Coblenz indefinitely.[142]

It is significant, however, that the primary factor in Harding's decision was the "general wish" of those around him and not what he envisaged as the self-interest of the United States.[143] As the president remembered it a few weeks later in private correspondence, "there was such an insistent appeal from various [Allied] sources, . . . and the Germans themselves . . . , that it was very hard to resist [leaving a contingent]."[144] In other words, Harding was largely responding to cries of distress and a shift in opinion, not to any preconceived notion on his part about what the interests of the United States required. Hughes, of course, may have believed that American economic and/or political interests were intimately bound up in Franco-German relations and European stability. Harding, accommodating individual that he was, either could not or would not calculate the self-interest of his country at such a distance.

But why had the weight of opinion that surrounded the president changed to such an extent since the previous March? One reason, certainly, was that the costs controversy had now disappeared from the news. Another significant factor was that few ordinary citizens realized the decision to withdraw was being reconsidered.[145] But clearly most important, in terms of strengthening the advocates of the occupation and weakening the critics, was the combination of distress and consensus that had developed in Europe. American attachment to the Old World may have been emotional and diverse, but it was still strong enough to build a favorable majority when a real crisis was occurring and when Europeans could agree, as they had regarding the occupation, on how the United States might assist them.[146]

9

ALLEN'S RESTRAINING FORCE, JUNE 1920–JUNE 1922

As regards the American troops, I feel that the consequences of their withdrawal might easily be of so
grave a nature that I would beg your Lordship to
consider whether it might not be possible to make
earnest and unofficial representations in Washington
with a view to their retention. . . . At present the
American representative and I act closely together
in all important matters, our views of what is right
and just being identical.

> Malcolm Robertson to the
> Marquess Curzon of
> Kedleston, July 15, 1921

Rolin-Jacquemyns said that the Americans' presence
on the Rhine modified the actions of the French; and
enabled him, sometimes against the wishes of his own
people, to follow our lead because he could say it
was the American view.

> Alanson Houghton Diary,
> April 18, 1922

During the same period that Americans were viewing their
Rhineland forces mainly as an instrument useful for bargaining, the military representatives of the United States at Coblenz had come to define themselves in much more ambitious
terms. If for a few months in 1920 the AFG had thought and
acted primarily as "observers," by 1921 General Allen and his
command had consciously embarked upon the role of inter-

national peacemaker and mediator. As Europe struggled to find its way toward peace, these Americans endeavored to serve their nation by working to diminish tensions in the storm center of the Continent.

Allen, in fact, contributed much to the functioning of the High Commission throughout this era. In collaboration with his colleagues and alone, this "unofficial" commissioner was notably effective in his efforts to restrain both the interventionist tendencies of the French and the obstructionist practices of the Germans. Strongly pro-French in the beginning, Allen came finally to resist the French interpretation of the occupation as vigorously as had Pierrepont Noyes. Yet in doing so he never lost his affection for the French, nor his ability to deal firmly and successfully with the Germans.

As we have noted, the cooperative mood that followed the Frankfurt incident of April 1920 had proved to be short-lived. By July, at Spa, tension had mounted to the point that the Allies had found it necessary to threaten the Germans with a seizure of the Ruhr before a schedule of coal deliveries could be agreed upon. Even more serious, the problem of reparations had been left untouched and had continued to be ignored as France devoted its primary attention to assisting Poland against Russia and to negotiating a military alliance with Belgium. In the autumn the elevation of Alexandre Millerand to the French presidency and Georges Leygues (a like-minded, if undistinguished Republican) to the premiership had only served to weaken the French government and to put off the possibility of further conferences. In Germany, the Fehrenbach regime had been plagued by a wave of separatist and radical agitation, given impetus by the new Prussian constitution of October.

With the first months of 1921, Britain, France, and Germany plunged into even more troubled regions as they fought their way to their first, tentative agreement on reparations. The French parliament had set the scene in January by recalling Aristide Briand (a moderate Republican) to his seventh ministry and rejecting a recent interim plan for the arrangement of German payments. Subsequently, after Lloyd George and Briand had suggested a "final" settlement of 226 billion marks, the Germans had responded with their 50 billion marks proposal of March—an offer that so provoked Lloyd George and Briand that they retaliated with the occupation of the three Ruhr ports and the establishment of military customs lines within the Rhineland. Then, at the beginning of May, after the Reparations Commission had reduced Allied terms to 132 billion marks, the two premiers renewed the threat to the Ruhr in an attempt to force agreement. It was at this juncture that the Germans made their appeal for arbitration to President Harding, and it was after the United States had held aloof that the Reichstag could see no alternative to capitulation and an effort at "fulfillment."[1]

The struggles of the day, then, were waged both in and about the area of the Rhine, where they could not avoid affecting and being affected by the Allied occupation. Every decision of the Supreme Council that involved Germany invariably had its impact on the Rhineland. Every action of the occupation authorities, even in local matters, could not fail to react upon Allied reparations, security, or prestige. The Americans at Coblenz provided no exception to these general rules. By participating in the High Commission and by sharing in the control of territory, American representatives could not escape playing a part in the European drama.

The position of General Allen on the High Commission was actually a good deal more influential than one might have expected. Until the separate peace of October 1921, of course, the general's status could only be unofficial, and even after that date Secretary Hughes made no move to alter it although he might legally have done so. Nevertheless, the fact that American territory remained technically under a different covenant (first the armistice, later the Treaty of Berlin) gave Allen what amounted to a veto over the High Commission's attempts to formulate policy for the entire occupation. In addition, because the Commission met in Coblenz, within the American zone, the Allies were continuously at the mercy of the general with regard to their quarters and offices within that city.[2] These two factors, together with the respect Allen received as representative of a great power and the eagerness of the French to preserve the appearance of Allied unity, greatly strengthened the American's hand.

When he had been named to succeed Noyes, Allen had not at first interpreted his instructions to mean a basic change in American policy. Though Noyes's perception had been that "the Department [of State] wishes to end [our] real participation in this Commission work,"[3] Allen himself had emphatically disagreed. Not only had the general insisted, for example, on his right to sit (or have his representative sit) with the High Commission, but he had also arranged to take over a large part of his predecessor's administrative personnel.[4]

Yet, if Allen did not assume that Washington had altered its policy direction, he *was* aware that Noyes's opposition to French designs had become much too strenuous for the commissioner's superiors in the State Department. And this realization, together with Allen's loyalty to his former comrades-in-arms, led him to begin his work on the High Commission with caution and concern for Allied unity. Convinced that the Germans had derived much comfort from Noyes's attitudes as well as "courage to resist the demands of the Commission," he immediately made it clear to Reichskommissar von Starck that he had no intention of simply copying his predecessor's policies.[5] He also emphasized to his own assistants "that there must be teamwork in the High Commission . . . and that outsiders should never know of the differences that may arise there."[6]

As it happened, the new American representative soon had an opportunity to display his consideration for the French. Only three weeks after Allen had taken up his duties with the High Commission the State Department requested that he make an investigation of the allegations regarding Negro atrocities on the Rhine.[7] Allen's subsequent report, though confirming the presence of large numbers of colonial troops, remained distinctly pro-Allied in tone and accused the Germans of gross exaggeration, particularly in labeling all Africans "Negroes" and blaming them for heinous crimes.[8] When the document was made public in the winter of 1921 its accuracy was widely disparaged in the German press, but, as far as the French were concerned, it remained a useful vindication of their policy.[9] By 1921, however, Allen had come to view the German grievance as much more legitimate than he had previously acknowledged.[10]

Another indication of the general's early loyalty to the French, as well as of his diplomatic talents, was his role in the Dorten incident of July 1920. Here the precipitating factor had been the action of German authorities in arresting the separatist leader and removing him to unoccupied territory despite an Allied ordinance that forbade such procedures. The response of the High Commission had been to insist upon Dorten's return, but when Tirard and his subordinates had also asked for the expulsion of two Wiesbaden officials for complicity, Allen and Sir Harold Stuart had pointed to the ordinance that stipulated that "no official will be removed until he shall have an opportunity to present his defense."[11] After some haggling, it became evident that Tirard had received such peremptory instructions from his government that, as the American later put it, "we [had to] . . . find some way to protect him."[12] Allen therefore entered into direct negotiations with the Germans, urging upon Reichskommissar von Starck and Oberpräsident von Groote the necessity of an apology to the Commission and prosecution of the individuals responsible for the abduction.[13] Then, after the German government had adopted his suggested course, the general proposed to his Allied colleagues that charges against the Wiesbaden officials be dropped. It required several weeks of deliberation, but the French ultimately agreed.[14]

Cooperation on the High Commission became even easier for Allen in the fall and winter of 1920 when the Germans reversed their earlier attitudes toward the occupation with several months of calculated obstruction. Why Berlin acted as it did is not easily explained, but serious inflationary pressures, the resurgence of separatist feelings, the nationalism of the Fehrenbach coalition, and the repudiation of "Wilsonism" by the American electorate all contributed to the motivations that lay behind the policy. The German effort was initiated in October and November with an extended attack from governmental benches in the Reichstag upon the expenditures, controls, requisitions, and moral problems of the Rhineland occupation.[15] Following this, Chancellor Fehrenbach and Foreign Minister Walter Simons went out of their way during speeches in Cologne and Aachen to criticize both the Treaty of Versailles and the Allies. When the High Commission complained to von Starck at such statements being made in occupied territory, the Reichskommissar not only declined to give a satisfactory explanation but returned to Berlin to preside at a public meeting where it was decided to give the controversial speeches further publicity.[16] In December the Allied ambassadors, with American support, protested both the Cologne and Aachen incidents to the Foreign Ministry in Berlin, but with no noticeable impact on German attitudes.[17] Indeed, by January lack of cooperation on the part of the

National Property Administration (the office that managed governmental properties) had forced the High Commission to suspend seven of its officials and to enact an ordinance enabling occupying authorities to requisition property from mayors and other officials in emergencies.[18]

If the American observer on the High Commission had demonstrated that he could work harmoniously with the Allies, however, he never unquestionably accepted the perspective of Paris. Allen had long possessed "almost a feeling of pity" for the French, but he had also been keenly aware that their anxiety regarding Germany might have undesirable consequences.[19] Thus he distrusted the French army intensely, and he encouraged Tirard whenever possible to resist the long arm of Marshal Foch.[20] Concerned in June that his own appointment might encourage the French military, Allen had soon been gratified to realize that "civil policy" from an American general could have a peculiarly instructive effect upon his fellow officers and commissioners.[21] Yet he was disappointed at the inability of Tirard to pursue a consistently liberal course in dealing with the Germans. Whether the matter for decision was how to pay for billets or how to distribute charity, Allen discovered that nationalist pressures on Tirard and his "desire to see France profit by the war" handicapped his good intentions.[22]

With the coming of the reparations crisis of 1921, Allen found himself more frequently in active opposition to French policy than in the past. At the beginning of March, for example, he and the Belgian commissioner, Baron Rolin-Jacquemyns, were involved in warding off Tirard's attempt to achieve a rather summary dismissal of Reichskommissar von Starck. That formidable Prussian had annoyed the French over the past year with a constant stream of protest notes, and now, with bitterness at a new high, Tirard took advantage of von Starck's failure to arrange the return of certain fugitives to seek his recall and the abolition of his office. Because it was obvious to Allen and Rolin-Jacquemyns that what Tirard really desired was to weaken German resistance to French power in the Rhineland, the two men insisted on giving von Starck a hearing and additional warnings.[23] Only in April, after a new deadline had been set and broken, were the American and Belgian commissioners willing to join in asking that Allied approval of von Starck's appointment be revoked.[24] Despite this, they not only took a strong stand for continuing the position of Reichskommissar (pointing out to their superiors that the office performed a vital function in providing information about occupation policies in all four zones), but persuaded the new British commissioner, Malcolm Robertson,[25] to do the same.[26] These opinions were to be influential in convincing the Council of Ambassadors to accept the appointment of von Starck's successor, Prince Hermann von Hatzfeld-Wildenburg, who assumed office in September 1921.[27]

On other occasions during these critical weeks Allen was to fight the French alone, and not without success. Rolin-Jacquemyns was unpredictable, and Robertson, Allen thought, was "at nearly all times . . . too antagonistic towards Germany."[28] The general found that, even without them, he could sometimes "completely change" Tirard's approach to problems."[29] Largely as the result of Allen's efforts, for instance, the French refrained from demanding a six-month jail term for the director of the National Property Administration. Intervention by the American also led the High Commission to revoke a decision to reestablish control over the movement of persons between occupied and unoccupied territory.[30]

As far as the March sanctions of the Supreme Council were concerned, Allen could only acquiesce, but he did insist on certain arrangements in the American zone and he did retain certain feelings of reservation. As Malcolm Robertson reported it at the time, "[Allen] has informed [the] High Commission in confidence that he hopes to be able to allow it to establish customs posts in his area. He has not asked United States Government for instructions and hopes not to receive any.... [He] insists that all three Allied nationalities shall be represented in American area, not [simply] one.... "[31] In point of fact, Allen *had* advised Secretary of State Hughes that, in his view, permitting Allied customs posts within the Coblenz zone was "not wholly inconsistent" with the American position,[32] and Hughes in turn had been willing to adopt a similar attitude.[33] Even so, Allen remained concerned about the Rhineland's being cut off from Germany and, as soon as Berlin had accepted the reparations ultimatum of May, he joined Robertson in a lengthy effort to obtain the removal of the sanctions.[34]

By the beginning of summer, Robertson had swung so far from his previous Francophilia that he and Allen were able to construct a working alliance similar to the one that Stuart and Noyes had earlier achieved. Indicative of the new friendliness between the two men was Allen's statement to Colonel Repington (a British journalist) in May that "he and Robertson were 19 out of 20 times in agreement, although they never discuss matters in advance."[35] Even more revealing was Robertson's dispatch to the Foreign Office on July 15, 1921:

> As regards the American troops, I feel that the consequences of their withdrawal might easily be of so grave a nature that I would beg your Lordship to consider whether it might not be possible to make earnest and unofficial representations at Washington with a view to their retention. ... *At present the American representative and I act closely together in all important matters, our views of what is right and just being identical.* Should I have no American colleague, and should the French troops occupy the whole length of the Rhine, my French colleague would be in a strong position to argue that, as it was the business of the High Commission to provide for the safety, requirements, and maintenance of the Armies of Occupation, and as his army was by far the most numerous ..., his view should prevail on all important matters. ...[36]

The French premier at American headquarters—1918
(l. to r., Pershing, Tardieu, Clemenceau, Foch, Weygand).

Pre-Armistice negotiations in Paris, October/November, 1918 (Col.
House and Gen. Bliss sit 5th and 6th from left on far side; Lloyd
George and Clemenceau sit across from them).

American troops entering Trier, December, 1918.

American color guard accompanied by German youngsters in Coblenz,
December, 1918.

President Woodrow Wilson with President Raymond Poincaré of France in Paris, December, 1918.

Generals Mangin and Dickman inspect French troops in Germany, Winter/Spring, 1919.

Pierrepont Noyes (left), American Rhineland Commissioner, and Wallace Day, American Deputy Commissioner, Autumn, 1919.

The American section of the Rhineland Commission, Coblenz, Autumn, 1919.

Sir Harold Stuart, British Rhineland Commissioner and High
Commissioner, 1919/1920.

Malcolm Robertson, British High
Commisioner, 1920/1921.

General Henry T. Allen and Paul Tirard, French Rhineland Commissioner and High Commissioner.

Members and staff of the High Commission at a reception given by General Allen, 1922 (Tirard, Allen, Rolin-Jacquemyns, and Kilmarnock stand l. to r. in front).

Secretary of State Charles Evans Hughes and President Warren G. Harding, March, 1921.

Ambassador Henry Fletcher, 1922.

Undersecretary of State William Phillips, April, 1922.

American troops on parade in Coblenz, 1922.

Hauling down the American flag at Ehrenbreitstein,
January, 1923.

It was unfortunate, both for Robertson and for his relationship with the American general, that his own star as a commissioner was on the wane. His tougher attitude toward the French had come too late to save him from criticism by the German government, conveyed behind his back to his superiors in London.[37] What is more, his obvious shift in allegiance seems to have alienated him from both the pro-French and pro-German factions in the Foreign Office, where a division similar to that in American opinion was developing. His requests during the summer of 1921 for a more vigorous British presence on the Rhine (i.e., more visiting dignitaries, more troops) only served to estrange him from the "low-profile" men in the Foreign Office.[38] At the same time, his previous record, together with the protest of the Germans, was enough to render him suspect with officials more sympathetic to Berlin.[39] As a result, despite the fact that he was guilty of no more than the same subtle drift from French sympathies that Noyes and Allen had experienced, Robertson's tour as commissioner was brought to a quick end in the autumn.

In the Coblenz zone itself, the American army remained both active and satisfied during 1920 and 1921 without deeply disturbing the lives of the inhabitants. Though neither soldier nor civilian could be sure from one day to the next that constant rumors of pending American withdrawal were only that,[40] the size of Allen's force held remarkably steady at about 15,000 men, while everyone submitted to the uncertainties concerning the future with considerable grace.[41] The *Amaroc News* caught the humor of the situation by claiming that its headlines had "unofficially moved more troops to and fro between the United States and Germany than any other set of Houdinis in captivity."[42]

A variety of activities contributed to the good military morale. There was no shortage of drill and training, even if most of the youngsters of earlier months had either matured in their service or been ordered home.[43] Vocational and educational programs also continued to absorb attention.[44] Athletics were encouraged, especially football and boxing among the men and polo among the officers, while American entrants in inter-Allied competitions were extraordinarily successful.[45] Service organizations like the Salvation Army offered a crowded schedule of entertainment.[46]

Above all, though, it was the standard of living that persuaded the average soldier or officer that he was fortunate to be on occupation duty. On a typical payday, a private could exchange his thirty-five dollars for, say, 1,800 marks, and range the streets of Coblenz buying everything from marzipan to cognac (now illegal at home). American wealth and the shortage of German men also allowed the ordinary soldier marked success with local women, and by the end of 1920 fully a tenth of the command had married *Rheinlanderinnen.* Though the officers were largely excluded from social intercourse with Germans, many could afford to bring over wives from the United States and to develop a vigorous social life of their own.[47]

Administratively, the American military government continued to promulgate the ordinances of the High Commission and to enforce them with relatively little difficulty. Though the "effectiveness" of the Americans may have been due as much to German hostility toward the French as to their own efforts, such statistics as the following demonstrate the ease with which the American zone was managed:[48]

German officials suspended, 1920–1921, at the request of—

French	Belgians	British	Americans
16	2	1	4

German appointments vetoed, 1920–1921, at the request of—

French	Belgians	British	Americans
19	9	0	0

German publications prohibited, 1920–1921, at the request of—

French	Belgians	British	Americans
79	7	10	1

Politically, Allen's regime limited itself to such endeavors as preventing the local Independent Socialists from joining the Third International, and arresting Communists who attempted to hold political meetings without giving legal notice.[49] Economically, its principal activity lay in the arbitration of industrial disputes.[50]

Meanwhile, the population of the Coblenz area remained reasonably pleased with the American occupation. The merchants obviously appreciated the free-spending soldiers, and young women were certainly willing to marry them.[51] German police copied the traffic-control methods of the MPs;[52] German youths were reported to have taken up the American version of the "manly art of self defense."[53] There were complaints about the critical housing shortage, of course, but these were not registered with any kind of vehemence.[54]

In unoccupied Germany, by contrast, reactions to the occupying army were more mercurial and more vigorous. Judging from the opinions voiced, Germany ran the gamut in 1920–1921 from admiration to anger and back to admiration regarding the Americans. If the summer of 1920 brought mutterings in the conservative press about the rule of Mammon in "Rhenish Dollarika,"[55] still the German government revealed how much it valued the American presence on the Rhine by unexpectedly assuming responsibility for Allen's operating expenses on the High Commission.[56] By November, nonetheless, the public campaign against all four occupations had reached the point that even the AFG could not escape censure in the Reichstag. Dr. Johannes Bell of the Center Party claimed that the money Americans were throwing away bred moral degeneracy in the Coblenz area, while Majority Socialist members complained of billeting requirements so unrealistic that a single Yankee lieutenant could requisition an entire villa.[57]

Hostility toward the Americans came to a climax in January and February 1921 as the result of several different factors, including the likelihood of American withdrawal, the publication of Allen's report on the black horror, and the complications surrounding the army's attempt to seize a military deserter living in the neutral zone. The last was a kind of Dorten incident in reverse, except that the American agents who (unknown to Allen) sought to kidnap Grover Cleveland Bergdoll were, in their turn, arrested by local police, convicted in state courts, and given (suspended) sentences.[58] In later years, Tirard asserted that the German press had been much kinder to the Americans than it would have been to the French in a similar situation, but contemporary evidence indicates that the AFG was severely criticized during these weeks for the Bergdoll affair and other "mistaken policies."[59] By March Allen was convinced that the Germans were "wholly ignorant" of his "moderating influence" on the High Commission,[60] although, paradoxically, it was at this very moment that German opinion began to reflect more recognition of American "helpfulness." Indeed, the general's efforts in the spring won him considerable adulation in Berlin governmental circles while the refusal of the United States to join in seizing the Ruhr ports greatly impressed the German public.[61] Even Harding's failure to intervene in the reparations crisis in April could not deprive the American occupation of increased German respect.

General Allen could thus look back with some satisfaction in the summer of 1921 on his first year as a "political" personage. If he had been powerless to solve the reparations dispute, forestall the Allied sanctions, or prevent the removal of von Starck, he had nevertheless done much to head off peremptory action by the High Commission with regard to the imprisonment of the German state property director, the appointment of the Reichskommissar, and the imposition of circulation controls. He had also given the public a better perspective on the black horror propaganda, helped to mediate the Dorten incident, and efficiently administered his zone of occupation. Such accomplishments undeniably contributed much to making the German attempt at "fulfillment" possible.[62]

With Chancellor Wirth's acceptance of the Allied ultimatum in May 1921, Germany abandoned a year of covert resistance to the provisions of the treaty, and Europe entered upon its first real *détente* since the end of the war. Wirth and Walther Rathenau, his most prominent minister, now dedicated themselves to meeting disarmament and reparations obligations, hoping that when the economic strain began to tell upon Germany the Allies would be wise enough to lessen their demands. In Paris, the receipt of the first money payment did have a sweetening effect on Premier Briand's attitudes, but French statesmen remained loath either to give up the sanctions on the Rhine or to abide by the recent German victory in the Silesian plebiscite. Not until the Paris conference in August was Lloyd George able to persuade Briand to lift the Rhenish customs lines, and even then the British were compelled to accede to the indefinite occupation of the Ruhr ports and the submission of the Silesian dispute to the League of Nations. Meanwhile, the economy of the Reich had been showing new signs of life, a German-American peace treaty had finally been achieved, and Rathenau and Louis Loucheur (the French minister of economics) had negotiated an agreement substituting certain reparations in kind for cash indemnities.

Despite this progress, neither the spirit of compromise nor the German economy was strong enough to endure the shocks of the second half of 1921. Violent opposition to fulfillment among German nationalists led to the assassination of Matthias Erzberger in August and to renewed tension between Berlin and Munich regarding extremism in Bavaria. Separatist activity flared up again in various parts of the Reich, inevitably encouraging the French to assist that movement within the Rhineland. In October the League's decision to award one-third of Silesia to Poland had a particularly disastrous effect on Germany, generating widespread fear of economic decline and serious fluctuations of the mark. Wirth's plans for a new tax program now met a storm of criticism from his countrymen, and when the chancellor failed to obtain either a domestic or foreign loan he was forced to concede that Germany could not meet its January reparations payment. This news, together with French disappointments at the Washington Conference, shocked Briand into a new aware-ness of his own country's weakness, with the result that the Quai d'Orsay began discussions in London aimed at the renegotiation of the Anglo-French Pact of 1919. Yet when Briand went to Cannes with Lloyd George in January 1922, the French Chamber of Deputies took fright that he might not demand enough of either Germany or England and it rose up to force the fall of his government.

The new premier, Raymond Poincaré (a conservative Re-publican), pursued French security so doggedly that European anxieties were soon perceptibly increased. Though he sent representatives to the Genoa economic conference of April 1922, his concern lest Germany escape its obligations was so intense that it virtually ensured the failure of that meeting. Though he continued to negotiate with Britain in regard to an alliance, his insistence on guarantees for eastern Europe made agreement difficult, and recriminations resulting from the Genoa conference and the German-Soviet understanding at Rapallo put an Anglo-French treaty almost beyond reach. In Germany, both the economy and the political consensus deteriorated de-spite the receipt of a partial reparations moratorium in January and Wirth's success in winning a new tax law from the Reichs-tag. In May the Reparations Commission finally approved a second reparations extension and a foreign loan for Germany, but there was no assurance of the latter until a lender could be obtained.[63]

"One cannot help but sympathize with France," Allen had written General Pershing a year before, in May 1921, "but there has never been a time when she needs the counsel of the United States more than now."[64] Thus, even with the first great reparations crisis past and Germany promising fulfillment, the American commander on the Rhine knew that French fear and French desire had not necessarily been channeled to pacific purposes. Paris had yet to approve an equitable settlement in Silesia or to provide substantial incentives for the German economy. Briand had still to relinquish the sanctions of March 1921 or to abandon French designs upon the Rhineland. Furthermore, Allen realized that none of these things could be accomplished without pressure on France from the Allies.[65]

He himself did as much as possible during the summer of 1921 to encourage the revocation of the sanctions and to limit their enlargement. Admittedly, the more Allen and Robertson emphasized to Tirard that there was no longer any legal reason to retain the Ruhr ports or administer German customs,[66] the more it became apparent that the French would not lightly abandon a chance for both reaping profit and encouraging separatism.[67] Even so, the Americans and British were able in May to prevent Tirard from extending the permanent jurisdiction of the High Commission to the Düsseldorf area.[68] More important, in July Allen, Robertson, and Rolin-Jacquemyns successfully opposed Tirard's attempt to secure endorsement for a new customs arrangement that would have given France a veto over German import regulations in the west.[69]

During August 9 to 13, at the Paris conference of Lloyd George and Briand (actually a meeting of the Supreme Council), the American general probably made a further contribution to the reduction of the sanctions. Allen was present as an adviser to the American observer, Ambassador George Harvey, who had come to France from his post in Britain expecting to utter no more than pleasantries. Yet Lloyd George and Lord Curzon no sooner saw General Allen than they expressed a desire to have his testimony presented to the conference, knowing full well that his "expert" opinions would strengthen their case against the situation in the Rhineland.[70] A somewhat apprehensive Harvey finally obtained Secretary Hughes's permission by cable for such a procedure,[71] although as it turned out, before Allen could be called, British concessions on the Silesian problem had cleared the way for a French promise to end the commercial sanctions.[72] Nevertheless, Allen remained convinced that Briand's awareness of what he might have said was influential in shaping French reactions.[73]

The actual lifting of the special tariff in the Rhineland did not come until the end of September 1921, following several weeks of French procrastination. Germans, British, Belgians, and Americans were vastly irritated by the delay, and Hughes himself, with uncharacteristic energy, inquired of Allen about the possibility of forcing the French hand by unilateral action.[74] Still, Briand required a weapon against possible commercial discrimination,[75] and he insisted before abandoning the sanctions that the Allies obtain supervisory rights over Rhenish foreign trade. When Berlin finally capitulated on this point in September, it meant that France had succeeded in permanently broadening the powers of the High Commission, which until the sanctions of March 1921 had never been legally involved in the economic affairs of the left bank except as they threatened public order.[76]

Unhappily, the solution of the customs controversy did not presage a period of reduced tension or of lessened need for "restraining influences" in the occupied area. The League's Silesian decision was only a few days off, the German reparations failure only weeks away, and in the face of such developments even moderates like Briand and Wirth felt compelled to allow their subordinates to protect their national interests vigorously. During the last months of Briand's tenure in office, Allen found himself constantly moving back and forth from the French to the German side of disputes in his attempts to keep both parties from overreaction. The ratification of peace between Germany and the United States had no perceptible impact on his course. Nor was he noticeably affected by the quality of relations between Rhinelanders and American troops, which reached a peacetime low during the autumn of 1921. If his voice in occupation councils carried somewhat less weight than heretofore, this was largely a result of the constant rumors of American withdrawal and the actual reduction of his forces.

On occasion Allen did find it desirable to cooperate with the French in tightening Allied control over the Rhineland. In September, for example, because certain newspapers from unoccupied Germany had been so persistently insulting to French troops, he supported a new ordinance that permitted the exclusion of journals, on a second offense, for more than the three months previously stipulated.[77] Allen also endorsed the High Commission's decision to veto Berlin's attempt to appoint teachers from East Prussia and Silesia to positions in the Rhenish schools. In doing this he was by no means as concerned as were the French with protecting separatism; he simply shared with all the Allies an aversion to Germans who had been bred in the overheated nationalism of the Polish frontier.[78]

Yet the American also found it necessary to oppose French interference in German public affairs. On the one hand, he and his British colleague (first Malcolm Robertson, later Lord Kilmarnock) continued a longstanding effort to prevent Tirard from forcing additional ordinances upon the High Commission every time the local situation appeared to change.[79] On the other hand, Allen became increasingly irritated about the failure of French military leaders to respect the rules that *had* been established. "In plain language," he noted in October, "we [have been] violating our own ordinances and failing to admit it, much less punish our officials when they [are] wrong."[80] He recognized the demands that French politics made upon Tirard, but he nonetheless often felt obliged to press the French commissioner to take disciplinary action against his own subordinates.[81]

One of the most publicized cases of French meddling in German government, and an affair regarding which General Allen opposed Tirard for many months, had its beginnings in the late autumn of 1921. On December 5, Joseph Smeets, a Rhenish separatist and editor, had been arrested by German authorities and charged with libel against the president of the Reich. Everyone knew, of course, that there was more involved than simply libel, but Smeets *had* been notoriously reckless in his charges against German leaders. Therefore, when Tirard, after a conference with Briand, demanded that the High Commission judge the case "politically" and intervene to release the prisoner, neither Allen nor the new British commissioner, Lord Kilmarnock,[82] could do other than oppose the move. At this point Tirard attempted to exclude the "observer" Allen from the discussion, but the American responded not only by reminding the French commissioner of his (Allen's) official position in Coblenz but also by arranging to have his objections to the release of Smeets entered formally in the record.[83] At length, Anglo-American opposition and the rising anger of the German public forced Tirard to work out a compromise with the Reichskommissar that allowed German courts to try Smeets upon the proviso that any sentence given would be a "normal" one.[84] The case was far from resolved, however, and would return to plague the Commission during 1922.

On the heels of the Smeets incident a controversy arose in which Allen found himself restraining the French even more directly. When Rhenish railway employees threatened a wage strike at the end of December, the French High Command convinced both Tirard and Rolin-Jacquemyns that the railroads should be placed under martial law and personnel requisitioned for essential traffic. Allen, however, foresaw that such military control would be as difficult to remove as the sanctions of the previous spring, and he not only successfully delayed its proclamation, but, after the walkout began on December 30, proceeded to requisition labor in the American zone under an earlier ordinance of the High Commission. Then, after the strike had quickly ended, he insisted, much to French annoyance, on the lifting of his own order, thereby compelling the High Commission to withdraw its order also.[85] "Possibly," he concluded afterwards, "[my] efforts . . . have been of greater good to the peace and to the Rhineland than anything [I have] thus far accomplished. . . ."[86]

Nevertheless, with Poincaré's accession to power in January 1922, French policy became more demanding and Allen's situation more difficult. The new premier's hard line was evident on all fronts: at Cannes, at Genoa, in the unsuccessful negotiations for the proposed Anglo-French pact, and even in the Allied attempt to exclude the United States from reimbursement of occupation costs. In Berlin Foreign Minister Rathenau found himself driven frantic by daily protests from Paris, frequently regarding technicalities.[87] On the Rhine, Allen began to encounter more vigorous tactics on the High Commission as well as increased pressure from the French military to bring their forces into the Coblenz zone.

At the end of January the general returned from an official trip to Rome to discover that the French were once again attempting to use the threat of a railway strike to obtain a decision in favor of martial law. This time Tirard, Rolin-

Jacquemyns, and General Payot were pressing for both military seizure of the railroads and a new ordinance to relegate such matters permanently to the High Command. With Kilmarnock somewhat indecisive, only Allen's vigorous objections prevented his colleagues from relinquishing control to the army.[88] Yet feelings were strained, and a few days later when the AFG published a German strike decree over Tirard's objections, Allen had to fend off a claim by the Frenchman that the entire American area should by rights be under High Commission jurisdiction.[89]

In the meantime, the French army was finally to succeed in penetrating the American zone. As early as October 1921 Washington's decision to reduce the size of the AFG had brought General Degoutte to Coblenz to "suggest" the necessity of maintaining Allied strength along the Rhine.[90] Allen had been able to refuse the offer of assistance on that occasion, but in February 1922 a surprise cable cutting his forces to 2,000 men put him in a most untenable position. Allen recognized that if the French did not now insist on taking part of the American zone or at least on stationing a number of troops there, they would be implicitly admitting that the total forces in the Rhineland (some 140,000) were much in excess of the need. Fortunately, he was able to capitalize on General Degoutte's desire to preserve the "alliance" to drive a hard bargain with the Frenchman. It was agreed that certain French forces would be put under Allen's command, that the city of Coblenz would be off limits to these units, and that the boundaries of the American zone would remain unchanged.[91]

Now and then during these months it must have seemed to Allen that he was becoming almost as lonely a figure as Pierrepont Noyes had been before him. Not only had his command been steadily diminished in number, but neither his colleagues, superiors, nor allies had provided him with consistent support in his attempts to mediate and assuage. In mid-December he had twice asked the ambassador in Paris, Myron T. Herrick, for advice and suggestions, but the latter's distrust of Germany was so intense that he could only endorse French policy almost without reservation.[92] Despite Allen's specific requests to Washington for directions,[93] communications from the state and war departments were vague and open-ended, leading him to conclude at times that they wished him to go farther than they dared specify, on other occasions that they did not know or care what he was attempting to do.[94] In later months he was told by Henry P. Fletcher, Harding's crony and the former undersecretary of state, that no one at home had been "expert" enough to advise him about Europe.[95]

The Belgian and British commissioners often only added to Allen's task. Though Rolin-Jacquemyns was independent in spirit and no tool of Tirard, on the important issues he was frequently forced to bow to pro-French pressure emanating from Brussels.[96] Throughout the winter and spring of 1921–1922, for instance, he apparently found it imperative to support the French concerning both Smeets and the railway strikes.[97] At the same time, the British representative, in Allen's opinion, showed "neither backbone nor intelligence." Kilmarnock was usually ready to surrender to Tirard's "steamroller," unless supported by both Allen and Rolin-Jacquemyns.[98]

The French and German representatives gave the American less cooperation than they probably would have preferred to give. On several occasions Tirard appeared to have serious doubts about the policies he pursued, but he did not always possess the power to modify his course.[99] Though he confessed great respect for Allen's good sense (going so far as to urge in April 1922 that the general be attached as an adviser to the American embassy in Paris in the event the AFG were withdrawn), he was infrequently in a position fully to exploit or profit from it.[100] As for the Germans, though Foreign Minister Rathenau had instructed Allen indirectly that Berlin favored

an "official" status for the American commissioner[101] and
though the general had relayed this information to Washington, Allen advised his informant that "any action R. might take
would probably defeat the ends he had in view."[102] Only after
President Harding had announced the recall of all remaining
troops in March 1922 did the Berlin government conclude
that it had nothing to lose and much to gain by openly requesting the United States (1) to reverse its recent decision and (2)
to allow Allen to become official.[103]

Indeed, as a result of Harding's action in March almost all
parties clarified the extent to which they endorsed American
representation in Coblenz. When the newly appointed Undersecretary of State William Phillips visited London on his way
home in April, he was told at the Foreign Office that the British strongly desired to retain the AFG but had been uncertain
as to how a formal note to that effect might be received in
Washington.[104] A few days earlier the Belgian high commissioner had informed Phillips (as well as Ambassador Houghton) that his country very much wanted a continued
American presence on the Rhine.[105] The French government
also forwarded a message to the State Department expressing
regret at the ending of the occupation. As Ambassador Herrick
pointed out to Allen, however, the French note contained no
suggestion that the matter should be reconsidered.[106] "The
Belgians are undoubtedly in favor of my remaining . . . ," the
general confided to his diary, "but the French are doubtful as
to whether or not my stay would . . . be an obstacle to their
efforts."[107]

Encouraged by these new evidences of support and chal-
lenged by mounting international tension, Allen continued
his "moderating" efforts despite the president's decision for
recall. As the Genoa conference disintegrated and Poincaré
became steadily more insistent on receiving the reparations due
May 31, Allen recognized that French activities in Germany

pointed to "an ever increasing intention of dominating the Rhineland."[108] He therefore warned Herrick against supporting the recently renewed French attack upon the German office of Reichskommissar, and he described for him indications of French plans for economic exploitation in the occupied region.[109] In April Allen and Kilmarnock successfully opposed Franco-Belgian efforts to quash the continuing German prosecutions of the separatist Smeets.[110] In May, he joined Kilmarnock and Rolin-Jacquemyns in resisting a French-sponsored directive from the Council of Ambassadors that required the destruction of allegedly strategic railways.[111] Normally, however, Rolin-Jacquemyns was in league with Tirard, even at the risk of disregarding ordinances, whereas "Kilmarnock either says nothing or agrees [with the French]."[112] It was a frustrating situation, and Allen could only watch with relief at the end of May as the Reparations Commission granted Germany a second moratorium, and Poincaré decided to pass up a "golden" opportunity to occupy the Ruhr.

Allen's attempts at reducing misunderstanding had been both assisted and hampered throughout the year by the army of which he was commander. The presence of American troops had made it possible for him to be more than simply an observer on the Rhineland High Commission. Yet, in the autumn and winter of 1921, when relations between the AFG and Rhenish civilians had deteriorated badly, the army itself had seemed to be undermining whatever German patience with the occupation Allen's diplomacy had achieved. Furthermore, the following spring, after strenuous American efforts had helped to improve German attitudes, the arrival of French units in the Coblenz sector had engendered considerable ill will between the armies of the Allies themselves.

American soldiers continued to live so well that they were quite happy with their surroundings. The ordinary doughboy earned as much as a German white-collar worker and often had enough money left over to invest in local business.[113] When he was not buying souvenirs or stocks, he could go touring, attend one of several fine schools, or wander down to the YMCA "hut" for bowling or a dance. The city of Coblenz was agreeably Americanized, with shoeshine parlors, barber shops, pie and waffles in the restaurants—and no American laws against alcoholic beverages.[114]

In spite of all this and partly because of it, serious friction began to appear in the latter part of 1921. There were a number of contributing factors, including German disappointment at the Treaty of Berlin's failure to "repudiate" the Treaty of Versailles and irritation at Harding's lack of interest in "assisting" Europe.[115] However, the basic reason for the strained relations was that the return of peace had brought so little change in the occupation. Investigations disclosed few new complaints per se but revealed the public's increasing sense of grievance at several longstanding problems: (1) the housing demands of American families and welfare organizations, (2) the misconduct of soldiers, especially their drunkenness in restaurants and on trains, (3) the "harshness" of military courts toward Germans, (4) the inflation and shortages that accompanied the American "buying out" of local stores, and (5) the domineering manners of officers and officers' wives. It was argued, in short, that while the end of the war should have brought a new consideration for civilians, the Americans had remained no less demanding than before.[116] In October and again in December Allen recognized the validity of these contentions by issuing orders requiring tighter military discipline and "courteous treatment of the inhabitants" within the zone.[117] By the beginning of 1922 these measures, together with a flicker of German hope in Washington's intentions, had helped to create better feelings.[118]

The constant threat and actuality of American troop withdrawal seem to have had an ambivalent effect upon civilian-military relationships. The fact that French occupation was always "around the corner" made many Rhinelanders more appreciative of the American army's size and motivations.[119] Still, so much uncertainty as to the future did leave soldiers and civilians somewhat uneasy with each other. Rumors of recall circulated repeatedly from July through November 1921 and from the following March to the end of May,[120] while the actual reductions after November 1921 lent much credibility to these stories. Although in that month there were almost 13,000 men in the AFG, by February 1922 the number had fallen to 5,000 and by July to only 1,200.[121] Perhaps it was no accident that the greatest difficulties in Rhenish-American relations coincided with the most rapid departure of military personnel.

The entry of French detachments into the zone may have established a favorable comparison for the Americans, but it did little to endear the two groups to each other. Within a few days after the arrival of the new units on April 11, Allen was complaining that "only one battalion of French ... makes more noise with [its] trumpets and drums than did all my troops a few months since...."[122] The French continually attempted to do things at variance with American custom, and only Allen's stubborn refusal to allow this forestalled the complete overthrow of existing arrangements.[123]

In contrast to previous years, citizens of unoccupied Germany reacted more favorably to the American occupation in 1921 and 1922 than did the population of the zone itself. Several explanations can be advanced. The almost simultaneous advent of new governments in Germany (Wirth) and the United States (Harding) had encouraged each nation to shake off a certain amount of past distrust. Then, too, Allen's sympathetic attitude toward the former foe had at last begun to attract public attention within Germany. And if Yankee

227

soldiers and officers were a little more obnoxious than in earlier days, this change was not keenly felt outside the Rhineland and faded into insignificance beside the fact that they, unlike their French associates, possessed no motives subversive to the Reich.

Of course, Germany east of the Rhine continued to be intensely critical of the Allied occupation, particularly of the lingering economic and military sanctions, the assistance given to separatism, the cost and size of the occupying armies, the requisition of homes and schools, and the presence of colonial troops.[124] In September 1921 the German Treasury emphasized in a special report to the Reichstag that the occupation had already cost almost four billion gold marks, money that could well have gone into reparations.[125] In December, the criminal courts of Cologne suspended all cases for an entire week in protest at the High Commission's interference with the Smeets case.[126] In March 1922 the Foreign Ministry in Berlin protested both the Allied retention of the Ruhr ports and the size of the forces on the left bank, inquiring pointedly if an army of 140,000 was really necessary to deal with an unarmed country.[127]

Occasionally criticism spilled over to include the Americans, as in the Reichstag debates of April 1922, when a Rhenish Democrat commented bitterly that it was coldhearted of the United States, with a "colored" problem of its own, to countenance the French use of Negro troops in occupation.[128] The German press could also be quite scathing about Allen's men, especially in the wake of public displeasure with the Treaty of Berlin or with American failure to attend the Genoa conference. In September 1921 the Center Party's *Germania* became so abusive of the AFG's misbehavior and "limitless" demands that two weeks later it felt obliged to qualify some of its own statements.[129] In March 1922 the conservative *Der Tag* predicted that only the "frivolous elements" of the population—jilted fiancées and barbershop assistants—would "mourn the passing of the doughboy."[130]

Despite such editorials, however, most of the German fury at the occupation was vented on the French and most of the hope for amelioration was placed on the Americans and British. Foreign Minister Rathenau, in particular, believed that only American participation in European affairs could bring France back to "sanity" and solve the dilemma of reparations.[131] For this reason, in the spring of 1922, Rathenau had not only hoped for American attendance at Genoa but had also been particularly anxious to keep American forces at Coblenz. When he had informed Washington in April that he wanted the army to remain as long as any in the Rhineland, he was offering a carefully weighted judgment regarding the American occupation.[132]

For two eventful years since America had rejected the Treaty of Versailles, General Allen and his troops had remained on the Rhine, continually buffeted, yet exerting a positive influence on those around them. Perhaps without always realizing it, they had contributed to the solution of several American dilemmas, facilitating, for example, both the achievement of a separate peace with Germany and the attainment of an inter-Allied agreement regarding occupation costs. Still, as they themselves clearly perceived, their greatest contribution had been in helping to reduce tension in an area of the world peculiarly important to America. They had accomplished this objective despite their steadily dwindling strength and a lack of specific directions from the Wilson and Harding administrations. They had achieved it in at least three different ways: by furnishing a model of an occupation without hidden objectives, by opposing extremism on the part of Allied and German representatives, and by allying with whichever side or group remained moderate at the moment. Though it would be wrong to overemphasize the extent to which this handful of soldiers altered European politics, their success in forestalling the seizure of Rhenish railways, lengthening the official life of the Reichskommissar, softening the German campaign against the black horror, and effecting other constructive actions should not be overlooked.

It had been far from an easy or simple role for these Americans to fill. Troop discipline had not always been exemplary, nor Allen's diplomacy even-handed. In fact, as time went on the American commander had found himself driven from his pro-French feelings closer and closer to the belief of his predecessor Noyes that the peace would never be secure as long as France was in the Rhineland.

Nevertheless, in the spring of 1922, when President Harding had attempted to withdraw the last few units left in Germany, the British, Belgians, and Germans had spoken out in protest and even the French had become concerned. With emotions growing stormier, the AFG had become a sort of balance wheel for all of them. Its presence also lent substance to the hope that the United States would one day return to provide succor for Europe.

10

THE LAST PHASE, JUNE 1922–JANUARY 1923

> Our contingent on the Rhine is a moraine of the
> Democratic age of blunders in Europe.
> > Ambassador Henry P. Fletcher to
> > President Warren G. Harding,
> > August 8, 1922

> . . . the presence of American troops, although few
> in number, [is] of the greatest aid in maintaining a
> reasonable attitude [on the Rhine].
> > The German Ambassador, Otto
> > Wiedfeldt, to Secretary of State
> > Charles Evans Hughes, October
> > 23, 1922

> Harding, by the withdrawal, has forcefully protested
> before the world against these French acts of violence
> [in the Ruhr].
> > Berliner Tageblatt,
> > January 11, 1923

> The Secretary [Hughes] seemed a little discouraged
> at the newspaper attacks on our policy towards
> France and wondered whether we could have done
> anything different.
> > Undersecretary of State William
> > Phillips, January 12, 1923

Throughout the remainder of 1922 the American occupation
in Germany lived to some extent on borrowed time. The arguments that had formerly justified the endeavor in Washing-

231

ton were no longer heard, and if the growing tension in Europe brought policymakers an increasing appreciation of their army's "stabilizing influence," it also bred a greater fear of involvement in hostilities. Such worries not only plagued the president in later months but also finally prompted congressional internationalists to join isolationists in attacking the posture of "half in, half out." Nevertheless, despite evident dangers and concern, the president and Secretary Hughes persisted in their Atlantic "straddle" until the ultimate crisis came (January 1923). In the process they became increasingly cognizant of the need for a more positive American policy in the future.

Being "half in" had other beneficial effects. General Allen not only continued to maintain a regime noteworthy for its noninterference in civil affairs but also continued, with intermittent success, his efforts to prevent violations of the Rhineland Agreement. As it had in the past, the American presence encouraged the British commissioner (and occcasionally the Belgian representative) to oppose the exploitation of the occupation. Moreover, in the end, the very timing of the American withdrawal dealt a stunning blow to the ill-conceived Ruhr venture.

In the weeks following June 1, 1922, Washington did not sustain the decision to leave American forces at Coblenz without considerable trepidation. The president continued to be uneasy about the wisdom of involvement, and critics of the arrangement had little difficulty in obtaining his attention. His anxiety about his legislative program in Congress and the approaching November elections only rendered him more sensitive to criticism.[1]

To be sure, the friends of the occupation persisted in making their voices heard. Former ambassador to Turkey Henry Morgenthau was widely quoted in the press when he praised

Allen's establishment as a "valuable essential" to the peace.[2] Ex-governor Frank Lowden, returning to the United States from Europe, made a number of speeches that were highly complimentary to American representation on the Rhine.[3] General Harbord, in cables to General Pershing, reiterated his opinion that the AFG was a "great moral and restraining force" in a situation "full of potentialities."[4]

Still, events were not cooperating with the individuals who held these views. In June Congress applied additional pressure for the recall of overseas forces by enacting an appropriations bill that reduced the army by another 10,000 men.[5] In August the British government incurred considerable ill will in the United States by offering (in the so-called Balfour Note) to abandon its European debts and reparations if British creditors (like the United States) would cancel their own holdings.[6] During the same period the European situation had veered dangerously toward confrontation as a London conference reached no accord on reparations and Poincaré blustered ominously.

By the middle of August, Harding was ready to agree with the criticisms of the Rhineland occupation received from his good friend Henry Fletcher, formerly undersecretary of state and now ambassador in Brussels. Though Fletcher admitted that Allen's force might serve as a "check" upon the French, he reasoned, rather amazingly, that "no direct national interest is served [by the occupation] aside from our deep concern in the recovery and re-establishment of Europe." British and French views on reparations would probably not be reconciled, he contended, but even if they were, when Washington asked for its army costs, "I very much fear that we shall not be paid at all." Fletcher had concluded that the entire affair was against the letter and spirit of the Monroe Doctrine and that, for every day there, the troops ran a greater risk of becoming entangled in violence.[7] To this the president replied on August

24, 1922: "I think perhaps we had the right hunch when the original order was made to withdraw [last March]. . . . [Since] it is very clear that their presence might involve us, . . . we are watching closely and are prepared to withdraw on very short notice."[8] A few days later, in correspondence with Undersecretary Phillips regarding the European situation, Harding wrote that he would be pleased to be promptly notified "when you think the moment has arisen for us to quietly order the withdrawal."[9]

In September the president became even more decided about ending the occupation. General Harbord's final report to the War Department had emphasized that "we are not there [in Germany] in the interest of any country but our own,"[10] but Secretary of War Weeks forwarded this to Harding with a very different opinion from General Peyton C. March, the touring former chief of staff. According to March, most of the matters that Allen thought he had settled at Coblenz had actually been adjusted by the diplomats in Paris, London, and Berlin. Furthermore, March asserted, though Allen possessed a "gigantic staff which could handle the affairs of an army corps," American officers in Germany were really "doing nothing except [playing] polo."[11] To this Weeks added for Harding, "as you know, I am in favor of getting out altogether and hope you will so decide."[12] The answer of the president on September 16 was quite specific: "We ought to arrange to withdraw . . . as soon as the Secretary of State has returned [from Brazil] and can pave the way for doing so without our action being given unusual significance."[13] Three weeks later, after talking with Secretary Hughes, Harding was still determined to act immediately.[14]

But it was not to be so simple. When Secretary Weeks intimated to the press in October that "the boys would be home by Christmas,"[15] the German government responded by suggesting that American withdrawal would be a violation of the nation's moral obligation to help its former enemy.[16] Premier Poincaré also complained,[17] and Undersecretary Phillips reminded Harding that France as yet had neither ratified the Washington treaties nor expressed its readiness to consult about war debts.[18] Congress itself proceeded to confuse the picture, for when Congressman John Tilson (R-Conn.) defended the importance of the American army in Germany, his speech was vigorously applauded by his colleagues in the House.[19] By October 21 President Harding had once again reversed himself on the occupation question. "I confess there is some merit to the German contention about our obligation," he wrote to Hughes, and "I recognize also the necessity of dealing diplomatically with the situation as it relates to France."[20]

Nonetheless, it was hardly a month before there was a new rumor of American withdrawal,[21] the origin of which remains to some extent a mystery. Perhaps it stemmed from the fact that on November 8 representatives of Britain, France, and Italy had finally promised Hughes to enter into negotiations about American army costs.[22] Or possibly it was related to the obviously increasing American concern at the deterioration of European affairs.[23] It may even have been connected with the bitter argument over the black horror that had erupted in November between Senator Gilbert Hitchcock (D-Neb.) and the visiting former premier Georges Clemenceau.[24] Whatever the source, at the president's press conference of December 1, 1922, Harding felt compelled to explain that the administration would not recall American troops as long as such action might be considered a gesture related to any European crisis.[25]

The European crisis to which he referred had been many months in the making. By the summer of 1922, a year of German fulfillment had produced only deficits and inflation in western Europe, pushing both Germany and its neighbors to the edge of economic disaster. The "new start" of the Genoa conference led to little but disagreement among the participating nations. Though Germany (like the entire continent) was in desperate need of capital and relief from obligation, the French remained unwilling to grant their traditional enemy more than the briefest respite, at least not without new and radical guarantees of ultimate payment.

The hopes engendered by a temporary moratorium in June quickly evaporated. A committee of international bankers attempting to arrange a loan for Germany adjourned without success in a matter of days.[26] On June 24, the foreign minister of the Reich, Walther Rathenau, was assassinated by right-wing extremists, and a period of political turbulence and confusion ensued.[27] Though late July saw the Reparations Commission exact Germany's agreement to added financial controls, August and the London conference brought Poincaré's demand that France receive a series of "productive pledges" (e.g., revenue from German forests and state mines) as a condition of further moratorium.[28] Rebuffed by Lloyd George, the French premier returned to Paris to indulge himself in two weeks of aggressive talk that sent the mark plummeting amid rumors that he was about to seize the Ruhr. Only the temporary defection of the Belgians from their French allies permitted the Reparations Commission to accept German treasury bonds at the end of August and postpone the crisis for six months.[29]

There followed an autumn of much maneuvering but little amelioration. The British pursued a plan for a two-year moratorium; German industrialists held discussions with French businessmen; and foreign financial experts were summoned to Berlin to study the problems of the mark.[30] In November the Wirth government advanced a proposal closely patterned upon the viewpoint of the experts, envisaging (1) reparations in accord with capacity to pay, (2) a three- or four-year moratorium, (3) an international loan to Germany, and (4) restoration of full German economic sovereignty in the occupied area.[31] Yet, though Wilhelm Cuno, the nonparty conservative who succeeded Wirth in late November, was quick to endorse his predecessor's suggestions,[32] the French by this time were in no mood for bargaining. Even the demise of Lloyd George's government in October only increased their impatience,[33] for they knew that the new prime minister, Andrew Bonar Law, was not as formidable an antagonist as the stormy Welshman had been.[34] When the British made a final effort to break the stalemate by offering to cancel the debts they held, Poincaré simply refused to cooperate, pointing out that the reparations due his nation from Germany were much greater than the French debt to Great Britain.[35]

Despite the centrality of the reparations issue, much more than economics was at stake during this period. Lingering behind discussion of money was the old French hope that any sanctions against the Reich would turn out to be more than sanctions, at least as far as the Rhineland was concerned. Hidden behind negotiations was a fear on the part of Berlin and other capitals that the French still schemed against German unity.

Understandably, as anxiety grew, the struggle on the Rhine was waged with increasing ferocity. The French attempted in a number of ways to strengthen their position in western Germany and to encourage and support the separatist movement.[36] They argued that the fifteen-year term of occupation had not yet begun;[37] they utilized the High Commission to protect commercial advantages and civilian allies like Smeets;[38] and they spent large sums of money to finance separatist newspapers and propaganda designed to impress the region with Gallic "culture."[39] The Germans labored diligently to counteract such French activity. Political parties, Rhenish and German, sponsored rallies denouncing separatism;[40] the chancellor and the foreign minister publicly opposed changes in the status of the left bank;[41] and the Reichskommissar protested repeatedly about occupation costs and the practices of colonial troops.[42]

In such a situation American participation in the occupation remained of great significance to all of the antagonists. The Germans were now more certain than ever that General Allen constituted a valuable brake upon the French, and they repeatedly expressed their interest in keeping him on the Rhine. Chancellor Wirth, Foreign Minister Rathenau, State Secretary (in the Foreign Ministry) Edgar Haniel, Commissioner von Hatzfeld, Prussian Minister of the Interior Carl Severing—all informed Allen in personal conversations that the American occupation was highly beneficial to the Reich.[43] At one point in the summer, Wirth himself told Ambassador Houghton that Allen's presence would be crucial in helping to forestall a Rhenish coup.[44] Meanwhile, criticism of the AFG had almost disappeared from the German press, and the praise was often impressive. In December 1922 the *Berliner Börsenzeitung* was delighted that another rumor of withdrawal had proven false, because, the newspaper asserted, Americans were helping to limit the French "passion for military encroachments" and had recently even prevented them from building barracks in Coblenz.[45]

The French were admittedly more ambivalent than the Germans about the Yankees. The military command in particular had come to find the Americans "unbearable,"[46] and well-founded rumors circulated that Allen had become *persona non grata* among higher governmental echelons.[47] However, responsible officials in Paris remained convinced that French-American differences on the Rhine could not outweigh the value in the symbolic maintenance of the wartime alliance. Commissioner Tirard assured Allen of this fact several times during 1922,[48] and as late as October Poincaré publicly repeated the same thing to Ambassador Herrick.[49]

The British and Belgian governments were more reticent than in earlier months about the American occupation, but there can be little doubt that they still found it useful. In November, for example, the British ambassador to Brussels, Sir George Graham, emphasized to Allen the "great importance attaching to the continuation of the Stars and Stripes on Ehrenbreitstein."[50] Belgian leaders did not dare talk too openly of restraining France, but it is clear that they were not especially eager to have the path cleared for additional sanctions or an invasion of the Ruhr.[51]

On the Rhineland High Commission General Allen was in the thick of the discussions and decisions, although he refrained from opposing every proposal with which he disagreed. On the contrary, as he noted in his diary, "hardly a session passes that [I] do not [accept] some measure at variance with [my] views...simply because of [my] anomalous status here."[52] Yet Allen could be depended upon to fight the enactment of ordinances and the creation of conditions seriously repugnant to the Rhineland Agreement. On occasion he emerged victorious as, for example, when he thwarted Tirard's repeated attempts to have a forest census taken in the area of the left bank.[53] More commonly, Allen had to content himself with providing criticism, as he did in protesting the continued interference with the collection of the German customs.[54]

During the August reparations crisis the British and Belgian commissioners offered "serious resistance to Tirard" in several instances, and Allen lent them his support.[55] In the Momm affair the three men waged a futile effort to stop the French from removing the president of the Wiesbaden Bezirk (Dr. Momm) on an exaggerated charge of failing to preserve public order. The High Commission finally compromised its differences on Momm by asking Berlin to transfer him, but when that request was refused, the commissioners felt compelled to require his dismissal from office.[56] Subsequently

Allen and Kilmarnock were more successful on another front, defending Reichskommissar von Hatzfeld from French disparagement designed to undermine his position.[57] They also began a joint effort to prevent the Rhineland from being placed on French (not German) daylight savings time.[58]

With the coming of autumn, however, Allen discovered Kilmarnock's courage declining badly, while the Belgian commissioner gravitated steadily toward the French perspective. "If Kilmarnock will [only] make a fight and insist on the record showing his divergent views . . . there will be less of the steamroller," the American noted unhappily,[59] and he was even more disturbed that "Rolin has become the most radical member of the Commission toward Germany, perhaps because the opposition papers in Belgium have been attacking him recently."[60] The shift in positions was epitomized in the Franco-Belgian decision in September to forego compromise and adopt the French proposal on daylight savings time by majority vote (2 to 1). It was the first time since the High Commission came into existence that it had acted other than unanimously.[61]

What was worse, a second majority vote was soon forced upon the British and Americans by the determination of the French and Belgians to set aside the judgments of the German courts against the separatist Joseph Smeets.[62] Once again Allen put his objections on the record, but neither Allen's nor Kilmarnock's pleas could dissuade Tirard and Rolin-Jacquemyns from taking action. Allen and Kilmarnock contended that such a direct intimidation of the German judiciary was an open invitation to Smeets and his followers to violate German laws.[63] As it developed, not only did this prediction prove correct,[64] but the Smeets decision inflamed German opinion more than anything the High Commission had ever done. The government of the Reich protested vehemently in London, Brussels, and Paris,[65] while both the Prussian Diet and German

Reichstag resounded with extensive criticism. Chancellor Wirth described the Smeets intervention as an unnecessary, unacceptable insult to the Reich.[66]

Despite the increasing weakness of Allen's position, he was able even in the late months of 1922 to post notable accomplishments. For example, his contention that the Council of Ambassadors had neither legal power nor strategic reasons for its announced plans to destroy Rhenish railways helped to provoke a High Commission protest that induced the ambassadors to transmit their next recommendations via the several foreign ministries.[67] This procedure was first employed during the Passau-Ingolstadt incident of December 1922, when the Council of Ambassadors fined these Bavarian cities 1 million gold marks in penalty for public riots involving Allied inspecting officers. On this occasion the high commissioners were directed by their governments, at the insistance of the ambassadors, to seize the equivalent in revenues from the Bavarian Palatinate if the original fine were not paid within two days. Such a seizure would have taken the Commission far beyond the bounds of the Rhineland Agreement, but Allen did not feel obligated to object now that the responsibility had been clearly placed with the foreign offices.[68] He advised the Germans to pay the ambassadors' fine, and there is good evidence that his opinion was a factor in Berlin's decision to do so.[69]

None of Allen's policies, it should be emphasized, was the result of formal instructions from his own government. Indeed, the closest thing to directions he had obtained were two telegrams in June cautioning him about his statements to reporters that he opposed the use of colonial troops and that he considered a Ruhr occupation "too terrible to contemplate."[70] Allen's reports to Secretary Hughes (he reported twice a month) were never answered by Hughes directly, although Undersecretary Phillips did keep the general up-to-date on what was going on in Washington.[71] From the War Department General Harbord sent an occasional note of encouragement,[72] but Pershing was completely silent, and Secretary Weeks wrote only once to express general "approval for your course."[73] In Europe, while Allen found a new and helpful ally in Ambassador Houghton in Berlin, both Ambassadors Herrick (in Paris) and Fletcher (in Brussels) remained somewhat judgmental and distant.[74]

American administration of the Coblenz sector during this period was characterized chiefly by a struggle to ward off French interference. General Degoutte and his subordinates seemed preoccupied by a desire to make French presence in the area recognized, particularly at times when sanctions threatened or when separatist feeling appeared. Since Allen was convinced that such ostentation was not consistent with either the spirit of the occupation or the dignity of the United States, he fought unremittingly against it—rejecting, without compromise, French requests to hold torchlight parades, to carry bayonets while off duty,[75] and to bring in more troops than originally agreed upon.[76] Despite his best efforts, however, the streets were increasingly crowded with French officers and soldiers,[77] so much so that one Salvation Army worker reported that the Americans looked like a "tourist party" in their own zone.[78] By December, after disciplining an insubordinate French colonel, Allen vowed grimly that "the maximum of French show in this city has been reached for the duration of my stewardship."[79]

American troops had their problems with the Rhinelanders also. Housing congestion was acute enough in Coblenz that inhabitants often made unfavorable comparisons between the AFG and the more "considerate" British Army on the Rhine (BAOR) in Cologne.[80] Dissatisfaction with army provost courts reached such extremes that it led to a request by the German ambassador in Washington for copies of their regulations.[81] There was also considerable grumbling at the way in which some soldiers went on buying sprees, especially as the inflation became more severe and the exchange rate more favorable to foreigners.[82]

Despite such difficulties, as the year wore on, the bond between the "Sammies" and local citizens grew stronger. Aside from general factors, perhaps the arrival of the French in the zone was the most important reason for this development. Yet there were other explanations, not the least of which was the fact that with only 1,200 Americans left, each soldier had become more identifiable and usually a little more discreet. Several hundred German wives contributed much to mutual understanding,[83] and the army's gifts of clothes and food to the poor during the Christmas season earned widespread approval.[84]

On the international scene, December brought the final stage of the crisis that culminated in the French seizure of the Ruhr and American withdrawal from the Rhine. At the London conference, in the second week of the month, Poincaré flatly refused to grant a moratorium without "productive pledges," and, though another Allied meeting was arranged for Paris in January, few retained substantial hope of heading off French military action.[85] If events took no direction for a few days, Poincaré inched closer to decisive measures on December 26 when he pressured the Reparations Commission into declaring Germany in default on certain deliveries in kind.[86] In the interim, in desperation, Berlin had supplemented its recent reparations proposals with a secret overture to Washington suggesting an agreement among the Rhine powers not to make war without public plebiscite.[87] The Germans obviously hoped that the United States would urge this idea upon France as its own, but Hughes simply relayed the proposal to Paris and made no comment when Poincaré rejected it.[88]

The American government was much more interested in the situation, however, than this incident might indicate. After ignoring the Genoa conference the previous April and sitting out the summer, Secretary Hughes had finally concluded upon returning from Brazil that special efforts must be made to alter the train of developments in Europe. As a result, and with President Harding's blessing, Hughes had begun to weigh the courses of action that were open to the United States.

Some of his assistants had been most eager to act. Roland Boyden had cabled him from the Reparations Commission sessions in October urging that the United States "turn the scales" on Europe by calling an international economic conference to meet in Washington.[89] The same month Ambassador Houghton (with the endorsement of the visiting William R. Castle) had proposed that America cancel its war debts in return for disarmament and promises of nonaggression.[90]

Yet, during the autumn at least, Hughes was unwilling to look beyond narrow solutions or to go beyond informal overtures. He rejected the idea of an economic conference for fear that "unrelated" matters like American debts, tariffs, and subsidies would be discussed.[91] He turned down Houghton's suggestion because he did not think the American public would accept it. And since he believed that the way to achieve a workable arrangement was to get the issue of reparations into the hands of financial experts,[92] he tried, with the help of Ambassador Herrick and banker J. P. Morgan, to convince Poincaré that this was the proper course.[93] When, in late November, the French premier rejected these proposals, Hughes and Herrick decided that further American efforts before the Brussels conference (scheduled for January 15, but never held) would only be interpreted in Paris as coercion.[94]

Nevertheless, the rapid deterioration in European affairs made it difficult to remain passive. The president's cabinet had no sooner discussed the collapse of the London conference on December 12, than rumors of a possible American "initiative" were circulating widely in the press.[95] William Phillips reported to a friend "it is possible we may take a hand in the situation at least to the extent of letting France know fairly definitely our attitude toward their much advertised move into the Ruhr,"[96] and Hughes did warn the French ambassador that, in his opinion, the occupation of more territory was "a great danger to future peace."[97] Meanwhile, among certain sections of the public, there was a perceptible growth of sentiment favoring a more active policy. Twenty-two congressmen sponsored a bill to offer Germany $70 million in relief,[98] and the maverick Senator William E. Borah won considerable acclaim by introducing a resolution demanding an economic conference to succeed the Washington disarmament talks.[99]

In the end, Borah's suggestion and Poincaré's actions forced Hughes into the open. In a speech to the American Historical Association in New Haven on December 29, the secretary of state publicly appealed for the creation of an international committee of experts to determine how much Germany could pay.[100] Simultaneously, at the insistence of Hughes, President Harding urged the Senate (1) to reject the Borah resolution, (2) to endorse official American representation on the Reparations Commission, and (3) to grant more latitude to the United States War Debt Commission.[101]

The differences between Borah's and Hughes's attitudes can be clarified by examining their positions with regard to the occupation in Germany. Though the senator from Idaho was now considered something of a turncoat by isolationists, he not only had allowed his December resolution to be amended by Senator James Reed (D-Mo.) to require the withdrawal of the Rhineland army but also had taken advantage of the opportunity to attack the AFG as accomplishing "only what Versailles anticipated." Thus, Borah maintained a continuing contempt for power politics as a means of improving international relations. Like many of the Irreconcilables, he attributed Europe's difficulties to its political ambitions. While he was willing to help reorganize that continent if it would renounce its earlier pursuits, he saw no need to involve American military power in putting an end to European tensions.[102]

The secretary of state was less of a moralist and more of a realist than Borah. Granted, Hughes also had legalist tendencies, as he revealed in his unfortunate insistence on the payment of contracted debts. Yet the two inclinations did blend together on occasion, as they did when he strove for greater orderliness in the structuring of German reparations. And the Secretary's realism did become the dominant theme when it permitted him to leave an American battalion in a position to inhibit European antagonists during a particularly difficult period. At this juncture, his realism also allowed him to use the occupation as a lever in an even more explicit sense. On January 8, 1923, the secretary informed the French ambassador that a move by Poincaré into the Ruhr would mean definite American withdrawal from Germany.[103]

Unhappily for Hughes and his policy, the Senate had already taken matters into its own hands. On January 7, after Senator Borah had retracted his conference proposal (saying he did not wish to "embarrass" the president), Senator Reed had introduced a new resolution demanding that the AFG embark for home.[104] Two hours' debate revealed that senatorial opinion was badly divided, but a motion to refer the matter to committee was defeated 38 to 22, and the Senate then passed Reed's measure by a vote of 57 to 6. League Democrats had joined with isolationist Republicans (and Reed) to force the issue. The former voted "yes" because the Rhineland army was so much less than what they thought was necessary in the crisis; the latter because it was so much more. Both agreed that only trouble could result if the AFG remained in Europe. Administration Republicans were more considerate of the president's diplomacy than were the isolationists, but the crucial vote brought their latent fears to the surface. America clearly would not wait long to bring its soldiers back from Europe.[105]

In any case, probably only decisive intervention could have deterred the French from acting. Certainly neither Hughes's New Haven proposal nor the threat of troop withdrawal appear to have had much effect. Indeed, to the secretary of state's vast indignation, Poincaré publicly denied both that he had ever heard of the American plan before Hughes's December speech and that he had received an American warning regarding an invasion of the Ruhr.[106] Prior to this the Allied prime ministers had met in Paris in one last bid to reach understanding, but, with Belgian and Italian acquiescence, Poincaré had virtually broken off the talks.[107] On January 7, General Allen was informed by General Degoutte that French troops were beginning a concentration in the Rhineland.[108] Two days later the Reparations Commission voted 3 to 1 to declare the Germans in "willful default" on coal deliveries,[109] and on January 10 France announced to the world that it was sending its forces into the Ruhr to take control of the region's mines.[110]

"A dispatch received this morning from the Embassy in Paris was all that was necessary to reach the decision [regarding the AFG] . . . ," William Phillips recorded in his diary that day.[111] Secretaries Weeks and Hughes and the president met at the White House at 9:45 A.M.[112] and in slightly more than an hour the press had been informed that Allen's army would leave the Rhine.[113] No reasons were given at the time, but it is clear that since Washington's bluff had been called, Hughes could hardly afford not to carry out his earlier threat. In addition, the president and his advisers were undoubtedly impressed with congressional opinion, fearful of an incident at Coblenz, and angry at Poincaré for resorting to force. Above all, they must have realized that their troops could no longer "restrain" a France that had fully committed itself to action.[114]

Yet the absence of official explanation meant that the French, British, and German governments could each interpret the American action in a manner favorable to its own policies. This kind of interpretation was, of course, particularly difficult for the French, but Poincaré did make the attempt in his January 11 speech to the Chamber of Deputies, claiming that Harding had only carried out an intention that he had formed many months before.[115] In later years Tirard also argued that there was no connection between the Ruhr seizure and the American decision to leave,[116] but the evidence indicates that few Frenchmen saw it this way at the time. The French press was seriously aggravated with the United States and gave vent to such comments as, "To our friends and allies who came to fight on French soil, hail! To the occupiers of the Rhine who helped to frustrate the fruits of victory, good-by!"[117] When Roland Boyden proceeded to condemn the Ruhr invasion at the Reparations Commission, it seemed conclusive proof in France that the timing of the withdrawal could not have been coincidental.[118]

The British and Germans were more easily able than the French to view Harding's move as an endorsement of their positions. To the British, the Americans were clearly affirming that they shared the aversion to military sanctions that for so long had guided Whitehall's policy. In fact, during the next few weeks, Bonar Law was sorely tempted to follow suit and recall the British army from the Rhine.[119] To the Germans, on the other hand, America's withdrawal signified an open rebuke to France on the part of the Harding administration. Foreign Minister Frederic von Rosenberg had informed Ambassador Houghton on January 9 that although the AFG would be missed at Coblenz, there would be a "certain consolation" for Germany if a withdrawal could be viewed as the result of French aggression.[120] When word of the president's decision was received, therefore, the first response was one of joy. "A more emphatic protest is hardly conceivable," trumpeted the *Berliner Tageblatt*, and most of the Reich's press echoed this assertion.[121] It took a few days before second thoughts began to appear. By January 26 the nationalist *Lokal Anzeiger* was noting sorrowfully that the evacuation had made "the accomplishment of the criminal aims of our oppressors easier."[122]

In the United States the reaction to the long-postponed recall was mixed. Isolationist papers like Hearst's *San Francisco Examiner* welcomed the move as "the best possible news in many a day,"[123] but so conservative a journal as the *New York Tribune* could complain that "our moral power was crippled when we struck our colors...."[124] The administration press ranged in tone from the delight of the *San Francisco Chronicle* ("The President had [decided] wisely....")[125] to the doubt of the *Wall Street Journal* ("it can only give the most humiliating offense to the French").[126] Democratic opinion was even more splintered. The *Cleveland Plain Dealer* charged that the president "renders the United States an advocate of the Anglo-German entente,"[127] but the *Atlanta Constitution* endorsed the return of the troops in the name of political "consistency."[128] The *New Republic* felt that Harding had had "every reason" to "warn France of our disapproval,"[129] but the *Christian Science Monitor* thought that the affair should teach the administration "the lesson of procrastination."[130] Even though Congress was more favorable than the press to Harding's decision, divisions of opinion remained very much in evidence among the lawmakers.[131]

In short, though Republicans were still largely pro-French and Democrats mainly pro-German, circumstances had conspired to fracture the old alliance of opposites with regard to the occupation. Republicans who previously had supported the occupation out of loyalty to France were now split not only by anxiety about violence and respect for the president's policy but also by the realization that the French themselves often saw the American army as a potential obstacle. Democrats who earlier had stood for the occupation out of friendship for Germany were now divided not only by fear of hostilities but also by recognition of the fact that the Germans saw an advantage in an American departure that took the form of a protest against the French.[132] As far as the American people were concerned, then, there was no clear-cut verdict about the virtue of withdrawing General Allen's force from the Rhine.

If the secretary of state assumed that the AFG was merely packing up, however, he was soon to discover otherwise. On January 11, as the French industrial mission moved into Essen, General Allen had called the high commissioners together on his own initiative to discuss the possibility of stimulating last-minute Franco-German conversations.[133] Tirard had said that he was certain Poincaré was still disposed to negotiate,[134] and, in Allen's opinion (as expressed in a cable), "the seriousness of the situation . . . and the way in which the High Commission is connected with the new occupation . . . [indicated] the usefulness of an expression from that source."[135] Hughes's first reaction to Allen's initiative is not recorded, but it is known that on the fourteenth he instructed Boyden in Paris not to express any views whatever, even in a purely personal capacity.[136] The next morning the French chargé brought in a message from Poincaré complaining that Allen's actions were "inappropriate,"[137] and the secretary hastened to wire Coblenz that the situation was far too "delicate" for any proposal "without explicit instructions from the Department."[138] Allen had expected such an injunction,[139] and he replied by conveying his "deep regret that my intentions [*sic*] should have annoyed you."[140] Yet it is an interesting reflection on Hughes's frame of mind that over a year later he and Ambassador Herrick devoted considerable discussion to Allen's statement in his *Journal* that his efforts in January 1923 had "met with an unsympathetic reception in Washington. . . ."[141]

So Allen was reduced for the first time to the status of a mere observer. Kilmarnock also had been instructed to abstain from participation on the High Commission, and he and Allen now watched silently as Tirard and Rolin-Jacquemyns acted to seize productive pledges (for example, coal taxes and state forests) on the left bank and to cope with passive resistance by Germans both there and in the Ruhr.[142] Tension increased sharply, particularly after January 20, when Berlin directed governmental employees to disregard new Allied ordinances and the High Commission retaliated with a series of expulsions of Rhenish officials that ultimately numbered in the hundreds.[143]

This period was much more active for the AFG than for its commanding general. According to the press, headquarters at Coblenz was like a domestic-relations court, with German women clamoring to marry soldiers before the American departure.[144] Claims for the support of illegitimate children, requests for work and charity, demands for payment of overdue bills—all suddenly mushroomed in number.[145] Yet there were plaudits too. A letter from Chancellor Cuno to Allen emphasized that "the German government appreciates highly the spirit in which you have administered the authority vested in you."[146] The mayor of Coblenz was lavish in his praise of the Americans,[147] as were the German press and the official French press in Mainz.[148] When Old Glory was lowered for the last time on Ehrenbreitstein on January 24 and the Eighth Infantry marched down to the Coblenz station, Allen paused to note "the genuine sorrow depicted on the faces of both allies and Germans."[149]

A peculiar kind of postscript followed. With the American army gone, the population of Coblenz assumed that American

control had ended, and students gave vent to nationalist feelings by attacking the printing plants of several separatist journals. In fact, however, though Allen had intended to hand over
the zone to the French commander on January 24, the latter
had found it impossible to accommodate him. It was therefore
necessary for Allen to disperse the demonstrators with a
few dozen MPs, and until January 27, when the transfer of
authority was finally accomplished, the general lived in some
apprehension that he might not be able to maintain order in
Coblenz.[150] Even by that date, he had not been apprised that
Washington had definitely decided upon his personal recall.
A letter from Undersecretary Phillips in December had led
him to believe that he might be allowed to continue as an observer,[151] and perhaps he also was aware that Chancellor Cuno
has asked the secretary of state to permit him to remain in
Coblenz as "moral protection" for Germany.[152] The possibility had not been seriously considered by the State Department,
but Allen did not receive a cable directing him to withdraw
from the High Commission until February 1, 1923.[153] He
attended his last meeting and read a message of farewell on
February 6.[154]

Meanwhile, the army continued on its homeward journey.
At Antwerp the troops received Belgian honors as they board-
ed the *St. Mihiel*, their "Noah's Ark," taking with them
wives, babies, horses, police dogs, monkeys, fish, and furni-
ture.[155] Out on the Atlantic they entertained themselves with
editions of the *Seagoing Amaroc* and with activities like the
burial of Aleck J. Corkscrew, a commemoration of their return to a Prohibition-blighted land. On February 7, 1923, their
crossing ended in Savannah harbor, where the governor of
Georgia turned out to welcome them and express thanks that
America at last was out of Europe.[156]

These final six months of occupation had been the most

difficult of all for the participants. Fewer in number than ever before, the American forces had seemed to ride almost helplessly upon the growing wave of French fear and resentment. Their presence may have preserved a semblance of normality for the Coblenz zone and it may have retarded French momentum and moderated German resistance, but it had been far from capable of preventing the Ruhr invasion.

Nevertheless, the occupation and the crisis it rode played an important role in awakening a reluctant administration to accept a greater responsibility in European affairs. If the awakening had not come early enough to forestall the immediate disaster, and if, from the standpoint of 1939, it would never come fully enough, particularly in political matters, still it was a noticeable and portentous shift. Though Hughes remained committed to a formal and primarily economic picture of America's foreign ties (as he clearly demonstrated during these weeks by his abandonment of a military observer [Allen] while protecting a financial observer [Boyden], who had also come under attack from the internationalist-isolationist coalition),[157] the secretary of state *had* kept American troops in Germany for substantially political reasons, and in the end he had even used their withdrawal as a threat against the French. These policy departures, his New Haven address, his defense of Boyden, and his flexibility in the British debt negotiations just beginning, revealed a new American recognition of the truth in a contemporary journalist's assertion that "our advice alone leaves Europe cold."[158] In this realization lay the roots of the Dawes Plan of 1924.

CONCLUSION

> . . . so long as the Americans remained at Coblenz
> there was an outward and visible sign that America,
> or some people in America at least, were thinking of
> the war fought and the peace signed in common, and
> so long as they remained all hope of American coop-
> eration in the hard work of peace was not abandoned.
>
> Charles Repington, in the
> (London) *Daily Telegraph*,
> January 25, 1923

> One thing is plain. America, however reluctantly, is
> preparing anew to take an open, active part in the
> settlement of European questions.
>
> William Castle, Western European
> desk officer, Department of State,
> March 1923

American troops had left Coblenz as the Franco-German
antagonism on the Rhine entered upon its climactic phase.
During the next nine months the two countries were to lock
themselves in the bitterest of struggles, France attempting to
take its reparations by direct action and at the same time to
reinvigorate the Rhenish separatists, Germany endeavoring to
mobilize its citizens in a passive resistance to the invader. By
September 1923, economic confusion and inflation had reached
such proportions that it was impossible for the Germans to
continue in their effort, and a new chancellor, Gustav Stresemann, announced the abandonment of opposition and the
granting of concessions. Thus France was outwardly victorious in its sanctions, but the price had been enormous in terms

of both the havoc wrought in Germany and the weakening of France's own economy.

At this point, finally, Europe was ready for a more pacific approach to the solution of its problems. October 1923 saw the beginning of financial consultations that resulted during the next year first in the acceptance of Hughes's New Haven ideas and then in their embodiment in the Dawes Plan. On the political side, the same period witnessed the initiation of direct talks between the western capitals and Berlin, negotiations leading ultimately to an agreement at Locarno in October 1925 in which France, Germany, Britain, and Italy all undertook to recognize and guarantee the Rhine frontier.

The Dawes Plan and Locarno Pact had their weaknesses, but they made further progress possible, both along the Rhine and in relations among the western powers. The Ruhr and Ruhr ports were evacuated by the Allies in the summer of 1925, shortly before the conference at Locarno, and the Rhineland High Commission simultaneously announced a relaxation of its regulations upon the local citizenry. The next year the northern (or Cologne) tier of the occupied territory was returned to German control, this being in accord with the Treaty of Versailles. The remainder of the Rhineland was evacuated in 1930, the southern part five years ahead of schedule as a reward for German ratification of the Young reparations settlement.

In the intervening years, the memory of the American occupation on the Rhine had assumed different forms and different meanings. In the United States the protracted dispute over reimbursement of army costs,[1] the publication of Allen's *Journal* in 1923,[2] and the appearance of his second book in 1927[3] helped to color the Rhineland history in a way that reinforced growing doubts about the motivations of the Allies. In Britain, in Belgium, and in France, meanwhile, these same events contributed to a substantial disenchantment with the Americans.⁴ Particularly in France, where the timing of the withdrawal was well remembered, the public developed an extremely hostile picture of the occupation and of its commander. Feeling in Paris was so intense that in 1924 when it seemed possible Allen might return to France as an escort to the American olympic team, Ambassador Herrick felt compelled to write to Hughes in order to prevent the general's appointment.⁵

The situation was almost the reverse in Germany, where Allen's *Journal* was recognized as an unexpected windfall and was immediately translated for use as ammunition against the French.⁶ The revelations warmed many German hearts toward the Americans, as did, in the postcrisis months, the memory that the Americans had chosen to withdraw their troops so as to strike a blow against the Ruhr invasion.⁷ Even so, most Germans remained persuaded that the United States could have done much more for European peace than it actually accomplished during these years. And such a conviction, reinforced by the vehement xenophobia of the Right, contributed to a lingering resentment regarding the earlier activities of the AFG. Though Chancellor Wilhelm Marx recalled in 1929 that the "Americans almost at once, and the English shortly afterwards, [had] attempted to make the occupation . . . bearable,"⁸ rightwing authors still dwelt at length upon the rawness, extravagance, and crudeness of the "big children" who had occupied Coblenz.⁹

The story of the Rhineland experience is both complex and ironic. Americans had never intended to join in an occupation of Germany after World War I. At the end of the fighting they had become involved in an advance to the Rhine primarily out of their desire to "beat the Hun" and as a result of Colonel House's failure to perceive that French leaders hoped to use this armistice arrangement to facilitate the detachment of the left bank and its incorporation into their defenses. At the Paris Peace Conference President Wilson had opposed an independent Rhineland and Prime Minister Lloyd George an occupation, but Premier Clemenceau's insistence on security for France had ultimately led to a compromise requiring Allied troops to stay on for fifteen years. Once having agreed to this, Wilson recognized several cogent reasons for American participation: to ensure the preservation of German unity, to render the occupation as moderate as possible, to mitigate French fears of Germany, and to see that Germany obeyed the treaty. He apparently believed that opposition at home could be minimized by shifting the duty to the League of Nations within a few years. That he had no wish to use the occupation as an instrument to change the German people was evidenced by his championing of Pierrepont Noyes's proposal for a civilian High Commission limited in power to the protection of the occupying forces. It was the French acceptance of this principle of civilian control for the occupation that made it possible for Wilson and Lloyd George to remain committed to the original compromise.

But why did an America that had rejected the Treaty of Versailles retain an army for more than four years in Germany? Humorist Will Rogers offered an explanation in 1922 when he suggested that the troops were still in Europe "because two of them weren't married yet."[10] In retrospect it is clear that the occupation owed its longevity to many factors, some temporary, others relatively permanent. Originally, in 1920 and 1921, Wilson and Harding had refrained from altering the situation primarily in order to preserve a diplomatic lever for the negotiation of peace with Germany. Later, during the Washington Conference of 1921–1922, the administration had avoided making changes on the Rhine so as not to disturb the French and jeopardize bargaining on disarmament and other matters. Following this, in the spring of 1922, after the reimbursement of American army costs had become an issue, Harding had maintained an occupation because Hughes said that the threat of withdrawal would help him in obtaining the moneys due the United States. In the meantime, many of their countrymen had developed considerable pride in providing "selfish" Europeans with a firsthand example of true "Americanism." Other citizens, under the impact of skidding farm prices, had become convinced of the need for a "mediating influence" in an area where it might encourage trade. Finally, in the summer and fall of 1922, when European pleas made it apparent that a genuine international crisis was imminent, the administration had sensed that it was unwise to withdraw the troops and possibly to upset the delicate balance. Still, the president had been extremely irresolute and only an alliance of pro-French and pro-German feelings among the public had enabled him to pursue the course he did.

If there had been reasons to maintain the army, other factors had encouraged recall. Harding originally had had strong tendencies toward withdrawal, as he had made clear in Des Moines during the campaign of 1920. His traditionalist beliefs decreed that Americans should remain apart from Europe, and he knew that the public not only wanted to demobilize but also entertained the gravest doubts about the desirability of peacetime involvement abroad. As president, he had felt the pressure of congressional drives for disarmament and economy as well as the weight of the Irreconcilables' campaign against all vestiges of Versailles. He had also become increasingly disgusted with the Allies as reports of French "extravagance," "racist" policies, and "connivance" with separatists filtered home from the Rhineland, and as the British and French revealed an inclination to deprive the United States of its army costs. It was difficult for Harding to understand how the Europeans could be so "ungrateful," and it was particularly galling for him to see the United States rewarded not only with a lack of appreciation overseas but also with mounting danger that its forces might be involved in hostilities. The end of the occupation was obviously in sight when Hughes attempted to forestall the invasion of the Ruhr by threatening to withdraw. Indeed, after France had acted on the morning of January 10, 1923, the administration had little choice but to schedule the departure of the troops.

What were the results and meaning of the American occupation, then, for both Europe and the United States? To begin with, the compromise that was involved in creating and preserving the arrangement was vital to the success of the Paris Peace Conference. Then again, Americans exerted a crucial moderating influence within successive occupations, defending civilian control, strengthening the more temperate of their allies, and in effect reassuring both Berlin and Paris that the worst of their fears would not come to pass. On the other hand, it may also be true that the failure of France to obtain its reparations was due in part to the way in which the American and British presence inhibited Paris from invoking sanctions against the Reich. Furthermore, the American withdrawal in January 1923 presumably intensified, even if it also shortened, the ensuing struggle within the Ruhr.

The occupation had other effects in Europe as well. The coming of American and Allied troops to Germany in December 1918 undoubtedly weakened the political revolution within that country, although the impact in the unoccupied regions may actually have been greater than that in the occupied. The existence of an American zone and the impartiality of its officers also helped to frustrate the scheming of Rhenish separatists, both in May 1919 and during the months that followed. Beyond this, the Americans can be given some credit for the fact that the French seizure of the Ruhr came as late as 1923 and thus posed no greater threat to German unity than it did.

The occupation on the Rhine also had an impact on the

United States. For one thing, its very existence after 1919 helped to prevent both the Wilson and Harding administrations from entirely neglecting the course of European affairs. When Hughes became secretary of state he may have chosen to ignore the League of Nations and refused to mediate the reparations dispute, but, of necessity, one of his first decisions was whether or not to allow the Allies to enforce sanctions against the Germans within the American zone. In succeeding years General Allen's bimonthly reports from Coblenz may have been seldom answered, but they were carefully read, even in the White House.[11] Hughes's increasingly pro-German attitude must be partially explained as the result of his concern regarding French policy as it related to the Rhineland. Furthermore, the need to safeguard the AFG was obviously a factor in alerting him to the possibility of an American initiative in the reparations crisis.

The changes wrought in American public opinion were not so manifest. Granted, the thousands of troops who participated in the occupation brought home much new sympathy for their enemies and a new distaste for their allies. However, only 15 percent of the AEF served in Germany, and if the consistently anti-German line of the American Legion is any indication, this minority was submerged in a vastly larger number of veterans who derived considerable psychic satisfaction from preserving wartime enmities. Though most Americans at Coblenz after 1919 came to have a deep respect for the German point of view, it should be remembered that many of these men, especially the officers, remained abroad until 1923, affecting domestic affairs only indirectly.[12] Moreover, if a considerable number of individuals developed unfavorable perspectives on the Allies as a result of the black-horror affair and the costs dispute, the response of the public to the Ruhr invasion demonstrated convincingly that even in 1923 the nation retained considerable loyalty to the victors and the victory of 1918.

Conclusion

It is in the realm of what could have been, however, that the American occupation in Germany is perhaps most provocative. Today it is widely agreed that, given both the Treaty of Versailles and the failure of the Senate to ratify it, a successfully "stabilizing" American foreign policy during 1920–1923 would have required an attack upon the two most destructive features of the European situation: the burden of reparations and the insecurity of France. The easiest solution, obviously, would have been for the United States to reduce (or to bargain with) the war debts that made reparations necessary and to ratify the alliance that Wilson had earlier signed with France. Once these courses of action had been rejected, however, the only possible answer lay in other attempts at reducing Franco-German tensions and at strengthening the European economy. In these matters, of course, the American occupation could have performed a useful service. Alone it would not have resolved the grand dilemma, but supported more adequately from home (with 10,000 troops, say, and a strong high commissioner) and supplemented, for example, with publicly guaranteed private loans to Germany and other nations, it could have been a significant factor in heading off the Ruhr invasion.

It is unfortunate that the president and secretary of state did not recognize the need for active intervention until the very end, if even then. They had failed to take real advantage of the period from May 1921 to January 1922 when moderate governments were still in power in both Berlin and Paris. Subsequently they had not only refused to go to the Genoa conference, but had also reduced the size of the army in occupation and limited themselves to tentative and largely informal overtures. That Harding and Hughes were gaining insight from the struggle of the antagonists does not lessen their considerable responsibility for failing to prevent the Ruhr tragedy.

Notes

CHAPTER 1

[1] *New York Times*, September 17, 1918, p. 5.

[2] Robert E. Osgood, *Ideals and Self Interest in America's Foreign Relations* (Chicago, 1953), pp. 78–81, 277–81; John Milton Cooper, Jr., *The Vanity of Power: American Isolationism and the First World War, 1914–1917* (Westport, Conn., 1969), pp. 7–32.

[3] See Daniel J. Boorstin, *America and the Image of Europe: Reflections on American Thought* (New York, 1960), pp. 19–39.

[4] George M. Cohan's song "Over There" gives some indication of the distance Americans felt from the fight. This is not to say that "isolationists" could not develop emotional attachments to countries overseas, they did form such attachments during the postwar years. Or, to be more precise, liberal isolationists followed liberal internationalists to an extent in "identifying" with Germany, while conservative isolationists paralleled conservative internationalists to an extent in retaining wartime loyalties to France. On the other hand, some Americans remained "irreconcilable" (i.e., largely unattached) in their isolationism.

[5] Osgood, pp. 125–53; Cooper, pp. 59–63; Lloyd E. Ambrosius, "Wilson, the Republicans, and French Security after World War I," *Journal of American History* 59 (September 1972): 341–52.

[6] For example, see Henry Cabot Lodge, ed., *Selections from the Correspondence of Theodore Roosevelt and Henry Cabot Lodge, 1884–1918* (New York, 1925), p. 539.

[7] "Shall the Peace League Include Germany?" *Literary Digest* 59 (October 12, 1918): 11–12. See also David H. Burton, "Teddy Roosevelt's Social Darwinism and Views on Imperialism," *Journal of the History of Ideas* 26 (March 1965), 103–18.

[8] Osgood, pp. 23–42; Christopher Lasch, *The American Liberals and the Russian Revolution* (New York, 1962), pp. vii–xvi. Lasch does point up the extent to which progressive forces at the time were divided among themselves, but it is clear that neither his "war liberals" nor his

"anti-imperalists" (who were really isolationists) foresaw the difficulty democracy would have in establishing itself in Germany.

9 For example, see Walter Weyl, *The End of the War* (New York, 1918), 157–231.

10 "Passing Sentence on the Kaiser and His People," *Literary Digest* 59 (October 26, 1918):14.

11 For two of the more "realistic" works of the day, see Thorstein Veblen, *An Inquiry into the Nature of Peace and the Terms of Its Perpetuation* (New York, 1917), 116–17; and Horace Meyer Kallen, *The Structure of Lasting Peace: An Inquiry into the Motives of War and Peace* (Boston, 1918), pp. 82–84, 104–10. Robert E. Osgood (pp. 17–20) argues persuasively that an optimist-pessimist polarity has been a continuing characteristic of American internationalism in this century. W. L. Dorn, in "The Debate over American Occupation Policy in Germany in 1944–1945," *Political Science Quarterly* 72 (1957): 484–85, offers substantiating evidence from a later period.

12 Earl S. Pomeroy, "Sentiment for a Strong Peace, 1917–1919," *The South Atlantic Quarterly* 43 (October 1944): 325–37; Arno J. Mayer, *Politics and Diplomacy of Peacemaking: Containment and Counterrevolution at Versailles, 1918–1919* (New York, 1967), pp. 55–60.

13 George Harvey, "Beware the Peace Drive," *North American Review* 208 (October 1918): 495.

14 *Literary Digest* 59 (October 12, 1918):11–12.

15 Arthur Willert, *The Road to Safety: A Study in Anglo-American Relations* (London, 1952), p. 175.

16 *Literary Digest* 59 (October 12, 1918): 11–12. A minor but significant factor in explaining American willingness to accept the unexpected occupation was the way in which the Rhine had become one of the two or three most common symbols of the day for Germany and "Germanness." One can get some sense of this from two American war songs that date from 1918: "When Pershing Eats That Melon on the Rhine," and "Just Like Washington Crossed the Delaware, General Pershing Will Cross the Rhine."

17 United States, Congress, *Congressional Record*, 65th Cong., 2nd sess., November 11, 1918, 56:11542.

18 *New York Times*, November 14, 1918, p. 12.

19 Wilson made the statement on July 21, 1917. See Ray Stannard Baker, *Woodrow Wilson, Life and Letters*, 8 vols. (New York, 1927–1939), 7:43.

Notes to Chapter One

[20] The best discussions of Wilson's efforts are in Osgood, pp. 273–91; Arno J. Mayer, *Wilson vs. Lenin: Political Origins of the New Diplomacy, 1917–1918* (Cleveland, 1964), pp. 329–93; Mayer, *Politics and Diplomacy,* pp. 33–116; and N. Gordon Levin, Jr., *Woodrow Wilson and World Politics: America's Response to War and Revolution* (New York, 1968), pp. 13–119. See also Lawrence Evans, *United States Policy and the Partition of Turkey, 1914–1924* (Baltimore, 1965), pp. 49–85.

[21] Baker, 7:254.

[22] Mayer, *Wilson vs. Lenin,* pp. 339–40; Lawrence E. Gelfand, *The Inquiry: American Preparations for Peace, 1917–1919* (New Haven, 1963), pp. 134–53. The Department of State played a relatively minor role in these studies; note John L. Snell, "Wilson's Peace Program and German Socialism, January-March 1918," *Mississippi Valley Historical Review* 38 (September 1951):200–12.

[23] The most accessible compilation of Inquiry documents is to be found in United States, Department of State, *Papers Relating to the Foreign Relations of the United States: The Paris Peace Conference, 1919,* 13 vols. (Washington, D. C., 1942–1944), 1:9–118. For discussion, see Gelfand, pp. 181–200.

[24] The Bolsheviks had broadcast the text of the Franco-Russian agreement over the Petrograd radio in December 1917; copies of the relevant documents had been forwarded to Washington by the American ambassador in Russia on December 5, 1917 (arriving December 27, 1917); see Jere Clemens King, *Foch versus Clemenceau: France and German Dismemberment, 1918–1919* (Cambridge, Mass., 1960), p. 13; United States, Department of State, *Papers Relating to the Foreign Relations of the United States: 1917,* 2 vols. (Washington, D.C., 1932), sup. 2, 1:493–507 (hereafter cited as *FRUS: 1917*). Of course, the president may not have learned of these negotiations before his speech (January 8, 1918), but it is clear that they were under discussion in governmental circles about this time. Indeed, William Harbutt Dawson's *Problems of the Peace,* which was published in London in January 1918 and widely reviewed in the United States, reported that French Premier Alexandre Ribot had told the French Chamber of Deputies (July 31, 1917) that the tsar had promised "to leave us free to seek guarantees against further aggression, not by annexing to French territories on the left bank of the Rhine, but by making of those territories, if need be, an autonomous State, protecting us as well as Belgium against invasion from beyond the Rhine." See also Mayer, *Wilson vs. Lenin,* pp. 208–12.

Notes to Chapter One

²⁵ The Fourteen Points address is in Ray Stannard Baker and William E. Dodd, eds., *The Public Papers of Woodrow Wilson*, 6 vols. (New York, 1925–1927), 5:155–62.

²⁶ Walter Lippmann to Secretary of War Newton D. Baker, June 9, 1919, Newton D. Baker Papers, Library of Congress.

²⁷ For Wilson's speeches, see H. W. V. Temperley, ed., *A History of the Peace Conference at Paris*, 6 vols. (London, 1920–1924), 1:431–48. References are to p. 444.

²⁸ See Mayer, *Politics and Diplomacy*, pp. 33–52, 84–89, 167–87; and Pierre Renouvin, "L'Opinion publique en France pendant la guerre 1914–1918," *Revue d'histoire diplomatique* 84 (October–December 1970):289–336. See also Lady Algernon Gordon Lennox, ed., *The Diary of Lord Bertie of Thame, 1914–1918*, 2 vols. (London, 1924), 2:301; Marcel Berger and Paul Allard, *Les Secrets de la censure pendant la guerre* (Paris, 1932), pp. 367–71; and John M. Sherwood, *Georges Mandel and the Third Republic* (Stanford, Calif., 1970), pp. 26–31.

²⁹ For information on this, see Robert Dell, *The Left Bank of the Rhine* (London, 1919); King, *Foch versus Clemenceau*, pp. 1–12; and Pierre Renouvin, "Les Buts de guerre du gouvernement français (1914–1918)," *Revue historique* 235 (January–March 1966):1–38.

³⁰ See Renouvin, "Buts de guerre"; Georges Suarez, *Briand: Sa vie—son oeuvre—avec son journal et de nombreux documents inédits*, 6 vols. (Paris, 1938–1952), 4:127–35; Mermeix [Gabriel Terrail], *Le Combat de trois* (Paris, 1922), p. 191; Clarence Jay Smith, Jr., *The Russian Struggle for Power, 1914–1917* (New York, 1956), pp. 459–66; Erwin Hölzle, "Das Experiment des Friedens im ersten Weltkrieg, 1914–1917," *Geschichte in Wissenschaft und Unterricht* 8 (August 1962):465–522; and Mayer, *Wilson vs. Lenin*, pp. 206–14.

³¹ In his "Buts de guerre," Pierre Renouvin contends that the Rhineland policy of Briand was abandoned by his immediate successors and only reclaimed by Clemenceau at the time of the peace conference. The evidence of the armistice period indicates, however, that while "Clemenceau refrained from committing himself publicly to these goals, [he did work] towards them privately" (Peter S. Stern, "France's Bid for Security and Order" [paper delivered at the meeting of the Pacific Coast Branch of the American Historical Association, Portland, Oregon, August 31, 1966]). André Tardieu, Clemenceau's closest associate at the conference, argues for the essential continuity of French policy in *La Paix* (Paris, 1921), pp. 30–241. See also Mayer, *Politics and Diplomacy*, 170–87.

[32] Balfour's interview with Ambassador Paul Cambon occurred ca. July 2, 1917; his remarks in Parliament date from December 19, 1917, see Great Britain, Foreign Office, *Papers respecting Negotiations for an Anglo-French Pact*, Cmd. 2169 (London, 1924), p. 4. See also David Lloyd George, *Memoirs of the Peace Conference*, 2 vols. (New Haven, 1939), 1:252; W. M. Jordan, *Great Britain, France, and the German Problem, 1918–1939* (New York, 1944), pp. 170–72.

[33] For the impact of the war on Britain, see Caroline Playne, *Britain Holds On, 1917–1918* (London, 1933); A. J. P. Taylor, *English History, 1914–1945* (Oxford, 1965), pp. 34–161; and Arthur Marwick, *The Deluge: British Society and the First World War* (London, 1965). For discussion of what British statesmen were thinking about the peace in 1917–1918, see Harold I. Nelson, *Land and Power: British and Allied Policy on Germany's Frontiers, 1916–1919* (London, 1963), pp. 7–50, and V. H. Rothwell, *British War Aims and Peace Diplomacy, 1914–1918* (Oxford, 1971), pp. 59–287.

[34] Mayer, *Wilson vs. Lenin*, pp. 310–28. See also Seth P. Tillman, *Anglo-American Relations at the Paris Peace Conference of 1919* (Princeton, N. J., 1961), pp. 26–31, and Rothwell, pp. 147–55. For Lloyd George's address (January 5, 1918), see United States, Department of State, *Papers Relating to the Foreign Relations of the United States: 1918*, one vol. and 2 supplements (Washington, D. C., 1930–1933), sup. 1, 1:4–7 (hereafter *FRUS: 1918*).

[35] Sir Frederick B. Maurice, *The Armistices of 1918* (London, 1943), p. 29; Harry R. Rudin, *Armistice, 1918* (New York, 1944), pp. 89–96; Pierre Renouvin, *L'Armistice de Rethondes: 11 Novembre 1918* (Paris, 1968), pp. 118–22.

[36] Arthur Frazier (diplomatic liaison at the Supreme War Council) to Secretary of State Robert Lansing, October 9, 1918, *FRUS: 1918*, sup. 1, 1:351. See also British War Cabinet Minutes, October 11, 1918, CAB 23/8/484; and Charles E. Callwell, *Field Marshall Sir Henry Wilson*, 2 vols. (New York, 1927), 2:133–35. The German note of October 5 and president Wilson's note of October 8, 1918 are in *FRUS: 1918*, sup. 1, 1:338–43.

[37] Frazier to Lansing, October 9, 1918 (two messages), *FRUS: 1918*, sup. 1, 1:352–53. See also Lord Hankey, *The Supreme Command, 1914–1918*, 2 vols. (London, 1961), 2:855.

[38] These four generals (representing France, Britain, Italy, and the United States) stood in a staff relationship to the Supreme War Council. See David Trask, *The United States in the Supreme War*

Notes to Chapter One

Council: American War Aims and Inter-Allied Strategy, 1917–1918 (Middletown, Conn., 1961), pp. 38–46.

[39] Frazier to Lansing, October 7, 1918, *FRUS: 1918*, sup. 1, 1:344; General Tasker Bliss to Adjutant General, War Department, October 7, 1918, United States, Department of the Army, *United States Army in the World War*, 17 vols., (Washington, 1948), 10:4–5 (hereafter cited as *Army in the World War*). See also David Lloyd George, *War Memoirs*, 6 vols. (London, 1933–1937), 6:3275–76; Maurice, pp. 29–30; Jordan, p. 14.

[40] Bliss to Adjutant General, October 8, 1918, in *Army in the World War*, 10:6–7; War Cabinet, October 11, 1918, CAB 23/8/484; Tasker Bliss, "The Armistices," *American Journal of International Law* 16 (1922):509–22; Maurice, p. 31; Jordan, p. 14; and Trask, p. 154.

[41] Bliss to Baker, October 23, 1918, Woodrow Wilson file, Newton Baker Papers. An earlier letter in a similar vein is Bliss to Baker, October 9, 1918, Tasker Bliss Papers, Library of Congress.

[42] Whereas Foch told Marshal Haig (and later claimed in his memoirs) that *he* had taken the initiative in submitting his views upon the armistice, Clemenceau's military adviser recorded that the marshal had been asked to do so by the French premier. On this, see Robert Blake, *The Private Papers of Douglas Haig* (London, 1952), p. 330; Ferdinand Foch, *Mémoires pour servir à l'histoire de la guerre de 1914–1918*, 2 vols. (Paris, 1931), 2:270; and J. J. H. Mordacq, *La Vérité sur l'armistice* (Paris, 1929), p. 39.

[43] Foch's note is in Lloyd George, *War Memoirs*, 6:3276–78. See also Frazier to Lansing, October 9, 1918, *FRUS: 1918*, sup. 1, 1:351; Foch, 2:270–72; Mordacq, p. 70; and Jordan, p. 15.

[44] War Cabinet, October 11, 1918, CAB 23/8/484; Lloyd George, *War Memoirs*, 6:3278; Hankey, 2:854; Callwell, p. 134; Jordan p. 15.

[45] The (second) German note of October 12 and President Wilson's note of October 14 are in *FRUS: 1918*, sup. 1, 1:357–58.

[46] War Cabinet, October 14, 1918, CAB 23/8/485; Lady Wester Wemyss, *Life and Letters of Admiral of the Fleet Lord Wester Wemyss* (London, 1935), pp. 398–99; Jordan, p. 17; and Sir Frederick Maurice, *Lessons of Allied Cooperation: Naval, Military, and Air, 1914–1918* (New York, 1942), pp. 394–95.

[47] British Ministerial Conference, October 19, 1918, CAB 23/17/29X, and October 21, 1918, CAB 23/17/30X; War Cabinet, October 21, 1918, CAB 23/14/489A; Stephen Roskill, *Hankey, Man of Secrets*, 2 vols. (London, 1970–1972), 1:614–21; Lloyd George, *War Memoirs*, 6:3299–3309; Callwell, p. 138; Blake, pp. 332–34.

[48] The generals were encouraged in their ambitions by president Raymond Poincaré, although, strangely enough, Poincaré disagreed with them about the wisdom of granting the Germans an armistice. See Mermeix, *Les Négociations secrètes et les quatre armistices avec pièces justificatives* (Paris, 1919), pp. 221–23; John J. Pershing, *My Experiences in the World War*, 2 vols., (New York, 1931), 2:369.

[49] Foch, 2:276–78; Maurice, *Armistices*, pp. 34–39.

[50] Clemenceau's reply was dated October 23, 1918. See René Michel M. Lhopital, *Foch, l'armistice et la paix* (Paris, 1938), pp. 33–36; Raymond Recouly, *Foch: My Conversations with the Marshal* (New York, 1929), pp. 42–44; King, *Foch versus Clemenceau*, pp. 13–15; and Jere Clemens King, *Generals and Politicians: Conflict between France's High Command, Parliament, and Government, 1914–1918* (Berkeley, 1951), pp. 239–41.

[51] Mordacq, pp. 73–74; Jordan, p. 18. The (third) German note of October 20 and President Wilson's note of October 23, 1918, are in *FRUS: 1918*, sup. 1, 1:380–82.

[52] The idea for the meeting of the generals was originally Clemenceau's, and apparently was not approved by the British War Cabinet until October 25, after he had already arranged for the conference. It is ironic that at this point the War Cabinet insisted on replacing his rather loose instructions with the "more severe" language of President Wilson's third note (requiring that the armistice terms "fully protect the interests of the peoples involved and ensure to the Associated Governments the unrestricted power to safeguard and enforce the details of the peace...."); War Cabinet, October 25, 1918, CAB 23/14/491A.

[53] Maxime Weygand, *Foch* (Paris, 1947), pp. 258–59. See also Poincaré, 10:401.

[54] Blake, pp. 335–36.

[55] Notes on Conference at Senlis, October 25, 1918, in *Army in the World War*, 10:19–23; Pershing to Adjutant General, October 25, 1918, Woodrow Wilson Papers, Library of Congress; Pershing, 2:360–63; Maurice, *Armistices*, pp. 45–46; Jordan, pp. 18–22.

[56] Or, as Pershing put it in his memoirs, "Although I was in favor of demanding the surrender of the German armies, I accepted this as a conference to decide upon the terms in case an armistice should be granted" (Pershing, 2:360). On this, see Francis Bullitt Lowry, "Pershing and the Armistice," *Journal of American History* 55 (September 1968): pp. 281–82. That Pershing might have been able to

sense something wrong, if he had tried, is indicated by Haig's reaction to the Senlis meeting: "It struck me too that the insistence of the two French generals on [occupying] the left bank of the Rhine means that they now aim at getting hold of the Palatinate as well as of Alsace Lorraine!" (Blake, p. 336).

[57] Mordacq, p. 75; Foch, 2:282–83; Tardieu, 69.

[58] See n. 41 above. Lloyd George's personal appeal of October 21, that Wilson not commit the Allies, may also have encouraged the president's suspicions. See Baker, 8:500–501; Tillman, p. 43; Nelson, pp. 69–70.

[59] Sir William Wiseman, "Notes of an Interview with the President at the White House, October 16, 1918," Edward M. House Papers, Yale University. See also Willert, p. 175. In an October 14 conversation with Sir Eric Geddes, First Lord of the Admiralty, Wilson had predicted that the statesmen would have to modify the proposals of the military experts in order to avoid "inexcusably humiliating" the Germans. See Lloyd George, *War Memoirs*, 6:3290. Note also War Cabinet, October 15, 1918, CAB 23/8/486.

[60] Anne W. Lane and Lewis H. Wall, eds., *The Letters of Franklin K. Lane* (Boston, 1922), pp. 293–96; Baker, 8:500–509.

[61] Baker, 8:520–21.

[62] The most satisfactory biography of House is the chapter entitled "Sphinx in a Soft Hat: Edward M. House," in Louis W. Koenig, *The Invisible Presidency* (New York, 1960).

[63] Charles Seymour, ed., *The Intimate Papers of Colonel House*, 4 vols. (Boston, 1928), 4:64–66.

[64] Ibid., p. 83.

[65] Bliss to House, October 28, 1918, Bliss Papers.

[66] Edward M. House Diary, October 26, 1918, House Papers. See also Blake, p. 337.

[67] House Diary, October 27, 1918; Seymour, *Intimate Papers*, 4:94, 114–17, 145–47; Bliss, pp. 509–22. It is true that Foch's scheme (and the later armistice) made provision for substantial German disarmament, but Bliss's argument was that if the Germans *were* defeated, they could hardly refuse to disarm completely, and that such a concession would render a military occupation unnecessary, put an early preliminary treaty (on military terms) within reach, and reduce the possibility of further bloodshed.

[68] Pershing, 2:364.

[69] Seymour, *Intimate Papers*, 4:116n; Baker, 8:578.

[70] House Diary, October 26, 1918.

[71] Memorandum, Admiral W. S. Benson to House, October 30, 1918, in House Papers; House Diary, October 29, 1918.

[72] Pershing to House, October 29, 1918; quotation is from second message, October 30, 1918; both in House Papers 11/52; Daniel R. Beaver, *Newton D. Baker and the American War Effort, 1917–1919* (Lincoln, Neb., 1966), pp. 204–05.

[73] W. Stull Holt, "What Wilson Sent and What House Received: Or Scholars Need to Check Carefully," *American Historical Review* 65 (April 1960): 469. Italics mine.

[74] Seymour, *Intimate Papers*, 4:150.

[75] Jacques De Launay, ed., *Secrets diplomatiques, 1914–1918* (Brussels, 1963), pp. 85–93. On pages 83–153 this volume reproduces interpreter Paul Mantoux's notes of the prearmistice conversations. These notes cover all sessions except those of October 30 (morning), November 1 (morning), and November 3, 1918. For the missing discussions, one must turn to Mermeix, *Négociations*; Seymour, *Intimate Papers*, 4:110–200; or to the notes taken by Sir Maurice Hankey, which form the basis of the Mermeix and Seymour versions and a copy of which can be found among the House papers.

[76] Seymour, *Intimate Papers*, 4:168–74. Premier Orlando had arrived in time for the afternoon session on October 30.

[77] Mordacq, p. 80.

[78] House to Wilson, October 30, 1918, in *FRUS: 1918*, sup. 1, 1:425–26.

[79] Seymour, *Intimate Papers*, 4:135–36. For similar remarks on other occasions, see pp. 111, 120.

[80] Ibid., p. 174.

[81] The marshal's project of October 27 had envisaged bridgeheads at Cologne, Coblenz, Mainz, and Strassburg.

[82] Mermeix, *Négociations*, p. 279.

[83] Seymour, *Intimate Papers*, 4:119–24; House to Lansing, November 1, 1918, in *FRUS: 1918*, sup. 1, 1:438; Nelson, pp. 80–82.

[84] Lloyd George had been pressuring his naval advisers for several days to reduce the very demands that he had encouraged them to make in mid-October. Still, he could not have been sure that the French would approve what he finally wished to require of the Germans. On this, see Foch, 2:284.

[85] Just how little reassurance Lloyd George should have taken from Clemenceau's pledge is indicated by a letter of the French am-

bassador in London to his brother, November 9, 1918: "This occupation will last not only until the conclusion of the peace, but until the conditions of this peace are accomplished, that is to say, for a period of several years" (Henri Cambon, ed., *Paul Cambon, Correspondance, 1870–1924*, 3 vols. [Paris, 1940–1946], 3:280).

⁸⁶ Seymour, *Intimate Papers*, 4:121–24. As Hankey recorded in his diary, "His [Foch's] clinching argument was that the soldiers would fight all right, should the peace negotiations fail, if they could start fair and square on the other side of the Rhine, but not otherwise" (Roskill, p. 625).

⁸⁷ Of course, this "dulling" was a relative thing and probably somewhat fleeting as far as Lloyd George was concerned. As late as October 26, 1918, he had remarked to his War Cabinet that "if the [armistice] gauge consisted of territory west of the Rhine, France would not be in any hurry to give it up, but would only be too glad of an excuse to retain it" (War Cabinet, October 26, 1918, CAB 23/14/491B).

⁸⁸ Rudin, Renouvin, and Mayer have not sufficiently emphasized the connection between the purely "military" matters of the armistice and the later peace terms, nor have such students of House's diplomacy as Trask or George and George. For more detail on the Armistice negotiations, see Keith L. Nelson, "What Colonel House Overlooked in the Armistice," *Mid-America* 51 (April 1969): 75–91. For a parallel, later view, see Inga Floto, *Colonel House in Paris: A Study of American Policy at the Paris Peace Conference 1919* (Aarhus, Denmark, 1973), pp. 25–60.

⁸⁹ Jordan, pp. 27–28.

⁹⁰ Erich Eyck, *A History of the Weimar Republic*, 2 vols. (Cambridge, Mass., 1962), 1:1–46.

⁹¹ Matthias Erzberger, *Erlebnisse im Weltkrieg* (Stuttgart, 1920), pp. 326–30; Klaus Epstein, *Matthias Erzberger and the Dilemma of German Democracy* (Princeton, N. J., 1959), p. 278.

⁹² Erzberger, p. 336.

⁹³ Maxime Weygand, *Le 11 Novembre* (Paris, 1932), pp. 60–61.

⁹⁴ Erzberger, p. 336; Weygand, pp. 58–68. Minutes are in Waffenstillstandskommission, *Der Waffenstillstand 1918–1919, Das Dokumentenmaterial der Waffenstillstandsverhandlungen von Compiègne, Spa, Trier und Brüssel*, 3 vols. (Berlin, 1928), 1:20–74. See also Erzberger's report to his government in Erich Matthias, ed., *Die Regierung des Volkgbeauftragten 1918/1919* (Düsseldorf, 1969), pp. 50–52.

Notes to Chapter Two

95 Erzberger, p. 335; Matthias, p. 52.

96 House to Lansing, November 9, 1918, in *FRUS: 1918*, sup. 1, 1:489.

97 Epstein, p. 279.

CHAPTER 2

1 United States, Army, *American Military Government of Occupied Germany, 1918–1920* (Washington, D. C., 1943), pp. 1–23 (hereafter cited as *Military Government*). This is the published version of the first volume of "American Military Government of Occupied Germany, 1918–1920," 4 vols., stencilled (Coblenz, 1921), hereafter cited as "Military Government." For a helpful, if somewhat nationalistic, history of the region, see Hermann Stegemann, *The Struggle for the Rhine* (New York, 1927).

2 On Rhenish separatism, see Jere Clemens King, *Foch versus Clemenceau: France and German Dismemberment, 1918–1919* (Cambridge, Mass., 1960), pp. 1–43, and Rudolf Morsey, *Die deutsche Zentrumspartei, 1917–1923* (Düsseldorf, 1966), pp. 111–28.

3 *Military Government*, pp. 105, 34–37.

4 For precise figures on American strength in Germany in 1918 and 1919, see file 462.00 R294/29, in Department of State (hereafter cited as SD) records, National Archives (hereafter NA), Record Group (hereafter RG) 59. For the size of the Allied occupying forces, see records of the British Imperial War Cabinet, December 3, 1918, CAB 23/42. According to Foch, the army included 17 French, 11 British, 10 American, and 4 Belgian divisions.

5 United States, American Expeditionary Force, Third Army, General Staff, "History of the Third United States Army, November 14, 1918–June 28, 1919" (n.p., n.d.), pp. 1–3; *Military Government*, pp. 25–27; Joseph T. Dickman, *The Great Crusade: A Narrative of the World War* (New York, 1927), pp. 195–99.

6 Henry T. Allen, *The Rhineland Occupation* (Indianapolis, 1927), p. 13.

7 Christian A. Bach and Henry Noble Hall, *The Fourth Division: Its Services and Achievements in the World War* (n.p., 1920), p. 216; William H. Amerine, *Alabama's Own in France* (New York, 1919), p. 220. See also AEF, "History of the Third United States Army," p. 8.

8 Bach and Hall, p. 216.

9 See the Third Army Intelligence summaries for November

273

20–23, 1918, in United States, Department of the Army, *The United States Army in the World War*, 17 vols. (Washington, D.C., 1948), 11:15–30 (hereafter cited as *Army in the World War*).

[10] *Military Government*, p. 35.

[11] Joint War History Commissions of Michigan and Wisconsin, *The 32nd Division in the World War, 1917–1919* (Madison, Wis., 1920), p. 133.

[12] Frank Freidel, *Over There: The Story of America's First Great Overseas Crusade* (Boston, 1964), p. 355.

[13] Ibid., pp. 356–57.

[14] *Military Government*, pp. 27–29.

[15] Francis P. Duffy, *Father Duffy's Story* (New York, 1919), p. 209.

[16] Ibid., p. 310; John H. Taber, *The Story of the 168th Infantry* (Iowa City, Iowa, 1925), p. 251; Freidel, pp. 357–58.

[17] Third Army Intelligence summaries, December 1–3, 1918, in *Army in the World War*, 11:50–57; Dickman, p. 212; Freidel, p. 365. For the German reception of French troops, which was also surprisingly cordial, see Charles F. Horne, ed., *The Great Events of the Great War* . . . (New York, 1923), vol. 7, *1918–1919*, pp. 2–21.

[18] *Military Government*, pp. 20–23, 40–44. See also Gregory Mason, "What the Germans Think and Say," *Outlook* 121 (February 5, 1919): 222–24; Louis Graves, "The American Soldier and the German Mind," *Atlantic* 123 (June 1919): 811–17; and Peter Berg, *Deutschland und Amerika 1918–1929: Uber das deutsche Amerikabild der zwanziger Jahre* (Lübeck, 1963), pp. 7–23.

[19] Joseph Mills Hanson, *South Dakota in the World War, 1917–1919* (n.p., 1940), p. 430.

[20] George Wythe, *A History of the 90th Division* (n.p., 1920), pp. 182–96.

[21] George H. English, *History of the 89th Division* (Denver, 1920), p. 263.

[22] *New York Times*, January 20, 1919; Bach and Hall, p. 233; Ferdinand Tuohy, *Occupied, 1918–1930: A Postscript to the Western Front* (London, 1931), p. 71.

[23] Taber, p. 257. See also, "If America Were Being Ruled as We Are Ruling Part of Germany," *Literary Digest* 61 (June 14, 1919): 90–93.

[24] *New York Times*, December 2, 1918, p. 1. The German press reported that the Americans had arrested the members of the soldier-

worker councils in Trier, but army records indicate that these groups had only been disarmed. See Wolf-Heino Struck, "Die Revolution von 1918/1919 im Erleben des Rhein-Main Gebietes," *Hessisches Jahrbuch für Landesgeschichte* 19 (1969): 397–98.

[25] Dickman, pp. 215–16; Bach and Hall, pp. 221–23. Cologne also was occupied ahead of schedule, because the British army responded to a similar invitation. See J. H. Boraston, *Sir Douglas Haig's Dispatches* (London, 1919), pp. 317–18.

[26] Third Army Intelligence summaries, December 8–12, 1918, in *Army in the World War*, 11:66–74; Taber, p. 253.

[27] There were three corps in the Third Army, with headquarters at Neuwied (III), Cochem (IV), and Wettlich (VII). The III Corps included the 1st, 2nd, and 32nd divisions; IV Corps included the 3rd, 4th, and 42nd divisions; and VII Corps included the 5th, 89th, and 90th divisions.

[28] For the text of the instructions, see *Army in the World War*, 10:85–91. For discussion, see Ernst Fraenkel, *Military Occupation and the Rule of Law: Occupation Government in the Rhineland, 1918–1923* (London, 1944), pp. 7–9.

[29] *Military Government*, pp. 46–49.

[30] Robert Blake, *The Private Papers of Douglas Haig* (London, 1952), p. 345. Foch's directives were supplemented by meetings of the Allied civil-affairs officers on November 22 and December 20, 1918 (minutes of the first are in *Army in the World War*, 10:139–41; minutes of the second are in the Tasker H. Bliss Papers, Library of Congress). The British representative at the first of these meetings reported the following reaction to Marshal Haig: "The French are anxious to be very strict,... [but we] must not forget that it is to our interest to return to Peace methods at once, to have Germany a prosperous, not an impoverished country. Furthermore, we ought not to make Germany our enemy for many years to come. Our Allies will turn our unpopularity to good account, if we do what they ask" (Blake, p. 345).

[31] For example, Fraenkel, pp. 28–34. Fraenkel contends that Allied antagonism to the councils played directly into the hands of reactionaries, encouraging the German High Command to order the dissolution of all councils in the neutral zone.

[32] The Majority Socialists appear to have been in control of most Rhenish councils; see the *New York Times*, December 3, 1918, p. 1; December 9, 1918, p. 1; December 23, 1918, p. 1; Eberhard Kolb,

Die Arbeiterräte in der deutschen Innenpolitik, 1918–1919 (Düsseldorf, 1962), pp. 109–113; and Helmut Metzmacher, "Der Novemberumsturz 1918 in der Rheinprovinz," *Annalen des historischen Vereins für den Niederrhein* 168–169 (1967): 259–65.

33 Arno J. Mayer, *Politics and Diplomacy of Peacemaking: Containment and Counterrevolution at Versailles, 1918–1919* (New York, 1967), pp. 96–116. The French, and Americans too, might have found it a good deal easier to sense the potentially reactionary nature of the Prussian administrative apparatus if the Ebert government in Berlin had been more aware of it. As it was, the Allies seem to have made their decisions in favor of the established authorities (over and against the soldier-worker councils) largely on technical grounds.

34 *Military Government*, p. 49. The American section continued to function at Coblenz after January 1920. See U.S. Army, American Forces in Germany, "American Representation in Occupied Germany, 1920–1921," 2 vols., stencilled (Coblenz? 1922), 2:233–37.

35 *Military Government*, pp. 49–50. Among the subcommissions appointed were the Inter-Allied Economic Commission, Inter-Allied Railway Commission, Inter-Allied Waterways Commission, Coal Distribution Commission, and Inter-Allied Military Food Commission.

36 *Military Government*, pp. 349–50. See also Paul Tirard, *Rapport sur l'administration des territoires occupés de la rive gauche du Rhin pendant l'armistice* ... (n.p., 1920), pp. 101–14; Jean Rousseau, *La haute Commission interalliée des territoires rhénans: ses origines, son organisation, ses attributions* (Mainz, 1923), pp. 24–27.

37 Paul Tirard (1879–1945), later president of the Inter-Allied Rhineland High Commission, had been an aide to the colonial minister and minister of justice before he went to Morocco as General Lyautey's chief civilian assistant in 1912. During the war he had been entrusted with the administrative reorganization of reconquered Alsace, and subsequently, with an economic mission to Russia.

38 A portion of the text is in *Military Government*, pp. 203–04.

39 Part of the text is in *Military Government*, pp. 32–34. The entire memorandum can be found in War Department (hereafter WD) records, Third Army file, Historical subdivision, box 19, NA, RG 120 (American Expeditionary Forces).

40 *Military Government*. pp. 204–06. The full text is in WD records, Third Army file, Historical subdivision, box 19, NA, RG 120.

41 Foch's and Pershing's proclamations are in *Military Government*, pp. 30–32.

[42] See ibid., pp. 103–05, 215–18. The Germans had their greatest difficulty with the sections pertaining to alcohol, sanitation, and travel.

[43] For much of the text, see ibid., p. 103–22.

[44] Allen, p. 49.

[45] These were published in Orders No. 1, Advance General Headquarters, December 13, 1918.

[46] The first division to be relieved was the 42nd (April 1, 1919), followed by the 32nd (April 8), and the 90th (May 6). The remainder stayed on until after the treaty was signed in June.

[47] The best discussion of this problem, although written from the standpoint of the OCCA, Third Army (Colonel I. L. Hunt), is in *Military Government*, pp. 66–85, 333–45. See also "Military Government," 2:224–87. After Advance Headquarters, AEF, was dissolved on June 1, 1919, the OCCA, Third Army (at Coblenz) assumed complete civil authority in the American zone.

[48] Thomas Bentley Mott, *Twenty Years as a Military Attaché* (New York, 1937), p. 254; Jere Clemens King, *Generals and Politicians: Conflict between France's High Command, Parliament and Government, 1914–1918* (Berkeley, 1951), pp. 243–48.

[49] Marshal Ferdinand Foch to the commanders-in-chief, November 16, 1918, and Brigadier General Fox Conner, G-3, to Major General James McAndrew, Chief of Staff, AEF, November 17, 1918, in *Army in the World War*, 10: 91, 101–102; Ferdinand Foch, *Mémoires pour servir à l'histoire de la guerre de 1914–1918*, 2 vols. (Paris, 1931), 2:325–30.

[50] See Major Paul Clark to Pershing, November 13, 14, 1918, Paul Clark Papers, Library of Congress. See also Colonel Thomas B. Mott to Pershing, November 29 and 30, 1918, in *Army in the World War*, 10:185–86, 193–94; and Ferdinand Foch Diary, December 6, 1918, Ferdinand Foch Papers, Bibliothèque Nationale, Paris.

[51] Pershing to Foch, November 28, 1918; Mott to General Maxime Weygand, November 28, 1918; Mott to Pershing, November 29, 1918; and Foch to Pershing, November 30, 1918, in *Army in the World War*, 10:169, 171–72, 185–86, 223.

[52] John J. Pershing Diary, December 6, 1918, John J. Pershing Papers, Library of Congress.

[53] See Mott to Edward M. House, December 3, 1918, in *Army in the World War*, 10:223–24. See also Dickman, pp. 208–10.

[54] Mott to House, December 3, 1918, Foch to Pershing, Decem-

ber 9, 1918, in *Army in the World War*, 10:223–24, 267–68; Pershing Diary, December 6, 7, 10, 11, 1918; Edward M. House Diary, December 4, 5, 1918, Edward M. House Papers, Sterling Library, Yale University.

55 Orders of Foch, December 8, 9, 1918, in *Army in the World War*, 10:259–65.

56 For example, see Bach and Hall, p. 226; Wythe, p. 182.

57 Pershing Diary, December 9, 1918. However, see Dickman, pp. 221–22.

58 Blake, p. 361 (diary entry for April 4, 1919). See also the reports of G-3, Third Army, April 30, 1919, in *Army in the World War*, 11:113–14.

59 Adjutant General to Pershing, December 2, 1918, in *Army in the World War*, 10:209. See also Secretary of War Newton Baker to Secretary of State Robert Lansing, February 11, 1919, Newton Baker Papers, Library of Congress.

60 Foch to Pershing, December 24, 1918; Pershing to Foch, December 26, 1918; Pershing to Baker, January 1, 1919, in *Army in the World War*, 10:347–50, 362–63, 406–407.

61 Memorandum of conversation between Pershing and Foch, December 23, 1918, and Pershing to Foch, April 8, 1919, in ibid., pp. 381–83, 967–68. For the most general of the relevant discussions in the Supreme War Council, see the minutes for the meeting of January 24, 1919, in United States, Department of State, *Papers Relating to the Foreign Relations of the United States: The Paris Peace Conference, 1919*, 13 vols. (Washington, D.C., 1942–1944), 3:705 (hereafter cited as *PPC*). Pershing's position was undoubtedly strengthened by a decision in London on January 24 to slow the demobilization of British armed forces. On this, see War Cabinet, January 28, 1919, CAB 23/9/521; Blake, pp. 350–53; and Charles E. Callwell, *Field Marshall Sir Henry Wilson*, 2 vols. (New York, 1927), 2:212–25.

62 Pershing to Foch, December 26, 1918; Pershing to Baker, January 1, 1919, in *Army in the World War*, 10:362–63, 406–407.

63 Minutes of meeting between Foch and Pershing, December 23, 1918, ibid., pp. 341–42; House Diary, December 26, 1918.

64 J. J. H. Mordacq, *Le Ministère Clemenceau: Journal d'un témoin*, 4 vols. (Paris, 1931), 3:19–20, 93–95 (entries for November 24, 1918 and January 23, 1919); Jane K. Miller, *Belgian Foreign Policy between Two Wars, 1919–1940* (New York, 1951), p. 177.

65 See Memorandum of conversation between Pershing and

Notes to Chapter Two

Foch, December 23, 1918; Mott to Weygand, December 27, 1918; Foch to Pershing, December 29, 1918; Conner to McAndrew, December 29, 1918; Brigadier General W. A. Bethel to McAndrew, December 30, 1918; and Pershing to Foch, January 12, 1919; in *Army in the World War*, 10:331–33, 368–69, 383–87, 483; Pershing to McAndrew, December 30, 1918, Pershing Papers; and Bliss Diary, December 23, 1918.

[66] Pershing Diary, January 20, 1919. On the attempted coup, see Mordacq, 3:87–88, 93–95, 121 (entries for January 12–14, 23, and February 9, 1919), and Henri Cambon, ed., *Paul Cambon, Correspondance 1870–1924*, 3 vols. (Paris, 1940–1946), 3:296–97.

[07] Pershing Diary, January 23, 1919; Foch to Pershing, January 25, 1919, in *Army in the World War*, 10:569–70. See also Pershing's final report to Baker, in United States, War Department, *Annual Report 1919*, 3 vols. (Washington, 1920), 2:602–603.

[68] Clark to Pershing, January 5, 1919, Clark Papers. See also Oswald G. Villard, *Fighting Years: Memoirs of a Liberal Editor* (New York, 1939), p. 389.

[69] Clark to Pershing, December 22, 1918, Clark Papers; Charles Mangin, "Lettres de Rhénanie," *Revue de Paris* 43 (April 1936): 487–88.

[70] Even before Christmas the French had been wondering if General Dickman's wife were "German." Later, they wondered about the general himself. See Clark to Pershing, December 23, 1918, Clark Papers; Joseph Grew to Bliss, January 17, 1919, Bliss Papers; and Acting Secretary of State Frank Polk to Gordon Auchincloss, for Pershing, January 18, 1919, House Papers, Peace Conference file. Pershing investigated Dickman's background and found "no known German connections"; Pershing to Baker, March 28, 1919, Pershing Papers. Nevertheless, on April 15 General Hunter Liggett was appointed to replace Dickman.

[71] Pershing to Dickman, December 22, 1918, Dickman to Pershing, December 25, 1918, Pershing Papers.

[72] Unsigned memorandum to Grew, January 22, 1919, in SD records, file 862.00/99, NA, RG 59; Joseph G. Grew and Walter Johnson, *Turbulent Era: A Diplomatic Record of Forty Years, 1902–1945*, 2 vols. (Boston, 1952), 1:372–74. See also Mangin, pp. 494–96.

[73] Pershing to House, January 25, 1919 (two letters), Pershing Papers.

[74] *Military Government*, pp. 155–67, 185–201.

[75] See Foch to Georges Clemenceau, January 3, 1919, and Foch to Minister of Commerce Lemery, January 15, 1919, in Tirard, p. 27.

[76] Clarence C. Stetson (representative of the United States War Trade Board in Paris) to the Secretary of State, December 14, 1918; second message, December 19, 1918; both in *Army in the World War*, 10:286–87, 318. A third message, December 25, 1918, is in *PPC*, 2:778.

[77] Acting Secretary of State to Ambassador in France, December 21, 1918; second message January 6, 1919; both in *PPC*, 2:771, 792.

[78] See Foch to commanders-in-chief, January 3, 1919, and minutes of a conference on economic questions, January 12, 1919, in *Army in the World War*, 10:420, 481–82. See also General Leroy Eltinge to McAndrew, January 8, 1919, and Eltinge to Pershing, January 17, 1919, in *Army in the World War*, 10:447–48, 508–509.

[79] Notes on conference and meeting of Luxemburg Commission, February 1, 1919, in *Army in the World War*, 10:627–28; André Isambert, "Les Provinces du Rhin pendant l'armistice," *Revue des sciences politiques* 42 (August–December 1919): 441–45. The first (and basic) trade regulations of the Luxemburg Commission date from January 18, 1919.

[80] Tirard, pp. 162–72; Fraenkel, pp. 16–21, 37–41.

[81] Tirard, pp. 162–72. See also Georges Blondel, *La Rhénanie, son passé, son avenir* (Paris, 1921), pp. 201–03; and Ernst Keit, *Der Waffenstillstand und die Rheinfrage 1918/1919* (Bonn, 1940), p. 138.

[82] Jean de Pange, "Notre Politique rhénane," *Le Correspondant* 285 (1921): 204; Robert E. Ireton, "The Rhineland Commission at Work," *American Journal of International Law* 17 (1923): 464.

[83] Charles Seymour, ed., *The Intimate Papers of Colonel House*, 4 vols. (Boston, 1928), 4:276–77.

[84] An interesting hint of American consideration for the Germans is provided by the following reminiscence of Franklin D. Roosevelt, dated May 23, 1942, and published in Elliott Roosevelt, ed., *F. D. R.: His Personal Letters, 1905–1945*, 2 vols. (New York, 1948), 2:1323–24.

We came around a bend in the river [in January 1919] and there was Ehrenbreitstein but no American Flag was flying over it. The flagstaff was bare. I got angrier and angrier as we approached Coblentz. We drove directly to the Headquarters of the Commanding General of the American bridgehead.

I strode into his room and before the poor man could say anything I demanded, in an angry voice, to know "Why the Hell the American Flag was not floating over Ehrenbreitstein." All of my thrill at the expected sight had been dashed to the ground.

He tried to explain to me that his orders were to take no action which would unduly excite or disturb the peace of mind of the German population in Coblentz or in the bridgehead and that he had, therefore, omitted the Flag for fear that it would arouse German sensibilities. . . .

As soon as I got to Paris I dashed around to General Pershing's hotel, told him my story and said to him, "This is wholly outside of my jurisdiction as Assistant Secretary of the Navy but I hope you will rectify what I think is a very grave error. The German people ought to know for all time that Ehrenbreitstein flew the American Flag during the occupation."

General Pershing smiled quietly and said, "You are right. It will be hoisted within an hour."

85 Letters of Instruction 4 (December 23, 1918), 6 (December 27), and 7 (December 27) to Civil Affairs Officers, in WD records, Third Army file, Historical subdivision, boxes 12 and 19, NA, RG 120 (American Expeditionary Forces). An almost complete collection of the Third Army's twenty-one letters of instruction (through May 1919), is to be found in these boxes. In some quarters the new regulations of late December were seen as a kind of "tightening up" by the Americans, but, if this was the case, the tightening was very moderate in scope; see "The Allied Armies in Germany," *Current History* 9 (February 1919): 234–35; and *New York Times*, December 24, 1918, p. 1; December 31, 1918, p. 10; and January 2, 1919, p. 3.

86 Letter of Instruction 2 (December 17, 1918) in WD records, Third Army file, Historical subdivision, box 19, NA, RG 120. See also "Military Government," 3:179–201.

87 "Military Government," 3:184–97. See memorandum by Eltinge for McAndrew, January 8, 1919, in *Army in the World War*, 10: 447–48.

88 *Military Government*, pp. 219–24.

89 Ibid., p. 117.

90 Letter of Instruction 14 (February 24, 1919), in WD records, Third Army file, Historical subdivision, box 12, NA, RG 120.

91 *Military Government*, p. 111.

92 Ibid., pp. 276–81.

93 Ibid., pp. 79–85.

94 Ibid., pp. 279, 282–88; "Military Government," 4:255–73. The British and Belgian figures stood halfway between the French and American.

95 General Malvern-Hill Barnum (acting chief of American Section, Inter-Allied Armistice Commission) to Pershing, February

10, 1919, in *Army in the World War*, 10:668–69. See also Minutes of the Financial Subcommittee of the Supreme Economic Council, February 26, 1919, in SD records, file 180.5201/1, NA, RG 256; and the note by E. F. Wise (British representative on the Supreme Economic Council), February 19, 1919, in Suda Lorena Bane and Ralph Haswell Lutz, *The Blockade of Germany after the Armistice,1918–1919* (Stanford, Calif., 1942), pp. 106–108.

[96] First session of the Supreme Economic Council February 25, 1919, in *PPC*, 10:7.

[97] Allen, p. 41. See also Frank M. Surface and Raymond L. Bland, *American Food in the World War and Reconstruction Period* (Stanford, Calif., 1931), pp. 193, 200; and *PPC*, 10:25–26, 36, 77, 81–83.

[98] *Military Government*, pp. 191–97. See also Fraenkel, p. 41. For a fuller discussion of labor policy, see Ireton, pp. 460–69.

[99] United States, Army, American Expeditionary Forces, General Staff, G-2, *Candid Comment on the American Soldier of 1917–1918 and Kindred Topics, by Germans* (Chaumont, 1919), pp. 27–30.

[100] *Army in the World War*, 11:143–44.

[101] Dickman, p. 240; Allen, p. 77; English, p. 277; James Greenleaf Adams, *Review of the American Forces in Germany* (Coblenz, 1921), pp. 6, 16.

[102] Dixon Wecter, *When Johnny Comes Marching Home* (Boston, 1944), p. 283.

[103] "The Doughboys Occupying Germany are Perfectly Calm but Homesick," *Literary Digest* 61 (June 21, 1919): 52–55.

[104] Amerine, p. 234.

[105] *New York Times*, February 14, 1919, p. 3; Tuohy, pp. 74, 114–5; Ambroise Got, *La Contre-révolution allemande* (Strassburg, 1920), pp. 23–24.

[106] "Military Government," 3:290.

[107] *Bitburger Zeitung*, of December 7, 1918, cited in editors of the *Army Times, The Yanks are Coming: The Story of General John J. Pershing* (New York, 1960), p. 140.

[108] Weekly censorship reports (February–June, 1919) of the Third Army, G-2, in WD records, Third Army file, historical subdivision, box 15, NA, RG 120. An excellent report on the general situation is Harry A. Franck, "Through Germany on Foot; Part II: Coblenz under the Stars and Stripes," *Harper's Magazine* 139 (August 1919): 311–25.

[109] "Military Government," 3:292–300; *New York Times*, April 5, 1919, p. 1.

CHAPTER 3

[1] Erich Eyck, *A History of the Weimar Republic*, 2 vols. (Cambridge, Mass., 1963), pp. 47–63; A. J. Ryder, *The German Revolution of 1918: A Study of German Socialism in War and Revolt* (Cambridge, 1967), pp. 140–217.

[2] See Alfred Milatz, *Wähler und Wahlen in der Weimarer Republik* (Bonn, 1967), pp. 29–39. The vote of 1920 stood in some contrast to that of 1912, the last national election, in which the Socialists received approximately 35 percent of the total, the Center, 16 percent, and conservative parties most of the remainder.

[3] In the elections of 1912 this area had cast a slightly higher percentage of its ballots for the Center Party and a somewhat smaller proportion for the Socialists.

[4] Eyck 1:64–79; Gerhard Schulz, *Zwischen Demokratie und Diktatur* (Berlin, 1963), pp. 101–212.

[5] Hans Sulzer (Swiss minister in Washington) to Secretary of State Robert Lansing, November 26, 1918 (four notes), in United States, Department of State, *Papers Relating to the Foreign Relations of the United States: The Paris Peace Conference, 1919*, 13 vols. (Washington, D.C., 1942–1944), 2:33–36 (hereafter cited as *PPC*).

[6] Gisbert von Romberg (minister in Switzerland) to the President of Switzerland, November 21, 1918, enclosing note of Foreign Minister Wilhelm Solf to American, British, and French governments, ca. November 19, 1918, in *PPC*, 2:40–43.

[7] Klaus Epstein, *Matthias Erzberger and the Dilemma of German Democracy* (Princeton, N. J., 1959), p. 291.

[8] Staatssekretär Paul von Hintze to Solf, November 12, 1918, in German Foreign Ministry (hereafter GFM) records, General Headquarters correspondence, file on "Friedensverhandlungen," serial no. (reel) 5449H.

[9] Harry Graf Kessler, *Tagebücher, 1918–1937* (Frankfurt 1961), p. 32 (entry for November 15, 1918).

[10] This is described in the (June 1919) report of Referat VIII of the Waffenstillstandskommission, *Der Waffenstillstand 1918–1919: Das Dokumentenmaterial der Waffenstillstandsverhandlungen von Compiègne, Spa, Trier und Brussell*, 3 vols. (Berlin, 1928), 2:86–202. (hereafter cited as *Waffenstillstand*).

[11] The transcript of this meeting (December 13, 1918) is in ibid., 1:125–29. See also Matthias Erzberger, *Erlebnisse im Weltkrieg* (Stutt-

gart, 1920), pp. 341–48; and General Pierre Nudant, "A Spa: journal du président de la commission interalliée d'armistice (1918–1919)," *La Revue de France* 2 (March 1925): 281.

[12] The transcript of this meeting (January 15, 1919) is in *Waffenstillstand*, 1:138–60. See also Erzberger, pp. 348–58. Nudant, p. 288; and Ferdinand Foch, *Mémoires pour servir à l'histoire de la guerre de 1914–1918*, 2 vols, (Paris, 1931), 2:329–30.

[13] Staatssekretär Edgar Haniel to Nudant, December 6, 1918, in *Waffenstillstand*, 3:180–81.

[14] See the summary of notes presented by the German Armistice Commission, January 17, 1919, in United States, Department of Army, *United States Army in the World War*, 17 vols. (Washington, D.C., 1948), 10:506–508 (hereafter cited as *Army in the World War*).

[15] General Hans von Hammerstein to Nudant, February 28, 1919, in *Army in the World War*, 10:763–64.

[16] General John J. Pershing to Edward M. House, February 10, 1919, John J. Pershing Papers, Library of Congress.

[17] General Wilhelm Groener to Walter Bacmeister, November 19, 1934, cited in Karl Dietrich Erdmann, *Adenauer in der Rheinlandpolitik nach dem ersten Weltkrieg* (Stuttgart, 1966), p. 39. For a discussion of Groener's role in general, see Otto-Ernst Schüddekopf, "German Foreign Policy between Compiègne and Versailles," *Journal of Contemporary History* 4 (April 1969): 182–89.

[18] Dorothea Groener-Geyer, *General Groener: Soldat und Staatsman* (Frankfurt, 1955), p. 136. The quote is from his diary, January 17, 1919.

[19] *PPC*, 12:9.

[20] Germany, Nationalversammlung, *Verhandlungen der verfassunggebenden deutschen Nationalversammlung, Stenographische Berichte*, February 14, 1919 (Berlin, 1920), 326:66–72. On Brockdorff-Rantzau's foreign policy, see Schüddekopf, pp. 189–97; Hajo Holborn, "Diplomats and Diplomacy in the Early Weimar Republic" in *The Diplomats, 1919–1939*, ed. Gordon A. Craig and Felix Gilbert (Princeton, N.J., 1953), pp. 120–53; and Ludwig Zimmermann, *Deutsche Aussenpolitik in der Ara der Weimarer Republik* (Göttingen, 1958), pp. 41–65.

[21] United States, Army, American Expeditionary Forces, General Staff, G-2, *Press Review* (n.p., 1917–1919), March 24, 1919, pp. 1–2.

[22] See GFM records, Weimar National Assembly period, file

for "Waffenstillstandsangelegenheiten—Besetzte Gebiete," serial no. (reel) 4665.

23 Romberg to Solf, December 13, 1918, in GFM records, Political Department, file for "Waffenstillstands—und Friedensverhandlungen," serial no. 4069 H.

24 Note, in evidence of German feelings, the comments made at the Reichskonferenz of November 25, 1918, by Foreign Minister Solf, ". . . there can be no doubt that . . . America's attitudes, and in particular those of President Wilson, will be of the greatest significance for the future. Economically and financially the whole world will be more or less dependent on the United States. This is the reason that we turned to Mr. Wilson when we saw that the war could no longer be prosecuted, and this is why we will have to be in touch with him during the peace conference too. We will be assisted by the fact that he alone of all the enemy statesmen has a genuine peace program and stands ready to carry it out" (reported in Erich Matthias, ed., *Die Regierung der Volksbeauftragten 1918/1919.* [Düsseldorf, 1969], pp. 155–56). See, in addition, the discussion in the cabinet meeting of January 21, 1919, reported in Charles B. Burdick and Ralph H. Lutz, *The Political Institutions of the German Revolution, 1918–1919* (New York, 1966), pp. 201–02:

> GROENER: The American Army is our firmest ally. It has had enough of the French. The two are absolutely incompatible in character. An American officer made the remark: 'We are done with the French for the next two hundred years.' It all comes from the fact that the French are filthy and the Americans are fanatics about cleanliness. Another reason is that the Americans were poorly lodged and received. Lastly, there was the bad treatment accorded the American command authorities by Foch. . . .
>
> ERZBERGER: The Americans are the ones most sympathetic to us, then the English, then the French, and then the Belgians. . . . [However,] one should not put too much faith in individual news items about American friendliness. Above all we cannot negotiate with them, since they are not represented in the [armistice] commission.

25 Whereas, for example, in December Konrad Adenauer, Oberbürgermeister of Cologne, had believed that "America alone" could prevent the creation of a buffer state on the Rhine, by February and March he had become persuaded that the British were more dependable than the Americans on this score; see Erdmann, pp. 28–48.

26 *Waffenstillstand,* 3:86–87.

27 Ibid., 3:200–01.

Notes to Chapter Three

[28] Erzberger to Nudant, April 19, 1919, *Army in the World War*, 10:985–87.

[29] *Waffenstillstand*, 3:92–107.

[30] Edward M. House Diary, December 9, 1918, in Edward M. House Papers, Sterling Library, Yale University. See also Wolfgang Elben, *Das Problem der Kontinuität in der deutschen Revolution* (Düsseldorf, 1965), pp. 103–06; and Arno J. Mayer, *Politics and Diplomacy of Peacemaking: Containment and Counterrevolution at Versailles* (New York, 1967), pp. 96–116. According to Elben and Mayer, there was even a conscious effort by German moderates and conservatives to use the threat of Allied military intervention as a means to control the German revolution.

[31] Wilhelm Groener, *Lebenserinnerungen: Jugend—Generalstab —Weltkrieg* (Göttingen, 1957), pp. 485–87. Adenauer even wired the president of the Reichstag, Konstantin Fehrenbach, on December 10, 1918, suggesting with disarming innocence that the Reichstag be convened in Limburg/Lahn or Coblenz, in the American zone of occupation, where it would be subjected neither to the pressures of the revolution nor the manipulations of the French; Erdmann, p. 37.

[32] *Press Review*, February 7, 1919.

[33] Ernst Fraenkel, "Das deutsche Wilsonbild," *Jahrbuch für Amerikastudien* 5 (1960): 69–83. As Fraenkel points out, there had also been some antagonism to Wilson.

[34] Some indication of this is given in Brigadier General George Harries to General Malvern-Hill Barnum, March 9, 1919, *Army in the World War*, 10:824–27.

[35] *Berliner Tageblatt*, March 19, 1919.

[36] *Tägliche Rundschau* (Berlin), April 10, 1919, in United States, Army, American Expeditionary Forces, General Staff, G-2, *Candid Comment on the American Soldier of 1917–1918 and Kindred Topics, by Germans* (Chaumont, 1919), pp. 27–30.

[37] *Rheinisch-Westfälische Zeitung* (Essen), May 26, 1919.

[38] *Lokal Anzeiger* (Berlin), May 22, 1919.

[39] Burdick and Lutz, pp. 270–71. The complete transcript, with additions from an alternative protocol, is in Hagen Schulze, ed., *Das Kabinett Scheidemann: 13. Februar bis 20. Juni 1919* (Boppard am Rhein, 1971), pp. 75–77. For the transcript of a further debate, on March 17, 1919, see Schulze, pp. 180–81.

[40] Alma Luckau, *The German Delegation at the Paris Peace Conference* (New York, 1941), pp. 28–29. Officially, the Paxkonferenz

was called Kommission für die Vorbereitung der Friedensverhandlungen.

[41] Ibid., pp. 32–33.
[42] Ibid., pp. 39–40.
[43] Ibid., pp. 41–46.
[44] The demand for a matching troop-free area in France and Belgium was apparently suggested by the General Staff. See the telegram from General Hans von Seeckt to Groener, April 21, 1919, in Friederich von Rabenau, *Seeckt: Aus seinem Leben 1918–1936* (Leipzig, 1940), p. 159.
[45] Luckau, pp. 199–202.
[46] See Keith L. Nelson, "The 'Black Horror on the Rhine': Race as a Factor in Post–World War I Diplomacy," *Journal of Modern History* 42 (1970): 606–09.
[47] *New York Times*, January 26, 1919, p. 9.
[48] Paul von Hindenburg, *Aus Meinen Leben* (Leipzig, 1920), p. 352.
[49] Wilson had been informed of the problem in a letter from General Bliss of May 19, 1919, in which Bliss stated, "no one who knows the degraded character of these (Senegalese)—desires to have American troops serve in any way in association with them" (State Department records, file 185.1711/31, NA, RG 256).
[50] Paul Mantoux, *Les Délibérations du conseil des quatres*, 2 vols. (Paris, 1955), 2:126.

CHAPTER 4
[1] The best exposition of Wilson's and Lloyd George's views at the beginning of the conference is the latter's report to the Imperial War Cabinet on their first meetings, dated December 30, 1918, in David Lloyd George, *Memoirs of the Peace Conference*, 2 vols. (New Haven, 1939), pp. 114–24.
[2] See Jere Clemens King, *Foch versus Clemenceau: France and German Dismemberment, 1918–1919* (Cambridge, Mass., 1969), pp. 19–20, for a translation of this memorandum. See also Georges Vial-Mazel, *Erreurs et oublis de Georges Clemenceau: l'affaire du Rhin* (Paris, 1931), pp. 206–08.
[3] See, for example, the Relevé des Consignes for October 25, 1918, in records of the French Censorship Service (Censure), Bibliothèque de Documentation Internationale Contemporaine, Paris. Note also Marcel Berger and Paul Allard, *Les Secrets de la censure pendant*

la guerre (Paris, 1932), pp. 367–71. That the censor was only partially successful in inhibiting agitation (both for and against various Rhineland "solutions") is evident from Georges Michon, *Clemenceau* (Paris, 1931), pp. 224–25; Pierre Miquel, *La Paix de Versailles et l'opinion publique française* (Paris, 1972), pp. 296–418; and George Bernard Noble, *Politics and Opinions at Paris, 1919: Wilsonian Diplomacy, the Versailles Peace, and French Public Opinion* (New York, 1935), pp. 242–60.

⁴ France, Assemblée Nationale, *Annales de la Chambre des Députés, Débats parlementaires*, December 29, 1918 (Paris, 1918), 107: 3732–34. For discussion, see Arno J. Mayer, *Politics and Diplomacy of Peacemaking: Containment and Counterrevolution at Versailles* (New York, 1967), pp. 170–87. Note particularly Clemenceau's comment that "though I will press certain claims ... I am not disposed to define these here ... because I may have to sacrifice some of them to a higher interest" (Mayer, p. 185).

⁵ The texts are in United States, Department of State, *Foreign Relations of the United States: The Paris Peace Conference, 1919*, 13 vols. (Washington, D.C., 1942–1944), 1:344–54 (hereafter cited as *PPC*), together with House's notes and David Hunter Miller's commentary (pp. 354–65).

⁶ *PPC*, 1:365–71. This note was sent from the State Department to the president at sea, on December 2; Ray Stannard Baker, *Woodrow Wilson and the World Settlement*, 3 vols. (Garden City, N.Y., 1922), 3:55. On its preparation, see Jules Laroche, *Au Quai d'Orsay avec Briand et Poincaré, 1913–1926* (Paris, 1957), pp. 62–63.

⁷ *PPC*, 1:385–406.

⁸ See, for discussion, Robert Binkley, "New Light on the Paris Peace Conference," *Political Science Quarterly* 46 (1931): 335–61; F. S. Marston, *The Peace Conference of 1919: Organization and Procedure* (London, 1944), pp. 35–59; and Harold Nelson, *Land and Power: British and Allied Policy on Germany's Frontiers, 1916–1919* (London, 1963), pp. 128–31.

⁹ Paul Cambon to Georges Clemenceau, November 14, 1918, in *Paul Cambon, Correspondance, 1870–1924*, ed. Henri Cambon, 3 vols. (Paris, 1940–1946), 3:282. See also J. J. H. Mordacq, *Le Ministère Clemenceau: journal d'un témoin*, 4 vols. (Paris, 1931), 3:6.

¹⁰ Lloyd George, 1:88. See also Raymond Poincaré, *Au Service de la France—neuf années de souvenirs*, 10 vols. (Paris, 1926–1933), 10:420.

Notes to Chapter Four

11 French Proposals for the Preliminaries of Peace with Germany, communicated by the French Ambassador, November 26, 1918, Sir George Foster Papers, National Archives, Ottawa, Canada. Clemenceau may have even contemplated playing it both ways simultaneously. Twice during November he had mentioned to Colonel House that he might need American support to battle the British for return of the Saar coal mines; see Edward M. House Diary, November 9 and 30, 1918, Edward M. House Papers, Sterling Library, Yale University.

12 Mordacq, 3:79. Foch had drawn up his memorandum (dated November 27, 1918) at the insistence of Clemenceau and with the help of Jacques Bardoux, who was convinced that "it was important, before the intervention of President Wilson, to achieve an understanding with Britain" (Jacques Bardoux, De Paris à Spa: La bataille diplomatique pour la paix française [Paris, 1921], pp. 51–54). A copy of the memorandum is in Mermeix [Gabriel Terrail], Le Combat des trois (Paris, 1922), pp. 205–10. Lloyd George gives excerpts from the marshal's oral statement in Memoirs, 1:78–80. Miquel, pp. 284–86, reprints a portion of the French procès verbal. See also Charles E. Callwell, Field Marshal Sir Henry Wilson, 2 vols. (New York, 1927), 2:153.

13 Lloyd George, Memoirs, 1:80.

14 British Imperial War Cabinet Papers, CAB 23/42, no. 43, December 18, 1918. This remark takes on added significance because on December 13 Clemenceau had informed the British ambassador in Paris, Lord Derby, that he was anxious to have a French frontier protected by an independent state with its neutrality guaranteed by the Great Powers; British War Cabinet Minutes, March 4, 1919, CAB 23/15, series A.

15 David Hunter Miller, My Diary at the Conference of Paris, 21 vols. (New York, 1924–1926), 1:163.

16 On this, see the statement by André Tardieu in Débats parlementaires, June 25, 1920, 112:2434–47; see also Lloyd George, Memoirs, 2:673; Ferdinand Friedensburg, "Die geheimen Abmachungen zwischen Clemenceau und Lloyd George vom Dezember 1918 und ihre Bedeutung für das Zustandekommen des Versailler Vertags," Berliner Monatsheft 16 (1938): 702–15; and Howard M. Sachar, The Emergence of the Middle East, 1914–1924 (New York, 1969), pp. 253–54. Note, in addition, Clemenceau's enigmatic complaint to Colonel House on the following March 12 that Lloyd George had "broken his word" on the Rhineland, Syria, and the division of reparations; House Diary, March 12, 1919.

Notes to Chapter Four

[17] Lord Esher to Marshal Sir Douglas Haig, December 8, 1918, in Reginald, Viscount Esher, *Journal and Letters*, 4 vols. (London, 1934–1938), 4:219–20. Esher was a retired British statesman living in Paris who was close to the court and cabinet as well as to the military leadership.

[18] Secretary of State Robert Lansing to General Tasker Bliss, December 16, 1918, reprinted in *PPC*, 1:296.

[19] Cary T. Grayson, *Woodrow Wilson, An Intimate Memoir* (New York, 1960), p. 60. The president may have been referring to reparations and other matters as well as to German boundaries.

[20] Reprinted in *PPC*, 1:371–78. This was received by the American embassy (London) on December 7, and cabled to Washington on December 10. Copies were sent to Colonel House in Paris between those two dates. Though the preamble from the original note was missing and several word changes had been made, the memorandum did retain its references to the Rhineland under section 4, "General Guarantee: (a) As safeguard for the carrying out the Preliminaries of the Peace, occupation of German territory; (b) Special military administration of the German territories on the left bank of the Rhine." On this, see Nelson, pp. 135–36.

[21] House's report to Wilson on the London conference is dated December 5, 1918, and is reprinted in *PPC*, 1:340–42. House's diary gives no indication that he was aware of what had transpired regarding the Rhineland. Indeed, before leaving for London, Clemenceau had called on the colonel to give him "his solemn word of honor that he would discuss no question of any importance with [Lloyd] George in London"; House Diary, November 30, 1918. That others were not as trusting as was House is evident from the reaction of Frank Cobb, who was present: "[Clemenceau] assured the Col[onel] nothing would happen at the London Conf[erence]. A great little humorist is G. C." (Frank I. Cobb Journal, November 30, 1918, Frank I. Cobb Papers, Library of Congress). On this, see Inga Floto, *Colonel House in Paris: A Study of American Policy at the Paris Peace Conference 1919* (Aarhus, Denmark, 1973), pp. 68–82.

[22] Lippmann to Sidney Mezes, December 5, 1918, in *PPC*, 1:287–88.

[23] Charles Seymour, *Letters from the Paris Peace Conference* (New Haven, 1965), p. 43 (diary entry of December 17, 1918).

[24] "Possible territorial changes in the German Empire" (sent to Bliss, December 24, 1918), Inquiry Papers, box 21, Sterling Library,

Yale University. See also Seymour, *Letters*, pp. 62–63, diary entry of December 21.

Later, on January 21, 1919, the experts of the delegation suggested as part of their summary "outline of tentative recommendations" (the so-called black book) "that in addition [to Alsace-Lorraine], territory in the basin of the Saar forming a part of Lorraine in 1814 be also restored to France," and "that within the territory west of the Rhine which shall continue to form a part of Germany: a) All fortifications be destroyed; b) The erection of new fortifications be forbidden; and c) The levy or presence of armed forces other than those strictly necessary for police purposes be forbidden." Alternately, it was recommended that "if the proposal for disarmament of the left bank of the Rhine be unacceptable, the fullest consideration be given to the proposal that the French frontier be extended northward to include most of the basis of the Saar [as well as] territory between the Lauter and the Queich, [and thereby] correspond to the frontier of 1814." The full text is in Miller, 2:213–14.

[25] Frederick C. Palmer, *Bliss, Peacemaker: The Life and Times of General Tasker Howard Bliss* (New York, 1934), pp. 354, 359, 368.

[20] Bliss to Secretary of War Baker, January 11, 1919, Newton Baker Papers, Library of Congress. Bliss was apparently the only American commissioner to take the Rhineland seriously. Witness his letter to Baker of December 24, 1918: "I think it likely that they intend to demand the cession of everything west of the Rhine, and they are going to get the appearance of backing from the native populations if they can do it in any way" (Tasker Bliss Papers, Library of Congress).

As for the others, Colonel House suggested to Clemenceau on January 7 that he restrain his countrymen from their advocacy of "foolish suggestions" such as American cancellation of war debts or French annexation of the Rhineland; Charles Seymour, ed., *The Intimate Papers of Colonel House*, 4 vols. (Boston, 1928), 4:270–71. Henry White, in a letter to Henry Cabot Lodge of January 14, registered his dismay at the fact that "one now hears a good deal about the whole of this side of the Rhine ..." (Allan Nevins, *Henry White: Thirty Years of American Diplomacy* [New York, 1930], p. 378). And President Wilson made only one known reference to the Rhineland before the peace conference began, reported indirectly by Lloyd George in his memorandum on their meeting after Christmas: "With regard to France, he [Lloyd George] did not think the President was prepared

to tolerate schemes for the control of the west bank of the Rhine..."
(Lloyd George, *Memoirs*, 1:119).

²⁷ France, Ministère des Affaires Etrangères, *Documents diplomatiques: Documents relatifs aux négociations concernant des garanties de sécurité contre une agression de l'Allemagne* (Paris, 1924), pp. 7–14, translated in André Tardieu, *The Truth about the Treaty* (Indianapolis, 1921), pp. 145–47. General Maxime Weygand testified that a copy was given to Colonel House; Maxime Weygand, *Mémoires*, 3 vols. (Paris, 1953–57), 2:37. For Foch's intentions see Ferdinand Foch Diary, December 31, 1918, Ferdinand Foch Papers, Bibliothèque Nationale, Paris. Note also the relevant comments of Marshal Joffre on January 8, 1919, as reported in *PPC*, 1:381–85.

²⁸ Robert Cecil to Earl Curzon, January 8, 1919, Marquess Curzon Papers, Kedleston Hall, Derby. The marshal did, however, go out of his way to make a statement about the Rhine to American correspondents at the time of the armistice renewal in Trier on January 18: "It is on the Rhine that we must hold the Germans. It is by using the Rhine that we must make it impossible for them to repeat their assault of 1914. The Rhine is the common barrier of all the Allies... The Rhine is the guarantee of peace" (*New York Times*, January 18, 1919, and January 19, 1919). Yet note the disclaimer of Foreign Minister Stephen Pichon a few days later: "Relative to the French attitude toward the holding of the left bank of the Rhine, M. Pichon declared that various published reports were premature and more or less incorrect. When his attention was called to remarks which Marshal Foch had recently made on the subject, M. Pichon said: 'Marshal Foch spoke in his personal capacity on this subject, and it has not yet been considered here'" (*New York Times*, January 27, 1919, pp. 1, 2). Raymond Recouly records that at the end of January he asked Pichon privately why the French had not yet made their demands regarding the frontiers of Germany, and that the latter responded: "M. Clemenceau has a plan for that.... All we have to do is trust him." (Raymond Recouly, *Le Mémorial de Foch: Mes entretiens avec le maréchal* [Paris, 1929], pp. 177–78).

²⁹ Mordacq, 3:117–18. Apparently Balfour passed on his doubts regarding French objectives to Colonel House on February 9; see Seymour, *Intimate Papers*, 4:345.

³⁰ Ibid.; Tardieu, pp. 170–71.

³¹ See Seth P. Tillman, *Anglo-American Relations at the Paris Peace Conference of 1919* (Princeton, N.J., 1961), pp. 101–33.

Notes to Chapter Four

[32] This interesting story is most completely and satisfactorily told by Francis Bullitt Lowry, "The Generals, the Armistice, and the Treaty of Versailles, 1919" (Ph.D. diss., Duke University, 1963), pp. 192–246. For relevant published material, see Seymour, *Intimate Papers*, 4:324–25; Robert Blake, *The Private Papers of Douglas Haig* (London, 1952), pp. 350–53; and *PPC*, 3:694–97, 704–14, 895–933, 970–79.

[33] See Henry Borden, ed., *Robert Laird Borden: His Memoirs*, 2 vols. (New York, 1938), p. 903; Blake, p. 353. On House's role during Wilson's absence, see Floto, pp. 116–63.

[34] It had been agreed before Wilson and Lloyd George left the conference that the Council of Ten would proceed with the drafting of a preliminary peace composed of only military terms; see *PPC*, 3: 370–79, 1000–1009. Foch, in effect, was trying to enlarge the preliminary treaty. See Foch Diary, February 14, 16, 1919.

[35] House to Wilson, February 19, 1919, in Seymour, *Intimate Papers*, 4:332–34. See also Mayer, pp. 450–62.

[36] Wilson to House, February 20, 1919, in House Papers; reprinted in Paul Birdsall, *Versailles Twenty Years After* (New York, 1941), pp. 200–01.

[37] Tillman, pp. 157–60. See also Baker, 1:301–03; Seymour, *Intimate Papers*, 4:336–42, 363–64; and Marston, pp. 13–45.

[38] To be sure, included among the military terms were provisions for the demilitarization of the Rhine; see Lowry, pp. 297–330; *PPC*, 4:183–90, 215–38.

[39] House to Wilson, February 23, 1919, in Seymour, *Intimate Papers*, 4:334.

[40] Ibid., pp. 346–47; diary entry of February 23, 1919.

[41] Ibid. For House's earlier attitude, see Seymour, *Intimate Papers*, 4:346; diary entry of February 19, 1919.

[42] Lord Balfour to House, February 25, 1919, House Papers; reprinted in Birdsall, pp. 202–03. When Balfour wrote this he had just received and read a "Memorandum of the French government on the fixation at the Rhine of the western frontier of Germany and on inter-Allied occupation of the Rhine bridges, February 25, 1919," reprinted in Great Britain, Foreign Office, *Papers respecting Negotiations for an Anglo-French Pact*, Cmd. 2169 (London, 1924), pp. 25–57; and in Tardieu, pp. 147–69. This had been prepared by Tardieu and constituted the first official French statement on the subject. House mentions having received it in a cable to Wilson of February 26, 1919;

Seymour, *Intimate Papers*, 4:351. The argument, roughly, was as follows: If Germany's aggressive tendencies were to be contained, the maritime powers had to have the assurance that French territory could not be overrun from the east within a few days. A limitation on German military forces would not be an adequate guarantee, since Germany's power had to be measured in terms of her population, strategic railways, fortresses, and in the last analysis, the transportation capacity of the Rhine bridges. In default of a league armed force, another defense was necessary. This could only be the Rhine. As for self-determination, the only assertion the French statement made was that no territorial annexation should occur against the desires of the inhabitants.

43 House Diary, February 27, 1919.

44 Vance C. McCormick, *Diaries of Vance C. McCormick...* (privately printed, n.d.), pp. 47–48. However, House recorded in his diary only that he and Tardieu had gotten "nearer together on the questions of the Rhenish republic" (House Diary, March 2, 1919). See also Arthur Walworth, *Woodrow Wilson: American Prophet and World Prophet* (New York, 1958), p. 280.

45 Lloyd George, *Memoirs*, 1:186–91.

46 House to Wilson, March 7, 1919, House Papers.

47 Wilson to House, March 10, 1918, House Papers. Charles Swem, to whom Wilson dictated this message, later reported that when the president described himself as "a little uneasy," he was putting it mildly. Actually, he was deeply concerned; Walworth, p. 280.

48 Lloyd George's notes on the conference of March 7 are in Lloyd George, *Memoirs*, 1:186–91. His discussions with the cabinet are in War Cabinet, February 28 and March 4, 1919, CAB 23/15, series A. On February 28 Lloyd George had inquired as to "what was the Foreign Office view of the proposition to set up a separate German republic West of the Rhine, the Republic to be entirely disconnected from Germany East of the River; and also of the further proposition that Germany should be compelled to relinquish all idea of union with the Germans of Austria. His own mind had not been made up on the matter, and he would like to discuss the whole question with the Cabinet before he returned to Paris. At present he inclined to the view of the Secretary of State for War [Winston Churchill], that we should give France all possible support in respect of her claims and desires in the West, so long as those claims did not leave a legacy of injustice which would rankle as Alsace-Lorraine had rankled." On March 4 Lloyd

George added that he was not convinced that the French government was "really behind" Foch's proposals for an occupation, "though they might appear to be supporting them. It was unlikely that France would accept permanently the burden of maintaining a garrison of something like 300,000 men on the Rhine. What we would say to the French was, that we were relying upon two things: first, the disarmament of Germany; and second, the League of Nations." The acting foreign minister, Lord Curzon, had urged with regard to the separation of the Rhineland that "it should be our policy to do our best for France and to support her claims with a view to diverting the French from their colonial enterprises." Both the secretary of state for war, Winston Churchill, and the chief of the Imperial General Staff, General Sir Henry Wilson, had also been sympathetic to the idea of a buffer state, the former adding that "if the French proposals were to be turned down at the Peace Congress he would prefer that the veto should be imposed by the United States."

[49] Lloyd George, *Memoirs*, 1:186–91.

[50] Seymour, *Intimate Papers*, 4:359. Lloyd George's confidante, Frances Stevenson, recorded in her diary on March 11: "He [Lloyd George] also told Kerr . . . that he [Kerr] was not to come to any arrangements at all with the French. D[avid] hopes by this means to make the French strike a bargain with him" (A. J. P. Taylor, ed., *Lloyd George: A Diary by Frances Stevenson* [New York, 1972], p. 171).

[51] Foreign Office, *Papers respecting Negotiations for an Anglo-French Pact*, pp. 59–67; Tardieu, pp. 172–75; Miller, Vol. 7, document 566.

[52] Lloyd George, *Memoirs*, 1:262–63.

[53] Seymour, *Intimate Papers*, 4:360. The idea of a British (and American) guarantee, however, had been in Lloyd George's head for some days. See War Cabinet, March 4, 1919, CAB 23/15, series A, for his statement that "if the United States and ourselves would guarantee France against invasion, France would be quite satisfied. This, however, was impossible, as the President would not hear of any entangling alliances."

[54] Thomas A. Bailey, *Woodrow Wilson and the Lost Peace* (New York, 1944), pp. 205–08.

[55] Nevins, p. 391; letter dated March 5, 1919.

[56] *New York Times*, January 28, 1919. The *Boston Herald* of December 10, 1918, had asserted, "we shall not grudge this police

Notes to Chapter Four

work nor its possible extension if it facilitates the formation of a government of the people and the establishment of peace. . . ."

[57] *Current History* 9 (March 2, 1919): 558.

[58] *Seattle Post Intelligencer*, January 30, 1919.

[59] The campaign against intervention in Russia had been gathering steam since December; see Mayer, pp. 331–39, 447–49. However, it had been manned largely by critics of the Left like Senators Hiram Johnson (R-Calif.) and Robert LaFollette (R-Wis.). Critics of the Right, like Senator Lodge (R-Mass.), came to support withdrawal from Europe only after they had become convinced that Wilson was not using armed force strongly enough against the Bolsheviks and/or Germans. On this, see Richard Coke Lower, "Hiram Johnson: The Making of an Irreconcilable," *Pacific Historical Review* 41 (November 1972): 505–26.

[60] Baker to Lansing, February 11, 1919, Newton Baker Papers.

[61] *San Francisco Chronicle*, April 12, 1919.

[62] Lloyd George, *Memoirs*, 1:265–66; Tardieu, pp. 176–77; Georges Clemenceau, *Grandeur and Misery of Victory* (New York, 1930), p. 235.

[63] On this, see Nelson, pp. 228–32. Nelson's supposition that even Colonel House did not know of the offer until March 26 would seem to be confirmed by the Auchincloss diary entry of March 22, 1919: "Tardieu came in to see the Colonel this afternoon. He and Clemenceau are very much excited about the settlement of the left bank of the Rhine question. I am afraid the Colonel got them a little too much worked up by holding out to them the hope that they might get something like a guarantee treaty" (Auchincloss Papers). See also Floto, pp. 179–85.

[64] Jacques De Launay, ed., *Louis Loucher: Carnets secrets, 1908–1932* (Brussels, 1962), p. 71; Tardieu, p. 177.

[65] De Launay, p. 72.

[66] Ibid., p. 73. That Lloyd George's conceptions were not much more "permanent" than Wilson's, if they were permanent at all, is attested by his remarks on the subject to the British imperial delegation on May 5, where he spoke (mistakenly) of the guarantee being for "a period of fifteen years." On this, see Nelson, pp. 245–46. Note also the revealing fact that when Wilson presented the guarantee pact to the United States Senate on July 29, 1919, he described it as a "temporary supplement" to the Versailles treaty; Ray Stannard Baker and William E. Dodd, eds., *The Public Papers of Woodrow Wilson*, 6 vols. (New York, 1925–1927), 1:555–56.

Notes to Chapter Four

[67] The memorandum was drawn up by Tardieu. See Tardieu, pp. 178–82, for the text.

[68] De Launay, p. 73.

[69] *PPC*, 11:121–33. (Meetings of the American commissioners, March 19, 20, 21, 1919). See also Seymour, *Intimate Papers*, 4:394–95, diary entry of March 20, 1919.

[70] Miller, 1:195–96; vol. 7, documents 559–64; Auchincloss Diary, March 22, 26, 1918, Auchincloss Papers; House Diary, March 23, House Papers.

[71] House Diary, March 27, 1919; reprinted in Nelson, pp. 231–32.

[72] Paul Mantoux, *Les Délibérations du conseil des quatres*, 2 vols. (Paris, 1955), pp. 50–51.

[73] Memorandum dated March 28, 1919, in Woodrow Wilson Papers, VIII-A, Library of Congress.

[74] Lloyd George, *Memoirs*, 1:266–73. See also Mayer, pp. 519–20.

[75] Lloyd George, ibid., pp. 274–76.

[76] "Amendments Proposed by France," House Papers, 29/47.

[77] Baker, 2:29–30, 46; Mayer, pp. 559–603.

[78] Great Britain, Parliament, *Parliamentary Debates, Official Report, House of Commons*, April 2, 1919, 114:1304–350; Lloyd George, *Memoirs*, 1:371–84; Mayer, pp. 604–46.

[79] Mordacq, 3:211–14; Baker, 2:39; Mayer, pp. 647–72.

[80] Ray Stannard Baker Diary, April 2, 3, 1919; Ray Stannard Baker Papers, Library of Congress; reprinted in Mayer, p. 572.

[81] House Diary, April 5, 1919.

[82] Mordacq, 3:205–06.

[83] Edward M. House and Charles Seymour, eds., *What Really Happened at Paris* (New York, 1921), p. 464.

[84] Birdsall, p. 209.

[85] Henry Wickham Steed, *Through Thirty Years, 1892–1922: A Personal Narrative* (Garden City, N. Y., 1925), pp. 311–13.

[86] Philip M. Burnett, *Reparations at the Paris Peace Conference from the Standpoint of the American Delegation*, 2 vols. (New York, 1940), 2:94–95. See also Minutes of the second and third meetings (March 11 and 13) of the Third Subcommittee of the Commission on Reparation of Damage, in Department of State (hereafter SD), file 181.13301, National Archives (hereafter NA), Record Group (hereafter RG) 256.

[87] On this, see Alexander L. George and Juliette L. George, *Woodrow Wilson and Colonel House: A Personality Study* (New York, 1956), pp. 254–56. See also Floto, pp. 186–214.

Notes to Chapter Four

89 Seymour, *Intimate Papers*, 4:401.

90 Ibid., p. 405; diary entry of April 8, 1919.

91 Mantoux, 1:203–07.

92 Ibid., pp. 209–10, 224–28. On this, see Nelson, pp. 249–81.

93 Mordacq, 3:214–15; Foch Diary, April 10, 1919. Clemenceau may also have been influenced by the fact that King Albert of the Belgians, in a session of the Council of Four on April 4, had opposed a lengthy occupation; Mordacq, 3:210–11; Paul Hymans, *Mémoires*, 2 vols. (Brussels, 1958), 1:392. On the general atmosphere during these days, note Sir William Wiseman's remark of April 8 that "since Saturday last [April 5] the position has substantially improved"; Wiseman to Lord Reading, April 8, 1919, in the Wiseman Papers, Sterling Library, Yale University. See also Stevenson's diary, April 5, 1919, in Taylor, p. 178.

94 Wilson to House, April 12, 1919, House Papers, 49/20. As Harold Nelson notes (*Land and Power*, pp. 239–40), the timing of this memorandum would appear to rule out the hypothesis that the April 11 French acceptance of the Monroe Doctrine amendment to the League Covenant had had anything to do with Wilson's acceptance of an occupation. See Birdsall, p. 213.

95 Memorandum on the Amendments proposed by France to the Agreement suggested by President Wilson regarding the Rhine Frontier, April 12, 1919; House Papers, 29/47.

96 House Diary, April 15, 1919.

97 Ibid.

98 Auchincloss Diary, April 15, 1919. Lloyd George later believed that "it was an essential part of the compromise" that Clemenceau would take action to inhibit the increasingly vicious attacks upon President Wilson that were being made in the French press (Lloyd George, *Memoirs*, 1:280). Lloyd George seems to have based his opinions on the published version of House's diary (see Seymour, *Intimate Papers*, 4:407–08). A careful reading of the diary indicates, however, that the bargain was complete before the subject of the press was even broached. Clemenceau's directions to the press were more a by-product than an element of the understanding. On this, see Mordacq, 3:222–23; Baker, pp. 79–81. See also the chapter by Jean-Baptiste Duroselle, in J. Joseph Huthmacher and Warren I. Sussman, eds., *Wilson's Diplomacy: An International Symposium* (Cambridge, 1973), pp. 19–44.

99 André Tardieu in *Le Temps*, September 15, 1921, p. 1.

Notes to Chapter Four

[100] Lloyd George, *Memoirs*, 1:280.

[101] Printed in *PPC*, 5:117–18. These were the future Articles 428–31 of the Treaty of Versailles.

[102] Mantoux, 1:318–19. See also *PPC*, 5:113–14.

[103] Lloyd George, *Memoirs*, 1:371–84; Sisley Huddleston, *Peace Making at Paris* (London, 1919), pp. 142–55; Mayer, pp. 627–32, 642–46.

[104] Jean Martet, *Clemenceau* (London, 1930), p. 148.

[105] Recouly, p. 205; Alexandre Ribot, *Journal d'Alexandre Ribot et correspondances inédites 1914–1922* (Paris, 1936), pp. 268–69. On April 14 and 15, Foch even attempted to browbeat the Belgian foreign minister, Paul Hymans, into pressuring the French government on behalf of an extended occupation; Notes of Paul Hymans on meeting with Foch, April 14 and 15, 1919, Paul Hymans Papers, Archives Generales du Royaume, Brussels, Belgium.

[106] Recouly, pp. 206–09. Foch's relations with Clemenceau are summed up in Foch Diary, April 10, 12, and 13, 1919.

[107] Clemenceau, pp. 131–32; Recouly, pp. 229–31; King, pp. 53–54.

[108] Mermeix, p. 226; Tardieu, pp. 187–89; Clemenceau, p. 125; Mantoux, 1:443–44; and King, pp. 56–59.

[109] Noble, pp. 254–55.

[110] Mordacq, 3:245; Mermeix, pp. 226–31; Recouly, pp. 198–204; Tardieu, p. 212; René Michel M. Lhopital, *Foch, l'armistice et la paix* (Paris, 1938), pp. 207–15; and King, pp. 61–64. The powers of the Reparations Commission regarding the occupation were defined in Article 430 of the treaty.

[111] Tardieu, pp. 209–12.

[112] *PPC*, 5:244–48.

[113] Ibid., p. 357. This later became Article 429, Part 3. On the controversy leading to its adoption, see Clemenceau, p. 237; and Miller, 19:485–89.

[114] See the articles by both men in *Le Temps* (Paris), September 12, 13, 15, 16, 18, 22, 1921.

[115] King, p. 65. Poincaré's letter is printed in English translation in Lloyd George, *Memoirs*, 1:281–84. It was not taken seriously by either the British or Americans.

[116] Recouly, pp. 223–28; Tardieu, pp. 189–94.

[117] Callwell, 2:183–86; *PPC*, 5:415. For French strategy, see Mordacq, 3:214–15. For an example of later suspicions, see Baker, 1:488 (Woodrow Wilson on June 3, 1919).

118 For example, Jan Christian Smuts to Lloyd George, May 5, 1919, in W. K. Hancock and J. van der Poel, eds., *Selections from the Smuts Papers*, 4 vols. (London, 1965), 4:149. Smuts had expressed great fear of an occupation "with an army to which there is no limit and for which Germany had to pay...."

119 Mantoux, 1:490, 2:8–9; *PPC*, 5:471; Callwell, 2:191.

120 See Minutes of the Subcommittee Dealing with Urgent Problems, March 19 and 22, 1919, in SD records, file 181.16101/2 and 5, NA, RG 256. Note also Burnett, vol. 1, document 257.

121 Armistice, Part I, Section IX, in H. W. V. Temperley, ed., *A History of the Peace Conference at Paris*, 6 vols. (London, 1920–1924), 1:463.

122 Minutes of Armistice Subcommission, January 9, 1919, in SD records, file 185.121/5, NA, RG 256.

123 German Armistice Commission to Inter-Allied Armistice Commission, March 14, 1919 (citing note of January), published in the United States, War Department, *The United States Army in the World War*, 17 vols. (Washington, D.C., 1948), 10:853–54. See also Memorandum of Major Lawrence Whiting to Norman Davis, March 29, 1919; 10:925–26.

124 Belgium had not yet received its much desired reparations priority. See Jane K. Miller, *Belgian Foreign Policy between Two Wars, 1919–1940* (New York, 1951), pp. 63–65; Minutes of Armistice Subcommission, February 27, 1919, in SD records, file 185.121/5, NA, RG 256.

125 Appendix A to Report of Supreme War Council, April 22, 1919, in *PPC*, 8:465–70.

126 David Hunter Miller, "Cost of American Troops on the Rhine," *Current History* 16 (July 1922): 614–16.

127 Ibid.; Memorandum to Bliss from DeLancey Kountze, April 17, 1919, Bliss Papers.

128 General Nudant to Chiefs of Armistice Missions, May 16, 1919, in *The United States Army in the World War*, 10:1107–08.

129 Miller, *Diary*, 1:155; vol. 6, documents 464, 465, 468, 477.

130 Minutes of Armistice Subcommission, February 28, 1919, in SD records, file 185.121/5, NA, RG 256.

131 Foch memorandum of May 9, 1919, Bliss Papers.

132 Bliss to Wilson, May 19, 1919, Bliss Papers.

133 Minutes of the Council of Four, May 29, 1919, in *PPC*, 6:108–11.

CHAPTER 5

1 General Leroy Eltinge to Pershing, January 17, 1919, in United States, Department of the Army, *The United States Army in the World War*, 17 vols. (Washington, D.C., 1948), 10:508–09 (hereafter cited as *Army in the World War*).

2 Memorandum of Wallace Day to the author, September 8, 1961. See also United States, Army, *American Military Government of Occupied Germany 1918–1920* (Washington, D.C., 1943), pp. 55, 350 (hereafter cited as *Military Government*. References to the original four-volume work, issued in stencilled form [Coblenz, 1920] are cited as "Military Government").

3 Draft of letter from Edward M. House to Lloyd George and Clemenceau, February 2, 1919, John J. Pershing Papers, Library of Congress.

4 Memorandum by W. H. Owen on the Inter-Allied Organization for the Administration of Occupied Territory, February 13, 1919, in Department of State (hereafter SD) records, file 185.001/48, National Archives (hereafter NA), Record Group (hereafter RG) 256.

5 *Military Government*, pp. 350–51; interview of author with Wallace Day, January 21, 1965.

6 Day to author, March 3, 1965. Day, who became deputy Rhineland commissioner in May, was born in 1891 in Leesville, Connecticut. In 1917 and 1918 served with the War Trade Board in Washington.

7 Day to author, September 8, 15, 1961.

8 *Military Government*, pp. 49–54. See also Pierrepont B. Noyes Diary (in the possession of his family, Oneida, New York), May 3, 1919.

9 Memorandum of E. F. Wise, April 5, 1919, in Minutes of Supreme Economic Council (hereafter SEC), April 7 and 9, 1919, in United States, Department of State, *Papers Relating to the Foreign Relations of the United States: The Paris Peace Conference, 1919*, 13 vols. (Washington, D.C., 1942–1944), 10:149–54 (hereafter cited as *PPC*). For a German discussion of what was occurring, see the report of Referat VIII of the Waffenstillstandskommission, *Der Waffenstillstand 1918–1919: Das Dokumentenmaterial der Waffenstillstandsverhandlungen von Compiègne, Spa, Trier und Brussell*, 3 vols. (Berlin, 1928), 2:86–202. See also Klaus Schwabe, *Deutsche Revolution und Wilson Friede: Die amerikanische und deutsche Friedensstrategie Zwischen Ideologie und Machtpolitik 1918/19* (Düsseldorf, 1971), pp. 480–89.

Notes to Chapter Five

[10] Day to author, February 2, 1962.

[11] After March 24 the Council of Ten (the two foremost delegates of France, Britain, Italy, Japan, and the United States) had been subdivided into the Council of the Heads of State (the Council of Four) and the Council of Foreign Ministers.

[12] Memorandum of Wise, *PPC*, 10:147–54. Tirard's preferences are discussed in Paul Tirard, *Rapport sur l'administration des territoires occupés de la rive gauche du Rhin pendant l'armistice.* . . . (n.p., 1920), pp. 101–14. See also Paul Tirard, *La France sur le Rhin: Douze années d'occupation rhénane* (Paris, 1930), pp. 97–101.

[13] See Minutes of the SEC, April 7 and 14, 1919, in *PPC*, 10:109, 160–61. The final recommendation is dated April 15, 1919; *PPC*, 10: 202–08.

[14] See Memorandum of the American section of the SEC, April 14, 1919, in *PPC*, 10:173–74. See also Alexander Legge to Bernard Baruch, April 16, 1919, in SD records, file 181.228/2, NA, RG 256; and Legge to Baruch (two letters), April 17, 1919, Bernard Baruch Papers, Princeton University Library.

[15] Minutes of the Council of Ten, April 21, 1919, *PPC*, 4:600. Many of the Americans were greatly surprised that the French agreed. See, for example, Vance McCormick, *Diaries of Vance C. McCormick* . . . (privately printed, n.d.), p. 72.

[16] Regarding this appointment, which was actually approved, see the correspondence among Baruch, Legge, Vance McCormick, and Joseph Grew, April 16–25, in SD records, file 181.228/2-8, NA, RG 256.

[17] Noyes (1870–1959) was president of Oneida Limited, a silverware manufactory of Oneida, New York. During the war he had been in Washington with the Fuel Administration and had had close contact with Baruch and Legge at the War Industries Board. He was the son of John Humphrey Noyes, founder of the Oneida Community.

[18] For the story of Noyes's "conversion" into a commissioner, see Pierrepont B. Noyes, *A Goodly Heritage* (New York, 1958), pp. 238–40. See also Noyes's Diary, May 4, 1919; and McCormick and Baruch to Joseph Grew, April 25, 1919, Baruch Papers.

[19] The words were Legge's; Noyes, *A Goodly Heritage*, p. 239; Noyes Diary, May 4, 1919.

[20] Noyes, *A Goodly Heritage*, pp. 239–40; Noyes Diary, May 6, 1919.

[21] Stuart had been home secretary in India before the war and

Notes to Chapter Five

during 1916–18 was with the Ministry of Food in London. He was fifty-nine in 1919.

[22] Noyes Diary, May 1 and 6, 1919.

[23] Noyes to Legge, May 2, 1919, in SD records, file 181.228/30, NA, RG 256.

[24] Noyes to Legge, May 8, 1919, in SD records, file 181.228/33, NA, RG 256. See also Baruch to Wise, May 10, 1919, Baruch Papers.

[25] Noyes Diary, May 8 and 10, 1919.

[26] Ibid., May 10, 1919.

[27] Ibid., May 17, 1919.

[28] Ibid., May 13, 1919. See also Noyes's final report to the Department of State, received March 16, 1921, in SD records, file 862t.01/245, NA, RG 59.

[29] Noyes Diary, May 26, 1919.

[30] Ibid., May 10, 1919. See also Tirard, *La France*, pp. 109–13.

[31] Ibid., May 13, 1919. For Paris decisions, see Minutes of Subcommittee on Germany, April 29, 1919, in SD records, file 180.05901/4, NA, RG 256.

[32] Noyes Diary, May 1, 1919. The story of Day's activities is contained in the memoranda of Day to the author, September 25, 1961, and January 31, 1962. His information reached the SEC on May 5, 1919 (see *PPC*, 10:230) but had been supplied by McCormick to the Superior Blockade Council a good deal earlier. The French waited to reply until June 2, 1919 (see *PPC*, 10:326–27, 337–39), at which time they "explained" that the shipments in question had been among stocks of goods manufactured in Alsace (as part of Germany) before the armistice. In actual fact, however, many of the carloads had been of cotton textiles, products that had been in short supply within Germany during the war. In this regard note McCormick's diary entry of May 19, 1919: "I think this great tenderness for Foch is due to suggestions from certain Cabinet Ministers, who want to play a lone game, in German commerce" (McCormick, *Diaries*, p. 88).

[33] Noyes Diary, May 17, 1919. See also the memorandum of the Subcommittee on Germany to the SEC, May 16, 1919, in *PPC*, 10:271.

[34] Noyes Diary, May 22 and 26, 1919. See also the Minutes of the SEC, May 19 and 26, in *PPC*, 10:271–95.

[35] Noyes Diary, May 27, 1919.

[36] General Tasker Bliss to General James W. McAndrew, May 1, 1919, in *Army in the World War*, 10:1069–72. See also the Minutes of the Council of Four, May 1, 1919, in *PPC*, 5:395; Paul Mantoux,

Les Délibérations du conseil des quatres, 2 vols. (Paris, 1955), 1:441–42, 2:8–9; and minutes of the Inter-Allied Committee on the Left Bank of the Rhine, May 31, 1919, in SD records, file 181.22401/1, NA, RG 256.

[37] Mantoux, 2:8–9. In early May the Council of Four had accepted Lloyd George's proposal that a general clause be inserted in the treaty to give a separate convention regarding the occupation full contractual force; Minutes of the Council of Four, May 1, 1919, in *PPC*, 5:395.

[38] Bliss to Baruch, May 22, 1919, Tasker Bliss Papers, Library of Congress; David Hunter Miller, *My Diary at the Conference of Paris*, 21 vols. (New York, 1924–1926), 19:490–94. That important officers in the British army much preferred military to civilian control of the peacetime occupation is indicated not only by the action of the military representatives at Versailles but also by the letter of General Sir William Robertson, commander of the British Army on the Rhine, to General Sir Henry Wilson, July 3, 1919, complaining with reference to the High Commission, of the complicated "legacy" that president Wilson had left the Rhineland; William R. Robertson Papers, Kings College Library, London. See, in addition, J. H. Morgan, *Assize of Arms: The Disarmament of Germany and Her Rearmament, 1919–1939* (New York, 1946), p 8.

[39] Pershing to Bliss, May 2, 1919, in *Army in the World War*, 10:1069–72.

[40] Noyes Diary, May 13, 1919. See also Bliss to Wilson, May 19, 1919, Bliss Papers.

[41] Noyes Diary, May 17, 1919.

[42] Ibid. For the text of Stuart's draft, see the appendix to J. Willard Raynesford, "Pierrepont B. Noyes, American Rhineland Commissioner" (senior thesis, Williams College, ca. 1942). Stuart's role should not obscure the fact that other British representatives were also making contributions to the conception of "civilianizing" the Rhineland. See, for example, the memorandum of S. P. Waterlow, May 4, 1919, in SD records, file 185.1711/19, NA, RG 256. This analysis suggested that there would be a continuing need for the "Rhineland Commission" after the peace.

[43] Noyes to Legge, May 17, 1919, Pierrepont B. Noyes Papers, Colgate University.

[44] Noyes Diary, May 17, 1919.

[45] Minutes of the Council of Four, May 29, 1919, in *PPC*, 6:108–11.

⁴⁶ Baruch to Wilson, May 17, 1919, and Bliss to Baruch, May 22, 1919, Baruch Papers.

⁴⁷ Bliss to Wilson, May 19, 1919, Bliss Papers.

⁴⁸ Wilson to Bliss, May 20, 1919, Woodrow Wilson Papers, Library of Congress.

⁴⁹ General John J. Pershing Diary, May 23, 1919, Pershing Papers. The discussion may also have touched upon General Mangin's recent activities with the Rhineland separatists.

⁵⁰ Noyes Diary, May 26, 1919. For memorandum, see appendix to Raynesford, "Pierrepont B. Noyes."

⁵¹ Noyes Diary, May 27, 1919.

⁵² The full text is in Minutes of the Council of Four, May 29, 1919, in *PPC*, 6:108–11.

⁵³ Noyes Diary, June 4, 1919.

⁵⁴ Minutes of the Council of Four, May 29, 1919, in *PPC*, 6:108–11. See also Mantoux, 2:253–54.

⁵⁵ The best descriptions of the separatists in this period are Jere Clemens King, *Foch versus Clemenceau: France and German Dismemberment, 1918–1919* (Cambridge, Mass., 1960), pp. 28–41; Günther Meinhardt, *Adenauer und der rheinische Separatismus* (Recklinghausen, 1962), pp. 7–27; Karl Dietrich Erdmann, *Adenauer in der Rheinlandpolitik nach dem ersten Weltkrieg* (Stuttgart, 1966), pp. 21–48; and Rudolf Morsey, *Die deutsche Zentrumspartei, 1917–1923* (Düsseldorf, 1966), pp. 117–28, 246–52.

⁵⁶ Hans Adam Dorten, "The Rhineland Movement," *Foreign Affairs* 3 (April 1925): 403.

⁵⁷ King, p. 42. See also Charles Mangin, "Lettres de Rhénanie," *Revue de Paris* 43 (April 1936): 500–14; and Hans Adam Dorten, "Le Général Mangin en Rhénanie," *Revue des deux mondes* 40 (July 1, 1937): 45–48.

⁵⁸ King, pp. 30–32. See also Marshal Emile Fayolle to Foch, March 6, 1919, in Miller, vol. 6, document 463, and Georges Vial-Mazel, *Erreurs et oublis de Georges Clemenceau: L'affaire du Rhin* (Paris, 1931), pp. 75–78.

⁵⁹ Erwin Goebel, *Die pfälzische Presse im Abwehrkampf der Pfalz gegen Franzosen und Separatisten, 1918–1924* (Ludwigshafen, 1931), pp. 34–90; Paul Jacquot, *General Gérard und die Pfalz (November 1918–Dezember 1919)* (Berlin, 1920), pp. 66–115.

⁶⁰ King, pp. 75–76. For statistics on the separatists and texts of their proclamations, see *Military Government*, pp. 291–315.

Notes to Chapter Five

[61] Mangin, pp. 517–18; King, pp. 80–84; Morsey, pp. 252–56. Resumés of Mangin's conversations with Dorten are in the Charles Mangin Papers, 149 AP 21, Archives Nationales, Paris. See also the report of Clemenceau's "investigator" Jules Jeanneny, May 27, 1919, in the Ray Stannard Baker Papers, Princeton University Library. Jeanneny attests that both Fayolle (Mangin's immediate superior) and Foch were aware of what Mangin was doing. To be sure, Fayolle was no "friend" of Mangin's, but Foch was, and had just visited him in Mainz, May 13–15; Emile Fayolle, *Cahiers secrets de la grande guerre* (Paris, 1964), pp. 328–29.

[62] Report of Jeanneny to Clemenceau, May 27, 1919, Baker Papers. See also Georges Clemenceau, *Grandeur and Misery of Victory* (New York, 1930), pp. 216–18.

[63] Report of Jeanneny to Clemenceau, May 27, 1919. Jeanneny's interviews with Mangin and with Colonel Denvignes (Mangin's emissary to Liggett) are reprinted in Georges Wormser, *La République de Clemenceau* (Paris, 1961), pp. 504–07. See also Hunter Liggett, *Commanding an American Army: Recollections of the World War* (Boston, 1925), pp. 142–44.

[64] Pershing Diary, May 22, 1919; telephone conversation between Liggett and Eltinge (in Paris), May 22, 1919, in *Army in the World War*, 10:1129. Wilson's letter to Clemenceau, dated May 23, 1919, is reprinted in Clemenceau, pp. 215–16. As a result of a misunderstanding on the phone between Liggett and Eltinge, Pershing and Wilson were under the impression that the "deputies" who had been scheduled to come to Coblenz were French instead of German. King, who follows Dorten's account, mistakenly attributes the source of this error to Noyes (King, pp. 85–86), but neither Noyes nor Liggett was confused about the matter; see Noyes Diary, May 22 and 27, 1919; Liggett, p. 144. Dorten later blamed the whole failure to secure American support upon this "error"; Hans Adam Dorten, *La Tragédie rhénane* (Paris, 1945), p. 70.

[65] Memorandum for Noyes from Major I. L. Hunt, officer in charge of civil affairs (OCCA), Headquarters, Third Army, June 4, 1919, Baruch Papers.

[66] Mangin was encouraging Dorten again as early as May 25, the day after the general had seen Jeanneny; Dorten, *Tragédie*, p. 71. Indeed, Mangin was so undaunted that he followed the same procedure with the British General Clive on May 30 that he had previously employed with Liggett, sending emissaries to warn Clive that the sep-

aratists were about to act. The result was as disastrous for Mangin as on the earlier occasion, for within twenty-four hours Clive was in Paris reporting to Lloyd George and being counselled to oppose separatist activity; Memorandum of General George S. Clive, described in Terence Prittie, *Konrad Adenauer, 1876–1967* (Chicago, 1971), pp. 47–48.

⁶⁷ Texts of German protests are in German Foreign Ministry (hereafter GFM) records, Weimar National Assembly (hereafter WNA) period, file for "Besetzte Gebiete im Westen," serial no. (reel) 4662. Though the Americans and British showed some antagonism to separatism (see the *New York Times*, June 5, 7, 1919), they were not as favorable to Berlin as Dorten and others supposed. Liggett, for example, not only forbade antiseparatist demonstrations (as well as separatist), but also banned local newspapers for accusing the French of aiding Dorten and enjoined the Prussian government from appointing a new and more "rhenish" provincial Oberpräsident. The principal motivation was clearly to maintain the status quo. See the *New York Times*, June 4, 8, 1919.

⁶⁸ Mangin, pp. 520–24; Clemenceau, pp. 218–25; King, 88–104. Clemenceau's reaction to Mangin was conveyed in a telegram from the Ministry of War, June 2, 1919. (Clemenceau was minister of war as well as premier.) The "famous" letter of June 1, 1919, which Mangin received on June 3 and which directed him to observe "complete neutrality in everything that has to do with purely political affairs," was written before Clemenceau knew of the "Wiesbaden revolution." A copy of this letter is in the Baker Papers.

The extent of Clemenceau's anger is conveyed in his remark of June 16, 1919 to Wilson and Lloyd George: "The Marshal has placed at Mainz and [Landau] two generals of whom one, Mangin, is a good soldier but a bad politician, while the other, Gérard, is a mediocre soldier and an execrable politician. He has placed them there with political intent. A policy of separatism is what he offers us" (Mantoux, 2:44).

⁶⁹ Germany, Nationalversammlung, *Verhandlungen der verfassunggebenden deutschen Nationalversammlung, Stenographische Berichte*, May 12, 1919 (Berlin, 1920), 327:1081–1111.

⁷⁰ E. L. Dresel to American Mission in Paris, May 10, 1919, in *PPC*, 12:110–21. General Harries to American Mission in Paris, April 30, 1919, in *PPC*, 12:86–87.

⁷¹ *Tägliche Rundschau*, May 8, 1919.

⁷² Germany, Auswärtiges Amt. [Foreign Ministry], Geschäft-

stelle fur die Friedensverhandlungen, *Ausserungen der zur Prüfung der Friedensbedingungen in Berlin eingesetzten Arbeitskommission* (Berlin, n.d.), pp. 16–20.

[73] See GFM records, WNA period, file for "Besetzte Gebiete im Westen," serial no. (reel) 4662. Observations of the German Delegation on the Conditions of Peace, dated May 29, 1919, is reprinted in *PPC*, 6:759–901.

[74] Alma Luckau, *The German Delegation at the Paris Peace Conference* (New York, 1941), pp. 302, 374–76.

[75] See Fritz T. Epstein, *Matthias Erzberger and the Dilemma of German Democracy* (Princeton, N.J., 1959), pp. 305–09. An interesting insight into the significance of the Rhineland Commission for these discussions is provided by the reports of what was said. Thus Colonel Arthur Conger's memorandum to his superiors, May 20, 1919, included the following excerpt from his own statement to Erzberger and Count Johann von Bernstorff, who was also present at the preliminary interview: "Sixth, that as regards the Government of the Occupied Territory, measures already taken in the establishment of the new board on economic control, which I described in brief, indicated that the Government of this territory would not be such as would be found either binding upon the people in the sense of a purely military government or one which would isolate the people economically from the rest of Germany."

Actually, Conger may have intimated a good deal more, since both Bernstorff and Ernst Langwerth, who talked to Conger's assistants, transmitted a somewhat different version to Brockdorff-Rantzau in Paris. Bernstorff reported (May 19) that "Conger contended that the treaty conditions would be much milder in practice than one might assume from the text; for example, a joint economic commission of the Allied powers is envisaged for the Rhineland which will prevent the military commanders from gaining influence, as well as forestall any attempts to make the region French." Langwerth reported (May 18) that, according to the Americans, "there was going to be a civil commission for the occupied territories in which the various Allies including America would participate and to which the military would be subordinate. This commission would see to it that local German authorities, as far as possible, would be able to function undisturbed, and that trade between this area and the rest of Germany would be able to develop freely." These reports have been published in Fritz T. Epstein, "Zwischen Compiègne und Versailles: Geheime amerikanische

Notes to Chapter Five

Militärdiplomatie in der Periode des Waffenstillstandes 1918/19," *Vierteljahrshefte für Zeitgeschichte* 3 (1955): 430–36.

[76] Smuts had written to Lloyd George on May 5, 14, 22, 1919, and to Wilson on May 14, 30, 1919, with regard to the occupation. See W. K. Hancock and J. van der Poel, eds., *Selections from the Smuts Papers*, 4 vols. (London, 1965), 4:149–209. He also wrote to Lloyd George about it on June 2, 3, 4, 1919, 4:215–21.

[77] David Lloyd George, *Memoirs of the Peace Conference*, 2 vols. (New Haven, 1939), 1:462–81.

[78] Ibid., pp. 464, 466, 480. For the full record, see the British Empire Delegation Minutes, May 30 and June 1, 2, 1919, in the Sir George Foster Papers, folder 143, Public Archives of Canada, Ottawa.

[79] Minutes of the Council of Four, June 2, 1919, in *PPC*, 6:141–45; Mantoux, 2:267–68.

[80] Minutes of the Council of Four, June 2, 1919, in *PPC*, 6:141–45; Mantoux, 2:267–68. See also Edward M. House Diary, May 30 and June 2, 1919, in Edward M. House Papers, Sterling Library, Yale University; André Tardieu, *The Truth About the Treaty* (Indianapolis, 1921), p. 196; and J. J. H. Mordacq, *Le Ministère Clemenceau: Journal d'un témoin*, 4 vols. (Paris, 1931), 3:292.

[81] Seth P. Tillman, *Anglo-American Relations at the Paris Peace Conference of 1919* (Princeton, N.J., 1961), pp. 349–62; Ray Stannard Baker, *Woodrow Wilson and the World Settlement, Written from His Unpublished and Personal Material*, 3 vols. (Garden City, N.Y., 1922), 2:111; Alexander L. George and Juliette L. George, *Woodrow Wilson and Colonel House: A Personality Study* (New York, 1956), pp. 264–65.

[82] Italics mine. For transcript of this meeting of June 3, see Baker, 3:469–504.

[83] Loucheur was minister of armament and aviation as well as a delegate to the Peace Conference. Davis was American Ambassador to Great Britain.

[84] Minutes of the Inter-Allied Committee of the Left Bank of the Rhine, May 31–June 9, 1919, in SD records, file 181.22401/1–6, NA, RG 256. Noyes Diary, June 9, 1919; Ernst Fraenkel, *Military Occupation and the Rule of Law: Occupation Government in the Rhineland, 1918–1923* (London, 1944), pp. 71–77. See also Schwabe, pp. 489–93.

[85] John Davis to Woodrow Wilson, June 10, 1919, Wilson Papers, VIII A.

[86] Minutes of the Inter-Allied Committee on the Left Bank of the

Rhine, May 31, and June 4 and 5, 1919. Foch's written comments of June 5 and 9, 1919 are printed in *PPC*, 6:386–89. His personal notebook would seem to indicate that his arguments were offered with considerable sincerity; see Ferdinand Foch Diary, May 31 and June 1, 1919, Ferdinand Foch Papers, Bibliothèque Nationale, Paris.

[87] Report of the Inter-Allied Committee on the Left Bank of the Rhine, June 9, 1919, is printed in *PPC*, 6:379–81. The convention and memorandum are in *PPC*, 6:381–86.

[88] Davis to Wilson, June 10, 1919, Wilson Papers.

[89] Ibid.

[90] Report of the Inter-Allied Committee on the Left Bank of the Rhine, June 9, 1919.

[91] Bliss to Wilson, June 6, 1919, in SD records, file 185.1711/46, NA, RG 256. Wilson responded with the hope that this would be possible; Wilson to Bliss, June 7, 1919, in Bliss Papers.

[92] Mantoux, 2:366–67.

[93] Ibid., 392–94; Minutes of the Council of Four, June 12, 1919, in *PPC*, 6:327–30, 343–44. Actually, there is the possibility that Clemenceau had committed himself to Lloyd George a day or so earlier, at least with regard to occupation costs. This might well be the meaning of the document of ca. June 10, which Lloyd George later published in his *Memoirs* (p. 486)—"the result of prolonged discussions between M. Loucheur and myself"—and which is obviously a preliminary draft of the "declaration" of June 16, 1919. (It stipulated occupation limits of 110,000 men and 240 million gold marks as well as an agreement not to hinder German trade.) This hypothesis might also explain why Lloyd George was generally optimistic about negotiations regarding the occupation when he met with the British Empire delegation on June 10, 1919. See the British Empire Delegation Minutes, June 10, 1919, Foster Papers.

[94] On June 11, Clemenceau complained that the projected convention was "too complicated" and suggested a "new" statute that Foch had drafted. On June 12, he promised that if his colleagues approved the proposals of the committee, he would accept them, although he preferred a shorter formula; Minutes of the Council of Four, June 11, 12, 1919, *PPC*, 6:294, 329.

[95] Minutes of the Council of Four, June 13, 1919, in *PPC*, 6:379–86. The amendment for Article V had been prepared by the president on his own typewriter; see Wilson Papers, VIII A, folder for June 10, 1919.

Notes to Chapter Five

[96] James T. Shotwell, *At the Paris Peace Conference* (New York, 1937), p. 369; Mantoux, 2:408–12.

[97] The text of the declaration of June 16, is in *PPC*, 6:521–22.

[98] The official reply dated June 16, 1919, is in *PPC*, 6:926–96. The convention was handed to the Germans at the same time as the reply.

[99] Davis had made this point to Wilson in his letter of June 10, 1919, Wilson Papers.

[100] The Germans had inquired on June 24, 1919 (after they had agreed to sign the treaty) as to when "negotiations" could begin with regard to the Rhineland Agreement. Upon being informed by the Allies that the agreement had to be signed at the same time as the treaty, they had submitted a formal protest on June 27, although they had intimated that they would not press their objections if conversations could take place later on the subject. See the Minutes of the Council of Four, June 25 and 27, 1919, *PPC*, 6:655, 730–34.

[101] This is clear from the Report of the German Peace Delegation to the German government on the Reply of the Allies, June 17, 1919, in Luckau, pp. 485–86.

[102] Ibid. Note also the comments of the financial and economic experts in their report to the German government, June 18, 1919: "The occupied territories are to be governed in the future in a way that is even more like a disguised annexation than would appear from the first draft" (Luckau, p. 489).

[103] Legationssekretär von Brentano to Matthias Erzberger, June 20, 1919, in the Weimar file of the German Armistice Commission records, Deutsches Zentralarchiv, Potsdam.

[104] John Maynard Keynes, *The Economic Consequences of the Peace* (New York, 1920), pp. 104–05.

[105] Statistics in SD records, file 462.00 R 294/29, NA, RG 59. See also *Army in the World War*, 11:144.

[106] "Military Government," 3:292–95.

[107] "Military Government," 3:296.

[108] *Amaroc News*, June 3, 1919.

[109] Arno J. Mayer, *Politics and Diplomacy of Peacemaking: Containment and Counterrevolution at Versailles, 1918–1919* (New York, 1967), p. 808. But see also John K. Zeender, "The German Center Party during World War I: An Internal Study," *Catholic Historical Review* 62 (1957): 467; and Morsey, pp. 180–95.

[110] Mayer, pp. 808–10.

[111] Epstein, p. 322; Mayer, p. 811–12.

CHAPTER 6

[1] Bliss and White stayed on in the French capital following Wilson's departure; Polk joined them from Washington in early July. The group was primarily concerned with preparing treaties for Austria, Bulgaria, and Turkey. See Seth P. Tillman, *Anglo-American Relations at the Paris Peace Conference of 1919* (Princeton, N.J., 1961), pp. 365–92; and David F. Trask, *General Tasker Howard Bliss and the "Sessions of the World," 1919* (Philadelphia, 1966), pp. 62–70.

[2] Minutes of the Council of Heads of Delegations, September 9, 1919, in United States Department of State, *Papers Relating to the Foreign Relations of the United States: The Paris Peace Conference, 1919*, 13 vols. (Washington, D. C., 1942–1944), 8:154–67 (hereafter cited as *PPC*).

[3] Britain and France were not waiting for ratification to release their businessmen, and it was the unanimous opinion of the State Department experts that even a few weeks headstart might mean a decided advantage. See United States, Department of State, *Papers Relating to the Foreign Relations of the United States: 1919*, 2 vols. (Washington, D. C., 1933), 2:234–40 (hereafter cited as *FRUS: 1919*).

[4] Noyes to American Commissioners, August 13, 1919, Pierrepont Noyes Papers, Colgate University Library.

[5] United States, Army, *American Military Government of Occupied Germany, 1918–1920* (Washington, D.C., 1943), p. 84. Actually, Allen did not arrive in Coblenz to take command until July 8, 1919; see Henry T. Allen, *My Rhineland Journal* (Boston, 1923), July 7, 8, 1919, pp. 8–9.

[6] Allen, *Journal*, July 8, 1919, p. 9.

[7] See statistics sheet in Department of State (hereafter SD) records, file 462.00 R294/29, National Archives (hereafter NA), Record Group (hereafter RG) 59.

[8] Henry T. Allen, *The Rhineland Occupation* (Indianapolis, 1927), p. 128.

[9] Secretary of War Newton Baker to President Woodrow Wilson, July 15, 1919, Newton Baker Papers, Library of Congress.

[10] The act had more than doubled the existing army, providing for 11,450 officers and 223,580 men. On this, see Edward M. Coffman, *The War to End All Wars: The American Military Experience in World War I* (New York, 1968), pp. 5–19. For the most complete published version of Baker's activities in 1919, see Edward M. Coffman, *The Hilt of the Sword: The Career of Peyton C. March* (Madison, Wis., 1966), pp. 175–97.

Notes to Chapter Six

[11] *New Orleans Times-Picayune*, June 17, 1919. Baker had said something quite similar when the administration bill had first been introduced in January 1919; United States, Congress, House of Representatives, Committee on Military Affairs, *Hearings on Army Reorganization*, 65th Cong., 3rd sess., 1919, p. 13.

[12] *New York Times*, August 19, 1919, p. 1.

[13] Ibid., June 17, 1919, p. 20.

[14] E. L. James in the *New York Times*, May 12, 1919, p. 1.

[15] Ibid., May 18, 1919, p. 14.

[16] Ibid., June 17, 1919, p. 1.

[17] *Boston Evening Transcript*, June 26, 1919.

[18] *New York Times*, July 30, 1919, p. 1.

[19] Thomas A. Bailey, *Woodrow Wilson and the Great Betrayal* (New York, 1945), pp. 7–8; see also Louis A. R. Yates, *United States and French Security 1917–1921* (New York, 1957), pp. 116–45.

[20] *Springfield Republican*, July 8, 1919.

[21] United States, Congress, *Congressional Record*, 66th Cong. 1st sess., August 23, 1919, 58:4502. Apparently the "declaration" was never submitted by the president to the Congress. On September 3, however, Wilson did transmit the agreement of June 13, 1919, defining the relations between the Allied military authorities and the Inter-Allied High Commission; see ibid., pp. 4886–887.

[22] Ibid., August 1, 1919, 58:3465; August 20, 1919, 58:4033–034.

[23] United States, Congress, Senate, Committe on Foreign Relations, *Hearings on the Treaty of Peace with Germany*, 66th Cong., 1st sess., 1919, pp. 549–50.

[24] Bailey, pp. 84–89.

[25] For example, Senate Joint Resolution 60, introduced by Senator Walter Edge (R-N.J.) on June 23, 1919, had excepted those individuals enlisting specifically for overseas; *Congressional Record*, 66th Cong., 1st sess., 58:1542.

[26] For example, Senate Resolution 181, introduced by Senator Medill McCormick (R-Ill.) on September 8, 1919. See ibid., 58:4997.

[27] See, for example, the speech of Representative William R. Wood (R-Ind.) on August 28, 1919, in ibid., 58:4461–62. The day before, Wood had introduced House Resolution 266, protesting against the sending of American forces to Silesia; ibid., August 27, 1919, 58: 4439.

[28] Ibid., September 29–30, 1919, 58:6068, 6122–28, 6147–49. See also the *New York Times*, September 30, 1919, p. 1.

29 On September 9, 1919, Senator Gilbert Hitchcock (D-Nebr.) had introduced Senate Joint Resolution 106, authorizing the president to use troops in Armenia; ibid., 58:5067.

30 Ibid., September 24, 1919, 58:5849.

31 *Nation* 109 (September 6, 1919): 323. For a helpful discussion of the Irreconcilables' attitudes and strategy, see Ralph A. Stone, "The Irreconcilables' Alternatives to the League of Nations," *Mid-America* 49 (July 1967): 163–73, as well as Ralph A. Stone, *The Irreconcilables: The Fight against the League of Nations* (Lexington, Ky., 1970), pp. 106–40.

32 *Congressional Record*, 66th Cong. 1st sess. October 17, 1919, 58:7054. There were also a number of Irreconcilables who tended to put France and French needs in a special category, as Lloyd E. Ambrosius points out in "Wilson, the Republicans, and French Security after World War I," *Journal of American History* 59 (September 1972): 345–48.

33 "Future Relations with Germany," *Literary Digest* 62 (July 5, 1919): 21–24.

34 *Nation* 109 (July 12, 1919): 27.

35 George Boas, "The Wonder of It," *Atlantic* 124 (September 1919): 376–81.

36 *New York Times*, November 8, 1919, p. 13.

37 *Boston Evening Transcript*, June 30, 1919.

38 *Philadelphia Public Ledger*, August 1, 1919.

39 *New York Times*, September 7, 1919, p. 11.

40 E.g. *New York Times*, September 15, 1919, p. 13; *New Yorker Staats-Zeitung*, September 15, 1919.

41 *New York World*, October 29, 1919. The first and second drafts of this article are in the clippings file of the Noyes Papers.

42 For example, *New Yorker Staats-Zeitung*, September 15, 1919.

43 Acting Secretary William Phillips to American Mission, October 25, 1919, in SD records, file 185.1711/112, NA, RG 256.

44 See Allen, *Journal*, October 2, 5, 1919, pp. 37–39; letter of Allen to General John J. Pershing, October 19, 1919, in John J. Pershing Papers, Library of Congress; dispatch of Phillips to American Mission, November 1, 1919, in Frank Polk Papers, Sterling Library, Yale University; and Secretary Robert Lansing to American Mission, November 4, 1919, in *FRUS: 1919*, 2:243.

45 Bliss to Allen, October 13, 1919, and Bliss to Polk, October 14, 1919. See also the correspondence between American Mission and

State Department, October 1–November 4, 1919, in *FRUS: 1919*, 2: 241–44; and Sally Marks and Dennis Dulude, "German-American Relations, 1918–1921," *Mid-America* 53 (October 1971): 216–20.

46 Lansing to Wilson, November 20, 1919, Woodrow Wilson Papers, VI, 40.

47 Edith Bolling Wilson to Lansing, undated, Wilson Papers, VI, 40.

48 Lansing to Wilson, November 26, 1919, Wilson Papers, VI, 40.

49 See the correspondence between Lord Curzon and Sir Eyre Crowe, December 6–8, 1919, in Great Britain, Foreign Office, *Documents on British Foreign Policy, 1919–1939*, First series, 17 vols. (London 1947–), 2:496–98 (hereafter cited as *DBFP*). See also Lansing to American Mission, December 6, 1919, in *PPC*, 11:692; and Lansing to American Mission, December 6, 1919, in SD records, file 763.72119/8124, NA, RG 59.

50 American Mission to Lansing, December 6, 1919, in *PPC*, 11:693.

51 Lansing to Wilson, December 7, 1919, in *PPC*, 11:695.

52 Edith Bolling Wilson to Lansing, December 8, 1919, in *PPC*, 11:696.

53 American Mission to Lansing, December 8, 1919, in *PPC*, 11:699–700; American Mission to Lansing, December 9, 1919, in SD records, file 763.72119/8198, NA, RG 59. See also Trask, p. 69.

54 German Peace Delegation to Allied Supreme Council, December 14, 1919, *DBFP*, 2:539–42.

55 Minutes of the Council of Heads of Delegations, October 28, 1919, in *PPC*, 8:784–86. Appendix A (8:795–96) gives Foch's letter to the Supreme Council of October 15, 1919.

56 Lansing to American Mission, November 4, 1919, in SD records, file 763.72119/7519, NA, RG 59.

57 Ambassador Jules Jusserand to Undersecretary Polk (in Washington), December 28, 1919, in SD records, file 763.72119/7519½, NA, RG 59.

58 Bliss to Polk, January 9, 1920, in SD records, file 763.72119/9181, NA, RG 59.

59 Ibid.

60 Noyes Diary, November 21, 1919.

61 Ibid., December 13, 1919; Sir Harold Stuart to Curzon, De-

cember 10, 1919, *DBFP*, vol. 5, no. 3110. The memorandum of four legal advisers, January 2, 1920, is in the Noyes Papers.
[62] *Military Government*, p. 361.
[63] Ibid.; Allen, *Journal*, January 5, 1920, p. 67.
[64] Noyes to Lansing, January 6, 1920, in SD records file 763.72119/8585, NA, RG 59.
[65] Lansing to Wallace, January 9, 1920, in SD records, file 763.72119/8567, NA, RG 59. The heart of the instructions was as follows: "This Government can not admit jurisdiction of that [High] commission over portion of Rhenish Provinces occupied by the American forces. Consequently, neither you [Noyes] nor Gen. Allen should issue any ordinances which conflict with or exceed the terms of the armistice, which the Department [of State] regards as continuing in force as to the United States. You should, however, maintain the closest touch with the high commission and endeavor in so far as possible to conform administrative regime within territory occupied by American forces to regime adopted by high commission for other portions of occupied territory."
[66] *Military Government*, p. 362. Allen, *Journal*, January 14, 1920, p. 71. See also Allen, *Rhineland Occupation*, pp. 116–26; Noyes Diary, January 24, 1920; and *DBFP*, vol. 9, nos. 1, 2, 8, 11.
[67] Sanford Griffith, "Occupying the Rhineland," *New Republic* 21 (January 7, 1920): 168–71.
[68] *New Yorker Staats-Zeitung*, January 16, 1920.
[69] *New York Times*, February 17, 1920, p. 8.
[70] Bailey, pp. 208–70.
[71] Noyes's longer messages to the Secretary of State are as follows: February 7, 1920, in Lansing Papers; February 27, 1920, in *FRUS: 1920*, 2:289; March 17, 1920, in SD records, file 862t.01/8, NA, RG 59; and April 23, 1920, in SD records, file 763.72119/9723, NA, RG 59. On March 6, 1920, Noyes had submitted a resignation to the department to be accepted if his superiors felt it necessary; Noyes to Acting Secretary, in *FRUS: 1920*, 2:296.
[72] Bailey, pp. 259–62; *Amaroc News*, March 10–12, 1920; for the text of the letter, see the *New York Times*, March 9, 1920.
[73] Wilson to Polk, March 15, 1920, in Wilson Papers. This statement indicates that Wilson was aware both of Premier Millerand's threat to extend the Rhineland occupation (made on February 6) and of French efforts at the London Conference (beginning February 12) to reach agreement on a seizure of the Ruhr. Noyes's telegram of

March 6, which directed attention to Millerand's proposals in London, had reached Washington on March 8, 1920.

74 Bainbridge Colby had taken the oath of office as secretary of state on March 23, 1920. For a discussion of his policies, see Daniel M. Smith, *Aftermath of War; Bainbridge Colby and Wilsonian Diplomacy, 1920-1921* (Philadelphia, 1970).

75 Wilson to Colby, April 8, 1920, in Bainbridge Colby Papers, Library of Congress. Of course, Wilson had rekindled his longstanding anger against the Allies as early as the previous summer. Lansing had noted in August that the president had complained, for the third time in a few weeks, of "the greed and utter selfishness" of the Allied powers; Robert Lansing Diary, August 20, 1919, Robert Lansing Papers, Library of Congress. Moreover, in the spring of 1920 Wilson does not seem to have had much sympathy for the Germans either. In April and May he had vetoed American participation in the San Remo and Spa conferences because Lloyd George had wanted to invite them; Wilson to Colby, April 23 and May 29, 1920, Colby Papers.

76 Wallace to the Acting Secretary of State, March 19, 1920, in SD records, file 862t.01/9, NA, RG 59.

77 Dresel to Colby, March 23, 1920, in SD records, file 862t.01/14, NA, RG 59.

78 Wallace to the Acting Secretary of State, March 19, 1920, in SD records, file 862t.01/9, NA, RG 59. See also, Allen, *Journal*, March 17 and 18, 1920, p. 91; and Noyes Diary, March 20, 1920.

79 Dresel to Colby, April 3, 1920, in SD records, file 862t.01/28, NA, RG 59.

80 Memorandum for Colby from Baker, April 6, 1920, Colby Papers.

81 See Baker to Colby, April 6, 1920, in Baker Papers; also Baker and Colby to Wilson, April 10, 1920, in Colby Papers. Note the memorandum of G. Howland Shaw (from the office of Undersecretary Polk), April 6, 1920, summarizing the cases for and against troop withdrawal, in SD records, file 862t.01/76, NA, RG 59.

82 See Noyes's telegram to Colby, April 23, 1920, in SD records, file 763.72119/9723, NA, RG 59. See also Noyes's statement in *Chicago Tribune*, April 28, 1920.

83 Noyes to Colby, April 23, 1920, in SD records, file 763.72119/9723, NA, RG 59.

84 "Now as to Noyes, he is a good American, a thoroughly honest man, and a man of quite a little initiative. On the other hand, he

is, to my mind, too impulsive and lacking in balance, and he is entirely without experience. . . . If I understand our present policy, it is to stand aloof from all direct participation in Commission work abroad. Yet, so far as I can see, and as in fact, Noyes told me, he acts practically as if he had a voice equal to that of the other Allied representatives" (Dresel to Polk, April 24, 1920, Polk Papers).

85 Castle to Polk, May 11, 1920, and Colby to Baker, May 13, 1920; both in SD records, file 462.00 R294/39, NA, RG 59. See also Castle to Dresel, May 18, 1920, Ellis L. Dresel Papers, Houghton Library; Dresel to Allen, June 8, 1920, in Henry T. Allen Papers, Library of Congress; and Wallace to Colby, May 12, 1920, in *FRUS: 1920*, 2:386.

86 Castle to Dresel, May 18, 1920, Dresel Papers. Polk later wrote of Noyes, "an excellent man, but the job was getting on his nerves," Polk to Dresel, June 2, 1920, Polk Papers. That President Wilson had nothing to do with relieving Noyes is indicated by the fact that Noyes was received socially in the former president's home on January 7, 1924, less than one month before Wilson died; see Noyes's memorandum on the visit, and Edith Bolling Wilson to Noyes, January 27, 1924, in the possession of the Noyes family, Oneida, New York.

87 Colby to Noyes, May 17, 1920, in *FRUS:1920*, 2:327.

88 This was House Resolution 500, adopted March 25, 1920; see *Congressional Record*, 66th Cong., 2nd sess., March 19, 1920, 59:4642–43, and March 25, 1920, 59:4814. See also the *Amaroc News*, March 27, 1920.

89 *Congressional Record*, 66th Cong., 2nd sess., April 1, 1920, 59:5101.

90 Ibid., April 14, 1920, 59:5661–67. Secretary Baker quickly called Kahn's attention to the fact that he (Kahn) had grossly overestimated the costs of the occupation in this debate, and Kahn inserted the secretary's letter in the *Congressional Record*, April 15, 1920, 59:5688.

91 Bailey, pp. 290–94. Congressman William E. Mason (R-Ill.) did introduce House Concurrent Resolution 55 on April 19, 1920, urging the withdrawal of American troops from Europe, but although this attracted some attention in the press, it was never acted upon; *Congressional Record*, 66th Cong., 2nd sess., April 19, 1920, 59:5881.

92 Bailey, pp. 290–94.

93 Baker to Allen, April 30, 1920, Allen Papers.

94 "French Watch on the Rhine," *Literary Digest*, 65 (April 24,

1920): 9–10. Castle wrote to Dresel, April 6, 1920, that "feeling in this country is bound to be deeply sympathetic with France because papers in general have stressed the dangers of German militarism. . . ." (Dresel Papers).

95 *Los Angeles Times*, April 15, 1920.

96 "French Watch on the Rhine," pp. 9–10.

97 *Nation* 110 (April 24, 1920): 535–36.

98 "The Problem of Germany," *New Republic*, 22 (April 28, 1920): 261–62.

CHAPTER 7

1 Minutes of the Heads of Delegations, July 26, 1919, in United States, Department of State, *Papers Relating to the Foreign Relations of the United States: The Paris Peace Conference, 1919*, 13 vols. (Washington, D.C., 1942–1944), 7:308 (hereafter cited as *PPC*).

2 Meeting of the Supreme Council, June 27, 1919, in Paul Mantoux, *Les Délibérations du conseil des quatres*, 2 vols. (Paris, 1955), 2:552.

3 Report of the Military Representatives, July 10, 1919, in Department of State (hereafter cited as SD) records, file 184.611/531, National Archives (hereafter NA), Record Group (hereafter RG) 256.

4 Memorandum of Marshal Ferdinand Foch to General Tasker Bliss, May 9, 1919, in Tasker Bliss Papers, Library of Congress.

5 John J. Pershing Diary, June 27, 1919, John J. Pershing Papers, Library of Congress; Bliss Diary, July 16, 1919, Bliss Papers.

6 Pershing Diary, June 30, 1919; Memorandum of conference with Foch, June 30, 1919, Pershing Papers. The stipulation regarding the one division was later to be altered.

7 See entry for July 2, 1919, in Henry T. Allen, *My Rhineland Journal* (Boston, 1923), p. 6.

8 Allen was born in Sharpsburg, Kentucky, in 1859 and was commissioned a lieutenant in 1882. Among his many assignments was a year as military governor of the island of Leyte during the Philippine insurrection (1901). For a brief biography, see United States, Army, American Forces in Germany, Assistant Chief of Staff, G-2, "American Representation in Occupied Germany, 1920–1921," 2 vols., stencilled (Coblenz?, 1922), 1:255–57 (hereafter cited as "American Representation: 1920–1921").

9 Bliss to President Woodrow Wilson, June 25, 1919, Bliss Papers.

Notes to Chapter Seven

[10] Bliss Diary, July 16, 1919.

[11] Memorandum of conference with Foch, July 25, 1919, Pershing Papers; Pershing Diary, July 25, 1919.

[12] Report of Allen, July 30, 1919, Bliss Papers, Allen, *Journal*, July 30, 1919, pp. 17–18. Ehrenbreitstein had assumed great symbolic significance because the huge American flag (30 x 35 feet) that flew above its walls could be seen for miles in all directions. Indicative of American feeling is the fact that the flag, which was taken down upon withdrawal of the United States army, January 24, 1923, was returned to the European Theater during World War II and raised again over Ehrenbreitstein, April 6, 1945.

[13] See Pershing to Foch, August 1, 1919, Bliss Papers; Pershing Diary, August 6, 1919; and Pershing to Foch, August 13, 1919, Frank Polk Papers, Sterling Library, Yale University.

[14] Pierrepont Noyes to Pershing, August 9, 1919, Pershing Papers; Noyes to Undersecretary of State Frank Polk, August 12, 1919, Polk Papers. See also Allen to Pershing, August 9, 1919, Allen Papers, Library of Congress.

[15] Pershing to Bliss, August 22, 1919, Pershing Papers; Foch to Pershing, August 27, 1919, Allen Papers.

[16] The four Kreise north of the Moselle had been evacuated by the Third Division on August 5; the bridgehead Kreise had been given up by the First Division on August 15. See the *New York Times*, September 5, 1919, and United States, Army, American Forces in Germany, *American Military Government of Occupied Germany, 1918-1920* (Washington, D.C., 1943), pp. 84–85 (hereafter cited as *Military Government*. References to the original stencilled version [Coblenz, 1920] are cited as "Military Government.")

[17] Allen, *Journal*, August 31, 1919, p. 30. During this same period the French had pressed the British to allow them to occupy Cologne but had found the latter unalterably opposed to giving up the city; see Earl Balfour to Earl Curzon (foreign secretary), August 14, 1919, S. P. Waterlow (Coblenz) to Curzon, August 27, 1919, in Great Britain, Foreign Office, *Documents on British Foreign Policy, 1919–1939*, 1st series, 17 vols., (London, 1947–), vol. 5, nos. 70, 84 and 97, respectively (hereafter cited as *DBFP*).

[18] Pershing to Allen, August 25, 1919, Pershing Papers.

[19] Pershing Diary, August 2, 1919.

[20] Allen to Pershing (Washington), October 19, 1919, Pershing Papers.

Notes to Chapter Seven

[21] Allen to Pershing (Washington), September 23, 1919, Pershing Papers.

[22] Allen to General Peyton C. March (Washington), December 20, 1919, Allen Papers.

[23] Polk to Allen, November 6, 1919, Allen Papers; Allen to Polk, November 11, 1919, Polk Papers; March to Allen, November 25, 1919, Allen Papers.

[24] *Military Government*, pp. 271–74. The elections took place in October and November 1919.

[25] Ibid., pp. 116–17.

[26] "Military Government," 3:261–62.

[27] *Military Government*, pp. 108–16.

[28] Ibid., pp. 203–08. About 100 marriages involving premarital pregnancy had been allowed during the spring and summer; ibid., pp. 208–10.

[29] "History of the American Forces in Germany," 2 vols. (n.p., n.d.), 1:50, in War Department (hereafter WD) records, American Forces in Germany (AFG) file, Historical subdivision, box 2, NA, RG 120 (American Expeditionary Forces).

[30] Censorship reports (July 11–19) of the AFG, G-2, in WD records, AFG file, Historical subdivision, box 5, NA, RG 120.

[31] *Military Government*, p. 237.

[32] United States, Army, AFG, Second Section, General Staff, "Weekly Digest" (74 nos., November 5, 1919–March 30, 1921), November 5, 1919.

[33] Allen to Pershing, August 1, 1919, Pershing Papers; Weekly Report, Allen to Bliss, October 28, 1919, Bliss Papers. The local police had been encouraged to take on more responsibility than they had held under the Prussian system.

[34] Matuschka (Coblenz) to Minister of Interior Eduard David, August 11, 1919, in University of California (hereafter UC) microfilm records of the German Foreign Ministry (hereafter GFM), file entitled "Beziehungen Vereinigten Staaten zu Deutschland," serial no. (reel) UC, I, 118; Matuschka to Staatssekretär Edgar Haniel, December 10, 1919, in University of Michigan (hereafter UM) microfilm records of the GFM, file entitled "Das besetzte Gebiet in West Deutschland," serial no. (reel) UM 146.

[35] *Neue Berliner Zeitung*, November 25, 1919.

[36] Matuschka to Haniel, December 10, 1919, in UM microfilm records of the GFM, serial no. (reel) UM 146.

[37] Polk to Secretary of State Robert Lansing, September 18, 1919, in SD records, file 185.1711/99a, NA, RG 256. Amedée Rousselier was appointed as French deputy commissioner. Malcolm Robertson became British deputy commissioner (see footnote 118).

[38] Lansing to Polk, October 27, 1919, in SD records, file 185. 1711/113, NA, RA 256. That there had been serious consideration given to finding another individual to serve is evident from John Foster Dulles's conversation with Lansing on July 10, 1919 (see Dulles Diary, John Foster Dulles Papers, Princeton University Library) as well as from Ellis Loring Dresel's letter to Dulles, September 24, 1919, Dulles Papers.

[39] Pierrepont Noyes Diary, (in the possession of his family, Oneida, New York) November 21, 1919. Baron Edouard Rolin-Jacquemyns, who was fifty-six at the time of his appointment, served as Belgian high commissioner until July 1925, when he resigned to accept a cabinet post in the Belgian government. His deputy until January 1922 was Fernand Cattoir; subsequently he was assisted by Count Raoul de Liedekerke.

[40] Noyes to Lansing, July 3, 1919, Bliss Papers; undated memorandum of Sir Harold Stuart, ca. July 1, 1919, Bernard Baruch Papers, Princeton University Library; Appendix to the seventeenth meeting of the Subcommittee on Germany, July 8, 1919, in SD records, file 180.05901/17, NA, RG 256.

[41] Noyes Diary, August 17, 1919.

[42] Ibid., November 21, 1919.

[43] Day's organizational arrangement, as actually established, included administrative subdivisions for labor, fuel, food, stolen property, communications, intelligence, and administration, as well as for economic and legal matters. Noyes himself headed up the fuel and food activities; Day was responsible for labor and stolen property; Addison Flint was in charge of intelligence as well as the several "Kreis men" (two of whom were actually intelligence operatives on duty in unoccupied Germany); Harry Kingston handled the finances and administration; and John Dolan was entrusted with communications. The group was supplemented by the military and legal advisers, Colonel David Stone and Major Manton Davis, both of whom Noyes had appointed on the recommendation of General Allen. The arrangement is recapitulated in detail in a memorandum of Wallace Day to the author, April 6, 1965.

[44] Noyes to Polk, August 27, 1919; Polk to Noyes, September 2 and 6, 1919, Pierrepont Noyes Papers, Colgate University.

[45] Noyes to Polk, August 28, 1919, Noyes Papers.

[46] Polk to Lansing, October 9, 1919, and December 9, 1919, in SD records, file 185.1711/104a, and 127 respectively, NA, RG 256; Noyes Diary, December 13, 1919.

[47] Noyes Diary, December 17, 1919; letters of Noyes to Allen, December 18, 1919, and Allen to Noyes, December 19, 1919, Noyes Papers.

[48] For example, see Assistant to Norman Davis (Assistant Secretary of the Treasury) to Swight (State Department), February 14, 1920, in SD records, file 763.72119/10656, NA, RG 59.

[49] Memorandum of Dresel to Polk, October 7, 1919, in SD records, file 185.121/24, NA, RG 256. See also Minutes of Heads of Delegations, September 30, 1919, *PPC*, 8:460; and November 24, 1919, *PPC*, 9: 320–21.

[50] Minutes of Heads of Delegations, December 9, 1919, *PPC*, 9:545–46. This dispute was to continue in muted form for many months.

[51] Tirard's first statement was summarized in the *Kölnische Zeitung*, October 24, 1919; his second was published as an interview in *La Petite Parisienne*, November 3, 1919.

[52] Minutes of Heads of Delegations, October 28, 1919, *PPC*, 8:784–96; Noyes Diary, November 21, 1919; Lansing to American Mission, November 4, 1919, in SD records, file 763.72119/7519, NA, RG 59.

[53] Noyes Diary, November 21, 1919.

[54] Actually, both Reichskommissar Carl von Starck and the Ministry of the Interior had urged the Foreign Ministry to make a formal protest in Paris. Because this occurred at the time of the crisis over the treaty protocol, however, Foreign Ministry officials had preferred to utilize the avenue of the press. See von Starck to Minister of the Interior Erich Koch-Weser, November 7, 1919; Unterstaatssekretär Theodor Lewald (Interior) to Foreign Minister Hermann Müller, November 11, 1919; and Unterstaatssekretär (Foreign Ministry) to Lewald, December 9, 1919; all in UM microfilm records of the GFM, series no. (reel) UM 146.

[55] Unterstaatssekretär (Foreign Ministry) to Lewald, December 9, 1919, in ibid.

[56] Curzon to Viscount Grey (Washington), December 2, 1919, in *DBFP*, vol. 5, no. 423.

[57] Conversation of Prime Minister David Lloyd George and Polk, November 29, 1919, in SD records, file 861.000/1175a, NA, RG 256.

Notes to Chapter Seven

⁵⁸ Lloyd George to Curzon, December 12, 1919, in Marquess Curzon Papers, Kedleston Hall, England. Just how well founded Lloyd George's concern actually was is revealed by the December 22, 1919, entry in Foch's diary (Ferdinand Foch Papers, Bibliothèque Nationale, Paris): "Saw Degoutte [Jean Degoutte, commander of the French Army of the Rhine]. The separatist movement is in preparation: Bavaria, Rhineland, Hannover: January or February. If it erupts, it will absorb part of Germany's military forces; in which case the Ruhr can be easily occupied and held by the Allies."

⁵⁹ Noyes to Tirard, November 10, 1919, Noyes Papers; Manton Davis to Undersecretary of State William Phillips, April 13, 1922, in John Dolan Papers, Hoover Library, Stanford University. In this regard note the undated memorandum of von Starck (ca. November 1, 1919) in which he predicts, with reference to Tirard's announced intentions, that "M. Tirard will presumably have ample opportunity in Coblenz to convince himself that the Americans are not so naïvely innocent as he seems to think they are . . . , but that they are just as much opposed as the British on the High Commission to allowing the expansion of France's special interests at the cost of the Rhenish population"; records of the Reichskommissar für die besetzten rheinischen Gebiete (hereafter RfdbrG), file entitled "Die interallierten Rheinlandkommission und die einzelnen Oberkommissare" (hereafter DiRudeO), Deutsches Zentralarchiv, Potsdam.

⁶⁰ Noyes Diary, November 21, 1919.

⁶¹ Ibid., December 17, 1919.

⁶² Ibid., December 14 and 17, 1919, January 24, 1920. See also Davis to Phillips, April 13, 1922, Dolan Papers.

⁶³ Noyes Diary, July 21, 1919.

⁶⁴ Ibid., November 21, 1919, and December 14 and 17, 1919. For a German report on this, see Alexander von Brandt (Coblenz) to Koch-Weser, December 10, 1919, in records of the RfdbrG, file entitled "Tätigkeitsberichte des Reichskommissar" (hereafter TdR).

⁶⁵ Noyes Diary, February 9 and 19, 1920. The French were more cooperative in regard to the shortages of food on the left bank. See *Military Government*, p. 354.

⁶⁶ Allen to Polk, November 3, 1919, Polk Papers.

⁶⁷ The most complete discussions of this are in the German records; see von Starck's reports to the German Ministry of the Interior, April 15, July 30, and October 27, 1920, in the records of the RfdbrG, TdR file. See also Noyes's final report to the State Depart-

Notes to Chapter Seven

ment, received March 16, 1921, in SD records, file 862t.01/24t, NA, RG 59 (hereafter cited as Noyes Report); and Jean de Pange, *Les Libertés rhénanes: pays Rhénans—Sarre—Alsace* (Paris, 1922), p. 112.

[68] See Noyes Report.

[69] Minutes of the Supreme Economic Council, September 20, 1919, in *PPC*, 10:567, 601–602. This German barrier, naturally, had its disadvantages for all parties concerned. It was painful for the Germans because it accomplished a longstanding French objective, splitting off the Rhineland from the Reich economically. It was troublesome to the French and Belgians because it drastically reduced their lucrative trade with the bulk of Germany. It was undesirable generally in that it recognized Berlin's inability to obtain Rhineland revenues that were sorely needed if Germany was to achieve financial stability.

[70] Tirard to President of Peace Conference (Georges Clemenceau), October 9, 1919, in SD records, file 185.1711/105, NA, RG 256. Most-favored-nation clauses were to be required of Germany under the treaty.

[71] *Military Government*, p. 353.

[72] Minutes of Heads of Delegations, December 6, 9, 17, 22, 1919, in *PPC*, 9:505–16, 545, 581, 591–92, 631–32.

[73] Albert Malaurie, "Un Année en Rhénanie," *Revue des deux mondes* 60 (1920): 112; Joseph Aulneau, *Le Rhin et la France* (Paris, 1921), pp. 340–53. An interesting aftereffect was that by mid-1920 France, Belgium, and Italy were accusing Germany of discriminating against their products in the licensing of foreign imports. For the relevant correspondence, see United States, Department of State, *Papers Relating to the Foreign Relations of the United States: 1920*, 2 vols. (Washington, 1935), 2:275–87. For a good summary of the entire problem, see Lord Kilmarnock's General Report on the Rhineland to Curzon, September 8, 1922, Curzon Papers.

[74] See Mantoux, 2:550.

[75] For texts of the German notes, see *PPC*, 7:218–29. See also Minutes of Committee on Left Bank of Rhine, July 11, 17, 28, and August 7, 1919, in SD records, file 763.72119/7186, NA, RG 59.

[76] Dulles to Ambassador John Davis (London), July 14, 1919, in SD records, file 185.1711/75A, NA, RG 256; Dulles to Lansing, July 16, 1919, in ibid., file 185.1711/77A, NA, RG 256; Dulles to Joseph Grew, July 25, 1919, Dulles Papers.

[77] For the Allied replies, see *PPC*, 7:212–18.

[78] For the German notes and replies to them, see *PPC*, 8:612–34.

Notes to Chapter Seven

79 The ordinances of the High Commission, as well as the accompanying instructions, were regularly published in the *Bulletin officiel* [Official Gazette] *de la haute commission interalliée des territoires rhénans* (Coblenz, 1920–1928). However, ordinances 1, 2, 3, 5, and 90, together with the Rhineland Agreement, are also available in Ernst Fraenkel, *Military Occupation and the Rule of Law: Occupation Government in the Rhineland, 1918–1923* (London, 1944), pp. 233–48.

80 For discussion, see Fraenkel, pp. 81–91.

81 Carl von Starck had been appointed Reichskommissar for the occupied regions (as well as representative of Prussia, Bavaria, Hesse, and Oldenburg) in June 1919, as part of an effort of the central governments to persuade the Rhineland that its interests were being represented vis à vis the occupation. He held that office until June 1921, at which time he resigned under Allied (mainly French) pressure. A native of Cassel, he was born in 1867.

In terms of organization, von Starck functioned as both ambassador and administrative coordinator. Thus, he not only represented the several ministries of interior to the High Commission, but he also served as the sole channel for the transmission of communications from local Rhenish agencies to the Allied authorities. In the national Ministry of Interior he was responsible, in the beginning, directly to the minister, and, after May 1921, to a Staatssekretär für die besetzten rheinischen Gebiete. See Fraenkel, pp. 111–16.

82 The Rhineland Commission had no sooner shown the proposed ordinances to von Starck in September 1919 than he had begun to protest their "severity." For a brief summary of his efforts, see the German note to the Supreme Council (Kurt von Lersner to Clemenceau), January 12, 1920, published in Great Britain, Foreign Office, *Protocols and Correspondence between the Supreme Council and the Conference of Ambassadors and the German Government and the German Peace Delegation between January 19, 1920 and July 17, 1920 . . .*, Cmd. 1325 (London, 1921), no. 4 (hereafter cited as *Protocols*). See also von Starck to Koch-Weser, January 13, 1920, in records of the RfdbrG, file entitled "Die interallierten Rheinlandkommission."

83 Von Lersner to Clemenceau, January 12, 1920, in *Protocols*, no. 4.

84 The Allied reply of March 2, 1920, is also in *Protocols*, no. 56. It complained vigorously about the "propaganda campaigns of the German press and certain high officials" against the ordinances of the High Commission.

⁸⁵ Polk to Noyes, October 30, 1919, Polk Papers. The Supreme Council formally endorsed the Tirard-Stuart plan on December 30, 1919; see *DBFP*, 2:632–39.

⁸⁶ T. H. Urwick (Coblenz) to Lord Hardinge (Foreign Office), October 9, 1919, *DBFP*, vol. 5, no. 177.

⁸⁷ Noyes Diary, November 21, 1919; Allen, *Journal*, December 8, 1919, pp. 57–58.

⁸⁸ Noyes to Lansing, January 9, 1920, in SD records, file 763. 72119/8585, NA, RG 59.

⁸⁹ Noyes Diary, January 24, 1920.

⁹⁰ "American Representation, 1920–1921," 2:11. To be sure, there continued to be Kreis officers in each of the Kreise who reported to the officer in charge of civil affairs (OCCA), Colonel I. L. Hunt, in Coblenz. For a delineation of the respective duties of the Kreis men and Kreis officers, see "Military Government," 4:325–29.

⁹¹ This was published in 33 sections as paragraph 58 of the AFG, Civil Affairs Bulletin, January 31, 1920. It was, of course, what remained of the original "Anordnungen" of December 1918. For the complete texts, see "Military Government," 4:10–122.

⁹² Noyes Diary, December 17, 1919.

⁹³ Oberpräsident Rudolf von Groote to von Starck, January 29, 1920, in records of the RfdbrG, DiRudeO file. The British also accepted what they considered an "unsatisfactory" solution rather than arguing the case and running the risk of having the United States withdraw; see Hardinge to the Earl of Derby, January 20, 1920, in *DBFP*, vol. 9, no. 11.

⁹⁴ Noyes Diary, December 17, 1919.

⁹⁵ Ibid., February 9, 1920, Pierrepont B. Noyes, *A Goodly Heritage* (New York, 1958), pp. 255–56.

⁹⁶ Noyes Diary, February 9, 1919; Allen to Noyes, February 8, 1920, Noyes Papers.

⁹⁷ F. S. Northedge, *The Troubled Giant: Britain among the Great Powers, 1916–1939* (New York, 1966), pp. 160–62; Edouard Bonnefous, *Histoire politique de la troisième république; L'après-guerre: 1919–1924* (Paris, 1959), pp. 92–142. Though the Bloc National (Conservatives and Republicans) controlled 376 of 616 seats in the Chamber of Deputies, Millerand preferred to stand to the center and to add support from the Radicals, who were to the left of the Bloc but to the right of the Socialists.

⁹⁸ *New York Times*, March 11, 1920, p. 1; March 12, 1920, p. 1;

Notes to Chapter Seven

March 16, 1920, p. 1; March 25, 1920, p. 1. See also the *Amaroc News*, March 23, 1920.

[99] Article in *Le Figaro*, March 25, 1920, Noyes Papers.

[100] Noyes Diary, February 19, 1920; Bonnefous, pp. 129–32, reports the text of Millerand's speech of February 6, 1920, in which he warned of a possible extension of the occupation.

[101] Noyes Diary, January 24 and February 18, 1920. This was reported to the State Department in Noyes's letter of February 27, 1920; *FRUS: 1920*, 2:291.

[102] Noyes Diary, February 23, 1920; Derby to Curzon, February 20, 1920, Curzon Papers; Notes on an Allied Conference, February 13, 1920, in *DBFP*, vol. 7, no. 4.

[103] Noyes to Colonel David Stone, February 6, 1920, Noyes Papers.

[104] Noyes Diary, February 18, 1920. The regulations regarding navigation, the French draft of which Wallace Day had completely reformulated in the space of one night in February, were later published as Ordinance 17 of the High Commission, April 1, 1920.

[105] Noyes Report; and Davis to Phillips, April 13, 1922, Dolan Papers. Davis also credits Noyes and Stuart with having forestalled a return of postal censorship (February 4, 1920). The controversy over the navigation ordinance had first arisen on February 11; the decision on the labor councils dates from early March. See the Minutes of the Inter-Allied Rhineland High Commission, February 4, 11, 14, and March 6, 7, 8, 1920, in the records of the Inter-Allied Rhineland High Commission, Stanford University.

[106] Noyes Diary, January 24 and February 9, 1920. See also Noyes to Acting Secretary of State, February 27, 1920, in *FRUS: 1920*, 2:292–93; and Davis to Phillips, April 13, 1922, Dolan Papers.

[107] Noyes to Acting Secretary of State, February 27, 1920, in *FRUS: 1920*, 2: 289. In October 1919 General Jean Marie Degoutte had been given command of the French Army of the Rhine, newly formed from the Eighth (Gérard) and Tenth (Mangin) Armies.

[108] Noyes to Lansing, February 7, 1920, Robert Lansing Papers, Library of Congress.

[109] Noyes to Acting Secretary of State, February 27, 1920, in *FRUS: 1920*, 2:289–96.

[110] Noyes to Acting Secretary of State, March 6, 1920, in *FRUS: 1920*, 2:296–97. Noyes submitted one further description of the situation on March 17, 1920; in SD records, file 862t.01/8, NA, RG 59.

[111] Noyes Diary, February 23, 1920.

Notes to Chapter Seven

[112] Curzon's minutes are in Stuart to Curzon, March 17, 1920, *DBFP*, vol. 9, no. 128. Stuart had reported that Allen had told him that Noyes and he (Allen) were being called to Paris to discuss Noyes's recent cables to Washington with Ambassador Wallace. According to Stuart, the general had spoken "with strong disapproval of Noyes's action, which he ascribed to his ignorance of affairs. . . ." It had been Stuart's feeling that "General Allen may attach too much importance to the incident." See also Allen, *Journal*, March 17 and 18, 1920, pp. 90–91.

[113] American military authorities, amazingly, did everything they could to discourage demonstrations favorable to the Ebert government within the American zone; see the *New York Times*, March 15, 1920, p. 1.

[114] See Werner T. Angress, "Weimar Coalition and Ruhr Insurrection, March-April 1920: A Study of Government Policy," *Journal of Modern History* 29 (March 1957): 1–20.

[115] For an excellent summary of Millerand's moves and British responses, see Foreign Office Memorandum of April 10, 1920 in records of the Foreign Office, Confidential Print: Germany, F.O. 408/1.

[116] See Ambassador Hugh Wallace to Secretary of State Bainbridge Colby, April 2 and 6, 1920, both in *FRUS: 1920*, 2:303, 311.

[117] Noyes to Colby, April 4, 1920, in *FRUS: 1920*, 2:307.

[118] Malcolm Robertson (1878–1951), a career foreign service officer, was appointed British deputy commissioner in December 1919 and succeeded Sir Harold Stuart as high commissioner in October 1920. He held the latter position for exactly one year before leaving to become British representative in Tangier.

[119] The gyrations of the Belgians are well explained by the correspondence in Belgium, Ministère des Affaires Étrangères, *Documents diplomatiques belges, 1920–1940*, 2 vols. (Brussels, 1964), 1:114–272 (hereafter cited as *Documents diplomatiques*). What had happened was that on April 6, 1920, France had expressed its willingness to relinquish the proposed French-Luxemburger customs union in return for Belgian support in the occupation of Frankfurt. See notes on conversation between Lloyd George and Emile Vandervelde, November 4, 1920, in *DBFP*, vol. 8, no. 94; Paul Hymans, *Mémoires*, 2 vols. (Brussels, 1958), 2:539–47; and Jonathan Helmreich, "The Negotiation of the Franco-Belgian Military Accord of 1920," *French Historical Studies* 2 (1964): 361–67.

[120] Noyes Diary, April 18, 1920; Noyes Report.

[121] Noyes Diary, April 28, 1920.

[122] Von Starck to German and Prussian Ministries of the Interior, January 14, 1921, in records of the Reichsministerium für die besetzten Gebiete (hereafter RMBG), file entitled "Denkschrift über die Verhältnisse im besetzten rheinischen Gebiet," Deutsches Zentralarchiv, Potsdam.

[123] Robertson to Curzon, April 8, 1920, in *DBFP*, vol. 9, no. 325. Rolin-Jacquemyns reported to his government on April 9 that relations between the British and Americans (Noyes and Robertson) were "tense and disagreeable"; Memorandum to Paul Hymans, April 9, 1920, in *Documents diplomatiques*, 1:251.

[124] Noyes Diary, April 28, 1920. See also Noyes Report.

[125] Colby to Wallace, April 12, 1920, in *FRUS: 1920*, 2:324. American correspondence on the Frankfurt occupation is published in *FRUS: 1920*, 2:297–325. It is interesting to note that Ambassador Wallace was so pro-French that he had even favored sending American troops into Frankfurt with the French; Baron de Gaiffier (ambassador in Paris) to Foreign Minister Paul Hymans, April 6, 1920, in *Documents diplomatiques*, 1:222.

[126] Derby to Curzon, April 11, 1920, Curzon Papers.

[127] Curzon to Derby, April 10, 1920, *DBFP*, vol. 9., no. 349; Keith Middlemas, ed., *Thomas Jones: Whitehall Diary* (London, 1969), 1:107–11 (entry for April 8, 1920). See also Lloyd George to his wife, April 9, 22, 1920: "The French have played the fool and we must act firmly with them if we are to keep out of great trouble. For the moment their papers and politicians are in full cry against me because I refuse to support their mad schemes for the destruction and dismemberment of Germany" (Kenneth O. Morgan, ed., *Lloyd George Family Letters, 1885–1936* [Cardiff, 1973], p. 191).

[128] Derby to Curzon, April 11, 1920, Curzon Papers. Millerand's public statement was on April 13. See Northedge, pp. 164–65.

[129] Baron Moncheur (London) to Hymans, April 13, 1920, in *Documents diplomatiques*, 1:269.

[130] Noyes Diary, April 28, 1920; Minutes of the IARHC, April 21 and 24, 1920. From von Starck's point of view, the continued expulsion of minor German officials from the occupied territory for alleged violations of Allied ordinances constituted one of the greatest grievances against the High Commission; von Starck's report to the German Ministry of the Interior, April 15, 1920, in the records of the RfdbrG, TdR file. For figures on this, see Fraenkel, pp. 129–31.

Notes to Chapter Seven

[131] Noyes to Colby, April 23, 1920, in SD records file 763.72119, NA, RG 59. Allen's reaction was one of amusement: "It would truly be worth something to see the President when he reads this cablegram if the State Department is bold enough to send it over to the White House"; Allen, *Journal*, April 28, 1920, p. 107.

[132] Noyes Diary, April 28, 1920.

[133] Colby to Noyes, May 17, 1920, in *FRUS: 1920*, 2:327; Noyes Diary, May 23, 1920. On May 22, Noyes requested clarification, pointing out that "the substitution of the American Commanding General as quasi-Commissioner would undo the work of a year, would stultify the President's former insistence on civilian control, [and] would, I believe, embarrass the High Commissioner of at least one other nation [i.e., Stuart]. . . ." The department responded on May 27 by assuring Noyes that the appointment of Allen as observer was "not an injection of the military element into what is and should remain a civilian commission. . . ." Still somewhat perplexed, Noyes submitted his resignation effective June 3, 1920. See *FRUS: 1920*, 2:327–28; Noyes Diary, June 3, 1920.

[134] AFG, *Weekly Digest*, March 10, 31, April 1, 15, 1920.

[135] Resumés of OCCA Reports, February 7 and April 3, 1920, in WD records, AFG file, Historical subdivision, box 541, NA, RG 120. The most complete information from the German side is in the bimonthly reports on public affairs submitted beginning April 1, 1920 by the Oberpräsident of the Rhineland province to the High Commission and American authorities (both in English). A complete file of these reports is in the records of the Oberpräsidium der Rheinprovinz, Abteilung 403, nr. 14804, Bundesarchiv, Coblenz. See also von Starck's reports to the German Ministry of the Interior, April 15, and October 27, 1920, in the records of the RfdbrG, TdR file.

[136] "American Representation, 1920–1921," 2:44.

[137] *Weekly Digest*, May 19, 1920.

[138] Albeit with some prodding from Pierrepont Noyes. Allen to Pershing, January 17, 1920, Pershing Papers; Noyes to Colonel Stone, January 17, 1920, Noyes Papers. See also von Starck's report to the German Ministry of the Interior, April 15, 1920, in the records of the RfdbrG, TdR file.

[139] *Weekly Digest*, February 18, March 17, April 1 and 15, May 12, 1920; "American Representation, 1920–1921," 1:46. See also Frank M. Surface and Raymond L. Bland, *American Food in the World War and Reconstruction Period* (Stanford, 1931), pp. 193–200. The Germans were particularly grateful to Pierrepont Noyes for his establishment of

child feeding stations, which distributed food provided by the Quakers through the good offices of Herbert Hoover; von Starck to Koch-Weser, June 3, 1920, in records of the RfdbrG, DiRudeO file.

[140] For use of the abbreviation, see Walter Steiner, "Die Rheinlandkommission" in Otto Peters, ed., *Kampf um den Rhein: Beiträge zur Geschichte des Rheinlandes und Seiner Fremdherrschaft, 1918–1930* (Mainz, 1930), pp. 90–92.

[141] Resumés of OCCA Reports, February 7, April 3, 1920 in WD records, AFG file, Historical subdivision, box 541, NA, RG 120.

[142] Peter Berg, *Deutschland und Amerika 1918–1929: Uber das deutsche Amerikabild der zwanziger Jahre* (Lübeck, 1963), pp. 47–62.

[143] *Berliner Börsenzeitung*, April 1, 1920.

[144] Von Starck to Koch-Weser, June 3, 1920, in records of the RfdbrG, DiRudeO file; Allen, *Journal*, June 21, 1920, p. 122.

[145] Allen to Colby, June 26, 1920, in SD records, file 862t.01/130, NA, RG 59. Allen reported to the State Department that he had seen von Starck and *von Groote* (Oberpräsident of the Rhine Province), but the entries in his *Journal* (June 21 and 26, August 6, 1920; pp. 122, 124, 138–39) make it clear that his callers had actually been von Starck and von Groenig (Regierungspräsident of Coblenz). Inasmuch as these were the first German officials that Allen had met during his year in Germany, the confusion is somewhat understandable.

[146] Minutes of the Conference at San Remo, *DBFP*, vol. 8, nos. 1–20. See also Northedge, pp. 165–67; Harold Nicolson, *Curzon: The Last Phase, 1919–1925* (Boston, 1934), pp. 225–26; and W. M. Jordan, *Great Britain, France and the German Problem, 1918–1939* (New York, 1944), pp. 45, 71.

[147] "American Representation, 1920–1921," 1:47.

[148] Wolfgang Hartenstein, *Die Anfänge der deutschen Volkspartei 1918–1920* (Düsseldorf, 1962), pp. 224–53.

CHAPTER 8

[1] Allen W. Dulles to E. L. Dresel, May 28, 1920 and August 24, 1920, E. L. Dresel Papers, Houghton Library, Harvard University. See also Wesley M. Bagby, *The Road to Normalcy: The Presidential Campaign and Election of 1920* (Baltimore, 1962), pp. 118, 129, 142, 146.

[2] Dulles to Dresel, July 28, 1920, Dresel Papers.

[3] Lithgow Osborne to Dresel, June 19, 1920, Dresel Papers. See also Robert K. Murray, *The Harding Era: Warren G. Harding and His Administration* (Minneapolis, 1969), pp. 75–80.

Notes to Chapter Eight

⁴ For example, *Syracuse Post Standard*, August 1, 1920, and *New York World*, August 17, 1920, Pierrepont Noyes Papers, Colgate University Library.

⁵ For example, *Harvey's Weekly* 3 (October 23, 1920): 31.

⁶ Walter Davenport, *Power and Glory: The Life of Boies Penrose* (New York, 1931), p. 323; but see Andrew Sinclair, *The Available Man: The Life behind the Masks of Warren Gamaliel Harding* (New York, 1965), p. 160.

⁷ Bagby, pp. 137–39, 144; Murray, pp. 54–59; Francis Russell, *The Shadow of Blooming Grove: Warren G. Harding in His Times* (New York, 1968), pp. 409–12.

⁸ *New York Times*, October 8, 1920, pp. 1, 2.

⁹ *Springfield Republican*, October 12, 1920.

¹⁰ *New York Times*, October 9, 1920.

¹¹ Thomas A. Bailey, *Woodrow Wilson and the Great Betrayal* (New York, 1947), pp. 327–33; Bagby, pp. 140–41; Murray, pp. 59–61.

¹² See Bagby, pp. 137, 154; and Sinclair, pp. 162–63.

¹³ For an indication of this, see the letters received by the Department of State (hereafter SD), file 862t.01/81, National Archives (hereafter NA), Record Group (hereafter RG) 59 (hereafter cited as SD letter file).

¹⁴ For the most complete discussion of this phenomenon, see Keith L. Nelson, "The 'Black Horror on the Rhine': Race as a Factor in Post–World War I Diplomacy," *Journal of Modern History* 42 (December 1970): 614–19.

¹⁵ This campaign was waged as far away as Argentina and Peru. See, for example, *El Terror Negro* (Buenos Aires, 1920); and Marchand Keifer, *El Terror Negro en Renania* (Lima, ca. 1922). The British Foreign Office, however, became and remained convinced that the propaganda was aimed primarily at Americans, "whose sense of the colour-line is so strong"; Cecil Harmsworth to Sir Frederick Hall, October 28, 1920, in Great Britain, Foreign Office (hereafter FO) records, General Correspondence: Political (hereafter GCP), F.O. 371/4799.

¹⁶ Proof that the German government subsidized a number of propaganda pamphlets can be found in the draft of a report to the Reichspräsident, September 9, 1923, Deutsche Volkspflege und Reichszentrale für Heimatdienst (July 1, 1922–December 14, 1923), papers of the Reichsministerium für die besetzten Gebiete (hereafter RMBG), Deutsches Zentralarchiv, Potsdam. The central importance of Morel's work in the propaganda is attested by Osborne to Dresel, June 19, 1920,

Dresel Papers. The most widely circulated of his statements was *The Horror on the Rhine* (London, 1920), which ran to at least eight editions and was translated into German, French, Italian, and Dutch. See also Robert C. Reinders, "Racialism on the Left: E. D. Morel and the 'Black Horror on the Rhine,' " *International Review of Social History* 12 (1968): 1–28.

[17] See the SD letter file; see also Marquis James, *A History of the American Legion* (New York, 1923), p. 204.

[18] *Literary Digest* 66 (August 28, 1920): 22. Though, in response to a request for information by President Wilson (June 15, 1920), reports had been received from both General Allen in Coblenz and Dresel in Berlin that tended to undercut the German claims, neither of these were made public until later. Extracts from Allen's report are in Henry T. Allen, *The Rhineland Occupation* (Indianapolis, 1927), pp. 319–22. See also Ambassador Hugh Wallace (Paris) to Colby, June 25, 1920, in United States, Department of State, *Papers Relating to the Foreign Relations of the United States: 1920*, 2 vols. (Washington, D.C., 1935), 2:329.

[19] Dudley Field Malone to Woodrow Wilson, October 18, 1920, Woodrow Wilson Papers, VI, 40, Library of Congress. Malone was assistant secretary of state under Wilson in 1913.

[20] *Christian Science Monitor*, October 28, 1920, p. 14. The so-called horror also received much attention in the German-American press; see the *New Yorker Staats-Zeitung*, October 7–9, 11–14, 1920.

[21] Otto Kannegiesser to William E. Borah, February 7, 1923, William E. Borah Papers, Library of Congress.

[22] Dresel to William R. Castle, November 4, 1920, Dresel Papers.

[23] Castle to Dresel, December 29, 1920 and January 21, 1921, Dresel Papers; David F. Houston, *Eight Years with Wilson's Cabinet, 1913–1920*, 2 vols. (New York, 1926), 2:95.

[24] Castle to Dresel, January 25, 1921, Dresel Papers.

[25] There is a faint possibility that Wilson continued to think of the occupation as a healthy obstacle to French ambition. On January 18, 1921, Josephus Daniels recorded in his diary after a cabinet meeting: "W W did not want Army reduced—said France would yet involve Europe in another war—that Foch and his party were determined to take the Rhine territory" (E. David Cronon, ed., *The Cabinet Diaries of Josephus Daniels, 1913–1921* [Lincoln, Neb., 1963], p. 588).

[26] Strength reports are to be found in War Department (hereafter WD) records, American Expeditionary Forces, American Forces in Germany file, Historical subdivision boxes, NA, RG 120.

[27] Memorandum from Adjutant General to Chief of Staff (General Peyton C. March), November 2, 1920, in WD records, Adjutant General's Office, AG 320.2 Germany Project (hereafter Ger) file, NA, RG 94.

[28] *New York Times*, January 13, 1921, p. 8.

[29] John Chalmers Vinson, *The Parchment Peace: The United States and the Washington Conference, 1921–1922* (Athens, Ga., 1955), pp. 46–54; John Chalmers Vinson, *William E. Borah and the Outlawry of War* (Athens, Ga., 1957), pp. 1–38; Robert James Maddox, *William E. Borah and American Foreign Policy* (Baton Rouge, 1969), pp. 85–92; Thomas H. Buckley, *The United States and the Washington Conference, 1921–1922* (Knoxville, 1970), pp. 3–19.

[30] Frederic L. Paxson, *Post-war Years: Normalcy, 1918–1923* (Berkeley, 1948), p. 185.

[31] See United States, Congress, *Congressional Record*, 66th Cong., 3rd sess., January 25 and February 2, 1921, 60:2015, 2455–456.

[32] Hamilton Holt, "The American Watch on the Rhine," *The Independent* 104 (December 4, 1920): 326–27, 347–49.

[33] *New York Times*, February 13, 1921, part 3, p. 1.

[34] *Congressional Record*, 66th Cong., 3rd sess., January 17, 1921, 60:1491, Senate Document 354. The resolutions (HJ Res. 433 and HJ Res. 438) had been introduced by Congressmen Frederick Britten (R-Ill.) on January 3, 1921, and James Sinclair (R-N.D.) on January 5, 1921, respectively.

[35] *Congressional Record*, 66th Cong., 3rd sess., February 15, 1921, 60:3172, Senate Document 397. The letter had been written to Congressman Stephen Porter (R-Pa.) on January 17, 1921.

[36] *New York Times*, February 11, 1921, p. 3.

[37] The best general discussion of Harding and foreign affairs is in Murray, pp. 129–69, 327–75; but see also John D. Hicks, *Republican Ascendancy: 1921–1933* (New York, 1960), pp. 23–49, 130–52; Selig Adler, *The Uncertain Giant, 1921–1941: American Foreign Policy between the Wars* (New York, 1965), pp. 1–68; and L. Ethan Ellis, *Republican Foreign Policy, 1921–1933* (New Brunswick, N.J., 1968), pp. 29–136.

[38] Note, for example, that the *Nation* complained of the "powerful Republican element" that opposed "conciliating Germany" (March 23, 1921), 26:86–88.

[39] Secretary of State Charles Evans Hughes to Dresel, March 29, 1921, in United States, Department of State, *Papers Relating to the Foreign Relations of the United States: 1921*, 2 vols. (Washington, 1936),

Notes to Chapter Eight

2:40 (hereafter *FRUS: 1921*); see also the unsigned memorandum for Hughes (from Castle?), March 24, (27?), 1921, in SD records file 462.00 R29/563, NA, RG 59. For background on Hughes's attitudes and policies, see Merlo Pusey, *Charles Evans Hughes*, 2 vols. (New York, 1951), 1:432–43; and Betty Glad, *Charles Evans Hughes and the Illusions of Innocence: A Study in American Diplomacy* (Urbana, Ill., 1966), pp. 123–62, 212–35. For particular reference to his relationship to the reparations question, see Dieter Bruno Gescher, *Die Vereinigten Staaten von Nordamerika und die Reparationen, 1920–1924* (Bonn, 1956); and Werner Link, *Die amerikanische Stabilisierungspolitik in Deutschland 1921–32.* (Düsseldorf, 1970), pp. 31–199.

⁴⁰ Castle to Dresel, March 30, 1921, Dresel Papers. When Edmund von Mach, director of "The American Campaign against the Horror on the Rhine," had attempted to obtain an interview with the new secretary of state in March 1921, he had been refused on grounds that his allegations were "mischievous and based on very slight foundation"; Assistant Secretary of State Fred Dearing to Edmund von Mach, March 23, 1921, in Warren G. Harding Papers, box 183, Ohio Historical Society, Columbus, Ohio.

⁴¹ The essential documentation on this period is in Great Britain, Foreign Office, *Documents on British Foreign Policy, 1919-1939*; First series, 1919–1930, 17 vols. (London 1947–   ), vol. 15, nos. 1, 30, 70, 77, 82, 84 (hereafter cited as *DBFP*). See also Viscount Edgar V. D'Abernon, *The Diary of an Ambassador*, 3 vols. (Garden City, N.Y., 1929–1931), 1:119–69; and the works cited in n. 1, Chap. 9.

⁴² *New York Times*, March 9, 1921, p. 2, and March 10, 1921, p. 12.

⁴³ See Hughes to Wallace, March 10, 15, and 19, 1921, and Castle to Hughes, March 15, 1921, in SD records, file 462.00 R29/517 and 552, NA, RG 59. See also Hughes to Wallace, March 23, 1921, in *FRUS: 1921*, 2:37.

⁴⁴ For correspondence regarding Germany's offer, see *FRUS: 1921*, 2:40–44. See also Sir Auckland Geddes to Earl Curzon, April 25, 1921 (two cables) *DBFP*, vol. 16, nos. 533, 535.

⁴⁵ Hughes to Ambassadors in London, Paris, and Rome, May 6, 1921, in SD records, file 462.00 R29/729, NA, RG 59. See also Geddes to Curzon, May 5, 1921, in *DBFP*, Vol. 16, no. 553.

⁴⁶ *Congressional Record*, 67th Cong., 1st sess., April 28, 1921, 61:752. Senator William King (D-Utah) commented in extension of remarks: "We throw away [with such a resolution] every weapon

which we may use, not for coercion, but to secure a just and righteous peace. Germany will regard this as an abandonment of our allies . . ." (Ibid., April 29, 1921, pp. 8318–330).

47 Kurt Wimer and Sarah Wimer, "The Harding Administration, the League of Nations, and the Separate Peace Treaty," *Review of Politics* 29 (January 1967): 16.

48 *Congressional Record*, 67th Cong., 1st sess., April 29, 1921, 61: 785.

49 Ibid., June 30, 1921, pp. 3288–289.

50 For correspondence regarding the negotiations of the Treaty of Berlin, July 5 to August 26, 1921, see *FRUS: 1921*, 2:5–29. Technically, this was a "treaty restoring friendly relations with Germany."

51 *New York Times*, July 5, 1921, p. 1.

52 *Congressional Record*, 67th Cong., 1st sess., July 20, 1921, 61: 4094. See also the *New York Times*, July 29, 1921, p. 1.

53 *Congressional Record*, 67th Cong., 1st sess., August 10, 1921, 61:4811–813.

54 *Freeman* 3 (July 20, 1921): 435.

55 *Wisconsin Times* (Milwaukee), August 18 and 20, 1921.

56 The fact that the Senate Foreign Relations Committee (probably with the Reparations Commission and Rhineland High Commission in mind) had added a reservation to the treaty specifying that the United States could not participate in any European body, agency, or commission without congressional approval seems to have had no appreciable calming effect upon the Irreconcilables; *New York Times*, September 24, 1921, p. 1; Wimer and Wimer, pp. 18–19.

57 *Congressional Record*, 67th Cong., 1st sess., September 24, 1921, 61:5879.

58 Ibid., October 17, 1921, 61:6375–380.

59 Ibid., October 18, 1921, 61:6436.

60 Ibid., September 24, 1921, 61:5771–780.

61 *New York Times*, July 30, 1921, p. 3.

62 He claimed that the Allies had already agreed to this in principle, since neither Japanese nor Italian troops had ever participated in the occupation. *Congressional Record*, 67th Cong., 1st sess., September 24, 1921, 61:5771.

63 *Washington Post*, September 26, 1921, p. 6.

64 See President Warren G. Harding to Weeks, June 1, 1921, and Weeks to Harding, June 6, 1921, both letters including copies of a poll of the American Legion's National Executive Committee. Weeks even

Notes to Chapter Eight

commented to the president on the "practically universal" opinion of the members in favor of continuing the occupation; Harding Papers, box 54. See also W. H. Hayes, Chairman, Military Policy Committee American Legion, to Hughes, June 9, 1921, in SD records file 862t.01/283, NA, RG 59.

[65] *Congressional Record*, 67th Cong., 1st sess., October 17, 1921, 61:6361–362; *New York Times*, September 27, 1921, p. 18.

[66] *Congressional Record*, 67th Cong., 1st sess., October 12, 1921, 61:6248–252.

[67] See, for example, the letters to the editor in *New York Times*, September 17, 1921, p. 12; September 24, 1921, p. 10; and September 27, 1921, p. 18; also an article, September 13, 1921, p. 24.

[68] Bernard Boylan, "Army Reorganization 1920: The Legislative Story," *Mid-America* 49 (April 1967): 115–28. See also Edward M. Coffman, *The Hilt of the Sword: The Career of Peyton C. March* (Madison, Wis., 1966), pp. 176–209.

[69] *New York Times*, June 8, 1921, p. 17. Senator Nathanial Dial (D-S.C.) attempted to attach a rider to the appropriations bill in accord with Reed's proposal, only to be turned back by the "constitutional" arguments of administration senators; *Congressional Record*, 67th Cong., 1st sess., June 8, 1921, 61:2249.

[70] Vinson, *Parchment Peace*, pp. 82–92; Maddox, pp. 92–96.

[71] Paxson, pp. 233–35; Murray, pp. 140–51.

[72] Murray, pp. 81–86, 199–226; John D. Hicks, *Rehearsal for Disaster: The Boom and Collapse of 1919–20* (Gainsville, Fla., 1964), pp. 68–86. See also Geddes to Curzon, March 18, 1921, in *DBFP*, vol. 16, no. 470.

[73] See, for example, the *Washington Post*, October 22, 1921, p. 5. This view, one might add, was widely encouraged and disseminated by General Allen and the other Americans in Coblenz; see Allen to Hughes, March 24, 1922, in *FRUS: 1922* (1938), 2:213; also Colonel David L. Stone to Joseph Defrees, October 14, 1921, and Stone to Silas Strawn, March 14, 1922, Myron T. Herrick Papers, Western Reserve Historical Association, Cleveland, Ohio.

[74] Henry T. Allen, *My Rhineland Journal* (Boston, 1923), October 5, 1921.

[75] *Congressional Record*, 67th Cong., 1st sess., October 17, 1921, 61:6356–357. See also "The American Farmer and Foreign Policy," *The Economist* (London) 94 (March 11, 1922): 493.

[76] On this, see Adler, pp. 18–21; John Higham, *Strangers in the Land: Patterns of American Nativism, 1860–1925* (New Brunswick,

N.J., 1955), pp. 265–82; Arno Mayer, "Post-War Nationalisms, 1918–1919," *Past and Present*, no. 34 (July 1966), pp. 114–18.

[77] Robert McCormick to Allen, April 6, 1921, Allen's unpublished journal, in Henry T. Allen Papers, Library of Congress. McCormick added, "[The American occupation] embodies the spirit and purpose of our country as our embassies and legations, too much under the sway of foreign social customs and aristocratic personal friends, unfortunately do not." Later in 1921, Cyrus Hall McCormick (Robert McCormick's cousin) wrote to Secretary Hughes of his conviction that the AFG represented the "truest Americanism"; Cyrus Hall McCormick to Hughes, August 27, 1921, in SD records file 862t.01/307, NA, RG 59.

[78] Harding to Henry P. Fletcher, October 11, 1921, Henry P. Fletcher Papers, Library of Congress.

[79] Harding had, to be sure, always been somewhat concerned about presidential prerogatives; for example, see Murray, p. 144. See also Weeks to Harding, June 6, 1921, in which the secretary of war complained about "unprecedented" congressional claims to control over the army; Harding Papers.

[80] Hughes to Harding, October 29, 1921, Harding to Hughes, October 31, 1921, both in SD records file 862t.01/432A and 433.

[81] See, for example, the *New York Times*, July 2, 1921, p. 1, and August 28, 1921, p. 3.

[82] Ibid., September 23, 24, 26, 1921.

[83] Ibid., October 23, 1921, p. 9. For correspondence (October 14–21, 1921) between Hughes and Weeks relating to the announcement, see SD records file 862.0146/1–3A, NA, RG 59.

[84] Vinson, *The Parchment Peace*, pp. 102–10; Murray, pp. 146–47; Buckley, pp. 20–47.

[85] Hicks, *Republican Ascendancy*, pp. 36–37.

[86] See Ambassador Jules Jusserand (Washington) to Premier Aristide Briand (Paris), October 27, 1921, in France, Ministère des Affaires Étrangères, *Documents diplomatiques: Conférence de Washington, juillet 1921–février 1922* (Paris, 1923), no. 32. Note that on October 28, 1921, Ambassador Myron T. Herrick (Paris) had cabled Hughes to caution him that France might decide to use "strong measures" of coercion against Germany if the French delegation returned from Washington without having received evidences of American sympathy; cited in Donald S. Birn, "British and French at the Washington Conference, 1921–1922" (Ph.D. diss., Columbia University, 1965), p. 209.

[87] The basic documentation is in *Documents diplomatiques*, nos.

70–78, and *FRUS: 1922*, 1:130–41. The story is in Buckley, pp. 104–26. For insight into American attitudes toward France at this time, see H. B. Welles, *Washington and the Riddle of Peace* (New York, 1922), p. 128; Elizabeth B. White, *American Opinion of France: From Lafayette to Poincaré* (New York, 1927), pp. 292–93; and Donald S. Birn, "Open Diplomacy at the Washington Conference of 1921–22: The British and French Experience," *Comparative Studies in Society and History* 12 (1970): 307–17.

[88] For indications of French concern on this score, see the *New York Times*, September 25, 1921, p. 2; and Hughes to Roland Boyden, March 16, 1922, in SD records file 462.00 R294/14, NA, RG 59. Note also that retiring ambassador to France Hugh Wallace, a strong proponent of continued occupation, had returned to Washington in the late summer and had "long talks" with Hughes about the AFG; Wallace to Allen, December 9, 1921, Allen Papers; Allen, *Journal*, July 4, 1921, pp. 220–21.

[89] Boyden to Hughes, September 21, 1921, in SD records file 462.00 R29/1049, NA, RG 59.

[90] *New York Times*, October 21, 1921, p. 16.

[91] As of this date, General Allen was directed to return an additional 3,200 men; see the Memorandum for Chief of Staff (General John J. Pershing) from Brigadier General William Lassiter, February 15, 1922, in WD records Adjutant General's Office, AG 370.5 Ger file, NA, RG 94. According to Allen (*Journal*, March 7, 1922, p. 325), Pershing himself was opposed to the reduction. The decision may well have been Harding's; see *New York Times*, March 21, 1922, p. 1.

[92] The documentation is in *DBFP*, vol. 16, chaps. 2, 5 and 6; but see also D'Abernon, 1:225–53.

[93] See, for example, D'Abernon, 1:291 (entry for March 14, 1922).

[94] See Hughes to Herrick, March 20, 1922 (with note for French government), in *FRUS: 1922*, 2:220.

[95] See Memorandum by Sir Cecil Hurst respecting the German-American Peace Treaty, October 1, 1921, in FO records, GCP, F.O. 371/7549.

[96] Record of an interview between the chancellor of the exchequer (Sir Robert Horne) and Paul Doumer (minister of finance), September 9, 1921, and Memorandum by R. F. Wigram on recent developments in Reparation, September 29, 1921, in *DBFP*, vol. 16, nos. 691, 710.

[97] Records by Mr. Fass (Treasury) of interviews with Belgian

Ministers, December 2 and 3, 1921, in *DBFP*, vol. 16, nos. 749 and 751.

[98] Boyden to Colby, August 2, 1920, in *FRUS: 1920*, 2:415. Note also Boyden to Colby, September 10, 1920 (two cables), 434–35.

[99] Boyden to Acting Secretary, December 15, 1920, in ibid., 338.

[100] For a good discussion of the general situation, see Arnold Toynbee, ed., *Survey of International Affairs, 1920–1923* (London, 1925), pp. 151–67. See also Hughes to Assistant Secretary of the Treasury Eliot Wadsworth, February 19, 1923, in *FRUS: 1923*, 2:110–34.

[101] Strictly speaking, these arrangements were not formally agreed upon until March 1922. The total British, French, and Belgian sum was stipulated at 200 million gold marks, thus leaving an opening for an American charge (among others) that, it was implied, might be collected independently. On this, see Boyden to Hughes, February 7, 1922, in SD records file 462.00 R294, NA, RG 59. See also the Allied Financial Agreement of March 11, 1922, in FO records, Confidential Print: Germany (hereafter CPGer), F.O. 408/7.

[102] This apportionment dealt with the debts accumulated up to April 30, 1921. For the period May 1, 1921–April 30, 1922, the Allies agreed to charge army costs against deliveries in kind already received.

[103] Toynbee, pp. 151–67.

[104] The British-French agreement, which dated from August 13, 1921, is reprinted in France, Ministère des Affaires Etrangères, *Documents diplomatiques: Documents relatifs aux réparations* (Paris, 1922), no. 17. It was never ratified by the French; see summary by Wigram of the reparations position, December 28, 1921, in *DBFP*, vol. 16, no. 767.

[105] The so-called (Loucheur-Rathenau) Wiesbaden Agreement of October 6, 1921.

[106] The scale was uniform, but Britain was to get a lump sum award of 2 gold marks per man per day in addition to her regular payment.

[107] The memorandum, dated December 22, 1921, is in *DBFP*, vol. 15, annex 3 to no. 111. Even under the revised distribution, the French were very dissatisfied that Belgium was receiving so much of the first proceeds; see D'Abernon, 1:241, 259. Lloyd George had told Walther Rathenau that he considered the Belgian priority a "stupidity" forced upon them by Woodrow Wilson at Versailles; Harmut Pogge von Strandmann, *Walther Rathenau Tagebuch, 1907–1922* (Düsseldorf, 1967), p. 268 (entry for December 2, 1921).

[108] The Cannes formulation, dated January 11, 1922, and the (final) Paris formulation, dated March 11, 1922, are in FO records, CPGer, F.O. 408/7.

Notes to Chapter Eight

[109] British army debts (to April 30, 1921) as of March 1922 stood at 693 million gold marks and French at 300 million gold marks (i.e., at approximately the estimated value of the Saar mines). The reason that France did not receive more than 140 million in cash was due to the order of payment: first, Britain received 500 million, second, France received 140 million, third, Belgium received 1 billion, fourth, Britain received enough to extinguish her debt (before which point, the money ran out), fifth, France received enough to extinguish her debt.

[110] See Doumer's statement to Horne to this effect, September 9, 1921, in *DBFP*, vol. 16, no. 691. See also the *Christian Science Monitor*, March 20, 1922.

[111] See, for example, Boyden to Hughes, July 15, 1921, in SD records file 462.00 R29/868; and Boyden to Hughes, February 7, 1922, file 462.00 R294/– . As the following exchange from the Inter-Allied conference at Lympne, June 20, 1920, reveals the Allies were not simply being altruistic in making such recognitions of right (*DBFP*, vol. 8, no. 27);

> Mr. [Austen] CHAMBERLAIN [Chancellor of the Exchequer] asked what was the position of America. Until the United States signed the treaty, had they any claim for the cost of their army of occupation under the treaty?
> Mr. [François] MARSAL [French Minister of Finance] said it was provided for under the terms of the armistice. . . .
> Mr. LLOYD GEORGE said it was undesirable to raise a point of this kind, as the Americans might take away their army of occupation.

[112] The first British draft reply to the United States (submitted to the French on May 2, 1922), suggested that "the most effective machinery for [settling these difficulties] would be the appointment of an official United States delegate on the Reparations Commission, but lengthy negotiations with Paris finally resulted in a less specific message being (jointly) sent, November 8, 1922; the Anglo-French correspondence is in FO records, CPGer, F.O. 408/7. Hints of even a more general British motivation are to be found occasionally in such minutes as that of R. Sperling, March 28, 1922: "The proper answer to the U.S.A. is that as they will do nothing to assist in the reconstruction of Europe, they cannot expect to get more money . . ." (FO records, GCP, F.O. 371/7548). For an indication of the French point of view, see Jacques Bardoux, *Lloyd George et la France* (Paris, 1923), pp. 396–98, and René Pinon, *Le Redressement de la politique française, 1922* (Paris, 1923), pp. 66–68.

[113] See Wigram's resumé, March 27, 1922, and S. P. Waterlow's

Notes to Chapter Eight

minutes, March 28, 1922, in FO records, GCP, F.O. 371/7548. See also "London Gets a Washington Bombshell," *Current Opinion* 72 (May 1922): 586–89.

[114] Curzon to Geddes, March 19, 1922, in FO records, CPGer, F.O. 408/7.

[115] Boyden to Hughes, March 14, 1922, in SD records, file 462.00 R294/14.

[116] This conference had been one of the results of the finance ministers' campaign to reduce existing expenses, but, according to a British Treasury official, its report had been "entirely valueless owing to the French refusing to discuss a diminution in the number of men, and the Americans refusing to discuss accepting from Germany less than the cost per man" (Memorandum by Fass of an interview with Italian ministers, December 9, 1921, in *DBFP*, vol. 16, no. 753). This apparently had not been clear to Boyden or Hughes, who anticipated using the report as a springboard to further discussions of both current expenses and past debts. See Boyden to Hughes, October 19, 1921, in SD records file 462.00 R29/1215; as well as Boyden to Hughes, February 7, 1922, and Hughes to Boyden, March 16, 1922, in SD records, file 462.00 R294/ and 14, NA, RG 59.

[117] Murray, pp. 360–62.

[118] Memorandum by E. Bell on Hughes's press conference, March 11, 1922, in SD records, file 462.00 R294/2b, NA, RG 59.

[119] *Congressional Record*, 67th Cong., 2nd sess., March 17, 1922, 62:4000–4003.

[120] *Chicago Tribune*, March 14, 1922, p. 7, and March 16, 1922, p. 1. The fact that the United States, with hardly a ripple of public notice, had maintained troops in China since the Boxer rebellion of 1900 (in 1922, there was one regiment) illustrates how much more seriously the United States took its relationship to Europe than its involvement in the Far East. See Louis Morton, "Army and Marines on the China Station: A Study in Military and Political Rivalry," *Pacific Historical Review* 29 (February 1960): 51–73.

[121] *St. Louis Post Dispatch*, March 17, 1922, March 19, 1922.

[122] For example, *Springfield Republican*, March 14, 1922; *Atlanta Constitution*, March 15, 1922.

[123] H. G. Chilton (Washington) to Curzon, March 31, 1922, in FO records, GCP, F.O. 371/7520.

[124] For example, *Washington Post*, March 11, 1922; *Chicago Tribune*, March 15, 1922; *Salt Lake City Tribune*, March 15, 1922.

Notes to Chapter Eight

[125] *New Orleans Times-Picayune*, March 17, 1922.

[126] Henry Fletcher to Allen, March 20, 1922, Allen Papers; Fletcher to Harding, August 8, 1922, Fletcher Papers; Russell, pp. 535–36.

[127] *Washington Post*, March 23, 1922, p. 4, and March 25, 1922, p. 3. The British assistant military attaché in Washington reported on March 31, 1922: "The President may have been influenced in his decision to withdraw the troops from Germany by a desire to emphasize the recent demand presented to the Allied Reparations Commission . . . , and also by the entire lack of sympathy in this country, especially in official circles, with the exaggerated military expenditures of France, but the prime motive for his action must be looked for in the ever present necessity of bending to the wishes of Congress . . ." (Major Charles Bridge to Ambassador Geddes, enclosed in the letter of Chilton to Curzon, March 31, 1922, FO records, GCP, F.O. 371/7520).

[128] Murray, p. 161; Buckley, pp. 180-84.

[129] Weeks to Hughes, March 21, 1922, in SD records, file 862t.01/ 368, NA, RG 59; Hughes to Harding, March 23, 1922, in *FRUS: 1922*, 2:211.

[130] Harding to Hughes, March 23, 1922, in *FRUS: 1922*, 2:213; Weeks to Hughes, March 23, 1922, in SD records, file 862t.01/369, NA, RG 59.

[131] Herrick (Paris) to Hughes, March 29, 1922, and Ambassador George Harvey (London) to Hughes, April 3, 1922, both in *FRUS: 1922*, 2:225. Actually, Harvey was involved in a peculiar and mysterious effort to offer Curzon special compensation for British cooperation on the cost question, but this occurred on March 19, 1922, before Harvey (or Hughes) could have known that the occupation might be a bargaining point, and therefore was probably with reference to a general settlement of war debts. See Curzon to Geddes, March 19, 1922, in FO records, CPGer, F.O. 408/7. What Hughes had in mind by way of reimbursement demands was spelled out on April 6, 1922, when he informed Harvey that it did not seem "too severe" to ask that the United States should have 300 million gold marks out of payments made: 100 million to be transferred immediately and the rest over two years; *FRUS: 1922*, 2:227.

[132] Allen to Hughes, March 24, 1922, and Harding to Hughes, April 1, 1922, in *FRUS: 1922*, 2:213–15.

[133] The note was conveyed informally in Dresel to Hughes, March 29, 1922, *FRUS: 1922*, 2:214; it is commented upon in Harding to Hughes, April 1, 1922 (second letter), in SD records file 862t.01/381. Later, when the formal text of Rathenau's note was received from the

German embassy, it also was forwarded from Hughes to Harding, May 1, 1922, in SD records, file 862t.01/399.

[134] Ambassador Alanson Houghton to Hughes, April 25, 1922, and Harding to Hughes, April 26, 1922, in *FRUS: 1922*, 2:216–17; Hughes to Harding, April 26, 1922, in SD records, file 862t.01/392.

[135] On the European situation, see D'Abernon, 1:293–335; F. S. Northedge, *The Troubled Giant: Britain among the Great Powers, 1916–1939* (London, 1967), pp. 178–79; and W. M. Jordan, *Great Britain, France and the German Problem, 1918–1939* (New York, 1944), pp. 76–82, 112–18.

[136] "Between you and me and no further, I have done my damnedest for General Allen and have had a long, three cornered talk . . . with the Secretary [Hughes] and Secretary Weeks, and another with General Pershing" (William Phillips to Fletcher, May 9, 1922, Fletcher Papers). See also Hughes to Harding, April 26, 1922, in SD records, file 862t.01/392.

[137] General James G. Harbord to Allen, April 21 and May 29, 1922, Allen Papers; Allen's unpublished journal, May 18 and 21, 1922, Allen Papers.

[138] Allen's unpublished diary, April 17 and May 18, 1922. Frank Lowden later assumed that his message had had considerable impact in Washington; see William T. Hutchison, *Lowden of Illinois*, 2 vols. (Chicago, 1957), 2:490. Tilson apparently stood in close relationship to the administration; see Allen, *Journal*, May 16, 1922, p. 358.

[139] Actually, in addition to the Germans, the British were the only ones to approach the State Department *directly* in the spring of 1922 on behalf of the American occupation; see R. A. Craigie to Curzon, June 9, 1922, in FO records, GCP, F.O. 371/7521.

[140] See Memorandum to Phillips from A. N. Young, May 26, 1922 and Memorandum to Hughes from Phillips, May 27, 1922, in SD records, file 862t.01/411 and 412, respectively, NA, RG 59.

[141] Phillips to Fletcher, May 9, 1922, Fletcher Papers. See Harding to Hughes, April 26, 1922, in *FRUS: 1922*, 2:217. Weeks too had begun to waver, if one can judge from Hughes's letter to him of May 29, 1922, in SD records, file 862t.01/436. Apparently both Weeks and Hughes had been impressed by an article by Charles H. Grasty in the *New York Times*, May 25, 1922.

[142] Hughes to Houghton, June 3, 1922, in *FRUS: 1922*, 2:218.

[143] The phrase is from Harding to Hughes, April 26, 1922, in *FRUS: 1922*, 2:217.

[144] Harding to Fletcher, August 24, 1922, Fletcher Papers.

Notes to Chapter Nine

[145] The possibility that the American occupation might be continued did not "leak" to the public until early May; see the *New York Times*, May 4, 1922, p. 21.

[146] The editors of the *New York Times* were representative of the emotionalism and superficial unity when they asserted on May 5, 1922: "If the Americans can perform a service to the world by postponing [the soldiers'] departure, it would be a pity to insist upon the order of recall."

CHAPTER 9

[1] Western European affairs of 1920–22 are described in Arnold Toynbee, ed., *Survey of International Affairs, 1920–1923* (London, 1925), pp. 5–203; Pierre Renouvin, *Histoire des rélations internationales; Les crises du xxᵉ siecle*, 2 vols. (Paris, 1957), 1:247–56; F. S. Northedge, *The Troubled Giant: Britain among the Great Powers, 1916–1939* (New York, 1966), pp. 160–84; Raymond J. Sontag, *A Broken World, 1919–1939* (New York, 1971), pp. 86–106; Harold Nicolson, *Curzon: The Last Phase, 1919–1925* (Boston, 1934), pp. 183–245; and Georges Suarez, *Briand: Sa vie—son oeuvre, avec son journal et de nombreux documents inedits*, 6 vols. (Paris, 1938–1952), 5:137–84. See also United States, Army, American Forces in Germany, "American Representation in Occupied Germany, 1920–1921," 2 vols., stencilled, (Coblenz?, 1922), 1:59–135 (hereafter cited as "American Representation, 1920–1921"); and U. S. Army, AFG, "American Representation in Occupied Germany, 1922–1923," stencilled, (Coblenz?, 1923), pp. 2–122 (hereafter cited as "American Representation, 1922–1923").

[2] As an illustration of General Allen's power in this regard, note the comments of the British ambassador in Paris during the negotiations that led to the formation of a trade-licensing body for the Rhineland: "I felt justified in suggesting this [that the new organization should sit in Coblenz, or failing this, in Cologne] as I had good reason to believe that General Allen is very unlikely to agree that there is sufficient accommodation available in Coblenz" (Lord Hardinge to Earl Balfour [acting foreign secretary], July 13, 1922, in Great Britain, Foreign Office (FO) records, Confidential Print: Germany (hereafter CPGer), F.O. 408/8). See also Henry T. Allen, *My Rhineland Journal*, (Boston, 1923), December 17, 1921, p. 291.

[3] Pierrepont Noyes Diary, June 3, 1920 (in possession of his family, Oneida, New York).

[4] Ibid., May 23 and June 3, 1920; Allen, *Journal*, May 19, 20, 22,

Notes to Chapter Nine

1920, pp. 112–13. Though Wallace Day returned to the United States with Noyes, most of Noyes's other assistants remained in Coblenz with Allen. Colonel David Stone was appointed Allen's deputy with the High Commission.

⁵ Allen, *Journal*, June 21, 1920, p. 122. Allen had concluded, perhaps on good evidence, that Noyes "immediately informed the Germans when he took their part"; see Allen to E .L. Dresel, March 14, 1921, E. L. Dresel Papers, Houghton Library, Harvard University.

⁶ Allen, *Journal*, June 6, 1920, p. 116; June 22, 1920, pp. 122–23.

⁷ Ibid., June 24, 1920, p. 123; Undersecretary of State Norman Davis to Ambassador Hugh Wallace (for Allen), June 22, 1920, in Department of State (hereafter SD) records, file 862t.01/121, National Archives (hereafter NA), Record Group (hereafter RG) 59.

⁸ United States, Congress, Senate, *Colored Troops in the French Army* . . . , 66th Cong., 3rd sess. (Senate Document 397).

⁹ Henry T. Allen, *The Rhineland Occupation* (Indianapolis, 1927), p. 322; Paul Tirard, *La France sur le Rhin: Douze années d'occupation rhénane* (Paris, 1930), pp. 219–20, 302–07; see also General Jean Degoutte to Allen, March 15, 1921, in Allen's unpublished journal, Henry T. Allen Papers, Library of Congress. In his memoirs, Tirard mistakenly asserts that Allen carried out this task on behalf of the High Commission.

¹⁰ Allen, *Journal*, April 18, 1921, p. 200.

¹¹ Ibid., August 1 and 2, 1920, pp. 135–36; Sir Harold Stuart to Earl Curzon (foreign secretary), July 31, 1920, in Great Britain, Foreign Office, *Documents on British Foreign Policy, 1919–1939*, First series, 17 vols. (London, 1947–   ), vol. 10, no. 187 (hereafter cited as *DBFP*). See also Ernst Fraenkel, *Military Occupation and the Rule of Law: Occupation Government in the Rhineland, 1918–1923* (London, 1944), pp. 117–18.

¹² Allen, *Journal*, August 3, 1920, p. 136. See also the Minutes of the Inter-Allied Rhineland High Commission, August 2 and 3, 1920, in the records of the Inter-Allied Rhineland High Commission, Stanford University.

¹³ Ibid., August 5, 1920, pp. 137–38; Allen to Secretary of War Newton D. Baker, August 10, 1920, in SD records, file 862t.01/166, NA, RG 59; Allen, *Rhineland Occupation*, pp. 218–19. For the German side, see the report of a meeting between Dr. Appelmann and Colonel Stone, August 2, 1920, in records of the Oberpräsidium der Rheinprovinz, Abteilung 403, Nr. 15009, Bundesarchiv, Coblenz. See also the

Notes to Chapter Nine

report of Reichskommissar Carl von Starck to the German Ministry of the Interior, October 27, 1920, in records of the Reichskommissar für die besetzten rheinischen Gebiete (hereafter RfdbrG), file entitled "Tätigkeitsberichte des Reichskommissars" (hereafter TdR), Deutsches Zentralarchiv, Potsdam.

¹⁴ Allen, *Rhineland Occupation*, p. 219; "American Representation, 1920–1921," 1:167–70.

¹⁵ See the report of Ministerialdirektor Sachs, October 7, 1920, in Peter Wulf, ed., *Das Kabinett Fehrenbach: 25. Juni 1920 bis 4. Mai 1921* (Boppard am Rhein, 1972), pp. 212–18; see also Germany, Reichstag, *Die Wunde in Westen. . . . Reichstagsitzung vom 6. November 1920* (Berlin, 1920), pp. 1–86. The British Foreign Office followed this very closely; see the extended comments on Malcolm Robertson's dispatch of October 26, 1920, as well as a military report of November 24, 1920, and the dispatch of Lord D'Abernon (ambassador in Berlin), November 25, 1920, in FO records, General Correspondence: Political (hereafter GCP), F.O. 371/4807.

¹⁶ Allen to Secretary of State Bainbridge Colby, November 29, 1920, in SD records, file 862t.01/218, NA, RG 59; Colonel Rupert Ryan to Curzon, November 27, 1920, and D'Abernon to Curzon, same date, in *DBFP*, vol. 10, nos. 241, 242.

¹⁷ D'Abernon to Curzon, December 6, 1920 (two messages), in *DBFP*, vol. 10, nos. 246, 247. See also Dresel to Colby, November 26, 28, December 4, 6, 1920, and Acting Secretary to Dresel, December 4, 1920, in United States, Department of State, *Papers Relating to the Foreign Relations of the United States: 1920*, 2 vols. (Washington, D.C., 1935), 2:335–37 (hereafter cited as *FRUS:1920*). For background on German motives regarding these speeches, see the remarks of Reichsminister Eduard David, May 25, 1920, in Martin Vogt, ed., *Das Kabinett Müller I: 27. März bis 21. Juni 1920* (Boppard am Rhein, 1971), pp. 282–83. See also the cabinet protocol of December 7, 1920, in Wulf, pp. 333–35.

¹⁸ Allen to Colby, January 18, 1921, in SD records file 862t.01/236, NA, RG 59; "American Representation, 1920–1921," 1:178–80. See also Robertson to Curzon, January 6, 1921, in *DBFP*, vol. 16, no. 566; and the Reichskommissar's report to the German and Prussian Ministers of Interior, January 14, 1921, in records of the RfdbrG, file entitled "Denkschrift über die Verhältnisse im besetzten rheinischen Gebiet."

¹⁹ Allen to General John J. Pershing, April 28, 1920, John J. Pershing Papers, Library of Congress.

²⁰ Allen, *Journal*, September 23, October 6, 1920, pp. 147, 154.

Notes to Chapter Nine

²¹ Ibid., June 2, 3, 1920, p. 116; Allen to Dresel, June 4, 1920, Dresel Papers; Allen to Baker, August 10, 1920, in SD records file 862t.01/166, NA, RG 59. Allen had decided in June to keep civilian Kreis representatives in the various Kreise and to relieve the local OCCAs of all duties except liaison with governmental agencies and courts in order to "prevent our administration [from] appearing too military"; Allen *Journal*, June 2, 1920, p. 116.

²² Ibid., October 6, 1920, p. 157.

²³ Memorandum of von Starck, March 5, 1921, in records of the Reichsministerium für die besetzten Gebiete (hereafter RMBG), file entitled "Den Reichskommissar für die besetzten rheinischen Gebiete," Deutsches Zentralarchiv, Potsdam; Allen, *Journal*, March 4, 7, 8, 1921, pp. 186–88; Allen to Dresel, March 14, 1921, Dresel Papers; and Robertson to Curzon, March 7, 1921, in *DBFP*, vol. 16, no. 592. See also the Minutes of the IARHC, March 4, 1921.

²⁴ Allen to Secretary of State Charles Evans Hughes, May 17, 1921, in SD records, file 862t.01/279, NA, RG 59. See also "American Representation, 1920–1921," 1:184–86.

²⁵ Malcolm Robertson had been appointed to succeed Sir Harold Stuart on October 10, 1920. Colonel Rupert Ryan had become deputy commissioner as of the same date.

²⁶ Ryan to Curzon, May 10, 1921, in FO records, GCP, F.O. 371/5882; Allen to Hughes, May 17, 1921, in SD records, file 862t.01/279, NA, RG 59; and Alexander von Brandt (Coblenz) to Ministry of the Interior, June 8, 1921, in RMBG records, file entitled "Den Reichskommissar für die besetzten rheinischen Gebiete."

²⁷ Auguste Saint Aulaire (French ambassador) to Curzon, June 1, 1921, and Curzon to Baron Moncheur (Belgian ambassador) and George Harvey (American ambassador), June 9, 1921, in FO records, GCP, F.O. 371/5883; Allen to Hughes, June 23, 1921, and Hughes to Harvey, June 27, 1921, in SD records, file 862t.01/303 and 287, respectively; Allen, *Journal*, July 7, 1921, p. 223. Prince Hermann von Hatzfeld-Wildenburg, a career diplomat, was born in 1867 and served as counselor of the embassy in Washington from 1906 to 1908. During the war he was a Red Cross delegate in Belgium and Bulgaria.

²⁸ Allen to Dresel, March 14, 1921, Dresel Papers.

²⁹ Allen to Pershing, March 10, 1921, Pershing Papers.

³⁰ Allen, *Journal*, March 4, 1921, p. 186; Allen to Dresel, March 14, 1921, Dresel Papers; "American Representation, 1920–1921," 1:185. See also the Minutes of the IARHC, March 4, 1921.

³¹ Robertson to Curzon, March 12, 1921, in *DBFP*, vol. 16, no. 460.

Notes to Chapter Nine

[32] Allen, *Journal*, March 8, 12, 18, 1921, pp. 188–91; Allen, *Rhineland Occupation*, pp. 204–10; see also Hughes to Allen, March 10, 19, 1921, and William R. Castle, Jr., to Hughes, March 15, 1921, in SD records file 462.00 R29/517 and 522 respectively, NA, RG 59.

[33] Hughes to Wallace (Paris), March 23, 1921, in *FRUS: 1921*, 2:37.

[34] Allen to Hughes, May 3, 1921, and May 17, 1921, in SD records file 862t.01/278 and 279, NA, RG 59. Robertson's views are reflected in Robertson to Curzon, May 17 and June 2, 1921, *DBFP*, vol. 16, nos. 621, 633.

[35] Charles á Court Repington, *After the War: A Diary* (Boston, 1922), pp. 231–32 (entry for May 24, 1921). See also Allen, *Journal*, August 9, 1921, p. 237, and Viscount Edgar V. D'Abernon, *The Diary of an Ambassador*, 3 vols. (Garden City, N.Y., 1929–1931), 1:217 (entry for September 26, 1921).

[36] Robertson to Curzon, July 15, 1921, in FO records, CPGer, F.O. 371/5973.

[37] Count Albrecht von Bernstorff (Foreign Ministry representative with the Reichskommissar and nephew of the former ambassador to the United States) suggested confidentially in London in June 1921 that a "stronger personality" at Coblenz would be in the interests of both Britain and Germany; see Bernstorff to German Foreign Ministry, August 17, 1921, in German Foreign Ministry (hereafter GFM) records, period after 1920, Office of the Reichsminister, file entitled "Besetztes Rheinland," container 1469.

[38] See Malcolm Robertson to Gladys Robertson, May 17 and 25, 1921, in the Sir (Malcolm) Arnold Robertson Papers, in possession of the family, Windsor, England. See also the comment of Sir Eyre Crowe, July 6, 1921, on Robertson to C. H. Tufton (London), July 2, 1921, in FO records, GCP, F.O. 371/5972. On the split in British opinion, note D. C. Watt, *Personalities and Policies: Studies in the Formulation of British Foreign Policy in the Twentieth Century* (South Bend, 1965), pp. 43–4, 211–14. See also John C. Cairns, "A Nation of Shopkeepers in Search of a Suitable France," *American Historical Revue* 79 (June 1974): 710–43.

[39] See S. P. Waterlow's comments, June 29, 1921, on a note from Sir Edward Grigg (prime minister's secretary), June 28, 1921, in FO records, GCP, F.O. 371/5857.

[40] See, for example, United States, Army, American Forces in Germany, *Weekly Digest* (Coblenz, 1919–1921), August 5, 1920.

Notes to Chapter Nine

[41] "American Representation, 1920–1921," 2:41.

[42] United States, Army, AFG, Military Intelligence Division, General Staff, *Christmas 1921* (Coblenz, 1921), p. 7 (hereafter cited as *Christmas 1921*).

[43] Memorandum from Captain H. E. Osann to Assistant Chief of Staff, G-2, November 12, 1921, in War Department (hereafter WD) records, Adjutant General's Office, AG 383 Germany Project (hereafter Ger) file, NA, RG 94; "American Representation, 1920–1921," 2: 315–19.

[44] Hamilton Holt, "The American Watch on the Rhine," *The Independent* 104 (December 4, 1920): 326–27, 347–49; "American Representation, 1920–1921" 2:327–34.

[45] See General Peyton C. March to Allen, July 27, 1920, Peyton C. March Papers, Library of Congress; Allen, *Journal*, May 12, 1921, p. 205; "American Representation, 1920–1921," 2:319–22. Allen, once called by a friend "the horseman of the U.S. Army," was himself an extremely active polo player; Robert Lee Bullard Diary, March 22, 1919, in Robert Lee Bullard Papers, Library of Congress.

[46] Edward A. Steiner, "Shifting Clouds," *The Independent* 105 (July 18, 1921): 637, 655–56; "American Representation, 1920–1921," 2:278–89.

[47] Holt, pp. 326–27, 347–49; Steiner, pp. 637, 655–56; "American Representation, 1920–1921," 2:41.

[48] "American Representation, 1920–1921," 1:219–23, 227–29. In judging these statistics, the reader must bear in mind that during this period the relative size of the zones was as follows:

French	57 Kreise	3,100,000 people
Belgian	18 Kreise	1,400,000 people
British	8 Kreise	1,250,000 people
American	7 Kreise	500,000 people

The suspensions and vetoes were carried out under Ordinance 29 (enacted July 1920). The press supervision was carried out under Ordinance 3 (January 1920) and 97 (September 1921). The publications include thirty-eight books and fifty-nine newspapers, the prohibition of the latter ranging in span from fifteen days to permanent. See also Reichsministerium für die Besetzten Gebiete, *Liste der von der interallierten Rheinlandkommission in Coblenz für das besetzte Gebiet verbotenen Bücher, Lichtbildstreifen und Zeitungen* (Berlin, 1925).

[49] Allen to Colby, September 18, 1920, and February 22, 1921, in

SD records, file 862t.01/187 and 256, NA, RG 59. See also "American Representation, 1920–1921," 1:75.

⁵⁰ "American Representation, 1920–1921," 1:70; 2:231–40.

⁵¹ Ibid., 2:42–49. Between October 1, 1919 and January 1, 1922 there were 1,527 applications to marry submitted by American soldiers. Of these, 767 were approved by Army headquarters.

⁵² Holt, pp. 326–27, 347–49.

⁵³ *Weekly Digest*, October 7, 1920.

⁵⁴ See reports of the Reichskommissar, October 27, 1920, in records of the RfdbrG, TdR file.

⁵⁵ Rhenanus, "In Rhenish Dollarika," *Der Tag*, translated in *Living Age* 303 (August 7, 1920): 334–36.

⁵⁶ On July 27, 1920, the War Department had cabled Allen that the inability of the State Department to provide funds would compel him to reduce his staff and replace civilians with military personnel in the American section of the High Commission (at that time the section employed about forty-three civilians, including department chiefs, Kreis representatives, and secretarial help). In order to avoid this necessity, Allen, to the delight and surprise of the State Department, persuaded the German custodian of state property to take over his current expenses. See the Memorandum of William Castle to A. N. Young, December 15, 1921, in SD records file 826t.01/432, NA, RG 59. See also the cables between Allen and Colby, July 28, 30, and August 2, 1920, in *FRUS: 1920*, 2:330–31.

⁵⁷ See Press Report, Dresel to Colby, November 8, 1920, in SD records file 862.9111/173, NA, RG 59; see also *Die Wunde im Westen*, pp. 1–86.

⁵⁸ See "American Representation, 1920–1921," 1:102–13; Allen, *Journal*, January 29, February 17, March 26, 27, 30, and April 2, 1921, pp. 178, 182, 192–95; see also *Chicago Tribune* (Paris edition), January 31, 1921. The *Tribune*, particularly, was outraged when Allen "apologized" to the German government for the Bergdoll affair, and it continued to urge sterner measures until the very end of the trial in March.

⁵⁹ Tirard, p. 218; news item of the *New York Herald* Bureau, Berlin, February 1, 1921, in Allen's unpublished journal, Allen Papers.

⁶⁰ Allen to Dresel, March 14, 1921, Dresel Papers.

⁶¹ Memorandum by Walter Simons, March 9, 1921, in GFM records, period after 1920, Office of the Reichsminister, file entitled "Besetztes Rheinland," container 149; Press Report, Dresel to Hughes, March 7, 1921, in SD records file 862.9111/189, NA, RG 59.

[62] Though in 1920 Allen had been more sympathetic to the French than President Wilson, by 1921 the general was clearly more pro-German than was Harding. So far did Washington and Coblenz respond to different pressures.

[63] Particularly useful for European diplomacy in the 1921–1922 period are J. P. Selsam, *The Attempts to Form an Anglo-French Alliance, 1919–1924* (Philadelphia, 1936), pp. 1–64; Ernst Laubach, *Die Politik der Kabinette Wirth 1921/22* (Lübeck, 1968), pp. 9–314; and David Felix, *Walther Rathenau and the Weimar Republic: The Politics of Reparations* (Baltimore, 1971), pp. 8–146.

[64] Allen to Pershing, May 26, 1921, Pershing Papers.

[65] Allen to Pershing, August 22, 1921, in SD records file 862t.01/437, NA, RG 59.

[66] For example, see Allen to Hughes, May 17, 1921 and July 20, 1921, in SD records file, 862t.01/279 and 308, respectively, NA, RG 59.

[67] Jean de Pange, *Les Libertés rhénanes: Pays rhénans—Sarre—Alsace* (Paris, 1922), pp. 114–23; Karl Wachendorf, *Zehn Jahre Fremdherrschaft am deutschen Rhein: Eine Geschichte der Rheinlandbesetzung von 1918–1928* (Berlin, 1928), pp. 107–17.

[68] Allen to Hughes, May 17, 1921, in SD records, file 862t.01/279, NA, RG 59.

[69] Allen to Hughes, July 20, 1921, in SD records, file 862t.01/308, NA, RG 59; Allen, *Journal*, July 13, 1921, p. 226.

[70] Allen, *Journal*, August 10, 1921, pp. 238–40. Robertson, in a letter to his wife during the conference, noted that "General Allen made a splendid impression on Lord Curzon, and Mr. Lloyd George wants him put forward, but Mr. Harvey has not the courage!" Malcolm Robertson to Gladys Robertson, August 10, 1921, Robertson Papers.

[71] Harvey (London) to Hughes and Hughes to Harvey, August 12, 1921, in SD records file 763.72119/11416, NA, RG 59.

[72] Transcripts of the conference are published in *DBFP*, vol. 15, nos. 92–104.

[73] Allen, *Journal*, August 12, 1921, p. 242; Allen to Pershing, August 22, 1921, in SD records, file 862t.01/437, NA, RG 59.

[74] Hughes to Allen, September 17, 1921, in SD records, file 462.00 R29/1038, NA, RG 59. Allen discouraged such a course. Yet he remarked to the British ambassador in Berlin that he was surprised at Washington's "energetic attitude"; see extract from Lord D'Abernon's Diary, September 24, 1921, in *DBFP*, vol. 16, no. 705.

[75] According to the French, German customs authorities had been

Notes to Chapter Nine

discriminating against French merchants ever since the 'hole in the West' was closed in April 1920. See the report of Minister of Economics Robert Schmidt to the German Ministry of the Interior, August 25, 1921, in RMBG records, file entitled "Aufhebung der wirtschaftlichen Sanktionen."

[76] See the correspondence during September-December 1921, in *DBFP*, vol. 16, nos. 689–709, 715–17, 724, 742, 759. See also Fraenkel, pp. 97–104.

[77] Allen to Hughes, September 19, 1921, in SD records file 826.01/ 313, NA, RG 59. This was Ordinance 97.

[78] Allen, *Rhineland Occupation*, pp. 175–76; Fraenkel, p. 124. For data on the appointments in question, see Ryan to Curzon, November 24, 1921, in FO records, GCP, F.O. 371/6038. Later, in January 1922, the High Commission established a committee under Colonel Stone to look into "reactionary tendencies" in local education. As Lord Kilmarnock reported it, "Considerable relief has been caused in German circles by the fact that the American representative has been appointed chairman . . ." (Lord Kilmarnock to Curzon, January 24, 1922, in FO records, CPGer, F.O. 408/7).

[79] The fact that sixty-nine ordinances were enacted during the twelve months from May 1920 to May 1921, and only twenty-eight during the next twelve months, may be tribute to a stiffening Anglo-American attitude. See Allen, *Rhineland Occupation*, p. 156.

[80] Allen, *Journal*, October 14, 1921, p. 268.

[81] Ibid., October 14, 15, 1921, pp. 268–69; see also Allen, *Rhineland Occupation*, p. 156.

[82] Lord Kilmarnock succeeded Malcolm Robertson as British High Commissioner on December 1, 1921. Born in 1876, he had been appointed to the British Foreign Service in 1900. His most recent tour of duty had been as chargé d'affaires in Berlin (since January 10, 1920).

[83] Allen, *Journal*, December 6, 8, 9, 1921, pp. 284–86; Allen to Hughes, December 9, 1921, and Allen to Ambassador Myron T. Herrick, December 14, 1921, both in Myron T. Herrick Papers, Western Reserve Historical Society, Cleveland, Ohio; Allen, *Rhineland Occupation*, pp. 325–32. See also the Minutes of the IARHC, December 2, 5, 6, 8, 1921.

[84] Allen, *Journal*, December 17, 1921, p. 291.

[85] Ibid., December 29, 31, 1921, and January 1, 3, 1922, pp. 297–300; "American Representation, 1922–1923," pp. 162–67. See also the Minutes of the IARHC, January 4, 1922.

[86] Allen, *Journal*, December 30, 1921, p. 297. This was also the claim of Manton Davis (Allen's legal adviser) in a letter to Undersecretary of State William Phillips, April 13, 1922, in John Dolan Papers, Stanford University.

[87] D'Abernon, 1:291 (entry for March 14, 1922).

[88] Allen, *Journal*, January 30, 1922, p. 136; Allen to Pershing, February 24, 1922, Pershing Papers; "American Representation, 1922–1923," 167–69.

[89] Allen, *Journal*, February 3, 9, 10, 1922, pp. 317–19.

[90] Ibid., December 15, 1921, pp. 287–89; Allen to Pershing, December 17, 1921, Pershing Papers.

[91] Allen, *Journal*, February 17, 18, 1922; Allen to Undersecretary of State Henry Fletcher, February 23, 1922, in SD records file 862t.01/382, NA, RG 59; Allen to Herrick, March 1, 1922, Herrick Papers. Degoutte and Foch attempted in March to infringe upon this agreement but abandoned the effort when Harding made his decision to withdraw; see Allen, *Journal*, March 1, 18, 24, 1922, pp. 324, 331, 337; also General J. G. Harbord to Allen, March 31, 1922, Allen Papers.

[92] Allen to Herrick, December 9, 14, 1921, and Herrick to Allen, December 20, 1921, all in Herrick Papers. See also Allen, *Journal*, December 23, 1921, p. 294. Herrick sent these letters and his reply on to the State Department, where one of Castle's assistants thought the ambassador's letter to Allen "sane and helpful"; see memorandum of R. H. N. (Norbeck?) to Castle, January 10, 1922, in SD records file 862t.01/463, NA, RG 59.

[93] For example, Allen to Hughes, December 5, 1921, Herrick Papers.

[94] Allen, *Journal*, February 17, 18, and March 16, 1922, pp. 321, 331.

[95] Ibid., May 24, 1922, p. 362.

[96] For example, Allen, *Journal*, December 9, 1921, p. 286; April 6, 1922, pp. 344–45; October 28, 1922, p. 460.

[97] Allen to Hughes, December 9, 1921, Herrick Papers; Allen, *Journal*, December 30, 1921, January 30, February 9, 1922, pp. 297, 316, 318.

[98] Allen to Pershing, February 24, 1922, Pershing Papers. Kilmarnock seems to have had a somewhat higher opinion of Allen than Allen of him, if we can judge by the latter's report to Curzon of February 21, 1922: "I earnestly hope, moreover, that the present reduction of American troops does not indicate an intention on the part of the United

Notes to Chapter Nine

States Government to withdraw completely from participation in the occupation of the Rhineland. Such a withdrawal would entail a serious weakening of the elements which contribute towards a reasonable application of the Rhineland Agreement" (FO records, CPGer, F.O. 408/7).

99 For example, Allen, *Journal*, December 6, 1921, p. 285; April 19, 1922, p. 349.

100 Ibid., April 28, 1922, p. 353. See also Allen to Herrick, April 16, 1922, Herrick Papers, and Allen, *Journal*, April 16, 1922, p. 348.

101 Ibid., February 22, 1922, p. 323; Allen to Pershing, February 24, 1922, Pershing Papers. See also Kilmarnock to Curzon, February 21, 1922, in FO Papers, CPGer, F.O. 408/7.

102 Allen, *Journal*, February 22, 1922, p. 323.

103 A representative of Rathenau discussed the draft cable with Allen before it was sent; Allen, *Journal*, March 23, 1922, p. 336. It was transmitted informally by Dresel to Hughes, March 29, 1922, and formally by the German Embassy in Washington to Hughes, April 24, 1922, in SD records file 862t.01/377 and 399, NA, RG 59.

104 Undersecretary of State William Phillips's memorandum on the occupation, May 27, 1922, in SD records file 862t.01/412, NA, RG 59 (hereafter cited as Phillips Memorandum). Foreign office feeling is reflected by the comments on Kilmarnock to Curzon, February 21, 23, 1922, both in FO records, CGP, F.O. 371/7520.

105 Phillips Memorandum. Houghton's interviews with the Belgian, British, and French commissioners, all of whom praised American representation, are recorded in the Alanson Houghton Diary, April 18, 1922, Alanson Houghton Papers (in possession of his family, Corning, New York). See also Houghton to Hughes, April 25, 1922, in *FRUS: 1922*, 2:216.

106 Herrick to Allen, April 7, 1922, Herrick Papers.

107 Allen, *Journal*, April 25, 1922, p. 352.

108 Allen to Herrick, April 10, 1922, Herrick Papers.

109 Ibid.; see also Allen, *Journal*, March 27, 1922, p. 337.

110 Allen, *Journal*, April 11, 1922, pp. 344–47; "American Representation, 1922–1923," p. 17; Allen, *Rhineland Occupation*, pp. 325–32.

111 Allen to Hughes, June 12, 1922, in SD records file 862t.01/425, NA, RG 59; Allen, *Rhineland Occupation*, pp. 229–31; Gerhard Pink, *The Conference of Ambassadors, Paris, 1920–1931* (Geneva, 1942), pp. 169–71.

112 Allen, *Journal*, May 12, 1922, p. 356.

Notes to Chapter Nine

[113] "Happy Days for the American Troops on the Rhine," *Literary Digest* 71 (October 1, 1921): 44–47.

[114] Mary Vane Turner, "Sidelights on Coblence. Amaroc to la France," *Queen's Quarterly* (Kingston, Ontario) 33 (1925): 53–59.

[115] Report of Major Bagby, G-2, November 26, 1921, included in a letter from Chief of Staff, AFG, to all unit commanders, December 9, 1921 (hereafter cited as Bagby Report); see also the Memorandum from H. H. to Assistant Chief of Staff, G-2, AFG, on October 31, 1921; and the Memorandum from H. E. Osann to Assistant Chief of Staff, G-2, AFG, November 12, 1921; all in WD records, Adjutant General's Office, AG 383 Ger file, NA, RG 94.

[116] Bagby Report. See also the detailed report of the Oberbürgermeister of Coblenz to the Prussian Minister of the Interior, September 7, 1921, in records of the RMBG, file entitled "Lageberichte der Behörden."

[117] Chief of Staff, AFG, to all unit commanders, October 11, 1921, and December 9, 1921; both in WD records, Adjutant General's Office, AG 383 Ger file, NA, RG 94.

[118] "American Representation, 1920–1921," 1:60–63. See, for example, the attitude of the *Frankfurter Zeitung*, February 9, 1922.

[119] See the undated reflections by a German regarding the AFG (probably written in November 1921) in WD records, American Expeditionary Forces, AFG file, Office of the Adjutant, box 538, NA, RG 102.

[120] *Christmas 1921*, pp. 8–9; also, United States, Army, American Forces in Germany, Second Section, General Staff, *Weekly Bulletin of Political and Economic Information* (Coblenz, 1919–1923), March 23, 1922, p. 11.

[121] Secretary of War John W. Weeks to Hughes, October 14, 1921, in SD records file 862.0146/1, NA, RG 59; corrected memorandum from Brigadier General William Lassiter to the Chief of Staff (General Pershing), February 17, 1922, in WD records, Adjutant General's Office, AG 370.5 Ger file, NA, RG 94; strength reports of the AFG may be found in WD records, American Expeditionary Forces, AFG file, Historical Headquarters boxes, NA, RG 120.

[122] Allen, *Journal*, April 22, 1922, p. 350.

[123] For example, ibid., June 19, 1922, p. 377; see also Allen to Herrick, October 27, 1922, Herrick Papers.

[124] See the speech of President Ebert, April 25, 1922, in Friedrich Ebert, *Schriften, Aufzeichnungen, Reden: Mit unveröffentlichten*

Notes to Chapter Ten

Erinnerungen aus dem Nachlass, 2 vols. (Dresden, 1926), 2:232–34; or the comments in the Reichstag, September 27, 30, 1921 in Germany, Reichstag, *Verhandlungen des Deutschen Reichstags, Stenographische Berichte* (Berlin, 1921), 351:4572.

[125] Leonard Woolf, "Germany and the Cost of Occupation," *Contemporary Review* 121 (January 1922): 114–16.

[126] See the *Kölnische Zeitung*, December 13, 1921.

[127] German note to the Allied powers, March 4, 1922, in GFM records, period after 1920, Office of the Staatssekretär, file entitled "Interallierte Kommission," container 2369.

[128] Reichstag, *Verhandlungen des Deutschen Reichstags*, April 6, 1922 (Berlin, 1922), 354:6943–46. On May 29, 1922, Tirard delivered a note to Reichskommissar Hatzfeld complaining about continued comments of this kind by the member in question (Adolf Korrell of the Democratic Party). Correspondence between Tirard and Hatzfeld is in GFM records, Embassy in Washington, file entitled "Besatzungstruppen," series AHA I, reel 25.

[129] *Germania* (Berlin), September 20 and October 4, 1921.

[130] *Der Tag* (Berlin), March 15, 1922.

[131] Allen, *Journal*, September 24, 1921, p. 258; December 1, 1921, p. 282; Willis F. Johnson, *George Harvey, A "Passionate Patriot"* (Boston, 1929), p. 310; and D'Abernon, February 6, 1922, 1:267.

[132] Rathenau's note to Hughes, March 29, 1922, is in Dresel to Hughes of the same date, in SD records, file 862t.01/377, NA, RG 59. Rathenau admitted that he had welcomed previous reductions for the precedent they had set, but he now asserted that the withdrawal had gone far enough.

CHAPTER 10

[1] See the *New York Times*, June 5, 1922, p. 1; also, Henry T. Allen, *My Rhineland Journal* (Boston, 1927), May 17, 1922, p. 358. It is noteworthy that the decision of June 1 was not made known to the American press. See Undersecretary of State William Phillips to General Henry T. Allen, June 3, 1922, Henry T. Allen Papers, Library of Congress.

[2] *New York Times*, June 26, 1922, p. 3.

[3] See, for example, his address to a group of businessmen in Chicago, October 17, 1922, text in the Frank Lowden Papers, University of Chicago Library.

[4] General James G. Harbord to General John J. Pershing, August

1922 (no day given), James G. Harbord Papers, Library of Congress.

[5] *New York Times*, June 7, 1922, p. 2.

[6] Arnold Toynbee, ed., *Survey of International Affairs, 1920–1923* (London, 1925), p. 178; Frank H. Simonds, *How Europe Made Peace without America* (Garden City, N.Y., 1927), pp. 230–41; David Lloyd George, *The Truth About Reparations and War Debts* (London, 1932), pp. 96 ff.

[7] Ambassador Henry P. Fletcher to President Warren G. Harding, Henry P. Fletcher Papers, Library of Congress.

[8] Harding to Fletcher, August 24, 1922, Fletcher Papers.

[9] Harding to Phillips, August 31, 1922, in Department of State (hereafter SD) records, file 462.00 R29, National Archives (hereafter NA), Record Group (hereafter RG) 59.

[10] Memorandum for Secretary of War John Weeks from General Harbord, September 7, 1922, forwarded with letter from Weeks to Harding, September 9, 1922, Warren G. Harding Papers, box 183, Ohio Historical Society, Columbus, Ohio.

[11] General Peyton C. March to Weeks, August 28, 1922, Peyton C. March Papers, Library of Congress, forwarded with letter from Weeks to Harding, September 9, 1922, Harding Papers, box 183.

[12] Weeks to Harding, September 15, 1922, Harding Papers, box 183.

[13] Harding to Weeks, September 16, 1922; see also Harding to Weeks, September 16, 1922, both in Harding Papers, box 183.

[14] Harding to Weeks, October 6, 1922, Harding Papers, box 183. Harding's concern with a possible $650 million deficit in the national budget was undoubtedly a factor here; *New York Times*, September 20, 1922, p. 19.

[15] Allen, *Journal*, October 25, 1922, p. 458.

[16] Allen to Secretary of State Charles E. Hughes, October 19, 1922, forwarded with letter from Hughes to Harding, October 21, 1922, in SD records, file 862t.01/467, NA, RG 59.

[17] *New York Times*, October 23, 1922, p. 1.

[18] Phillips to Hughes, October 17, 1922, in SD records, file 862t.01/465, NA, RG 59.

[19] *Congressional Record*, 67th Cong., 2nd sess., September 14, 1922, 62:12919–2921.

[20] Harding to Hughes, October 21, 1922, in SD records, file 862t.01/460, NA, RG 59.

[21] *New York Times*, December 1, 1922, p. 3.

22 See Hughes to Assistant Secretary of the Treasury Eliot Wadsworth, February 19, 1923, in United States, Department of State, *Papers Relating to the Foreign Relations of the United States: 1923*, 2 vols. (Washington, D.C., 1938), 2:110–34 (hereafter cited as *FRUS: 1923*).

23 See, for example, the uneasiness of the *Nation*, 115 (November 8, 1922): 492.

24 *Washington Post*, November 23, 24, 25, 27, 28, 1922; *Congressional Record*, 67th Cong., 3rd sess., November 23 and 27, 1922, 63:49, 277–82, 289–96. The German Embassy in Washington had been responsible for giving Hitchcock much of the information on which he based his criticism of the French. See Ambassador Otto Wiedfeldt to Foreign Minister Frederic von Rosenberg, January 2, 1923, in German Foreign Ministry (hereafter GFM) records, Embassy in Washington, file on "Besatzungstruppen," series AHA I, reel 25.

25 Transcript enclosed in Phillips to Allen, December 2, 1922, in SD records, file 862t.01/961, NA, RG 59.

26 Ernst Laubach, *Die Politik der Kabinette Wirth 1921/22* (Lübeck, 1968), pp. 236–42; David Felix, *Walther Rathenau and the Weimar Republic: The Politics of Reparations* (Baltimore, 1971), pp. 147–58; and Werner Link, *Die amerikanische Stabilisierungspolitik in Deutschland 1921–32* (Düsseldorf, 1969), pp. 122–35.

27 United States, Army, American Forces in Germany (AFG), Assistant Chief of Staff, G-2, "American Representation in Occupied Germany, 1922–1923," stencilled (Coblenz?, 1923), pp. 44–47 (hereafter cited as "American Representation, 1922–1923"). See also Laubach, pp. 242–49; Felix, pp. 159–74.

28 The procès verbal of the London conference is in Great Britain, Foreign Office, *Minutes of the London Conference on Reparations, August, 1922* (London, Cmd. 2258 of 1924). See also Toynbee, pp. 66–68, 180; and Laubach, pp. 250–63.

29 Allen, *Journal*, August 14–31, 1922, pp. 412–21; Toynbee, pp. 181–83; Laubach, pp. 269–76; and Link, 144–48. On French foreign policy, see Auguste Saint Aulaire, *Confession d'un vieux diplomate* (Paris, 1953), pp. 593–649; Jules Laroche, *Au Quai d'Orsay avec Briand et Poincaré, 1913–1926* (Paris, 1957), pp. 156–71; Edouard Bonnefous, *Histoire politique de la troisième république; L'après-guerre: 1919–1924* (Paris, 1959), pp. 285–331; and Jules Chastenet, *Histoire de la troisième république*, 7 vols. (Paris, 1952–1963), 5:76–106.

30 Edgar V. D'Abernon, *The Diary of an Ambassador*, 3 vols. (Garden City, N.Y., 1929–1931), November 6, 10, 1922, 2:132–37; Toynbee, pp. 183–86; Laubach, pp. 276–306.

Notes to Chapter Ten

[31] D'Abernon, November 21, 1922, 2:141–42; Laubach, pp. 306–07.

[32] Carl Bergmann, *Der Weg der Reparation* (Frankfurt, 1926), p. 194. On Cuno's role in general, see Alfred Cornebise's useful article, "Cuno, Germany, and the Coming of the Ruhr Occupation: A Study in German–West European Relations," *Proceedings of the American Philosophical Society* 116 (December 1972): 502–31.

[33] Lord Hardinge (British ambassador in France) to Marquess Curzon, October 22, 1922, Marquess Curzon Papers, Kedleston Hall.

[34] See D'Abernon, 2:9.

[35] Minutes of the negotiations are in Great Britain, Foreign Office, *Inter-Allied Conferences on Reparations and Inter-Allied Debts, held in London and Paris, December 1922 and January 1923* (London, Cmd. 1812 to 1923). See also Toynbee, pp. 186–89; Bonnefous, pp. 331–44; and Ludwig Zimmerman, *Deutsche Aussenpolitik in der Ara der Weimarer Republik* (Göttingen, 1958), pp. 134–38.

[36] These were the explicit objectives of the secret and semiofficial "Dariac" report, compiled for Poincaré by the chairman of the Financial Commission of the Chamber of Deputies. This report was submitted May 28, 1922, and later became public in the columns of the *Manchester Guardian*, November 2, 1922, and March 5, 1923. The best discussion of the separatists is in Lord Kilmarnock to Curzon, August 4, 1923, Curzon Papers.

[37] See Alcide Ebray, *A Frenchman Looks at the Peace* (New York, 1927), pp. 139–54, 173–89.

[38] On the commercial situation, see Kilmarnock to Earl Balfour, July 24, 1922, in Great Britain, Foreign Office (FO) records, Confidential Print: Germany (hereafter CPGer), F.O. 408/8.

[39] Reichskommissar von Hatzfeld-Wildenburg to the Minister of the Interior (?), July 27, 1922, in GFM records, Embassy in Washington, file on "Besatzungstruppen," series AHA I, reel 25.

[40] "American Representation, 1922–1923," pp. 49, 97–99.

[41] Chancellor Wilhelm Cuno on November 24, 1922, Foreign Minister Walther Rathenau on June 21, 1922; see "American Representation, 1922–1923," pp. 38, 92.

[42] Regarding costs, see "Das Rheinland nach dem Versailler Vertrag" by Freiherr von Solemacher-Antweiler in Otto Peters, ed., *Kampf um den Rhein* (Mainz, 1931). The Germans were particularly incensed at the fact that the High Commission had now increased its staff to over 1,300 people. Regarding "outrages" by colonials, see Hatzfeld to Tirard, March 13, 1923, in GFM records, Embassy in Washington, file on "Besatzungstruppen," series AHA I, reel 25. Hatzfeld here makes refer-

ence to five protests on the same subject since August 1922.
⁴³ Allen, *Journal*, October 14, 20 and November 28, 1922, pp. 373–74, 447, 454, 484. Correspondence among officials of the Foreign Ministry included a great deal of praise of the Americans; see, for example, Gerhard von Mutius to Rosenberg, December 9, 1922, in GFM records, period after 1920, Office of the Reichsminister, file on "Besetztes Rheinland," container 1469.

⁴⁴ Diary of Alanson B. Houghton, July 26, 1922, Alanson B. Houghton Papers (in possession of his family, Corning, New York). The German government was extremely worried during the summer of 1922 that Britain might be changing its Rhenish policy in return for certain favors and that this change might clear the way for a separatist revolution. On this, see Staatssekretär Edgar Haniel to Ambassador Friedrich Stahmer (London), July 24, 1922, in GFM records, Embassy in Washington, file on "Besatzungstruppen," series AHA I, reel 25.

⁴⁵ *New York Times*, December 1, 1922, p. 3. On the German mood, see Princess Cantacuzene, "Between Kaiser and Democracy," *Saturday Evening Post* 195 (November 25, 1922): 89.

⁴⁶ J. J. H. Mordacq, *La Mentalité allemande: Cinq ans de commandement sur le Rhin* (Paris, 1926), p. 104.

⁴⁷ Memorandum of Henry Hossfeld to Allen, August 19, 1922, in SD records, file 862t.01/979, NA, RG 59.

⁴⁸ For example, Allen, *Journal*, October 25, 1922, p. 458.

⁴⁹ *New York Times*, October 23, 1922. André Tardieu and Jules Cambon, however, did not consider the presence of the AFG important because "America has no European policy"; Oscar T. Crosby to Allen, July 8, 1922, Allen Papers.

⁵⁰ Allen, *Journal*, November 11, 1922, pp. 469–70.

⁵¹ See Sir George Graham (British ambassador in Brussels) to Curzon, November 22, 25, 26, 1922, all in FO records, CPGer, F.O. 408/8. See also Allen, *Journal*, November 11, 1922, pp. 470–71.

⁵² Allen, *Journal*, July 26, November 28, 1922, pp. 400, 482–88.

⁵³ Ibid., August 12, 1922, p. 410. A census would have been useful in calculating "productive guarantees."

⁵⁴ Ibid., July 9, 18, 1922, pp. 391–96.

⁵⁵ Ibid., August 1, 1922, pp. 403–04.

⁵⁶ Ibid., August 1, 3, 18, 1922, pp. 403, 405, 414; and Kilmarnock to Curzon, August 14, 1922, in FO records, General Correspondence: Political (hereafter GCP), F.O. 371/7537. See also Henry T. Allen, *The*

Notes to Chapter Ten

Rhineland Occupation (Indianapolis, 1927), pp. 180–84; "American Representation, 1922–1923," pp. 171–74; and Ernst Fraenkel, *Military Occupation and the Rule of Law: Occupation Government in the Rhineland, 1918–1923* (New York, 1944), pp. 127–28.

[57] Allen, *Journal*, August 1, 3, 1922, pp. 403–05.

[58] Ibid., September 12, 1922, p. 427. The Rhineland had been on French time twice before, in the winters of 1920 and 1921, but on this occasion the French had expressed a desire that the change be permanent; see "American Representation, 1922–1923," pp. 178–79.

[59] Allen, *Journal*, September 27, 1922, p. 437. Allen was disturbed enough by Kilmarnock's indecisiveness that he criticized the British high commissioner both to a representative of the Foreign Office who was visiting Coblenz and to the British ambassador in Berlin; Allen to Houghton, October 26, 1922, Houghton Papers.

[60] Allen, *Journal*, October 28, 1922, p. 460.

[61] "American Representation, 1922–1923," pp. 178–80. In other words, this was the first time a British negative vote was not the equivalent of a veto.

[62] Allen, *Journal*, September 12, 22, 1922, pp. 427, 432; Allen, *Rhineland Occupation*, pp. 325–32; "American Representation, 1922–1923," pp. 156–61, 210–14; Fraenkel, p. 157; Allen to Hughes, October 2, 1922, in SD records file 862t.01/458, NA, RG 59. The Allied notification to the Germans is printed in Germany, Reichsministerium für die Besetzten Gebiete, *Dokumente zur Besetzung der Rheinlande*, 3 vols. (Berlin, 1925), 2:27.

[63] Allen to Hughes, October 2, 1922, in SD records, file 862t.01/458, NA, RG 59.

[64] "American Representation, 1922–1923," pp. 156–61.

[65] See Chancellor Joseph Wirth to Paris, London, and Brussels embassies, October 14, 1922, in GFM records, period after 1920, Office of the Reichsminister, file on "Besetztes Rheinland," container 1469.

[66] See Prussia, Landtag, *Sitzungsberichte des Preussischen Landtags*, October 23, 1922 (Berlin, 1922), 10:12875–2893; Germany, Reichstag, *Verhandlungen des Deutschen Reichstags, Stenographische Berichte*, October 23, 1922 (Berlin, 1922) 357:8872–876. See also Kilmarnock to Curzon, August 4, 1923, Curzon Papers.

[67] See Allen, *Journal*, October 30, November 15, 23, and December 19, 1922, pp. 461, 474–79, 498; Allen to Herrick, October 27, 1922, Myron T. Herrick Papers, Western Reserve Historical Society, Cleveland, Ohio; Allen to Houghton, December 2, 1922, Houghton Papers;

and Kilmarnock to Curzon, December 4, 1922, in FO records, CPGer, F.O. 408/8.

⁶⁸ Allen, *Journal,* December 8, 1922, p. 490; Gerhard Pink, *The Conference of Ambassadors, Paris, 1920–1931* (Geneva, 1942), p. 169.

⁶⁹ See Mutius to Rosenberg, December 9, 1922, unsigned memorandum of December 11, 1922, and memorandum of von Rintelen, December 11, 1922, all in GFM records, period after 1920, Office of the Reichsminister, file on "Besetztes Rheinland," container 1469.

⁷⁰ Allen, *Journal,* June 16, 22, July 12, 1922, pp. 374, 378, 392; *New York Times,* June 17, 1922, p. 4; June 19, 1922, p. 14.

⁷¹ Phillips to Allen, June 3, July 26, August 23, September 3, December 2, 1922, and January 3, 1923, Allen Papers. Allen also was able to confer with William R. Castle, Jr., in October during the latter's visit to Berlin; Allen, *Journal,* October 20, 21, 1922, pp. 452–55.

⁷² For example, Harbord to Allen, September 18, 1922, Allen Papers.

⁷³ Weeks to Allen, December 16, 1922, Allen Papers.

⁷⁴ See Houghton to Allen, May 27, August 28, September 8, and November 23, 1922, Allen Papers. Herrick, while no friend of the occupation, did not campaign actively against it; see Herrick to Allen, January 11, 1923, Herrick Papers.

⁷⁵ Allen, *Journal,* July 25, 31, 1922, pp. 399–402.

⁷⁶ By September 30, 1922, there were 4,641 French troops in the American zone; see report of that date in WD records, Adjutant General's Office, AG 350.05 Germany Project (hereafter Ger) file, NA, RG 94. Originally, Allen had accepted relatively few troops but he had been forced to be more accommodating in June. Even then, Degoutte had asked him to take over twice as many as he ultimately did; see Allen, *Journal,* February 18, 1922, p. 322; June 11, 1922, pp. 370–71.

⁷⁷ Harbord to Pershing, August 3, 1922, Harbord Papers.

⁷⁸ *New York Times,* January 16, 1923, p. 3.

⁷⁹ Allen, *Journal,* December 15, 16, 1922, pp. 436–37.

⁸⁰ Ludvig af Petersens, "In den besetzten Gebieten am Rhein und der Saar," *Deutsche Rundschau* 193 (October 1922): 12–28. Part of the difficulty lay in the number of retired American officers and American tourists who refused to leave Coblenz; see Report on Political and Economic Conditions in Coblenz, October 7, 1922, in SD records, Coblenz Post Records 1922, decimal 800, NA, RG 84.

⁸¹ Wiedfeldt to Hughes, November 21, 1922, and Hughes to Wiedfeldt, January 3, 1923, in GFM records, Embassy in Washington, file on "Besatzungstruppen" series AHA I, reel 25.

Notes to Chapter Ten

[82] Report on Political and Economic Conditions in Coblenz, October 7, 1922, January 19, 1923, in SD records Coblenz Post Records 1922, decimal 800, NA, RG 84.

[83] *New York Times*, January 16, 1923, p. 3; Memorandum of Lassiter to Assistant Chief of Staff, G-1, January 11, 1923, in WD records, Adjutant General's Office, AG 370.5 Ger file, NA, RG 94.

[84] "American Representation, 1922–1923," p. 237; *Washington Post*, December 4, 1922. Two good articles on the situation in the American zone are O. G. Villard, "Germany 1922: In the Occupied Territory," *Nation* 115 (August 2, 1922): 116–18, and Francis Rogers, "Verdun and Coblenz," *Outlook* 132 (September 13, 1922): 56–57.

[85] See Hardinge to Curzon, December 20, 1922, Curzon Papers; Toynbee, pp. 186–89; and David Glen White, "Einige Kapitel aus der Grossen Politik zur Zeit der Ruhrbesetzung" (Ph.D. diss., University of Berlin, 1939), pp. 23–28. For a description of the mood of despair which descended on the Rhineland in December, see the transcript involving Staatssekretär Eduard Hamm and Staatssekretär (for the Occupied Regions) Philipp Brugger, December 4, 1922, in Karl-Heinz Harbeck, ed., *Das Kabinett Cuno: 22. November 1922 bis 12. August 1923* (Boppard am Rhein, 1972), pp. 21–25.

[86] James Logan (Paris) to Hughes, January 5, 1923, in SD records, file 462.00, R29/2363. On Poincaré's attitudes, see Hughes Memorandum of December 26, 1922, in United States, Department of State, *Papers Relating to the Foreign Relations of the United States: 1922*, 2 vols. (Washington, D.C., 1937), 2:197–99 (hereafter cited as *FRUS: 1922*); and Herrick to Hughes, December 22, 1922, Herrick Papers.

[87] Correspondence is in *FRUS: 1922*, 2:203–11. See also Dieter Bruno Gescher, *Die Vereinigten Staaten von Nordamerika und die Reparationen, 1920–1924* (Bonn, 1956), pp. 134–35.

[88] On German intentions, see Max von Stockhausen, *Sechs Jahre Reichskanzlei, Von Rapallo bis Locarno: Erinnerungen und Tagebuchnotizen, 1922–1927* (Bonn, 1954), pp. 54–56; and Zimmerman, pp. 138–42. Cuno made his Rhine proposal public on December 31, 1922, after the French had leaked it to the press.

[89] Boyden to Hughes, October 14, 1922, in *FRUS: 1922*, 2:165.

[90] Houghton to Hughes, October 23, 1922, and Castle to Hughes, October 24, 1922, in *FRUS: 1922*, 2:171, 176. William R. Castle was the Chief of the Western European desk in the State Department.

[91] Hughes to Herrick and Boyden, October 17, 1922, in *FRUS: 1922*, 2:168–70.

[92] Hughes to Houghton, November 14, 1922, in *FRUS: 1922*, 2:181–82.

[93] Hughes to Herrick and Boyden, October 17, 1922, in *FRUS: 1922*, 2:168–70; and Hughes to Fletcher, October 18, 1922, in SD records, file 462.00 R296/2, NA, RG 59. See also Link, pp. 148–63.

[94] Herrick to Hughes, November 17, 1922, in *FRUS: 1922*, 2:185; Herrick to Hughes, November 24, 1922, and Hughes to Herrick, November 25, 1922, in SD records, file 462.00 R29/2199, NA, RG 50.

[95] Memorandum by Hughes on conversation with Ambassador Jusserand, December 14, 1922, in *FRUS: 1922*, 2:187.

[96] William Phillips to Warren Robbins (Berlin), December 13, 1922, in SD records, file 701.6211/595, NA, RG 59.

[97] Memorandum by Hughes on conversation with Ambassador Jusserand, December 14, 1922, in *FRUS: 1922*, 2:187.

[98] *Chicago Tribune*, December 15, 1922.

[99] John Chalmers Vinson, *William E. Borah and the Outlawry of War* (Athens, Ga., 1955), pp. 54–57; Robert James Maddox, *William E. Borah and American Foreign Policy* (Baton Rouge, 1969), pp. 129–35.

[100] Castle to Houghton, December 30, 1922, Houghton Papers; text of Hughes's speech is in *FRUS: 1922*, 2:199–202. See also Vinson, pp. 54–7; Gescher, pp. 135–37; and Link, pp. 163–76.

[101] *St. Louis Post Dispatch*, December 28, 1922. Hughes approved Harding's letter to the Senate of December 28, describing it as "most excellent"; Hughes to Harding, December 28, 1922, Charles E. Hughes Papers, Library of Congress.

[102] *New York Times*, December 28, 1922, p. 2; Maddox, pp. 125–26.

[103] Memorandum by Hughes of conversation with Ambassador Jusserand, January 8, 1923, in *FRUS: 1923*, 2:47; William Phillips Diary, January 8, 1923, William Phillips Papers, Houghton Library, Harvard University.

[104] *New York Times*, January 6, 1923.

[105] *Congressional Record*, 67th Cong., 4th sess., January 6, 1923, 64:1349–61. One of the most interesting indications of the international-ist attitude was Pierrepont Noyes's support of recall; see the *New York Times*, January 8, 1923, p. 3. Shortly after the Senate's vote, Senator Joseph Robinson (D-Ark.) summed up this view when he charged that "after refusing for two years to go in, we declined to come out"; *New York Times*, January 10, 1923, p. 3. Senator Reed, meanwhile, was threatening to renew the fight for recall through the army appropria-tions bill, due soon on the floor; *San Francisco Examiner*, January 3, 1923; *Philadelphia Public Ledger*, January 8, 1923.

Notes to Chapter Ten

[106] Phillips Diary, January 9, 1923, Phillips Papers; *New York Times*, January 10, 1923, p. 1.

[107] Minutes are in Great Britain, Foreign Office, *Inter-Allied Conferences on Reparations and Inter-Allied Debts*. See also Toynbee, pp. 193–201; White, pp. 34–43; and Bonnefous, pp. 343-44. To be sure, Bonar Law was widely blamed for ineptitude; see Curzon to Lord Crewe (British ambassador in Paris), January 5, 1923, Curzon Papers; and Keith Middlemas, ed., *Thomas Jones: Whitehall Diary*, 2 vols. (London, 1969), 1:233 (entry for March 9, 1923). Moreover, both French army documents and Poincaré's biographers tend to emphasize his uneasiness at the time; Jacques Chastenet, *Raymond Poincaré* (Paris, 1948), pp. 245–46; Pierre Miquel, *Poincaré* (Paris, 1961), pp. 456–57.

[108] Allen, *Journal*, January 7, 1923, p. 507.

[109] Toynbee, p. 201; White, pp. 43–48; Gescher, p. 142.

[110] *St. Louis Post Dispatch*, January 10, 1923; Gescher, pp. 143–48.

[111] Phillips Diary, January 10, 1923, Phillips Papers. See also William Phillips, *Ventures in Diplomacy* (Boston, 1953), pp. 114–16.

[112] Entry in Hughes's official appointment book, January 10, 1923, Hughes Papers.

[110] Phillips Diary, January 10, 1923, Phillips Papers; Phillips, pp. 114–16.

[114] Castle to Houghton, January 12, 1923, Houghton Papers. Still, Hughes told Jusserand that Harding's action did not reflect on American friendship for France, and when Borah later demanded an official protest against the Ruhr seizure, the administration refused on the grounds that it would only alienate the French; *New York Times*, January 24, 1923, p. 1.

[115] France, Assemblée Nationale, *Annales de la Chambre des Députés, Débats parlementaires*, January 11, 1923 (Paris, 1923), 119:12; *New York Times*, January 12, 1923, p. 1.

[116] Paul Tirard, *La France sur le Rhin: Douze années d'occupation rhénane* (Paris, 1930), p. 219.

[117] "End of Our Watch on the Rhine," *Literary Digest* 76 (February 17, 1923): 22. See also the memorandum of R. H. N. (Norbeck?) to Castle, January 31, 1923, in SD records, file 862t.01/1055, NA, RG 59.

[118] *New York Times*, January 10, 1923, p. 1, January 12, 1923, p. 3.

[119] *New York Times*, January 8, 1923, p. 1, and January 27, 1923, p. 1. The British were badly divided during January and February, with D'Abernon strongly in favor of British withdrawal, and Crewe and Kilmarnock as adamantly opposed; memorandum of February 6, 1923, in FO records, CPGer, F.O. 408/9. On Bonar Law's decision to stay, see

Middlemas, p. 231 (entry for February 22, 1922). See also the exchanges between Stahmer (London) and Rosenberg, January 22, 25, 26, 31, 1923, in GFM records, period after 1920, Office of the Reichsminister, file on "Besetztes Rheinland," container 1469.

[120] Rosenberg to Wiedfeldt, January 9, 1923, in GFM records, period after 1920, Office of the Reichsminister, file on "Besetztes Rheinland," container 1469.

[121] Press Report, Ambassador Alanson Houghton to Hughes, January 15, 1923, in SD records, file 862.9111/279, NA, RG 59.

[122] Houghton to Hughes, January 29, 1923, in SD records, file 826t.01/618, NA, RG 59. See also Cuno's qualms of January 23, 1923 in Harbeck, p. 186.

[123] *San Francisco Examiner*, January 11, 1923.

[124] "American Aloof as Europe Burns," *Literary Digest* 76 (February 10, 1923): 7–9. Former Governor Lowden was also of this view, arguing that America "had no right to haul down the flag"; *New York Times*, January 27, 1923, p. 1.

[125] *San Francisco Chronicle*, January 11, 1923.

[126] *Wall Street Journal*, January 11, 1923.

[127] *Cleveland Plain Dealer*, January 11, 1923.

[128] *Atlanta Constitution*, January 9, 1923.

[129] *New Republic* 33 (January 17, 1923): 183.

[130] *Christian Science Monitor*, January 8, 1923.

[131] For example, *Congressional Record*, 67th Cong., 4th sess., January 20, 27, 1923, 64:2087–088, 2598–602.

[132] See "American Public opinion concerning the French seizure of the Ruhr," *The Outlook* 133 (January 31, 1923): 210–12; Ernest H. Abbott, "A Samaritan in Search of an Inn," *The Outlook* 133 (January 24, 1923): 166–68; "America Aloof as Europe Burns," *Literary Digest* 76 (February 10, 1923): 7–9; and "American Opinion on the Ruhr," *The Spectator* 130 (April 7, 1923): 578–79. See also Sir Auckland Geddes (British ambassador in Washington) to Curzon, January 21, 25, February 8, 1923, in FO records, CPGer, F.O. 408/9; and Gescher, pp. 149–56.

[133] Allen, *Journal*, January 11, 12, 1923, pp. 514–17; Allen, *Rhineland Occupation*, pp. 282–86.

[134] Allen, *Journal*, January 11, 1923, pp. 514–15.

[135] Allen to Hughes, January 12, 1923, in *FRUS: 1923*, 2:51.

[136] Hughes to Boyden, January 14, 1923, in SD records, file 462.00 R29/2344, NA, RG 59.

[137] Phillips Diary, January 15, 1923, Phillips Papers. The British

had been as uninterested as the French in Allen's proposal, but had confined themselves to so informing their commissioner in Coblenz; see Kilmarnock to Curzon, January 12, 1923 (two telegrams); and Curzon to Kilmarnock, January 15, 1923, in FO records, GCP, F.O. 371/8702.

[138] Hughes to Allen, January 18, 1923, in *FRUS: 1923*, 2:52.

[139] Allen, *Journal*, January 18, 1923, pp. 522–23.

[140] Allen to Hughes, January 18, 1923, in SD records, file 862t.01/657, NA, RG 59.

[141] Herrick to Hughes, February 15, 1924, in SD records, file 862t.01/942, NA, RG 59. See Allen, *Journal*, January 18, 1923, p. 522.

[142] Allen, *Rhineland Occupation*, p. 274. Kilmarnock had in fact suggested to his government that the American posture of March 1921, be taken as a model for the British occupation. Colonel Ryan (British deputy commissioner) later made the same suggestion to Bonar Law personally; Kilmarnock to Curzon, January 11, 1923, and Memorandum of January 22, 1922, in FO records, CPGer, F.O. 408/9.

[143] "American Representation, 1922–1923," pp. 129–45; Allen, *Rhineland Occupation*, pp. 276–79.

[144] *New York Times*, January 14, 1923, p. 2.

[145] "American Representation, 1922–1923," p. 226.

[146] Reprinted in Allen, *Journal*, January 18, 1923, pp. 524–25.

[147] Reprinted in ibid., January 22, 1923, pp. 531–32.

[148] See ibid., January 13, 18, 19, 1923, pp. 518, 525–27.

[149] Ibid., January 24, 1923, pp. 537–38. See also *New York Times*, January 25, 1923, p. 1; *The Times* (London), January 25, 1923; and Katherine Tynan, *Life in the Occupied Area* (London, 1925), p. 202.

[150] Allen, *Journal*, January 22, 24–27, 1923, pp. 531, 536–42; "American Representation, 1922–1923," pp. 144–46.

[151] Allen had inquired of Phillips about the possibility on November 7, 1922, and Phillips had replied on December 2, 1922; both in SD records, file 826t.01/961, NA, RG 59.

[152] Houghton to Hughes, January 16, 1923, in SD records, file 862t.01/951, NA, RG 59.

[153] Hughes to Allen, January 31, 1923, in *FRUS: 1923*, 2:193; see also Hughes to Harding, February 2, 1923, in SD records, file 862t.01/583A, NA, RG 59. By this time it had become even clearer to Hughes that both Germany and France were determined on "no compromise"; see Houghton to Hughes, January 30, 1923, and Hughes to Harding, January 31, 1923, in SD records, file 862t.01/569, NA, RG 59.

[154] Allen, *Journal*, February 6, 1923, p. 555; minutes of this meeting

are included with Allen to Phillips, March 26, 1923, in SD records, file 862t.01/952, NA, RG 59.

¹⁵⁵ *St. Louis Post Dispatch*, January 13, 1923, p. 2; *New York Times*, January 26, 1923, p. 3.

¹⁵⁶ *New York Times*, February 8, 1923, pp. 1, 10.

¹⁵⁷ See the *New York Times*, January 20, 1923, p. 3; January 21, 1923, p. 2; and January 23, 1923, p. 1.

¹⁵⁸ E. L. James, in the *New York Times*, January 13, 1923, p. 3.

CONCLUSION

¹ An agreement with the Allies was finally negotiated on May 25, 1923, according to which the United States was to receive payment over a twelve-year period, beginning December 31, 1923. Payments lagged, however, and under the Dawes and Young plans the United States reduced their size in order to get them back on schedule. For a listing of the agreements, see United States, Department of State, *Papers Relating to the Foreign Relations of the United States: The Paris Peace Conference 1919*, 13 vols. (Washington, D.C., 1947), 13:778. The account of the United States as of July 1, 1941, stood as follows:

Total army and commission costs, 1918–23.... $292,663,435.79
Credits (cash or kind) 44,797,790.30
Under agreement of May 25, 1923............ 14,725,154.40
Under agreement of January 14, 1925 .... 39,203,725.89
Under agreement of June 23, 1930............ 12,069,631.84
Unpaid balance of the original $181,867,133.36

The correspondence regarding the original agreement is in United States, Department of State, *Papers Relating to the Foreign Relations of the United States: 1923*, 2 vols. (Washington, D.C., 1938), 2:110–92. For an instance of public reaction, see the *New York Tribune*, May 25, 1923, p. 20, which cites the statement of the chairman of the Republican National Committee that "The whole matter [of Europe promising to pay army costs] is a crooked deal."

² Henry T. Allen, *My Rhineland Journal* (Boston, [October] 1923). It was reviewed by R. H. Allen in the *Boston Transcript*, November 10, 1923, an anonymous reviewer in the *New York Times*, November 18, 1923, D. C. Seitz in the *New York World*, November 18, 1923, Ferdinand Schevill, in the *New Republic* 37 (January 9, 1924): 179, and Edward Krehbiel in the *American Historical Review* 29 (April, 1924): 604.

³ Henry T. Allen, *The Rhineland Occupation* (Indianapolis, 1927).

Notes to Conclusion

[4] British reviews of Allen's *Journal* include those in the (London) *Times Literary Supplement*, July 17, 1924, and *Manchester Guardian*, September 2, 1924.

[5] For this letter, see a confidential envelope in the Herrick correspondence of the Charles Evans Hughes Papers, Library of Congress.

[6] Henry T. Allen, *Mein Rheinland Tagebuch* (Berlin, 1925). Three years later, Allen's *Rhineland Occupation* was translated as *Die Besetzung des Rheinlands* (Berlin, 1928). Pierrepont Noyes's remembrances of the occupation, *While Europe Waits for Peace* (New York, 1920), had also been translated shortly after publication. The German title was *Wo Europa doch des Friedens harrt . . .* (Berlin, 1921).

[7] German reviews of Allen's *Journal* include those by Wilhelm Sollmann, in *Die Gesellschaft* 1 (1924): 179–81; Hajo Holborn, in *Archiv für Politik und Geschichte* 3 (1924): 679–82; and A. V., in *Europäische Gespräche* 2 (1924): 384–85. For a less formal reaction, see Fritz von Hake, *Frankreich im Rheinland: Der Versailler Vertrag ein fetzten Papier* (Berlin, 1925), pp. 23–36.

[8] Wilhelm Marx, "Rhineland Occupation," *Foreign Affairs* 7 (January 1929): 198–203. In 1965 General Allen was still remembered in the Coblenz region as the man who "rescued" the fortress Ehrenbreitstein from destruction by the French; see *Die Festung Ehrenbreitstein in Wort und Bild* (Coblenz, ca. 1960), p. 37.

[9] See Annelise Timmermann, *Die Rheinlandbesetzung in ihrer Wirkung auf die sozialausgaben der Städte* (Berlin, 1930); also Jakob Wenz, *Elf Jahre in Fesseln: die Leidengeschichte der Koblenzer Bevölkerung während der Besatzungszeit* (Coblenz, 1930), pp. 13–44.

[10] O. G. Villard, "Germany, 1922: In the Occupied Territory," *Nation* 115 (August 2, 1922): 116–18.

[11] Note, in this regard, Hughes's letter to Allen of March 3, 1923: "It has been of inestimable value to have the benefit of your mature judgment and opinion . . . and I deeply appreciate the manner in which, through your comprehensive reports, you have kept the Department in touch with the situation"; Allen, *Rhineland Occupation*, p. 295.

[12] Indeed, more than a few former American troops returned to Coblenz to become residents of the city; see the *Boston Herald*, August 26, 1923.

Bibliography

PRIVATE COLLECTIONS

I.   In the Library of Congress
Henry T. Allen Papers, Chandler Anderson Papers, Newton D. Baker Papers, Ray Stannard Baker Papers, Tasker H. Bliss Papers, William E. Borah Papers, Robert Lee Bullard Papers, Wilbur Carr Papers, Paul H. Clark Papers, Frank I. Cobb Papers, Bainbridge Colby Papers, Norman H. Davis Papers, Henry P. Fletcher Papers, James G. Harbord Papers, Leland Harrison Papers, Charles Evans Hughes Papers, Robert Lansing Papers, Peyton March Papers, John J. Pershing Papers, Charles P. Summerall Papers, Henry White Papers, Woodrow Wilson Papers, World War I Collection.

II.   In the Houghton Library at Harvard University
E. L. Dresel Papers, David Houston Papers, William Phillips Papers.

III.   In the Sterling Library at Yale University
Gordon Auchincloss Papers, Edward M. House Papers, Inquiry Papers, Frank L. Polk Papers, Sir William Wiseman Papers.

IV.   In the Princeton University Library
Ray Stannard Baker Papers, Bernard Baruch Papers, John Foster Dulles Papers.

V.   In the Hoover Institute Library, Stanford University
John A. Dolan Papers, Hans Adam Dorten Papers, Edwin F. Gay Papers, Louis Loucheur Papers, Rhineland Collection, Brand Whitlock Papers.

VI.   In Other American Locations
Benedict Crowell Papers. Western Reserve University Library.
Warren G. Harding Papers. Ohio Historical Society. Columbus, Ohio.
Myron T. Herrick Papers. Western Reserve Historical Society. Cleveland, Ohio.

372

Bibliography

Alanson B. Houghton Papers. In the possession of his family, Corning, New York.

Frank Lowden Papers. University of Chicago Library.

Sidney Mezes Papers. Columbia University Library.

Pierrepont B. Noyes Diary. In the possession of his family, Oneida, New York.

Pierrepont B. Noyes Papers. Colgate University.

VII. In the Public Archives of Canada, Ottawa
Sir Robert Borden Papers, Sir George Foster Papers.

VIII. In the Archives Générales du Royaume, Brussels, Belgium
P. Forthomme Papers, Paul Hymans Papers, Baron Edouard Rolin-Jacquemyns Papers.

IX. In Other European Locations
George Nathaniel Marquess Curzon Papers. In the possession of his family, Derby, England.

Ferdinand Foch Papers. Bibliothèque Nationale, Paris.

L. L. Klotz Papers. Bibliothèque de Documentation Internationale Contemporaine, Paris.

Erich Koch-Weser Papers. Bundesarchiv Coblenz, Germany.

Charles Mangin Papers. Archives Nationales de France, Paris.

Sir Malcolm Arnold Robertson Papers. In the possession of his family, Windsor, England.

Sir William Robertson Papers. Library of Kings College, London, England.

UNPUBLISHED DOCUMENTS

I. United States
   A. Department of State records in the Foreign Affairs Branch of the National Archives, Washington, D. C.
      1. Record Group 59 (General)
         462.00 R29 Reparations from Germany.
         462.00 R291 German Indemnity—Popular Comment.
         462.00 R294 Army Costs to be Paid by Germany.
         462.00 R296 Financial and Business Men's Committee.
         711.62119 Termination of War between the United States and Germany.
         763.72119 Termination of the War.
         862.00 Germany—Political and Economic Conditions.
         862.911 Newspapers, Germany.
         862.9111 Clippings, Germany.

862t.01 Government of Rhineland.
862t.01 P81 Government of Rhineland—Popular Comment.
2. Record Group 84 (Foreign Service Posts)
Coblenz Post Records 1922–1923, decimal 800 (reports)
Cologne Post Records 1922–1923, decimal 800 (reports)
3. Record Group 256 (American Commission to Negotiate Peace)
180.03301 Minutes of the Conference of Ambassadors.
180.059 Sub-Committee on Germany (Supreme Economic Council).
180.05901 Sub-Committee on Germany (Supreme Economic Council)—Minutes.
181.16101 Sub-Committee Dealing with Urgent Problems Necessary for Preliminary of Peace—Minutes.
181.224 Inter-Allied Committee on Left Bank of Rhine.
181.22401 Inter-Allied Committee on Left Bank of Rhine—Minutes.
181.22402 Inter-Allied Committee on Left Bank of Rhine—Reports.
181.228 Inter-Allied Commission on the Rhine Territory.
181.3101 Committee on the Execution of the Treaty—Minutes.
181.3102 Committee on the Execution of the Treaty—Reports.
181.32 Committee on Rhine Territory.
181.3202 Committee on Rhine Territory—Reports.
185.001 Questions Considered by the Conference, Negotiations with Germany.
185.121 Cost of Armies of Occupation.
185.1711 Occupation of the Rhine Territory.
B. War Department records in the World War I Branch, War Records Division, National Archives, Washington, D. C.
1. Record Group 94 (Adjutant General's Office)
Germany Project file (see boxes 241–246).
2. Record Group 120 (American Expeditionary Forces)
a) Third Army file
(1) Historical (see boxes 4, 6, 7, 12, 13, 15, 19).
(2) Decimal (see box 62).
b) American Forces in Germany file
(1) Historical Headquarters (see boxes 1–6). Note: box

2 contains a two-volume typewritten "History of the American Forces in Germany" (1919–1923).

    (2) Adjutant (see boxes 538–541).

    (3) G-2 (see box 816).

    (4) Civil Affairs (see boxes 1129–1135).

  c) Negative Intelligence for the American Commission to Negotiate Peace file (see box 317).

C. Records of the United States Army, at the Hoover Institute Library, Stanford, California.

1. United States. Army. American Expeditionary Force. Military Mission, Berlin. "Berlin Press Review." Stencilled. March–August 1919.

2. ———. American Expeditionary Force. Third Army. Second Section. General Staff. "History of the Third United States Army, November 14, 1918 to July 2, 1919." Stencilled.

3. ———. American Expeditionary Force. Third Army. Second Section. General Staff. "Summary of Intelligence," nos. 1–224, November 18, 1918–June 28, 1919. Stencilled. (Succeeded by "Daily Bulletin.")

4. ———. American Forces in Germany. Second Section. General Staff. "Bulletin of Military Information," nos. 1–109 (except 84, 94), November 5, 1919–May 18, 1922. Stencilled.

5. ———. American Forces in Germany. Second Section. General Staff. "Daily Bulletin," nos. 1–97 (several missing), June 29, 1919–October 7, 1919. Stencilled. (Replaced "Summary of Intelligence.")

6. ———. American Forces in Germany. Second Section. General Staff. "Daily Press Excerpts," nos. 1–111, September 11, 1922–December 31, 1922. Stencilled. (Replaced "Excerpts from the German Press.")

7. ———. American Forces in Germany. Second Section. General Staff. "Excerpts from the German Press," nos. 223–479, December 10, 1921–September 10, 1922. Stencilled. (Succeeded by "Daily Press Excerpts.")

8. ———. American Forces in Germany. Second Section. General Staff. "Strategic Reports," nos. 1–443 (many missing), June 26, 1920–December 31, 1922. Stencilled.

9. ———. American Forces in Germany. Second Section. General Staff. "Weekly Bulletin of Political and Economic Information," nos. 1–147, November 5, 1919–January 19, 1923. Stencilled.

10. ——. American Forces in Germany. Second Section. General Staff. "Weekly Digest," nos. 1–74, November 5, 1919–March 30, 1921. Stencilled.
11. ——. American Forces in Germany. Second Section. General Staff. "Weekly Digest of Censorship Information," nos. 19–29, November 8, 1919–January 17, 1920. Stencilled.

II. Great Britain
  A. Microfilm Records of the War Cabinet, 1916–1919, and Cabinet Papers, 1916, 1919–1922, available at the Public Record Office, London.
    1. Photographic Copies of Cabinet Papers, 1916 (CAB 37/154).
    2. War Cabinet Minutes, December 9, 1916–October 27, 1919 (CAB 23/1–17).
    3. Cabinet Conclusions, November 4, 1919–December 29, 1922 (CAB 23/18–32).
    4. Conferences of Ministers, November 13, 1919–October 6, 1922 (CAB 23/35–39).
  B. Microfilm Records of the Imperial War Cabinet, 1917–1918, available at the Public Record Office, London.
    1. Minutes of meetings, March 20, 1917–December 31, 1918 (CAB 23/40–42).
    2. Procès verbal of meetings, March 20, 1917–November 28, 1918 (CAB 23/43).
    3. Minutes, papers, and report of the two committees on terms of peace appointed by the Imperial War Cabinet, April 12, 1917 (CAB 21/77, 21/78).
  C. Microfilm Records of the Foreign Office, 1920–1923, available at the Public Record Office, London.
    1. Class F.O. 371: General Correspondence, Political.
    2. Class F.O. 408: Confidential Print: Germany.

III. France
  A. Records of the French censorship service, 1918–1919, in the Bibliothèque de Documentation Internationale Contemporaine, Paris.
    1. France, Censure, Agences et Fils spéciaux (August 17, 1918–October 10, 1919).
    2. France, Censure, Consignes (August 15, 1918–July 15, 1919).
    3. France, Censure, Relevé des Consignes (June 5, 1918–September 5, 1919).

Bibliography

B. Records of the French Army of the Rhine, in the Bibliothèque du Service Historique, Château de Vincennes.
   1. Armée française du Rhin. "Historique Sommaire de l'occupation des [territoires rhénans] par les armées alliées (1918–1930) rédigée par l'état-major de l'Armée du Rhin sous les ordres du Général Guillaumat." Bureau Cartographique du C.F.R. (G.C.T.A.), June 1930.
   2. Armée française du Rhin. "Une historique de l' "Occupation de la Ruhr," rédigée en 1923, au quartier général de Düsseldorf, sur l'ordre du Général Degoutte, précise et complète le présent travail, en tout ce qui a trait à cette opération. *Avec Pièces annexes.*" 16 vols.
C. Records of the French section of the Inter-Allied Rhineland High Commission, in the Bibliothèque de Documentation Internationale Contemporaine, Paris.
   1. Haut Commissariat de la République française. "Bulletin de Presse." December 1919–June 1922. Replaced by "Analyse de Presse" (July 1922–1923).
   2. Haut Commissariat de la République française "Bulletin d'Informations Économiques." Coblenz, 1920–1923.
   3. Haut Commissariat de la République française. "Bulletin mensuel des revues allemandes." January 1920–June 1922. Replaced by "Analyse des revues allemandes" (bimonthly) (July 1922–1923).
D. Records of the French section of the Inter-Allied Rhineland High Commission, in the Archives Nationales de France, Paris.
   1. Haut Commissariat de la République française, Archives du Secrétariat Général (folders 2889–4067).
   2. Haut Commissariat de la République française, Archives du Cabinet (folders 4227–4617).
   3. Haut Commissariat de la République française, Documentation commune au Secrétariat Général et au Cabinet, et des services annexes de la Haute Commission (folders 4618–4849).

IV. Inter-Allied Agencies
   A. Records of the Inter-Allied Rhineland Commission and the Inter-Allied Rhineland High Commission, at the Hoover Institute Library, Stanford, California.
      1. Inter-Allied Rhineland Commission, Minutes, Meetings 29–35, 37–39, 41–45, October 7, 1919–January 7, 1920.

Bibliography

2. Inter-Allied Rhineland High Commission, Minutes, Meetings 1–28, 36, 40, 43–44, 46–47, 49–50, 52–92, 106–17, 135, 163, 164, 166, January 11, 1920–January ?, 1923.

B. Records of the Inter-Allied Rhineland Commission and the Inter-Allied Rhineland High Commission, in the Archives Nationales de France, Paris.

1. Haute Commission Interalliée de Rhénanie, Secrétariat Général Interallié (folders 1–737).
2. Haute Commission Interalliée de Rhénanie, Centralisation (folders 738–800).
3. Haute Commission Interalliée de Rhénanie, Archives de la CITR et des Comités HCITR (folders 801–1395).
4. Haute Commission Interalliée de Rhénanie, Comités de Prestations (folders 1396–1545).
5. Haute Commission Interalliée de Rhénanie, Comité Financier des Gages (folders 1546–1974).

V. Germany
A. Microfilm Records of the German Foreign Ministry, available at the National Archives, Washington, D. C.
1. Records for the period before 1920:
   a) Political Department (Abteilung IA), 1867–1920.
      (1) "Beziehungen Vereinigten Staaten zu Deutschland." Serial number (reel) University of California I, 118. Covers November 1917–December 1919.
      (2) "Waffenstillstands– und Friedensverhandlungen." Serial number (reels) 4069, 4080, 4097, and 4099. Covers November 1918–December 1919.
      (3) "Das Besetzte Gebiet in West Deutschland." Serial number (reel) University of Michigan 146. Covers June 1919–March 1920.
   b) File established during the period of the Weimar National Assembly, February–August 1919.
      (1) "Waffenstillstandsangelegenheiten – Besetzte Gebiete." Serial number (reel) 4665. Covers February–March 1919.
      (2) "Friedensverhandlungen – Linksrheinischesgebiet." Serial number (reel) 4665. Covers February–April 1919.
      (3) "Separatistische Umtriebe in Deutschland." 13. Serial number (reel) 4665. Covers June 1–28, 1919.

c) German Peace Delegation file.

(1) "Die Rhein Linie." Serial number (reel) 4662. Covers April–July 1919.

(2) "Besetzte Gebiete im Westen." Serial number (reel) 4662. Covers April–June 1919.

d) Undersecretary Toepffer file.

"Amerika." Serial numbers (reels) 4628–4629. Covers January–May 1919.

2. Records for the period after 1920:

a) Office of the Reichsminister (Foreign Minister).

(1) "Besetztes Rheinland." Containers (reels) 1469–70. Covers October 1920–March 1923.

(2) "Das Ruhr Gebiet." Container (reel) 1524. Covers July 1920–January 1923.

(3) "Vereinigten Staaten von Amerika." Container (reel) 1489. Covers June 1920–August 1923.

b) Office of the Staatssekretär (in the Foreign Ministry). "Inter-allierte Kommission." Container (reel) 2369. Covers February–March 1922.

B. Microfilm Records of the German Foreign Ministry, Archives of the German Embassy at Washington, available at the National Archives, Washington, D. C.

1. "Besatzungstruppen." Series AHA I, Reel 25. Covers January 1922–September 1928.

2. "Besatztungskosten." Series AHA I, Reel 25. Covers February 1921–June 1930.

C. Records of the Waffenstillstandskommission, Reichskommissar für die besetzten rheinischen Gebiete, Reichsministerium für die besetzten Gebiete, and Rheinische Volkspflege, in the Deutsches Zentralarchiv, Potsdam, Germany.

1. Waffenstillstandskommission (folders 1–75, 173–208, 234–287, 333–351, 456–492, 603–676, 724–746, 831–920).

2. Reichskommissar für die besetzten rheinischen Gebiete.

a) Abteilung I (Z). Zeitungsausschnitte (folders 1688a–1769).

b) Abteilung II (folders 2152/12–2152/771).

c) Abteilung Preussen (folders 3039–3089).

3. Reichsministerium für die besetzten Gebiete.

a) Vorakten (folders 1–20).

b) Abteilung I alt (folders 288–976, 1047–1143).

c) Abteilung I neu (folders 1270–1713).

Bibliography

d) Abteilung II alt (folders 1–690, 1353–1389).
e) Abteilung II neu (folders 1547–1561).
4. Rheinische Volkspflege (folders 2153–2880).
D. Records of the Oberpraesidium der Rheinlande in the Bundesarchiv, Coblenz, Germany.
1. Weltkrieg und Nachkriegszeit (folders 13362, 13365, 13462, 13583, 14138, 14709, 15003).
2. Besatzungszeit (folders 13392, 13397–13398, 13451, 13452, 13578, 13586, 14710, 14719, 14725, 14726, 14736, 14740, 14798, 14800, 14801, 14804, 14805, 14817, 14822, 14829, 14831, 14909, 14925, 14926, 15009).

PUBLISHED DOCUMENTS

The location of certain rare works is cited as a convenience to the scholar. The Hoover Institute Library is abbreviated HIL; the Library of Congress, LOC.

Allied Powers. Reparations Commission. *Report on the Work of the Reparations Commission from 1920–1922.* London, 1923.
Belgium. Ministère des Affaires Étrangères. *Documents diplomatiques: Livres gris: Documents diplomatiques aux réparations (de décembre 1922 au 27 août 1923).* Brussels, 1923.
Belgium. Ministère des Affaires Étrangères. *Documents diplomatiques belges, 1920–1940.* 2 vols. Brussels, 1964.
Calmette, Germain, ed. *Recueil de documents sur l'histoire de la question des réparations; 1919–5 Mai 1921.* Paris, 1921.
France. Assemblée Nationale. *Annales de la Chambre des Députés. Débats parlementaires.* Vols. 107–119. Paris, 1918–1923.
France. Assemblée Nationale. *Annales du Sénat. Débats parlementaires.* Vols. 89–98. Paris, 1918–1923.
France. Ministère des Affaires Étrangères. *Documents diplomatiques: Conférence de Washington (juillet 1921–février 1922).* Paris, 1923.
France. Ministère des Affaires Étrangères. *Documents diplomatiques: Conférence économique internationale de Gênes (9 avril–19 mai 1922).* Paris, 1922.
France. Ministère des Affaires Étrangères. *Documents diplomatiques: Demande de moratorium du Gouvernement allemand à la Commission des Réparations (14 novembre 1922). Conférence de Londres (9–11 décembre 1922). Conférence de Paris (2–4 janvier 1923).* Paris, 1923.

Bibliography

France. Ministère des Affaires Étrangères. *Documents diplomatiques: Documents relatifs aux négociations concernant des garanties de sécurité contre une agression de l'Allemagne (10 janvier 1919–7 décembre 1923)*. Paris, 1924. Translated as *Urkunden über die Verhandlungen btr. die Sicherheitsbürgschaften gegen einen deutschen Angriff*. Berlin, 1924.

France. Ministère des Affaires Étrangères. *Documents diplomatiques: Documents relatifs aux réparations*. Paris, 1922.

Germany. Auswärtiges Amt. *Die den Allierten seit Waffenstillstand übermittelten deutschen Angebote und Vorschläge zur Lösung der Reparations–und Wiederaufbaufrage*. Berlin, 1923.

Germany. Auswärtiges Amt. *Die Separatistischen Umtriebe in den besetzten Gebiete; Notenwechsel zwischen der deutschen und der französischen Regierungen*. Berlin, 1924.

Germany. Auswärtiges Amt. Geschäftstelle für die Friedensverhandlungen. *Ausserungen der zur Prüfung der Friedensbedingungen in Berlin eingesetzten Arbeitskommission*. Berlin, n.d.

Germany. Auswärtiges Amt. Geschäftstelle für die Friedensverhandlungen. *Drucksache*. 51 volumes. Berlin, 1919. (Especially vols. 4, 9, 10, 11, 12, 18, 24, 27, and 47; of these, 4, 9, 11, 27 and 47 are available at HIL.)

Germany. Auswärtiges Amt und Reichsministerium des Innern. *Amtliche Urkunden zur Vorgeschichte des Waffenstillstandes 1918* (2nd edition, Berlin, 1924). Translated as *Preliminary History of the Armistice: Official Documents Published by the German National Chancellery by Order of the Ministry of State*. New York, 1924.

Germany. Nationalversammlung. *Verhandlungen der verfassunggebenden deutschen Nationalversammlung. Stenographische Berichte*. Vols. 326–43. Berlin, 1919–1920.

Germany. Reichsministerium des Innern. *Die Ausschreitungen der Besatzungstruppen im besetzten rheinischen Gebiet*. Berlin, 1923. (HIL)

Germany. Reichsministerium für die Besetzten Gebiete. *Denkschrift über die Ausschreitungen der Besatzungstruppen im besetzten Gebiet*. Berlin, 1925. (HIL)

Germany. Reichsministerium für die Besetzten Gebiete. *Liste der von der Interallierten Rheinlandkommission in Coblenz für das besetzte Gebiet verbotenen Bücher, Lichtbildstreifen und Zeitungen*. Berlin, 1925. (HIL)

Germany. Reichsministerium für die Besetzten Gebiete. *Dokumente zur Besetzung der Rheinlande. I. Die politischen Ordonnanzen der*

Bibliography

Interallierten Rheinlandkommission in Coblenz und ihre Anwendung in den Jahren 1920–24. II. *Eingriffe der Besatzungsbehörden in die Rechtspflege im besetzten Rheinland*. III. *Urkunden zum Separatistenputsch im Rheinland im Herbst 1923*. Berlin 1925. (HIL).

Germany. Reichstag. *Memorial on the Cost of the Occupation of the Rhineland up to the End of March 1921*. Leipzig, 1922. (HIL).

Germany. Reichstag. *Verhandlungen des Deutschen Reichstags. Stenographische Berichte* (1920–1924). Vols. 344–81. Berlin, 1920–1924.

Germany. Waffenstillstandskommission. *Der Waffenstillstand 1918–1919: Das Dokumentenmaterial der Waffenstillstandsverhandlungen von Compiègne, Spa, Trier und Brüssel*. 3 vols. Berlin, 1928.

Great Britain. Foreign Office. *Correspondence Regarding the Reimbursement of the Costs of American Army of Occupation*. Cmd. 1973. London, 1923.

Great Britain. Foreign Office. *Correspondence with the Allied Governments Respecting Reparation Payments by Germany*. Cmd. 1943. London, 1923.

Great Britain. Foreign Office. *Documents on British Foreign Policy, 1919–1939*. First series. 17 vols. London, 1947–.

Great Britain. Foreign Office. *Inter-Allied Conferences on Reparations and Inter-Allied Debts, held in London and Paris, December, 1922 and January, 1923. Reports and Secretaries' Notes of Conversations*. Cmd. 1812. London, 1923.

Great Britain. Foreign Office. *Minutes of the London Conference on Reparations, August 1922*. Cmd. 2258. London, 1924.

Great Britain. Foreign Office. *Papers respecting Negotiations for an Anglo-French Pact*. Cmd. 2169. London, 1924.

Great Britain. Foreign Office. *Protocols and Correspondence between the Supreme Council and the Conference of Ambassadors and the German Government and the German Peace Delegation between January 10, 1920 and July 17, 1920 respecting the Execution of the Treaty of Versailles of June 28, 1919*. Cmd. 1325. London, 1921.

Great Britain. Parliament. *British and Foreign State Papers, 1919–1923*. London, 1922–1926.

Great Britain. Parliament. *The Parliamentary Debates, Official Report, House of Commons* (1917–1923). Vols. 90–168. London, 1917–1923.

Harbeck, Karl Heinz, ed. *Das Kabinett Cuno: 22. November 1922 bis 12. August 1923*. Boppard am Rhein, 1972.

Inter-Allied Rhineland High Commission. *Bulletin officiel de la haute commission interalliée des territoires rhénans. Official Gazette of the*

Bibliography

Inter-Allied Rhineland High Commission. Vols. 1–4. Coblenz, 1920–1923.

Inter-Allied Rhineland High Commission. *Recueil des ordonnances, instructions, et décisions de la haute commission interalliée des territoires rhénans, January 20, 1920–August 1, 1923.* Mainz, 1923.

Italy, Ministero degli Affari Esteri. *I Documenti Diplomatici Italiani.* Series 6. November 5, 1918–October 30, 1922. Series 7. October 31, 1922–April 14, 1935. Rome, 1952–

Kolb, Eberhard, ed. *Der Zentralrat der deutschen sozialistischen Republik, 19. 12. 1918–8. 4. 1919: Quellen zur Geschichte der Rätebewegung in Deutschland 1918/1919.* Leiden (Holland), 1968.

Kraus, Herbert, and Gustav Rödiger, eds. *Urkunden zum Friedensvertrag von Versailles vom 28 Juni 1919.* 2 vols. Berlin, 1920–1922.

Mantoux, Paul. *Les Délibérations du conseil des quatres.* 2 vols. Paris, 1955.

Marchand, René, ed. *Un Livre noir; Diplomatie d'avant guerre et de guerre d'apres les documents des archives russes (1910–1917).* 3 vols. Paris, 1922–1934.

Matthias, Erich, ed. *Die Regierung des Volksbeauftragten 1918/1919: Quellen zur Geschichte des Parlamentismus und der politischen Parteien.* 2 vols. Düsseldorf, 1969.

Prussia. Landtag. *Sitzungsberichte des Preussischen Landtags (1921–1924).* Vols. 1–18. Berlin, 1920–1924.

Prussia. Statistisches Landesamt. *Besetzte Gebiete Deutschlands.* Berlin, 1925.

Schulze, Hagen, ed. *Das Kabinett Scheidemann: 13. Februar bis 20. Juni 1919.* Boppard am Rhein, 1971.

United States. Army. American Expeditionary Forces. General Staff, G-2. *Candid Comment on the American Soldier of 1917–1918 and Kindred Topics, by Germans.* Chaumont, 1919.

United States. Army. American Expeditionary Forces. General Staff, G-2. *City of Coblenz and Environs.* n.p., 1918(?).

United States. Army. American Expeditionary Forces. General Staff, G-2. *Press Review.* Nos. 1–473, December 12, 1919–June 6, 1919. n.p., 1917–1919.

United States. Army. American Forces in Germany. Assistant Chief of Staff, G-2. "American Representation in Occupied Germany, 1920–1921." 2 vols. Stencilled. Coblenz(?), 1922.

United States. Army. American Forces in Germany. Assistant Chief of Staff, G-2. "American Representation in Occupied Germany, 1922–1923." Stencilled. Coblenz(?), 1923.

383

Bibliography

United States. Army. American Forces in Germany. Military Intelligence Division. General Staff. *Christmas 1921*. Coblenz, 1921. (HIL)

United States. Army. Third Army and American Forces in Germany. Officer in Charge of Civil Affairs (Colonel I. L. Hunt). "American Military Government of Occupied Germany, 1918–1920." 4 vols. Stencilled. Coblenz, 1921. (The first volume was republished in Washington, 1943, and became known as the "Hunt Report.")

United States. Army. Army War College. Historical Section. *Order of Battle of United States Land Forces in the World War: American Expeditionary Force*. Washington, 1937.

United States. Army. Office of Military Government. Reports and Information Branch. The Historical and Documents Section. *Hunt Report Digest: American Military Government of Occupied Germany, 1918–1920*. United States Zone of Germany, January, 1946.

United States. Congress. *Congressional Record*. 65th to 67th Congresses. Washington, D.C., 1917–1923.

United States. Congress. Senate. *Colored Troops in the French Army: A Report from the Department of State Relating to the Colored Troops in the French Army and the Number of French Colonial Troops in the Occupied Territory*. 66th Congress. Third Session. Senate Document 397. Washington, D.C., 1921.

United States. Congress. Senate. *Hearings before the Committee on Foreign Relations, United States Senate: Treaty of Peace with Germany*. 66th Congress. First Session. Washington, D.C., 1919.

United States. Congress. Senate. *Report of the Conference between Members of the Senate Committee on Foreign Relations and the President of the United States, at the White House, August 19, 1919: Treaty of Peace with Germany*. 66th Congress. First Session. Senate Document 76. Washington, D.C., 1919.

United States. Department of the Army. *The United States Army in the World War*. 17 vols. Washington, D.C., 1948.

United States. Department of State. *Conference on the Limitation of Armament: Washington, November 12, 1921–February 6, 1922*. Washington, D.C., 1922.

United States. Department of State. *Papers Relating to the Foreign Relations of the United States*. Vols. for 1918–1923. Washington, D.C., 1933–1938.

United States. Department of State. *Papers Relating to the Foreign Relations of the United States: The Lansing Papers, 1914–1920*. 2 vols. Washington, D.C., 1939–1940.

Bibliography

United States. Department of State. *Papers Relating to the Foreign Relations of the United States: The Paris Peace Conference, 1919.* 13 vols. Washington, D.C., 1942–1944.

United States. War Department. *Annual Report, 1919.* 3 vols. Washington, D.C., 1920.

United States. War Department. *Annual Report, 1920.* 3 vols. Washington, D.C., 1921.

Vogels, Werner, ed. *Die Bestimmungen der interallierten Rheinlandoberkommission und der Besatzungsarmeen über Einquartierung, Requisitionen und Schaden.* Berlin, 1925.

Vogels, H., and Vogels, W., eds. *Das Rheinlandabkommen sowie die Verordnungen der Hohen Kommission in Coblenz: Dreisprachige Textausgabe.* Bonn, 1920.

Vogt, Martin, ed. *Das Kabinett Müller I.: 27. März bis 21. Juni 1920.* Boppard am Rhein, 1971.

Wulf, Peter. ed. *Das Kabinett Fehrenbach: 25. Juni 1920 bis 4. Mai 1921.* Boppard am Rhein, 1972.

NEWSPAPERS

Many of the standard American, British, French, and German newspapers of the era are cited in footnotes. The following is a list of publications that are also useful.

Adenauer Zeitung [scattered issues, 1921–1923, HIL]

Ahrweiler Zeitung [scattered issues, 1921–1923, HIL]

Amaroc News (American Forces in Germany, Coblenz), 1919–1923 [complete, HIL]

Andernacher Volkszeitung (Center Party) [scattered issues, 1921–1923, HIL]

Bendorfer Zeitung [scattered issues, 1921–1923, HIL]

Bridgehead Sentinel (First U. S. Division, Montabauer, Germany), 1919 [scattered issues, HIL]

Chicago Tribune (Paris, France) [1918–1923, LOC]

Coblenzer General Anzeiger [scattered issues, 1921–1923, HIL]

Coblenzer Volkszeitung (Center Party) [scattered issues, 1921–1923, HIL]

Coblenzer Zeitung (People's Party) [scattered issues, 1921–1923, HIL]

Cochemer Zeitung [scattered issues, 1921–1923, HIL]

Cologne Post (British Army of the Rhine, Cologne) [1921–1923, Imperial War Museum, London]

Bibliography

The Doughboy (Seventh Infantry Brigade, Adenau, Germany), 1919 [scattered issues, HIL]

L'Echo du Rhin (French section of the High Commission, Mainz), 1919–1923

The 51st Pioneers (Cochem, Germany), 1919 [scattered issues, HIL]

Fourth Corps Flare (Mayen, Germany), 1919 [scattered issues, HIL]

The Indian (Second U. S. Division, Neuwied, Germany), 1919 [scattered issues, HIL]

Kölnische Volkszeitung (Center Party), 1919–1923

Kölnische Zeitung (People's Party) [1918–1920, HIL]

Mainzer Tageblatt (Center Party) [scattered issues, 1921–1923, HIL]

Mayener Zeitung [scattered issues, 1921–1923, HIL]

Neuwieder Zeitung [scattered issues, 1921–1923, HIL]

New York Herald (Paris, France) [1918–1923, LOC]

Revue rhénane (French section of the High Commission, Mainz), 1921–1923

Rheinische Herold (Coblenz, Dorten Separatist) [scattered issues, 1920–1923, HIL]

Rheinische Republik (Cologne, Smeets Separatist) [scattered issues, 1923, HIL]

Der Rheinländer (Coblenz, Dorten Separatist) [scattered issues, 1920–1923, HIL]

The Skirmisher (Fourth Engineers, Dungenheim, Germany), 1918–1919 [scattered issues, HIL]

Stars and Stripes, The Official Newspaper of the A.E.F. (Paris, France), 1918–1919 [complete in HIL]

Watch on the Rhine (Third U. S. Division, Andernach, Germany), 1919 [scattered issues, HIL]

PUBLISHED LETTERS, DIARIES, MEMOIRS, AND BIOGRAPHIES

Allen, Henry T. *My Rhineland Journal.* Boston, 1923. Translated as *Mein Rheinland Tagebuch.* Berlin, 1925.

Aubert, Louis, et al. *André Tardieu.* Paris, 1957.

Baden, Prinz Max von. *Erinnerungen und Dokumente.* Stuttgart and Berlin, 1927.

Baker, Ray Stannard. *Woodrow Wilson, Life and Letters.* 8 vols. New York, 1927–1939.

———. *Woodrow Wilson and the World Settlement: Written from His Unpublished and Personal Material.* 3 vols. Garden City, N. Y., 1922.

Bibliography

—— and Dodd, William E., eds. *The Public Papers of Woodrow Wilson*. 6 vols. New York, 1925–1927.

Baldwin, Marian. *Canteening Overseas, 1917–1919*. New York, 1920.

Baruch, Bernard M. *Baruch*. 2 vols. New York, 1958–1960.

——. *The Making of the Reparation and Economic Sections of the Treaty*. New York, 1920.

Benoist, Charles. *Souvenirs*. 3 vols. Paris, 1934.

Bernstorff, Johann Heinrich von. *Erinnerungen und Briefe*. Zürich, 1936. Trans. *Memoirs of Count Bernstorff*. New York, 1936.

Blake, Robert. *The Private Papers of Douglas Haig*. London, 1952.

——. *The Unknown Prime Minister: The Life and Times of Andrew Bonar Law*. London, 1955.

Böttcher, Helmuth. *Walther Rathenau*. Bonn, 1958.

Bonham-Carter, Victor. *The Strategy of Victory, 1914–1918: The Life and Times of the Master Strategist of World War I, Field Marshal Sir William Robertson*. New York, 1964.

Boraston, J. H. *Sir Douglas Haig's Dispatches*. London, 1919.

Borden, Henry, ed. *Robert Laird Borden: His Memoirs*. 2 vols. New York, 1938.

Brockdorff-Rantzau, Count Ulrich von. *Dokumente und Gedanken um Versailles*. Berlin, 1922.

Bruun, Geoffrey. *Clemenceau*. Cambridge, Mass. 1943.

Bullard, Robert L. *Personalities and Reminiscences of the War*. New York, 1925.

Butler, J. R. M. *Lord Lothian (Philip Kerr): 1882–1940*. London, 1960.

Callwell, Charles E. *Field Marshall Sir Henry Wilson*. 2 vols. New York, 1927.

Cambon, Henri, ed. *Paul Cambon, Correspondance, 1870–1924*. 3 vols. Paris, 1940–1946.

Casey, Lady Maie. *Tides and Eddies*. London, 1966.

Cecil, Robert. *A Great Experiment: An Autobiography*. New York, 1941.

Chalmers, W. S. *The Life and Letters of David, Earl Beatty*. London, 1951.

Chastenet, Jacques. *Raymond Poincaré*. Paris, 1948.

Churchill, Randolph S. *Lord Derby, King of Lancashire: The Official Life of Edward, Seventeenth Earl of Derby, 1865–1948*. New York, 1960.

Clemenceau, Georges. *Grandeur et misères d'une victoire*. Paris, 1930. Translated as *Grandeur and Misery of Victory*. New York, 1930.

Bibliography

Coffman, Edward M. *The Hilt of the Sword: The Career of Peyton C. March*. Madison, Wis., 1966.

Cole, Margaret I. *Beatrice Webb's Diaries, 1912–1924*. London, 1952.

Collier, Basil. *Brasshat: A Biography of Field Marshal Sir Henry Wilson (1864–1922)*. London, 1961.

Cooper, Duff. *Haig*. London, 1936.

Cox, James M. *Journey Through My Years*. New York, 1946.

Crane, Katharine. *Mr. Carr of State: Forty-Seven Years in the Department of State*. New York, 1960.

Cronon, E. David, ed. *The Cabinet Diaries of Josephus Daniels, 1913–1921*. Lincoln, Neb., 1963.

D'Abernon, Viscount Edgar V. *The Diary of an Ambassador*. 3 vols. Garden City, N. Y., 1929–1931.

Daniels, Josephus. *The Wilson Era: Years of War and After, 1917–1920*. Chapel Hill, N. C., 1946.

Davenport, Walter. *Power and Glory: The Life of Boies Penrose*. New York, 1931.

Dawson, Warrington, ed. *The War Memoirs of William Graves Sharp, American Ambassador to France, 1914–1919*. London, 1931.

De la Rocca, Emmanuel de Peretti. "Briand et Poincaré: Souvenirs." *Revue de Paris*, année 43, vol. 6 (1936).

De Launay, Jacques, ed. *Louis Loucheur: Carnets secrets, 1908–1932*. Brussels, 1962.

Dickman, Joseph T. *The Great Crusade: A Narrative of the World War*. New York, 1927.

Dorten, Hans Adam. *La Tragédie rhénane*. Paris, 1945.

Duffy, Francis P. *Father Duffy's Story*. New York, 1919.

Dugdale, Blanche E. C. *Arthur James Balfour*. 2 vols. New York, 1937.

Ebert, Friedrich. *Schriften, Aufzeichnungen, Reden, mit unveröffentlichten Erinnerungen aus dem Nachlass*. 2 vols. Dresden, 1926.

Editors of the *Army Times*. *The Yanks Are Coming: The Story of General John J. Pershing*. New York, 1960.

Epstein, Klaus. *Matthias Erzberger and the Dilemma of German Democracy*. Princeton, N. J., 1959.

Erzberger, Matthias. *Erlebnisse im Weltkrieg*. Stuttgart, 1920.

Escholier, Raymond. *Souvenirs parlés de Briand*. Paris, 1932.

Esher, Reginald Baliol Brett, Viscount. *Journal and Letters*. 4 vols. London, 1934–1938.

Fayolle, Emile, *Cahiers secrets de la grande guerre*. Paris, 1964.

Felix, David. *Walther Rathenau and the Weimar Republic: The Politics*

Bibliography

of Reparations. Baltimore, 1971.

Foch, Ferdinand. *Mémoires pour servir à l'histoire de la guerre de 1914–1918.* 2 vols. Paris, 1931. Translated as *The Memoirs of Marshal Foch.* New York, 1931.

Freidel, Frank. *Franklin D. Roosevelt: The Ordeal.* Boston, 1954.

Fry, Anna Ruth. *A Quaker Adventure: A Story of Nine Years' Relief and Reconstruction.* London, 1926.

Gärtner, Margarete. *Botschafterin des guten Willens: Aussenpolitische Arbeit 1914–50.* Bonn, 1955.

Garraty, John A. *Henry Cabot Lodge: A Biography.* New York, 1953.

George, Alexander L., and George, Juliette L. *Woodrow Wilson and Colonel House: A Personality Study.* New York, 1956.

Glad, Betty. *Charles Evans Hughes and the Illusions of Innocence: A Study in American Diplomacy.* Urbana, Ill., 1966.

Godley, Sir Alexander. *Life of an Irish Soldier.* London, 1939.

Gollin, A. M. *Proconsul in Politics: A Study of Lord Milner in Opposition and in Power.* New York, 1964.

Grayson, Cary T. *Woodrow Wilson, An Intimate Memoir.* New York, 1960.

Grew, Joseph C., and Johnson, Walter. *Turbulent Era. A Diplomatic Record of Forty Years, 1902–1945.* 2 vols. Boston, 1952.

Groener-Geyer, Dorothea. *General Groener: Soldat und Staatsman.* Frankfurt, 1955.

Groener, Wilhelm. *Lebenserinnerungen: Jugend-Generalstab-Weltkrieg.* Göttingen, 1957.

Hancock, W. K., and van der Poel, J., eds. *Selections from the Smuts Papers.* 4 vols. London, 1965.

Harrington, General Sir C. *Lord Plumer.* London, 1935.

Hindenburg, Paul von. *Aus Meinem Leben.* Leipzig, 1920. Translated as *Out of My Life.* London, 1920.

Hoover, Herbert. *Memoirs of Herbert Hoover: The Cabinet and the Presidency, 1920–1933.* New York, 1952.

Houston, David F. *Eight Years with Wilson's Cabinet, 1913–1920.* 2 vols. New York, 1926.

Howe, Frederick C. *Confessions of a Reformer.* New York, 1925.

Hunter, Thomas Marshall. *Marshal Foch: A Study in Leadership.* Ottawa, 1961.

Hutchinson, William T. *Lowden of Illinois.* 2 vols. Chicago, 1957.

Hyde, Charles Cheney. "Charles Evans Hughes." In *The American Secretaries of State and Their Diplomacy,* edited by S. F. Bemis, vol. 10. New York, 1929.

Hymans, Paul. *Fragments d'histoire: Impressions et souvenirs.* Brussels, 1940.

———. *Mémoires.* 2 vols. Brussels, 1958.

Joffre, Joseph J. C. *Mémoires du Maréchal Joffre.* 2 vols. Paris, 1932. Translated as *The Personal Memoirs of Joffre, Field Marshal of the French Army.* New York, 1932.

Johnson, Willis F. *George Harvey, A "Passionate Patriot."* Boston, 1929.

Kessler, Harry Graf. *Walther Rathenau: Sein Leben und Sein Werk.* Berlin, 1928. Translated as *Walther Rathenau: His Life and Work.* New York, 1930.

———. *Tagebücher, 1918–1937.* Frankfurt, 1961. Translated as *The Diaries of a Cosmopolitan, Count Harry Kessler, 1918–1937.* London, 1971.

Kuehl, Warren F. *Hamilton Holt.* Gainsville, Fla., 1960.

LaFollette, Belle Case, and LaFollette, Fola. *Robert M. LaFollette, June 14, 1855–June 18, 1925.* 2 vols. New York, 1953.

Lane, Anne W., and Wall, Lewis H., eds. *The Letters of Franklin K. Lane.* Boston, 1922.

Lansing, Robert. *The Peace Negotiations: A Personal Narrative.* Boston, 1921.

Laroche, Jules. *Au Quai d'Orsay avec Briand et Poincaré, 1913–1926.* Paris, 1957.

Lee, Mary. "Young America: Letters of Mary Lee," *Atlantic* 124 (October 1919): 520–31.

Lennox, Lady Algernon Gordon, ed. *The Diary of Lord Bertie of Thame, 1914–1918.* 2 vols. London, 1924.

Lichten, Hans E. *Von Versailles zur UNO.* Bonn, 1962.

Liggett, Hunter. *Commanding an American Army: Recollections of the World War.* Boston, 1925.

Lloyd George, David. *The Truth about the Peace Treaties.* 2 vols. London, 1938. Published in the United States as *Memoirs of the Peace Conference.* 2 vols. New Haven, 1939.

———. *The War Memoirs of David Lloyd George.* 6 vols. London, 1933–1937.

Lodge, Henry Cabot, ed. *Selections from the Correspondence of Theodore Roosevelt and Henry Cabot Lodge, 1884–1918.* New York, 1925.

Maddox, Robert James. *William E. Borah and American Foreign Policy.* Baton Rouge, 1969.

Mangin, Charles. *Lettres de guerre.* Paris, 1950.

———. "Lettres de Rhénanie," *Revue de Paris* 43 (April 1936): 481–526.

Martet, Jean. *La Mort du Tigre*. Paris, 1930. Translated as *Georges Clemenceau*. London, 1930.

———. *Le Silence de M. Clemenceau*. Paris, 1929.

McCormick, Donald. *The Mask of Merlin: A Critical Biography of David Lloyd George*. New York, 1963.

McCormick, Vance C. *Diaries of Vance C. McCormick, Member of the American War Mission to Inter-Allied Conference in London and Paris in 1917; and Adviser to President Wilson at the Peace Conference in Paris, in 1919*. Privately printed, n.d.

Michon, Georges. *Clemenceau*. Paris, 1931.

Middlemas, Keith, ed. *Thomas Jones: Whitehall Diary*. 2 vols. London, 1969.

Miller, David Hunter. *My Diary at the Conference of Paris*. 21 vols. New York, 1924–1926.

Millin, Sarah Gertrude. *General Smuts*. 2 vols. London, 1936.

Miquel, Pierre. *Poincaré*. Paris, 1961.

Mordacq, J. J. H. *Clemenceau au soir de sa vie, 1920–1929*. 2 vols. Paris, 1933.

———. *La Mentalité allemande: Cinq ans de commandement sur le Rhin*. Paris, 1926.

———. *Le Ministère Clemenceau: Journal d'un témoin*. 4 vols. Paris, 1931.

———. *La Verité sur l'armistice*. Paris, 1929.

Morgan, Kenneth O., ed. *Lloyd George Family Letters, 1885–1936*. Cardiff, 1973.

Morgenthau, Henry. *All in a Life-Time*. Garden City, N. Y., 1922.

Morison, Elting E., et al., eds. *The Letters of Theodore Roosevelt*. 8 vols. Cambridge, Mass., 1951–1954.

Mosely, Leonard. *Curzon: The End of an Epoch*. London, 1960.

Mott, Thomas Bentley. *Myron T. Herrick: Friend of France; An Autobiographical Biography*. Garden City, N. Y., 1929.

———. *Twenty Years as a Military Attaché*. New York, 1937.

Murray, Arthur Cecil. *At Close Quarters: A Sidelight on Anglo-American Diplomatic Relations*. London, 1946.

Nayral de Bourgon, P. E. *Dix Ans de souvenirs (1914–1924)*. 7 vols. Nimes, 1930.

Nevins, Allan. *Henry White: Thirty Years of American Diplomacy*. New York, 1930.

———, ed. *The Letters and Journal of Brand Whitlock*. 2 vols. New York, 1936.

391

Bibliography

Newbolt, Henry. *Naval Operations.* 5 vols. New York, 1920–1931.

Nicolson, Harold. *Curzon: The Last Phase, 1919–1925.* Boston, 1934.

———. *Peacemaking, 1919.* New York, 1939.

Nollet, Général Charles M. E. *Une Expérience de désarmement: Cinq ans de contrôle militaire en Allemagne.* Paris, 1932. (LOC)

Noyes, Pierrepont B. *A Goodly Heritage.* New York, 1958.

Palat, B. E. *La Part de Foch dans la victoire.* Paris, 1930.

Paléologue, Georges Maurice. *La Russie des tsars pendant la grande guerre.* 3 vols. Paris, 1921–1922. Translated as *An Ambassador's Memoirs.* New York, 1924–1925.

Palmer, Frederick C. *Bliss, Peacemaker: The Life and Times of General Tasker Howard Bliss.* New York, 1934.

Pershing, John J. *My Experiences in the World War.* 2 vols. New York, 1931.

Persil, Raoul. *Alexandre Millerand (1859–1943).* Paris, 1949.

Petrie, Sir Charles. *The Life and Letters of the Right Hon. Sir Austen Chamberlain.* 2 vols. London, 1940.

Phelps, R. H. "Aus den Groener-Dokumenten: II. Die Aussenpolitik der O.H.L. bis zum Friedensvertrag," *Deutsche Rundschau* 8 (August 1950): 616–25.

Phillips, William. *Ventures in Diplomacy.* Boston, 1953.

Pogge von Strandmann, Harmut, ed. *Walther Rathenau Tagebuch 1907–22.* Düsseldorf, 1967.

Poincaré, Raymond. *Au Service de la France—neuf années de souvenirs.* Vol. 10. *Victoire et armistice.* Paris, 1933.

Prittie, Terence. *Konrad Adenauer, 1876–1967.* Chicago, 1971.

Pusey, Merlo. *Charles Evans Hughes.* 2 vols. New York, 1951.

Rabenau, Friedrich von. *Seeckt: Aus seinem Leben 1918–1936.* Leipzig, 1940.

Recouly, Raymond. *Le Mémorial de Foch: Mes entretiens avec le maréchal.* Paris, 1929. Translated as *Foch: My Conversations with the Marshal.* New York, 1929.

Reichert, J. W., ed. *Helfferichs Reichstagsreden 1922–1924.* Berlin, 1925.

Repington, Charles á Court. *After the War: A Diary.* Boston, 1922.

Ribot, Alexandre. *Journal d'Alexandre Ribot et correspondances inédites, 1914–1922.* Paris, 1936. (HIL)

Riddell, Lord George A. *Lord Riddell's Intimate Diary of the Peace Conference and After, 1918–1923.* New York, 1934.

Ronaldshay, Earl of. *The Life of Lord Curzon: Being the Authorized Biography of George Nathaniel Marquess Curzon of Kedleston, K.G.* 3 vols. London, 1928.

Bibliography

Roosevelt, Elliot. *FDR: His Personal Letters.* 3 vols. New York, 1947–1950.

Rosen, Friedrich. *Aus einem diplomatischen Wanderleben.* Wiesbaden, 1959.

Roskill, Stephen. *Hankey: Man of Secrets.* 2 vols. London, 1970–1972.

Russell, Francis. *The Shadow of Blooming Grove: Warren G. Harding in His Times.* New York, 1968.

Saint-Aulaire, Auguste. *Confession d'un vieux diplomate.* Paris, 1953.

Scheidemann, Phillipp. *Memoiren eines Sozialdemokraten.* 2 vols. Dresden, 1928. Translated as *The Making of a New Germany: The Memoirs of Philipp Scheidemann.* 2 vols. New York, 1929.

Seymour, Charles, ed. *The Intimate Papers of Colonel House.* 4 vols. Boston, 1928.

——. *Letters from the Paris Peace Conference.* New Haven, Conn., 1965.

Sharp, William Graves. *The War Memoirs of William Graves Sharp.* London, 1931.

Shotwell, James T. *At the Paris Peace Conference.* New York, 1937.

Sinclair, Andrew. *The Available Man: The Life behind the Masks of Warren Gamaliel Harding.* New York, 1965.

Steed, Henry Wickham. *Through Thirty Years, 1892–1922: A Personal Narrative.* Garden City, N. Y., 1925.

Stoeck, Christian. *Aus Meinen Erinnerungen an die Besatzungszeit der Stadt Trier . . .* Trier, 1930. (New York Public Library)

Suarez, Georges. *Briand: Sa vie—son oeuvre, avec son journal et de nombreux documents inédits.* 6 vols. Paris, 1938–1952.

——. *Herriot.* Paris, 1932.

Taylor, A. J. P., ed. *Lloyd George: A Diary by Frances Stevenson.* New York, 1971.

Taylor, H. A. *The Strange Case of Bonar Law.* London, 1932.

Terraine, John. *Ordeal of Victory.* Philadelphia, 1963.

Thwaites, General Sir W. "German Memories." *The Army Quarterly* 47 (October 1943): 115–22.

Tirard, Paul. *La France sur le Rhin: Douze années d'occupation rhénane.* Paris, 1930.

Trask, David F. *General Tasker Howard Bliss and the "Sessions of the World," 1919.* Philadelphia, 1966.

Tumulty, Joseph P. *Woodrow Wilson as I Know Him.* New York, 1921.

Turner, Henry Ashby. *Stresemann and the Politics of the Weimar Republic.* Princeton, N. J., 1963.

Bibliography

Tynan, Katharine. *Life in the Occupied Area*. London, 1925.

Villard, Oswald Garrison. *Fighting Years: Memoirs of a Liberal Editor*. New York, 1939.

Vinson, John Chalmers. *William E. Borah and the Outlawry of War*. Athens, Ga., 1957.

Von Stockhausen, Max. *Sechs Jahre Reichskanzlei, Von Rapallo bis Locarno: Erinnerungen und Tagebuchnotizen, 1922–1927*. Bonn, 1952.

Von Vietsch, Eberhard. *Wilhelm Solf: Botschafter zwischen den Zeiten*. Tubingen, 1961.

Walworth, Arthur. *Woodrow Wilson: American Prophet and World Prophet*. New York, 1958.

Washburn, Charles G. *The Life of John W. Weeks*. Boston, 1928.

Weygand, Maxine. *Foch*. Paris, 1947.

———. "Le Maréchal Foch et l'armistice." *Revue des deux mondes*, 7th period, 48 (November 1938): 1–29.

———. *Le 11 Novembre*. Paris, 1932.

———. *Mémoires*. 3 vols. Paris, 1953–1957.

Wheeler-Bennett, John W. *Wooden Titan: Hindenburg in Twenty Years of German History, 1914–1934*. New York, 1936.

Williams, Wythe. *The Tiger of France: Conversations with Clemenceau*. New York, 1949.

Wilson, Edith Bolling. *My Memoir*. Indianapolis, 1939.

Wrench, John Evelyn. *Alfred Lord Milner: The Man of No Illusions, 1854–1925*. London, 1958.

CONTEMPORARY BOOKS AND ARTICLES

Ackermann, Carl W. *Germany, The Next Republic?* New York, 1917.

Adams, James Greenleaf. *Review of the American Forces in Germany*. Coblenz, 1921.

"African Troops on the Rhine," *New Republic* 26 (March 9, 1921): 29–30.

"After the Ruhr Invasion—What?" *Literary Digest* 76 (January 20, 1923): 7–9.

A. I. [Andre Isambert?]. "Le Régime de l'occupation rhénane institué par le traité de Versailles." *Revue des sciences politiques* 44 (1921): 245–73.

"A la Ruhr." *New Statesman* 20 (December 16, 1922): 320–21.

Bibliography

Allehaut, Maurice. *Les Libertés dans les pays rhénans pendant l'occupation*. Paris, 1925.

Allen, Henry T. *The Rhineland Occupation*. Indianapolis, 1927. Translated as *Die Besetzung des Rheinlands*. Berlin, 1928.

———. "The Effect of Germany's Industrial Condition." *The Annals* 114 (July 1924): 7–9.

———. "We Must Not Secede from the World." *Survey* 52 (August 1, 1924): 417–19.

"The Allied Armies in Germany." *Current History* 9 (January 1919): 15–20; (February 1919): 234–35.

"Allied Occupation of the Rhinelands." *The Nation* 109 (August 9, 1919): 186–88.

"Along the Rhine." *The Independent* 105 (March 5, 1921): 237–38.

"America Aloof as Europe Burns." *Literary Digest* 76 (February 10, 1923): 7–9.

American Academy of Political and Social Sciences. "America and the Rehabilitation of Europe." *The Annals*, vol. 102 (July 1922).

———. "America's Relations to the European Situation." *The Annals*, vol. 108 (July 1923).

"The American Farmer and Foreign Policy." *The Economist* (London) 94 (March 11, 1922): 493.

"American Public Opinion Concerning the Seizure of the Ruhr." *The Outlook* 133 (January 31, 1923): 210–12.

"America's Part in the European Problem." *Current History* 17 (February 1923): 5, 727–29.

Amerine, William H. *Alabama's Own in France*. New York, 1919.

Angell, Norman. "How to Treat Germany." *The Dial* 66 (March 22, 1919): 279–82.

———. *The Political Conditions of Allied Success: A Plea for the Protective Union of the Democracies*. New York, 1918.

Anonymous [Paul Tirard]. "La France sur le Rhin," *Revue des deux mondes*. "I. La Leçon du passé," 48 (1928): 762–97. "II. L'occupation," 49 (1929): 112–39. "III. La Leçon du présent," 49 (1929): 372–400.

"A Parting Doughboy's Glance at the German on his Rhine." *Literary Digest* 62 (September 6, 1919): 82–83.

Apex. *The Uneasy Triangle: Four Years of Occupation*. London, 1931.

Aulneau, Joseph. *Le Rhin et la France*. Paris, 1921.

Bach, Christian A., and Hall, Henry Noble. *The Fourth Division: Its Services and Achievements in the World War*. n.p., 1920.

Bainville, Jacques. *Les Conséquences politiques de la paix*. Paris, 1920.

Bibliography

Balch, Emily Greene. *Approaches to the Great Settlement*. New York, 1918.

Baldwin, Elbert Francis. "Notes in the Rhineland." *The Outlook* 135 (December 5, 1923): 578–80.

———. "The American Forces in Germany." *The Outlook* 122 (August 27, 1919): 635–36.

Bardoux, Jacques. *De Paris à Spa: La bataille diplomatique pour la paix française (février 1919–octobre 1920)*. Paris, 1921.

———. *Lloyd George et la France*. Paris, 1923.

Barker, J. Ellis. "The Colored French Troops in Germany." *Current History* 14 (July 1921): 594–99.

Barrès, Maurice. *L'Appel du Rhin*. Paris, 1919.

———. *Le Génie du Rhin*. Paris, 1921.

———. *La Politique rhénane: Discours parlementaires*. Paris, 1922.

Barthou, Louis. *Le Traité de paix: Versailles 1919*. Paris, 1919.

Bass, John F., and Moulton, Howard G. *America and the Balance Sheet of Europe*. New York, 1922.

Bausman, Frederick. *Let France Explain*. London, 1923.

Beard, Charles A. *Cross Currents in Europe Today*. Boston, 1922.

Beck, James M. *The Reckoning: A Discussion of the Moral Aspects of the Peace Problem and of Retributive Justice as an Indispensable Element*. New York, 1918.

Bergmann, Karl. *Der Weg der Reparation: Von Versailles über den Dawesplan zum Ziel*. Frankfurt, 1926. Translated as *The History of Reparations*. London, 1927.

Beumelberg, Werner. *Deutschland in Ketten: Von Versailles bis zum Youngplan*. Berlin, 1931.

"The Black Troops on the Rhine." *The Nation* 112 (March 9, 1921): 365–66.

Blakeslee, George H. *The Recent Foreign Policy of the United States*. New York, 1925.

Bliss, Tasker H. "The Armistices." *American Journal of International Law* 16 (1922): 509–22.

Blondel, Georges. *La Rhénanie, son passé, son avenir*. Paris, 1921.

Boas, George. "The Wonder of It." *Atlantic* 124 (September 1919): 376–81.

Böhmer, Leo. *Die rheinische Separatistenbewegung und die französische Presse*. Stuttgart, 1928.

Boetticher, Friedrich von. *Der Kampf um den Rhein und die Weltherrschaft*. Leipzig, 1922.

Bibliography

Bourgeois, Léon. *Le Traité de paix de Versailles*. Paris, 1919.

Bouriand, Captain. *La Campagne allemande contre les troupes noires*. Mainz, 1922.

Braley, Berton. "Buddy Bosses the Boche: First Hand Impressions of the American Army of Occupation." *Sunset* 42 (July 1919): 45–46.

Briey, Comte Renaud de. *Le Rhin et le problème d'occident*. Brussels, 1922.

Bruggemann, Fritz. *Die rheinische Republik: Ein Beitrag zur Geschichte und Kritik der rheinischen Abfallbewegung während des Waffenstillstandes im Jahre 1918/1919*. Bonn, 1919. (HIL)

Bryan, William Jennings. "Our Responsibility for the Ruhr Invasion." *Current History* 17 (March 1923): 898–99.

Cantacuzene, Princess, Countess Speransky. "Between Kaiser and Democracy." *Saturday Evening Post* 195 (November 25, 1922): 23, 80,

Capper, Arthur. *The Agricultural Bloc*. New York, 1922. 83–86, 89–90.

———. "The American Farmer and Foreign Policy." *Foreign Affairs* 1 (June 15, 1923): 127–35.

Carles, Jacques. "L'Occupation interalliée des provinces du Rhin." *L'Opinion* 13 (1920): 300–303, 326–28, 357.

Cheradame, André. *The Essentials of an Enduring Victory*. New York, 1918.

Coblenz, Hermann. *Frankreichs Ringen um Rhein und Ruhr: Eine Schriftenreihe zur Abwehr*. Berlin, 1923. (HIL)

Colbeck, Alfred. "France, England, and the Rhineland." *Fortune* 115 (April 1921): 541–48.

"Collapsing: Germany and America." *The Nation* 115 (November 8, 1922): 492.

Collins, Louis L. *Minnesota in the War: History of the 151st Field Artillery, Rainbow Division*. St. Paul, Minn., 1924.

"Coloured Troops in the Occupied Provinces." *New Statesman* 17 (July 2, 1921): 353–54.

Comité d' Etudes. *Travaux du Comité d'Etudes*. 2 vols. Paris, 1918–1920.

Comité des Forges. *La Métallurgie et le traité de paix*. Paris, 1920.

Committee on Public Information. *War Information Series*. Nos. 1–18. Washington, D.C., 1917–1918.

"The Common People of Germany on the Peace Treaty." *Literary Digest* 62 (July 12, 1919): 70–76.

Cosmos. *The Basis of a Durable Peace*. New York, 1917.

Creel, George. *The War, the World, and Wilson*. New York, 1920.

Bibliography

Croly, Herbert. "American Withdrawal from Europe." *New Republic* 36 (September 12, 1923): 65–68.

Crosby, Oscar T. "French Policy since the Armistice." *The Annals* 114 (July 1924): 44–48.

Croy, Homer. "The Movie of the Rhine." *Saturday Evening Post* 191 (May 24, 1919): 41–42, 69.

Cuno, Rudolf. *Der Kampf um die Ruhr: Frankreichs Raubzug und Deutschlands Abwehr.* Leipzig, 1923.

Dariac, Adrien Louis. *The Dariac Report: Ruhr, Rhineland and Saar . . .* Manchester, England, 1923. (HIL)

Dawson, William Harbutt. "Can France and Germany be Reconciled?" *The Fortnightly Review* 112 (July 1, 1922): 1–17.

———. *Problems of the Peace.* London, 1918.

De Gruben, Baron Hervé. *Les Belges sur la Rhin.* Brussels, 1924. (HIL)

De Jaer, B. *L'Armée belge d'occupation et son droit de juridiction.* Liège, 1928.

Dell, Robert. *The Left Bank of the Rhine.* London, 1919.

Deutsche Minister und Abgeordnette. *Die Wunde im Westen . . . (Reichstagsitzung vom 6. November 1920).* Berlin, 1920. (HIL)

Distler, Heinrich. *Das deutsche Leid am Rhein.* Minden, 1921.

Dorten, Hans Adam. "Le Général Mangin en Rhénanie." *Revue des deux mondes,* 7th period, 40 (July 1, 1937): 39–67.

———. "The Rhineland Movement." *Foreign Affairs* 3 (April 1925): 399–410.

"The Doughboys Occupying Germany are Perfectly Calm but Homesick." *Literary Digest* 61 (June 21, 1919): 52–55.

Dreist, Paul. *Die Vergütung der Okkupationsleistungen — Recht und Rechtsgang auf dem Gebiet der Leistungen für die fremden Besatzungstruppen.* Berlin, 1922. (HIL).

Ebray, Alcide. *A Frenchman Looks at the Peace.* New York, 1927.

"End of Our Watch on the Rhine." *Literary Digest* 76 (February 17, 1923): 22.

English, George H. *History of the 89th Division.* Denver, 1920.

Erdmannsdörfer, Hans Gustav. *Der Kampf um Ruhr und Rhein: Deutsche Reparationen — französischen Rechtsbruch.* Berlin, 1923.

Erkelenz, Anton, ed. *Zehn Jahre deutsche Republik.* Berlin, 1928.

"Fair Play for Germany." *The Nation* 110 (April 24, 1920): 535–36.

Finch, George A. "The Costs of the American Army of Occupation on the Rhine." *American Journal of International Law* 17 (1923): 513–17.

Français de couleur sur le Rhin. Mainz, 1921.

"France's Terrible Black Troops." *Literary Digest* 66 (August 28, 1920): 22.

Franck, Harry A. "Through Germany on Foot." *Harper's Magazine* 139, pt. 1 (July 1919): 145–59, pt. 2 (August 1919): 311–25.

Frankfurter, Felix. "French Policy and Peace in Europe." *New Republic* 24 (October 6, 1920): 138–40.

"The French Occupation on the Rhine and in the Saar Valley." *Review of Reviews* 66 (December 1922): 661–62.

"French Watch on the Rhine." *Literary Digest* 65 (April 24, 1920): 9–10.

Frost, Stanley. *Germany's New War Against America.* New York, 1919.

Funck-Brentano, Frantz. *La France sur le Rhin.* Paris, 1919.

"Future Relations with Germany." *Literary Digest* 62 (July 5, 1919): 21–24.

Gannett, Lewis S. "The Horror on the Rhine Again." *The Nation* 113 (September 7, 1921): 264.

———. "Those Black Troops on the Rhine—and the White." *The Nation* 112 (May 25, 1921): 733–34.

Garvin, J. L. "Wanted—A Foreign Policy." *The Living Age* 324 (March 31, 1923): 750–51.

Gawthorne, E. E. "The British Army of the Rhine: A Retrospect." *Journal of the Royal United Service Institution* 74 (1929): 93–97.

"German Ways Puzzle Yanks Who Occupy Coblenz Sector." *Literary Digest* 60 (February 8, 1919): 73–78.

"Germany Informed that We Stand by Our Allies." *Literary Digest* 69 (April 16, 1921): 5–8.

Giese, Friedrich. "Der Reichskommissar für die besetzten Gebtiete: eine kritische Anregung." *Zeitschrift für Völkerrecht* 12 (1923): 447–59.

Goebel, Erwin. *Die pfälzische Presse im Abwehrkampf der Pfalz gegen Franzosen und Separatisten, 1918–1924.* Ludwigshafen, 1931.

"Good-bye to the Rhine." *The Outlook* 133 (January 24, 1923): 162.

Goring, Helmut. *Die Grossmächte und die Rheinfrage in den letzten Jahrhunderten.* Berlin, 1926.

Got, Ambroise. *La Contre-révolution allemande.* Strassburg, 1920.

Grabo, Carl H. *The World Peace and After.* New York, 1918.

Graves, Louis. "Leaves from a Coblenz Diary; Being Fragments from the Notebook of Heinrich Scheinstutzen, Apothecary." *Atlantic* 124 (July–August 1919): 76–83, 209–15.

———. "The American Soldier and the German Mind." *Atlantic* 123 (June 1919): 811–17.

Bibliography

Griffith, Sanford. "Occupying the Rhineland." *New Republic* 21 (January 7, 1920): 168–71.

Grimm, Friedrich. *Frankreich am Rhein: Rheinlandbesetzung und Separatismus im Lichte der historischen französischen Rheinpolitik.* Hamburg, 1931.

Haas, Eberhard. *Die Pfalz unter französischer Besetzung, 1918–1924.* Munich, 1925.

Hagemann, Johann Gerhard. *Das Rheinland und die Sozialdemokratie im Spiegel der mehrheitssozialistischen Presse von der Revolution bis zum Ruhreinbruch.* Quakenbrück, 1926.

Hanotaux, Gabriel. *Le Traité de Versailles du 28 Juin 1919: L'Allemagne et l'Europe.* Paris, 1919. (HIL)

"Happy Days for the American Troops on the Rhine." *Literary Digest* 71 (October 1, 1921): 44–47.

Hart, Albert Bushnell. "Can Germany be Regenerated?" *Forum* 61 (January 1919): 1–11.

Hartmann, Peter. *Französische Kulturarbeit am Rhein.* Leipzig, 1921. (HIL)

Harvey, George. "Beware the Peace Drive." *North American Review* 208 (October 1918): 493–97.

Helfferich, Karl. *Die Politik der Erfüllung.* Munich, 1922.

Herrmann, Georg. *Deutschlands Recht auf das linke Rheinufer.* Freienwalde an der Oder, 1923. (HIL)

Heyck, Hans. *Deutschlands Befreiungskampf 1918–1933.* Bielefeld und Leipzig, 1933.

Heyland, Karl. *Die Rechtstellung der besetzten Rheinlande.* Stuttgart, 1923.

Hill, David Jayne. "Germany After the War." *Scientific Monthly* 8 (April 1919): 311–20.

Holt, Hamilton. "The American Watch on the Rhine." *The Independent* 104 (December 4, 1920): 326–27, 347–49.

Horne, Charles Francis, ed. *The Great Events of the Great War . . .* New York, 1923. Vol. 7, *1918–1919.*

House, Edward M., and Seymour, Charles, eds. *What Really Happened at Paris.* New York, 1921.

Howe, Frederic C. "With the Armies of Occupation in Germany." *Scribner's Magazine* 65 (May 1919): 622–29.

Huddleston, Sisley. *Peace Making at Paris.* London, 1919.

Huget, Pierre. *Le Droit pénal de la rhénanie occupée.* Paris, 1923. (HIL)

Bibliography

Hughes, Charles Evans. "Some Observations on the Conduct of Our Foreign Relations." *American Journal of International Law* 16 (July 1922): 365–74.

———. *The Pathway of Peace: Representative Addresses Delivered during His Term as Secretary of State (1921–1925)*. New York, 1925.

Hugins, Roland. *The Possible Peace: A Forecast of World Politics after the Great War*. New York, 1916.

"If America Were Being Ruled as We Are Ruling Part of Germany." *Literary Digest* 61 (June 14, 1919): 90–93.

"In Germany with William Allen White." *Literary Digest* 61 (April 26, 1919): 64–66.

"In Occupied Germany." *Survey* 41 (March 1, 1919): 793–94.

Ireton, Robert E. "The Rhineland Commission at Work." *American Journal of International Law* 17 (1923): 460–69.

Isambert, André. "Les Provinces du Rhin pendant l'armistice." *Revue des sciences politiques* 42 (August–December 1919): 426–45.

"Is the Black Horror on the Rhine Fact or Propaganda?" *The Nation* 113 (July 1921): 44–45.

Izoulet, Jean. *Et pas de France (ni d'Angleterre et d'Amérique) sans Rhénanie!* Paris, 1920.

Jacquot, Paul. *General Gérard und die Pfalz (November 1918–Dezember 1919)*. Berlin, 1920.

Jaspar, Henri. "La Belgique et la politique occidentale depuis le traité de paix." *Revue belge* 2 (June 1924): 385–410.

Jastrow, Morris. *The War and the Coming Peace: The Moral Issue*. Philadelphia, 1918.

Johnson, Douglas W. *The Peril of Prussianism*. New York, 1917.

Joint War History Commissions of Michigan and Wisconsin. *The 32nd Division in the World War, 1917–1919*. Madison, Wis., 1920.

Kahn, Ernst. *Zwischen Waffenstillstand und Frieden: Ein wirtschaftlicher Rückblick und Ausblick*. Frankfurt, 1920. (Harvard Library)

Kallen, Horace Meyer. *The Structure of Lasting Peace: An Inquiry into the Motives of War and Peace*. Boston, 1918.

Kessler, Count Harry. *Germany and Europe*. New Haven, Conn., 1923.

Keynes, John Maynard. *The Economic Consequences of the Peace*. New York, 1920.

King, Joseph. *The History of the French Occupation of the Ruhr: Its Meaning and Consequences*. London, 1924. (HIL)

Koch-Weser, Erich. *Deutschlands Aussenpolitik in der Nachkriegzeit.*

Bibliography

Berlin, 1930. Translated as *Germany in the Post-war World*. Philadelphia, 1930.

Köhrer, Erich. *Rheinische Wirtschaftsnot*. Berlin, 1921.

Kuske, Bruno. *Rheingrenze und Pufferstatt: Eine volkswirtschaftliche Betrachtung*. Bonn, 1919. (HIL)

La Campagne contre les troupes noires. Mainz, 1921.

Laforêt, Claude. "Mayence—Notes d'un Occupant." *Mercure de France* 131 (January–February 1919): 650–57.

Latané, John H. *From Isolation to Leadership*. New York, 1922.

Laur, Francis. *Une Suisse rhénane? La seule garantie contre une guerre future entre la France et l'Allemagne*. Geneva, 1918–1919.

Lauzanne, Stephane. "The Black Troops." *The Outlook* 127 (March 16, 1921): 423–25.

Lersner, Freiherr von. *Versailles! Volkskommentar des Friedensdiktats*. Berlin, 1921.

Leyland, John. "The Allies, the Rhine, and the Ruhr." *The Nation and Athenaeum* 32 (December 23, 1922): 484–85.

Lichtenberger, Henri. *The Ruhr Conflict*. Washington, 1923.

Linnebach, Karl. *Deutsche und französische Okkupationsmethoden 1871–1873, 1920–?*. Berlin, 1925.

Lippmann, Walter. *The Political Scene: An Essay on the Victory of 1918*. New York, 1919.

Lloyd George, David. *Is It Peace?* London, 1923. Published in the United States as *Where Are We Going?* New York, 1923.

Lodge, Henry Cabot. "Foreign Relations of the United States, 1921–1924." *Foreign Affairs* 2 (June 15, 1924): 525–39.

"London Gets a Washington Bombshell." *Current Opinion* 72 (May 1922): 586–89.

Maccoby, Simon. "The Rhineland in Inter-Allied Negotiations during the War." *Contemporary Review* 125 (February 1924): 206–16.

Malaurie, Albert. "Une Année en Rhénanie." *Revue des deux mondes*, 5th period, 60 (November 1920): 96–127.

Manthey-Zorn, Otto. *Germany in Travail*. Boston, 1922.

Marcosson, Isaac. *The War after the War*. New York, 1917.

Markham, Violet R. "Occupation or Reparation?" *The Fortnightly Review* 112 (September 1922): 383–93.

———. *A Woman's Watch on the Rhine: Sketches of the Occupation*. London, 1920.

Marx, Wilhelm. "Rhineland Occupation." *Foreign Affairs* 7 (January 1929): 198–203.

Bibliography

Masefield, John. *The War and the Future.* New York, 1918.

Mason, Gregory. "Down the Rhine." *The Outlook* 121 (March 12, 1919): 428–29.

———. "From Metz to Mayence." *The Outlook* 121 (March 19, 1919): 477–79.

———. "How the Allies Govern Occupied Germany." *The Outlook* 121 (April 2, 1919): 558–59.

———. "What the Germans Think and Say." *The Outlook* 121 (February 5, 1919): 222–24.

McCormick, Medill. "Political Panaceas or Economic Remedies for Europe." *Saturday Evening Post* 195 (February 17, 1923): 22–23.

McGurdy, Charles A. *A Clean Peace: The War Aims of British Labor.* New York, 1918.

Mehrmann, Karl. *Zehn Jahre Fremdherrschaft am deutschen Rhein: Locarno–Thoiry–Genf in Wirklichkeit: Eine Bilanz der Rheinlandbesetzung.* Berlin, 1927. (HIL)

Mermeix [Gabriel Terrail]. *Les Négociations secrètes et les quatre armistices avec pièces justificatives.* Paris, 1919.

———. *Le Combat des trois.* Paris, 1922.

Miles, J. Saxon. *The Genoa Conference.* London, 1922.

Miller, David Hunter. "Cost of American Troops on the Rhine." *Current History* 16 (July 1922): 614–16.

"The Missing Formula." *New Republic* 26 (April 27, 1921): 250–52.

Mohendis, L. "La Rive gauche du Rhin et la reprise du commerce avec l'ennemi . . . d'hier." *Revue des sciences politiques* 42 (August–December 1919): 446–55.

Morel, E. D. *The Horror on the Rhine.* London, 1920.

Morgan, John H., and Spears, R. L. "The Problem of the Rhineland." *Journal of the Royal Institute of International Affairs* 4 (May 1925): 118–41.

"Mr. Borah Takes Sides." *The Outlook* 133 (January 31, 1923): 162.

Myers, Denys P. "France's Policy on the Rhine." *Current History* 17 (February 1923): 730–37.

Nast, Marcel. "L'Occupation des territoires rhénans par les troupes des alliés et des Etats-Unis pendant l'armistice." *Revue générale de droit international public* 28 (1926): 139–59.

Naunin, Helmut. *Die Besetzung der Stadt Duisburg durch belgische und französische Truppen nach dem Weltkrieg.* Berlin, 1930.

"The New Crisis in Europe." *The Outlook* 133 (January 17, 1923): 106–17.

Bibliography

Nichols, Bruce. "France's Rhineland Republic." *New Republic* 36 (September 5, 1923): 39–40.

Nock, Albert J. *The Myth of a Guilty Nation.* New York, 1922.

Nolan, J. Bennett. "Germany Revisited." *Atlantic* 127 (January 1921): 106–13.

Nourse, Edwin G. *American Agriculture and the European Market.* New York, 1924.

Nowak, Karl F. *Versailles.* Berlin, 1927.

Noyes, Pierrepont B. *A Practical Business Solution to the European Crisis: An Address* . . . New York, 1923.

———. "The Effect of French Policies on Present Day European Situation." *The Annals* 114 (July 1924): 26–28.

———. "Justice to Germany and France." *The Nation* 112 (January 19, 1921): 92–101.

———. *While Europe Waits for Peace.* New York, 1920. Translated as *Wo Europa doch des Friedens harrt* . . . Berlin, 1921.

Oberhauser, Robert. *Der Kampf um die Rheinpfalz.* Leipzig, 1932.

Ossenbruck, A. *Deutschland–Protektorat Englands und Amerikas?* Munich, 1919. (HIL)

P. G. "American Opinion on the Ruhr." *The Spectator* 130 (April 7, 1923): 578–79.

Pange, Jean de. *Les Libertés rhénanes: Pays Rhénans–Sarre–Alsace.* Paris, 1922.

"Passing Sentence on the Kaiser and His People." *Literary Digest* 59 (October 26, 1918): 14.

Patillo, George. "Rubbing Elbows with Heinie." *Saturday Evening Post* 191 (May 24, 1919): 3, 4, 111–16.

"The Peace with Germany." *Current Opinion* 71 (October 1921): 409–13.

People's Council of America for Democracy and Peace. *Report of the First American Conference for Democracy and Terms of Peace.* New York, 1917.

Peters, Otto, ed. *Kampf um den Rhein: Beiträge zur Geschichte des Rheinlandes und seiner Fremdherrschaft, 1918–1930.* Mainz, 1930.

Petersens, Ludvig af. "In den besetzten Gebiete am Rhein und der Saar." *Deutsche Rundschau* 193 (October 1922): 12–28.

Picard, Roger. *L'Allemagne et la France.* La Flèche, 1924.

Pierrefeu, Jean de. *Le GQC, secteur I.* 2 vols. Paris, 1920–1922. Translated as *French Headquarters, 1915–1918.* London, 1924.

Pinon, René. *Le Redressement de la politique française, 1922.* Paris, 1923.

———. "Territorial Claims of France." *Atlantic* 123 (March 1919): 398–407.

Poincaré, Raymond. *Histoire politique: Chroniques de quinzaine.* 4 vols. Paris, 1922.

———. "Since Versailles." *Foreign Affairs* 7 (July 1929): 519–31.

Powers, Harry H. *The Great Peace.* New York, 1918.

"The President's Reply and the People's Reply." *Literary Digest* 59 (October 19, 1918): 7–10.

"The Problem of Germany." *New Republic* 22 (April 28, 1920): 261–62.

Prothero, Sir George W., ed. *Peace Handbooks.* 155 vols. London, 1920.

Pyszka, Hannes. *Der Ruhrkreig.* Munich, 1923.

Recouly, Raymond. *La Barrière du Rhin: Droits et devoirs de la France pour assurer sa sécurité.* Paris, 1923. (HIL)

Reichert, J. W., ed. *Rathenaus Reparationspolitik: Eine kritische Studie.* Berlin, 1922.

Reilly, H. J. *Americans All: The Rainbow at War.* Columbus, Ohio, 1936.

Renaud, Jean. *Aux Pays occupés.* Paris, 1920.

Rheinische Frauenliga. *Farbige Franzosen am Rhein.* 4th ed. Berlin, 1923.

Rhenanus. "In Rhenish Dollarika." *Living Age* 306 (August 7, 1920): 334–36.

"Rhineland Occupation Terms Modified." *Current History* 11 (October 1919): 101–104.

"The Rhine's Black Horror Faded." *Literary Digest* 69 (June 25, 1921): 14.

"Right and Wrong of the Ruhr Invasion." *Literary Digest* 76 (January 27, 1923): 7–11.

Rogers, Francis. "Verdun and Coblenz." *The Outlook* 132 (September 13, 1922): 56–57.

Rogers, Lindsay. *The War Aims of the United States: A Study Outline.* New York, 1918.

Roosevelt, Theodore. *Roosevelt in the Kansas City Star: Wartime Editorials by Theodore Roosevelt.* Boston, 1921.

Rousseau, Jean. *La haute Commission interalliée des territoires rhénans; ses origines, son organisation, ses attributions.* Mainz, 1923.

Roz, Firmin. "La Crise de la paix aux Etats Unis et les relations franco-américaines." *Revue des deux mondes,* 6th period, 11 (September 15, 1922): 307–28.

Sarrail, M. "Les Têtes de pont du Rhin." *Revue politique et parlementaire* 104 (July 1920): 40–49.

Bibliography

Scheidewin, Wolfgang. *The Burden of Military Occupation in the Rhineland, Representative Cases and Statistics Compiled from the Memoranda of the German Ministry of Finance.* Leipzig, 1923.

Schmid, C. C. "Zehn Jahre fremder Besatzung am Rhein." In *Zehn Jahre deutsche Geschichte 1918–1928.* Berlin, 1928.

Schmitt, Carl. *Die Rheinlande als Objekt internationaler Politik.* Cologne, 1925. (HIL)

Schmitz, Joseph. "Eine neue Einmischung der Rheinlandkommission in die sozialen Verhältnisse des besetzten Gebietes," *Rheinischer Beobachter* (1922), pp. 312–13.

Schücking, Levin L. "France, Germany and the Occupation of the Rhineland." *New Statesman* 18 (January 28, 1922): 467–69.

Schulte, Aloys. *Frankreich und das linke Rheinufer.* Stuttgart, 1918.

Seventh Field Artillery. *History of the Seventh Field Artillery, World War 1917–1919.* New York, 1929.

Sevestre, Norbert. "Une Campagne de propagande allemande, 'La honte noire,' " *Revue des deux mondes,* 5th period, 60 (September 15, 1921): 417–33.

Seymour, Charles. "America's Responsibility to Germany." *Atlantic* 133 (June 1924): 824–32.

Siegfried, André. *Post-War Britain: A French Analysis.* London, 1924.

Simon, Hugo Ferdinand. *Reparation und Wiederaufbau.* Berlin, 1925.

Simonds, Frank H. "Europe's New Crisis." *The American Review of Reviews* 67 (February 1923): 151–62.

———. *How Europe Made Peace without America.* Garden City, N. Y., 1927.

Society of the Fifth Division. *The Official History of the Fifth Division, U.S.A.* Washington, D.C., 1919.

Society of the First Division. *History of the First Division during the World War, 1917–1919.* Philadelphia, 1922.

Solemacher-Antweiler, Viktor Freiherr von. *Die abgetretenen und besetzten Gebiete im deutschen Westen: Tatsachen und Zahlen.* Berlin, 1925.

Springer, Max. *Frankreich und seine "Freunde" am Rhein.* Leipzig, 1923.

———. *Loslösungsbestrebungen am Rhein, 1918–1924.* Berlin, 1924.

Stegemann, Hermann. *Under the Yoke of Foreign Rule: Sufferings of the Rhineland Population.* Leipzig, 1923–1924. (HIL)

———. *Der Kampf um den Rhein . . .* Stuttgart, 1924. Translated as *The Struggle for the Rhine.* New York, 1927.

Bibliography

Street, C. J. C. *Rhineland and Ruhr*. London, 1923.

Strobel, Rudolf. *Sanktionen und Rheinzollinie: Eine politischwirtschaftliche Studie*. Munich, 1922.

Stulpnagel, Otto von. *The French Terror: The Martyrdom of the German People on the Rhine and Ruhr*. Berlin, 1923. (HIL)

Taber, John H. *The Story of the 168th Infantry*. Iowa City, Iowa, 1925.

Tardieu, André. *Devant l'Obstacle: L'Amérique et nous*. Paris, 1927. Translated as *France and America*. New York, 1927.

———. "The Policy of France." *Foreign Affairs* 1 (September 1922): 11–28.

———. *La Paix*. Paris, 1921. Translated as *The Truth about the Treaty*. Indianapolis, 1921.

Temperley, H. W. V., ed. *A History of the Peace Conference at Paris*. 6 vols. London, 1920–1924.

Thayer, William Roscoe. *Volleys from a Non-Combatant*. New York, 1919.

Thiallet, Frances. *La haute Commission interalliée des territoires rhénans et la conciliation des conflits collectifs du travail*. Coulommiers, 1928.

Timmermann, Annelise. *Die Rheinlandbesetzung in Ihrer Wirkung auf die Sozialausgaben der Städte*. Berlin, 1930. (HIL)

Tirard, Paul. *L'Art français en Rhénanie pendant l'occupation, 1918–1930*. Strasbourg, 1930.

———. *Rapport sur l'administration des territoires occupés de la rive gauche du Rhin pendant l'armistice . . .* n.p., 1920 (HIL)

"To Help France Watch the Rhine." *Literary Digest* 62 (July 19, 1919): 22.

"To Punish Hun Frightfulness." *Literary Digest* 59 (October 19, 1918): 10–11.

Toynbee, Arnold, ed. *Survey of International Affairs, 1920–1923*. London, 1925.

Troeltsch, Ernst. "Public Opinion in Germany," *Contemporary Review* 123 (May 1923): 578–83.

Tuohy, Ferdinand. *Occupied, 1918–1920: A Postscript to the Western Front*. London, 1931.

———. "France's Rhineland Adventure." *Contemporary Review* 138 (1930): 29–38.

Turner, John Kenneth. *Shall It Be Again?* New York, 1922.

Usher, Roland. *The Winning of the War*. New York, 1918.

Veblen, Thorstein. *An Inquiry into the Nature of Peace and the Terms of Its Perpetuation*. New York, 1917.

Bibliography

Vanard, Robert. *L'Occupation des territoires rhénans et le droit privé.* Paris, 1922.

Vial-Mazel, Georges. *Erreurs et oublis de Georges Clemenceau: L'affaire du Rhin.* Paris, 1931.

———. *Le Rhin: Victoire allemande.* Paris, 1921.

Villard, O. G. "Germany 1922: In the Occupied Territory." *The Nation* 115 (August 2, 1922): 116–18.

Viviani, René. *As We See It.* London, 1923.

Vogels, Werner. "Die Organe der Allierten im besetzten Rheinland." *Preussisches Verwaltungsblatt* 42 (1921): 413–15.

Von Hake, Fritz. *Frankreich im Rheinland: Der Versailler Vertrag ein fetzen Papier.* Berlin, 1925.

Wachendorf, Karl. *Zehn Jahre Fremdherrschaft am Deutschen Rhein: Eine Geschichte der Rheinlandbesetzung von 1918–1928.* Berlin, 1928.

Wächter, Gerhardt. *Französische Truppen am Rhein, eine Gefahr für den Frieden Europas.* Heidelberg, n. d.

Warren, Maude Radford. "American Rule in the Rhineland." *Saturday Evening Post* 191 (May 3, 1919): 135, 139, 143.

"The Watch on the Rhine." *The Nation and Athenaeum* 32 (November 11, 1922): 225–26.

Weber, H. A. *Besetztes Gebiet.* Baden Baden, 1931.

Welles, H. B. *Washington and the Riddle of Peace.* New York, 1922.

Wentzcke, Paul. *Rheinkampf.* 2 vols. Berlin, 1925.

Wenz, Jakob. *Elf Jahre in Fesseln: Die Leidengeschichte der Koblenzer Bevölkerung während der Besatzungszeit.* Coblenz, 1930.

Weyl, Walter. *The End of the War.* New York, 1918.

"What Can America Do?" *The New Statesman* 20 (January 13, 1923): 420–21.

"What Drove Belgium into the Ruhr." *Literary Digest* 76 (February 17, 1923): 20–21.

"What Harding's Victory Means to Europe." *Literary Digest* 67 (November 20, 1920): 22–23.

"What Helping Europe Means." *New Republic* 33 (January 10, 1923): 158–60; 33 (January 17, 1923): 183; 33 (January 24, 1923): 209.

"What Occupation is for Germany." *The Living Age* 310 (September 3, 1921): 560–61.

"What To Do With Germany." *The Public: A Journal of Democracy* (December 14, 1918), pp. 1495–496.

Woolf, Leonard. "Germany and the Cost of Occupation." *Contemporary Review* 121 (January 1922): 114–16.

Bibliography

Wythe, George. *A History of the 90th Division*. n.p., 1920.

Zwendelaar, A. *La Belgique jusqu'au Rhin*. Brussels, 1916.

HISTORIES, TREATISES, AND SCHOLARLY ARTICLES

Abrams, Richard, M. "United States Intervention Abroad: The First Quarter Century." *American Historical Review* 79 (February 1974): 72–102.

Adler, Selig. "Isolationism since 1914." *American Scholar* 21 (Summer 1952): 335–44.

———. *The Isolationist Impulse: Its Twentieth Century Reaction*. London, 1957.

———. *The Uncertain Giant, 1921–1941: American Foreign Policy between the Wars*. New York, 1965.

———. "The War Guilt Question and American Disillusionment, 1918–1923." *Journal of Modern History* 23 (March, 1951): 1–28.

Allard, Paul. *Les Dessous de la guerre, révélés par les comités secrets*. Paris, 1932.

Ambrosius, Lloyd E. "Wilson, the Republicans, and French Security after World War I." *Journal of American History* 59 (September 1972): 341–52.

Angell, James W. *Financial Foreign Policy of the United States*. New York, 1933.

———. *The Recovery of Germany*. New Haven, Conn., 1929.

Angress, Werner T. *Stillborn Revolution: The Communist Bid for Power in Germany, 1921–1923*. Princeton, N. J., 1963.

———. "Weimar Coalition and Ruhr Insurrection, March–April, 1920: A Study of Government Policy." *Journal of Modern History* 29 (March 1957): 1–20.

Artaud, Denise. "A propos de l'Occupation de la Ruhr." *Revue d'histoire moderne et contemporaine* 17 (January–March 1970): 1–21.

Auld, George P. *The Dawes Plan and the New Economics*. Garden City, N. Y., 1928.

Bagby, Wesley M. *The Road to Normalcy: The Presidential Campaign and Election of 1920*. Baltimore, 1962.

Bailey, Thomas A. *Woodrow Wilson and the Great Betrayal*. New York, 1945.

———. *Woodrow Wilson and the Lost Peace*. New York, 1944.

Bander, Ingram. "Sidney Edward Mezes and the Inquiry." *The Journal of Modern History* 2 (1939): 199–202.

409

Bibliography

Bane, Suda Lorena, and Lutz, Ralph Haswell. *The Blockade of Germany after the Armistice, 1918–1919.* Stanford, Calif., 1942.

Bariéty, Jacques. "Les Reparations allemandes après la première guerre mondiale: Objet ou prétexte a une politique rhénane de la France (1919–1924)." *Bulletin société d'histoire moderne* 72 (March-May 1973): 21–33.

Baumont, Maurice. *La Faillite de la paix, 1918–1939.* 2 vols. Paris, 1945.

Beaver, Daniel R. *Newton D. Baker and the American War Effort, 1917–1919.* Lincoln, Neb., 1966.

Beaverbrook, Lord. *The Decline and Fall of Lloyd George.* Des Moines, Iowa, 1963.

Becker, Howard. "Das Deutschlandbild in Amerika." *Politische Studien* 115 (November 1959): 737–47.

Benz, Wolfgang. *Suddeutschland in der Weimarer Republik.* Berlin, 1970.

Berbusse, Edward J. "Diplomatic Relations between the United States and Weimar Germany, 1919–1929." Ph.D. diss., Georgetown University, 1952.

Berg, Peter. *Deutschland und Amerika 1918–1929: Uber das deutsche Amerikabild der zwanziger Jahre.* Lübeck, 1963.

Berger, Marcel, and Allard, Paul. *Les Dessous du traité de Versailles (d'après les documents inédits de la censure française).* Paris, 1933.

———. *Les Secrets de la censure pendant la guerre.* Paris, 1932.

Beyerhaus, G. *Die Europa-politik des Marshalls Foch.* Leipzig, 1942.

Billington, Ray A. "The Origins of Middle Western Isolationism." *Political Science Quarterly* 60 (March 1945): 44–64.

Binkley, Robert A. "New Light on the Paris Peace Conference." *Political Science Quarterly* 46 (1931): 335–61.

———. "Reactions of European Public Opinion to Woodrow Wilson's Statesmanship from the Armistice to the Peace of Versailles." Ph.D. diss. Stanford University, 1927.

Binoux, Paul. *La Question rhénane et la France.* Paris, 1946.

Birdsall, Paul. *Versailles Twenty Years After.* New York, 1941.

Birn, Donald S. "British and French at the Washington Conference, 1921–1922." Ph.D. diss. Columbia University, 1965.

———. "Open Diplomacy at the Washington Conference of 1921–2: The British and French Experience." *Comparative Studies in Society and History* 12 (1970): 297–319.

Boas, George. "Human Relations in Military Government." *Public Opinion Quarterly* 7 (Winter 1943): 542–54.

Bibliography

Bonnefous, Edouard. *Histoire politique de la troisième république; L'après-guerre: 1919–1924.* Paris, 1959.

Boorstin, Daniel J. *America and the Image of Europe: Reflections on American Thought.* New York, 1960.

Boylan, Bernard. "Army Reorganization 1920: The Legislative Story." *Mid-America* 49 (April 1967): 115–28.

Brandes, Joseph. *Herbert Hoover and Economic Diplomacy: Department of Commerce Policy, 1921–1928.* Pittsburgh, 1962.

Brecht, Arnold. *Federalism and Regionalism in Germany: The Division of Prussia.* London, 1945.

Bretton, Henry L. *Stresemann and the Revision of Versailles: A Fight for Reason.* Stanford, Calif., 1953.

Brogan, D. W. *France Under the Republic.* New York, 1940.

Bruch, Werner Friedrich. *The Social and Economic History of Germany, 1888–1938.* London, 1938.

Buchanan, Russell. "American Editors Examine American War Aims and Plans in April 1917." *Pacific Historical Review* 9 (September 1940): 253–65.

Buckley, Thomas H. *The United States and the Washington Conference, 1921–1922.* Knoxville, 1970.

Buehrig, E. H., ed. *Wilson's Foreign Policy in Perspective.* Bloomington, Ind., 1957.

Burdick, Charles B., and Lutz, Ralph H., eds. *The Political Institutions of the German Revolution, 1918–1919.* New York, 1966.

Burnett, Philip M. *Reparation at the Paris Peace Conference from the Standpoint of the American Delegation.* 2 vols. New York, 1940.

Burton, David H. "Teddy Roosevelt's Social Darwinism and Views on Imperialism." *Journal of the History of Ideas* 26 (March 1965): 103–118.

Bury, J. P. T. *France, 1814–1940.* Philadelphia, 1949.

Cairnes, John C. "A Nation of Shopkeepers in Search of a Suitable France." *American Historical Review* 79 (June 1974): 710–43.

Carleton, William G. "Isolation and the Middle West." *Mississippi Valley Historical Review* 33 (December 1946): 377–90.

Carr, E. H. *Britain: A Study in Foreign Policy from the Versailles Treaty to the Outbreak of the War.* London, 1939.

———. *International Relations since the Peace Treaties.* London, 1937.

Carsten, Francis Ludwig. *Revolution in Central Europe, 1918–1919.* Berkeley, 1972.

Bibliography

Castillon, Richard. *Les Réparations allemandes: Deux Expériences, 1919–1932, 1945–1952*. Paris, 1953.

Chastenet, Jacques. *Histoire de la troisième république*. 7 vols. Paris, 1952–1963.

Churchill, Winston. *The Aftermath*. New York, 1929.

Cleveland, Robert E. "French Attitudes toward the German Problem, 1914–1919," Ph.D. diss., University of Nebraska, 1956–1957.

Coffman, Edward M. *The War To End All Wars: The American Military Experience in World War I*. New York, 1968.

Cohen, Warren Ira. *The American Revisionists: The Lessons of Intervention in World War I*. Chicago, 1967.

Cooper, John Milton, Jr. *The Vanity of Power: American Isolationism and World War I, 1914–1917*. Westport, Conn., 1969.

Cornebise, Alfred E. "Cuno, Germany, and the Coming of the Ruhr Occupation . . ." *Proceedings of the American Philosophical Society* 116 (December 1972): 502–31.

———. "Some Aspects of the German Response to the Ruhr Occupation, January-September 1923." Ph.D. diss., University of North Carolina, 1966.

Cowan, Laing Gray. *France and the Saar, 1680–1948*. New York, 1950.

Cox, Frederick J. "The French Peace Plans, 1918–1919: The Germ of the Conflict between Ferdinand Foch and Georges Clemenceau." In *Studies in Modern European History in Honor of Franklin Charles Palm*. Edited by Frederick J. Cox et al. New York, 1956.

Craig, Gordon, and Gilbert, Felix, eds. *The Diplomats, 1919–1939*. Princeton, N. J., 1953.

Crosby, Gerda Richards. *Disarmament and Peace in British Politics, 1914–1919*. Cambridge, Mass., 1957.

Curry, George. "Woodrow Wilson, Jan Smuts, and the Versailles Settlement." *American Historical Review* 66 (July 1961): 968–96.

Curti, Merle. *Peace or War*. New York, 1936.

Dahlin, Ebba. *French and German Public Opinions on Declared War Aims, 1914–1918*. Stanford, Calif., 1933.

Daines, Franklin David. "The Rhineland Policy of France." Ph.D. diss., University of California, Berkeley, 1930.

Davis, Rodney O. "Lloyd George: Leader or Led in British War Aims, 1916–1918." In *Power, Public Opinion and Diplomacy: Essays in Honor of Eber Malcolm Carroll*, edited by Lillian Parker Wallace and William C. Askew. Durham, N. C., 1959.

412

Bibliography

De La Gorce, Paul-Marie. *The French Army: A Military-Political History*. New York, 1963.

De Launay, Jacques, ed. *Secrets diplomatiques, 1914–1918*. Brussels, 1963.

De Loménie, E. Beau. *Le Débat de ratification du traité de Versailles*. Paris, 1945.

DeWeerd, Harvey A. *President Wilson Fights His War: World War I and American Intervention*. New York, 1968.

Dorn, W. L. "The Debate Over American Occupation Policy in Germany in 1944–1945." *Political Science Quarterly* 72 (1957): 481–501.

Duroselle, Jean-Baptiste. *From Wilson to Roosevelt: Foreign Policy of the United States, 1913–1945*. Cambridge, Mass., 1963.

———. *Les Relations franco-allemandes de 1914 à 1939*. Paris, 1967.

Elben, Wolfgang. *Das Problem der Kontinuität in der deutschen Revolution*. Düsseldorf, 1965.

Elcock, Howard. *Portrait of a Decision: The Council of Four and the Treaty of Versailles*. London, 1972.

Ellis, L. Ethan. *Republican Foreign Policy, 1921–1933*. New Brunswick, N. J., 1968.

Epstein, Fritz T. "Germany and the United States: Basic Patterns of Conflict and Understanding." In *Issues and Conflicts: Studies in Twentieth Century American Diplomacy*, edited by George L. Anderson. Lawrence, Kansas, 1965.

———. "Zwischen Compiègne und Versailles, geheime amerikanische Militärdiplomatie in der Periode des Waffenstillstandes 1918/1919." *Vierteljahrshefte für Zeitgeschichte* 3 (July 1955): 412–45.

Erdmann, Karl Dietrich. *Adenauer in der Rheinlandpolitik nach dem ersten Weltkrieg*. Stuttgart, 1966.

Erger, Johannes. *Der Kapp-Lüttwitz Putsch*. Düsseldorf, 1967.

Evans, Laurence. *United States Policy and the Partition of Turkey, 1914–1924*. Baltimore, 1965.

Eyck, Erich. *Geschichte der Weimarer Republik*. 2 vols. Zurich, 1954–1956. Translated as *A History of the Weimar Republic*. 2 vols. Cambridge, Mass., 1963.

Favez, Jean-Claude. *Le Reich devant l'occupation franco-belge de la Ruhr en 1923*. Geneva, 1969.

Feis, Herbert. *The Diplomacy of the Dollar: First Era 1919–1932*. Baltimore, 1950.

Fisher, Ernst F. "Road to Rapallo: A Study of Walther Rathenau and

Bibliography

German Foreign Policy, 1919–1922." Ph.D. diss., University of Wisconsin, 1952.

Flandin, Pierre-Etienne. *Politique française, 1919–1940*. Paris, 1947.

Flechtheim, Ossip. *Die kommunistische Partei Deutschlands in der Weimarer Republik*. Offenbach, 1948.

Floto, Inga. *Colonel House in Paris; A Study of American Policy at the Paris Peace Conference 1919*. Aarhus, Denmark, 1973.

Först, Walter. *Das Rheinland in preussischer Zeit*. Cologne, 1965.

Fontaine, Arthur. *French Industry during the War*. New Haven, 1926.

Fraenkel, Ernst, ed. *Amerika im Speigel das deutschen Politischen Denkens* . . . Cologne, 1959.

———. "Das deutsche Wilsonbild." *Jahrbuch für Amerikastudien* 5 (1960): 66–120.

———. *Military Occupation and the Rule of Law: Occupation Government in the Rhineland, 1918–1923*. London, 1944.

François-Poncet, André. *De Versailles à Potsdam: La France et le problème allemand contemporain, 1919–1945*. Paris, 1948.

Frasure, Carl M. *The British Policy on War Debts and Reparations*. Philadelphia, 1940.

Freidel, Frank. *Over There: The Story of America's First Great Overseas Crusade*. Boston, 1964.

Friedensburg, Ferdinand. "Die geheimen Abmachungen zwischen Clemenceau und Lloyd George vom Dezember 1918 und ihre Bedeutung für das Zustandekommen des Versailles Vertrags," *Berliner Monatsheft* 16 (1938): 702–15.

Friedrich, Carl J., et al. *American Experiences in Military Government in World War II*. New York, 1948.

Gachot, Edouard. *La Dispute du Rhin de l'antiquité à nos jours*. Paris, 1952.

Garston, J. "Armies of Occupation: II." *History Today* 2 (July 1961): 479–89.

Gedye, G. E. R. *The Revolver Republic: France's Bid for the Rhine*. London, 1930.

Gelfand, Lawrence E. *The Inquiry: American Preparations for Peace, 1917–1919*. New Haven, 1963.

Gescher, Dieter Bruno. *Die Vereinigten Staaten von Nordamerika und die Reparationen, 1920–1924*. Bonn, 1956.

Gordon, Harold J., Jr. *The Reichswehr and the German Republic, 1919–1926*. Princeton, N. J., 1957.

414

Bibliography

Gottleib, W. W. *Studies in Secret Diplomacy During the First World War*. London, 1957.

Graebner, Norman A. *An Uncertain Tradition: American Secretaries of State in the Twentieth Century*. New York, 1961.

Graham, Frank D. *Exchange, Prices, and Production in Hyper-Inflation: Germany 1920–1923*. Princeton, 1930.

Graml, Hermann. "Die Rapallo-Politik im Urteil der westdeutschen Forschung," *Vierteljahrshefte für Zeitgeschichte* 18 (1970): 366–91.

———. "Europa zwischen den Kriegen," in *Deutsche Geschichte seit dem ersten Weltkrieg*. 2 vols. Stuttgart, 1971.

Grassmuch, George L. *Sectional Biases in Congress in Foreign Policy*. Baltimore, 1951.

Grimm, Friedrich. *Poincaré am Rhein*. Berlin, 1940.

Grossman, Paul. *Im Kampf um den Rhein, 1918–1930*. Frankfurt a.M., 1933.

Haig, R. H. *The Public Finances of Post-War France*. New York, 1929.

Hammond, Paul Y. *Organizing for Defense: The American Military Establishment in the Twentieth Century*. Princeton, N. J., 1961.

Hankey, Lord. *The Supreme Command, 1914–1918*. 2 vols. London, 1961.

———. *The Supreme Control at the Paris Peace Conference, 1919*. London, 1963.

Hanson, Joseph Mills. *South Dakota in the World War, 1917–1919*. n.p., 1940.

Hardinge of Penshurst, Lord. *Old Diplomacy*. London, 1947.

Hartenstein, Wolfgang. *Die Anfänge der deutschen Volkspartei 1918–1920*. Düsseldorf, 1963.

Harvey, James C. "The French Security Thesis and French Foreign Policy from Paris to Locarno, 1919–1925." Ph.D. diss., University of Texas, 1955.

Helmreich, Jonathan E. "Belgian Diplomatic Style: A Study in Small Power Diplomacy." Ph.D. diss., Princeton, 1961.

———. "The Negotiation of the Franco-Belgian Military Accord of 1920." *French Historical Studies* 3 (1964): 360–78.

Henry, Laurin L. *Presidential Transitions*. Washington, 1960. Gainsville, Fla., 1964.

Hicks, John D. *Rehearsal for Disaster: The Boom and Collapse of 1919–1920*. Gainsville, Fla., 1964.

———. *Republican Ascendancy, 1920–1932*. New York, 1960.

Bibliography

Higham, John. *Strangers in the Land: Patterns of American Nativism, 1860–1925*. New Brunswick, N. J., 1955.

Hoag, G. L. *Preface to Preparedness: The Washington Conference and Public Opinion*. Washington, 1949.

Hoelzle, Erwin. "Das Experiment des Friedens im ersten Weltkrieg, 1914–1917." *Geschichte in Wissenschaft und Unterricht* 8 (August 1962): 465–522.

Holborn, Hajo. *American Military Government: Its Origins and Policies*. Washington, 1947.

Holt, W. Stull. "What Wilson Sent and What House Received: Or Scholars Need to Check Carefully." *American Historical Review 65* (April 1960): 569–71.

Howard, Michael. *The Continental Commitment: The Dilemma of British Defence Policy in the Era of the Two World Wars*. London, 1972.

Howard, T. H. "Tales of the E.O.T.A.: The British Army of the Rhine." *Army Quarterly* 47 (1943–1944): 759–70.

Hughes, Judith M. *To the Maginot Line: The Politics of French Military Preparation in the 1920's*. Cambridge, Mass., 1971.

Huthmacher, J. J., and Susman, Warren I., eds. *Wilson's Diplomacy: An International Symposium*. Cambridge, Mass. 1973.

Jacobson, Jon. *Locarno Diplomacy: Germany and the West, 1925–1929*. Princeton, N. J., 1972.

Jaffe, Lorna. "British Policy towards Germany, 1919–1922." Ph.D. diss., Yale University, 1968.

James, Marquis. *A History of the American Legion*. New York, 1923.

Jordan, W. M. *Great Britain, France and the German Problem, 1918–1939*. New York, 1944.

Kastning, Alfred. *Die deutsche Sozialdemokratie zwischen Koalition und Opposition 1919–1923*. Paderborn, 1970.

Keit, Ernst. *Der Waffenstillstand und die Rheinfrage 1918/1919*. Bonn, 1940.

Kennan, George F. *Soviet-American Relations, 1917–1920*. 2 vols. Princeton, 1956-.

King, Jere Clemens. *Generals and Politicians: Conflict between France's High Command, Parliament and Government, 1914–1918*. Berkeley, 1951.

———. *Foch versus Clemenceau: France and German Dismemberment, 1918–1919*. Cambridge, Mass., 1960.

Klein, Peter. *Separatisten an Rhein und Ruhr . . .* (East) Berlin, 1961.

Bibliography

Koenig, Louis W. *The Invisible Presidency.* New York, 1960.

Köller, Heinz. *Kampfbündnis an der Seine, Ruhr und Spree: Der gemeinsame Kampf der KPF und KPD gegen die Ruhrbesetzung 1923.* (East) Berlin, 1963.

Kolb, Eberhard. *Die Arbeiterräte in der deutschen Innenpolitik, 1918–1919.* Düsseldorf, 1962.

Kollman, Eric C. "Walther Rathenau and German Foreign Policy; Thoughts and Actions." *Journal of Modern History* 24 (June 1952): 127–42.

Krüger, Wilhelm. *Die englische-französischen Spannungen bei der Lösung der orientalischen Frage, 1922.* Berlin, 1940.

Landauer, C. "The Bavarian Problem in the Weimar Republic, 1918–1923," *The Journal of Modern History* 16 (1944): 93–115, 205–23.

Lang, Reuben Clarence. "Die Meinung in der USA über Deutschland im Jahr des Ruhrkampfes und des Hitlerputsches." *Saeculum* 17 (1966): 402–16.

Lasch, Christopher. "American Intervention in Siberia: A Reinterpretation." *Political Science Quarterly* 67 (June 1962): 205–23.

———. *The American Liberals and the Russian Revolution.* New York, 1962.

Laubach, Ernst. *Die Politik der Kabinette Wirth 1921/22.* Lübeck, 1968.

Lefranc, Georges. *Le Mouvement socialiste sous la troisième republique.* Paris, 1963.

Leopold, Richard W. "The Mississippi Valley and American Foreign Policy, 1890–1941." *Mississippi Valley Historical Review* 37 (March 1951): 625–42.

Leuchtenberg, William E. *The Perils of Prosperity, 1914–1932.* Chicago, 1958.

Levin, N. Gordon, Jr. *Woodrow Wilson and World Politics: America's Response to War and Revolution.* New York, 1968.

Lhopital, René Michel M. *Foch, l'armistice et le paix.* Paris, 1938.

Link, Arthur S. *Wilson the Diplomatist: A Look at His Major Foreign Policies.* Baltimore, 1957.

Link, Werner. *Die amerikanische Stabilisierungspolitik in Deutschland 1921–32.* Düsseldorf, 1969.

———. "Die Ruhrbesetzung und die wirtschaftpolitischen Interessen der USA." *Vierteljahrshefte für Zeitgeschichte* 17 (July 1969): 372–82.

Linke, Horst Günther. *Deutsch-sowjetische Beziehungen bis Rapallo.* Cologne, 1970.

Lloyd George, David. *The Truth about Reparations and War Debts.* London, 1932.

417

Bibliography

Lower, Richard Coke. "Hiram Johnson: The Making of an Irreconcilable," *Pacific Historical Review* 41 (November 1972): 505–26.

Lowry, Francis Bullitt. "The Generals, the Armistice, and the Treaty of Versailles, 1919." Ph.D. diss., Duke University, 1963.

———. "Pershing and the Armistice." *Journal of American History* 55 (September 1968): 281–91.

Luckau, Alma. *The German Delegation at the Paris Peace Conference.* New York, 1941.

Lutz, Ralph Haswell, ed. *The Fall of the German Empire, 1914– 1918.* 2 vols. Stanford, Calif., 1932.

———. *The German Revolution, 1918–1919.* Stanford, Calif., 1922.

Maehl, William Harvey. "The German Socialists and the Foreign Policy of the Reich from the London Conference to Rapallo." *Journal of Modern History* 19 (March 1947): 35–54.

Mangin, Louis Eugene. *La France et la Rhin, hier et aujourdhui.* Geneva, 1945.

Mantoux, Etienne. *The Carthaginian Peace, or the Economic Consequences of Mr. Keynes.* New York, 1952.

Margulies, Herbert F. "The Election of 1920 in Wisconsin; The Return to 'Normalcy' Reappraised." *Wisconsin Magazine of History* 38 (Autumn 1957): 15–22.

Marks, Sally, and Delude, Denis. "German-American Relations, 1918– 1921," *Mid-America* 53 (October 1971): 211–26.

Marlowe, John. *Perfidious Albion: The Origins of Anglo-French Rivalry in the Levant.* London, 1971.

Marston, F. S. *The Peace Conference of 1919: Organization and Procedure.* London, 1944.

Martin, Laurence W. *Peace without Victory: Woodrow Wilson and the British Liberals.* New Haven, 1958.

Marwick,Arthur. *The Deluge: British Society and the First World War.* London, 1965.

Maurice, Sir Frederick B. *Lessons of Allied Cooperation: Naval, Military, and Air, 1914–1918.* New York, 1942.

———. *The Armistices of 1918.* London, 1943.

Mayer, Arno. *Wilson vs. Lenin: Political Origins of the New Diplomacy, 1917–1918.* Cleveland, 1964.

———. *Politics and Diplomacy of Peacemaking: Containment and Counterrevolution at Versailles, 1918–1919.* New York, 1967.

———. "Post-War Nationalisms, 1918–1919." *Past and Present*, No. 34 (July 1966): 114–26.

Bibliography

McFadyean, Sir Andrew. *Reparations Reviewed*. London, 1930.

McKay, Donald C. *The United States and France*. Cambridge, Mass., 1951.

Medlicott, W. N. *British Foreign Policy since Versailles*. London, 1940.

Meinhardt, Günther. *Adenauer und der rheinische Separatismus*. Recklinghausen, 1962.

Merritt, Richard L. "Woodrow Wilson and 'the Great and Solemn Referendum,' 1920." *Review of Politics* 27 (January 1965): 78–104.

Metzmacher, Helmut. "Der Novemberumsturz 1918 in der Rheinprovinz," *Annalen des historischen Vereins für den Niederrhein* 168–169 (1967): 135–265.

Meyer, Henry Cord. *Five Images of Germany: Half a Century of American Views on German History*. Washington, 1960.

Milatz, Alfred. *Wähler und Wahlen in der Weimarer Republik*. Bonn, 1967.

Miller, Jane K. *Belgian Foreign Policy between Two Wars, 1919–1940*. New York, 1951.

Miquel, Pierre. *La Paix de Versailles et l'opinion publique française*. Paris, 1972.

Mock, James R. and Cedric Larson. *Words That Won the War: The Story of the Committee on Public Information, 1917–1919*. Princeton, N. J., 1939.

Möckelmann, Jürgen. *Deutsch-amerikanische Beziehungen in der Krise. Studien zur amerikanischen Politik im ersten Weltkrieg*. Frankfurt, 1967.

Morgan, John H. *Assize of Arms: The Disarmament of Germany and Her Rearmament, 1919–1939*. New York, 1946.

Morsey, Rudolf. *Die deutsche Zentrumspartei, 1917–1923*. Düsseldorf, 1966.

Morton, Louis. "Army and Marines on the China Station: A Study in Military and Political Rivalry." *Pacific Historical Review* 29 (February 1960): 51–73.

Moulton, Harold G., and Pasvolsky, Leo. *War Debts and World Prosperity*. Washington, 1932.

Mowat, Charles Loch. *Britain between the Wars, 1918–1940*. Chicago, 1955.

Mowen, Howard Alden. "Rhenish Separatism, 1919–1923: A Study in the Franco-German Problem." Ph.D. diss., Western Reserve University, 1955–1956.

Bibliography

Murray, Robert K. *Red Scare: A Study in National Hysteria, 1919–1920.* Minneapolis, 1955.

———. *The Harding Era: Warren G. Harding and His Administration.* Minneapolis, 1969.

———. *The Politics of Normalcy: Governmental Theory and Practice in the Harding-Coolidge Era.* New York, 1973.

Nelson, Harold I. *Land and Power: British and Allied Policy on Germany's Frontiers, 1916–1919.* London, 1963.

Nelson, Keith L. "The 'Black Horror on the Rhine': Race as a Factor in Post–World War I Diplomacy." *Journal of Modern History* 42 (December 1970): 606–27.

———. "What Colonel House Overlooked in the Armistice." *Mid-America* 51 (April 1969): 75–91.

Nobecourt, Jacques. *Une Histoire politique de l'armée.* 2 vols. Paris, 1967.

Noble, George Bernard. *Policies and Opinions at Paris, 1919: Wilsonian Diplomacy, the Versailles Peace, and French Public Opinion.* New York, 1935.

Northedge, F. S. *The Troubled Giant: Britain among the Great Powers, 1916–1939.* London, 1967.

Obermann, Karl. *Die Beziehungen des amerikanischen Imperialismus zum deutschen Imperialismus in der Zeit der Weimarer Republik (1918–1925).* (East) Berlin, 1952.

Oertzen, Peter von. *Betriebsräte in der Novemberrevolution.* Düsseldorf, 1963.

Osgood, Robert E. *Ideals and Self Interest in America's Foreign Relations.* Chicago, 1953.

Parrini, Carl P. *Heir to Empire: United States Economic Diplomacy, 1916–1923.* Pittsburgh, 1969.

Paxson, Fredric L. *Post-war Years: Normalcy, 1918–1923.* Berkeley, 1948.

Piggott, Julian. "The Rhineland Republic." *History Today*, pt. 1, 3 (December 1953): 817–22; pt. 2, 4 (January 1954): 11–19.

Pingaud, Albert. *Histoire diplomatique de la France pendant la grande guerre.* 3 vols. Paris, 1938.

Pink, Gerhard. *The Conference of Ambassadors, Paris, 1920–1931.* Geneva, 1942.

Playne, Caroline. *Britain Holds On, 1917–1918.* London, 1933.

Pollard, James E. *The Presidents and the Press.* New York, 1947.

Pomeroy, Earl S. "Sentiment for a Strong Peace, 1917–1919." *The South Atlantic Quarterly* 43 (October 1944): 325–37.

Bibliography

Prittwitz und Gaffron, Friedrich W. *Deutschland und die Vereinigten Staaten seit dem Weltkrieg.* Leipzig, 1934.

Quirk, Robert E. *An Affair of Honor: Woodrow Wilson and the Occupation of Vera Cruz.* Lexington, Ky., 1962.

Rain, Pierre. *L'Europe de Versailles (1919–1939): Les traités de paix—leur application—leur mutilation.* Paris, 1945.

Reinders, Robert C. "Racialism on the Left: E. D. Morel and the 'Black Horror on the Rhine.' " *International Review of Social History* 12 (1968): 1–28.

Renouvin, Pierre. *L'Armistice de Rethondes: 11 Novembre 1918.* Paris, 1968.

———. *Les Crises du XXᵉ siècle.* 2 vols. Paris, 1957. The first volume has been translated as *War and Aftermath, 1914–1929.* New York, 1968.

———. "Les Buts de guerre du gouvernement français (1914–1918)." *Revue historique* 235 (January-March 1966): 1–38.

———. "L'Opinion publique en France pendant la guerre 1914–1918." *Revue d'histoire diplomatique* 84 (October-December 1970): 289–336.

Reynolds, Bernard T. *The Saar and the Franco-German Problem.* London, 1934.

Reynolds, Philip A. *British Foreign Policy in the Inter-war Years.* London, 1954.

Rieselbach, Leroy N. "The Basis of Isolationist Behavior." *Public Opinion Quarterly* 24 (Winter 1960): 645–57.

Robertson, John Henry. *The "Office": A Study of British Foreign Policy and Its Makers, 1919–1951.* London, 1958.

Rodman, Barbee-Sue M. "British Public Opinion and the German Question, 1918–1920." Ph.D. diss., Radcliffe College, 1957–1958.

Rogers, James H. *The Process of Inflation in France, 1914–1927.* New York, 1929.

Rosenberg, Arthur. *Geschichte der deutschen Republik.* Karlsbad, 1935. Translated as *A History of the German Republic.* London, 1936.

Rothstein, Andrew. *British Foreign Policy and Its Critics, 1830–1950.* London, 1969.

Rothwell, V. H. *British War Aims and Peace Diplomacy, 1914–1918.* Oxford, 1971.

Rudin, Harry R. *Armistice, 1918.* New York, 1944.

Ryder, A. J. *The German Revolution of 1918: A Study of German Socialism in War and Revolt.* Cambridge University, 1967.

Sachar, Howard M. *The Emergence of the Middle East, 1914–1924.* New York, 1969.

Bibliography

Salewski, Michael. *Entwaffnung und Militärkontrolle in Deutschland, 1919–1927.* Munich, 1966.

Scherer, André and Grunwald, Jacques, eds. *L'Allemagne et les problèmes de la paix pendant la première guerre mondiale.* Paris, 1962.

Schieber, Clara. *The Transformation of American Sentiment toward Germany, 1870–1914.* Boston, 1923.

Schmidt, Hans. *The United States Occupation of Haiti, 1915–1934.* New Brunswick, N. J., 1971.

Schmidt, Royal J. *Versailles and the Ruhr: Seedbed of World War II.* The Hague, 1968.

Schoenthal, Klaus Ferdinand. "American Attitudes towards Germany, 1918–1932." Ph.D. diss., Ohio State University, 1959.

Schüddekopf, Otto-Ernst. "German Foreign Policy between Compiègne and Versailles." *Journal of Contemporary History* 4 (April 1969): 181–97.

Schulz, Gerhard. *Zwischen Demokratie und Diktatur.* 2 vols. Berlin, 1963–.

———. *Revolutions and Peace Treaties, 1917–1920.* New York, 1972.

Schuman, Frederick L. *War and Diplomacy in the French Republic.* New York, 1931.

Schwabe, Klaus. *Deutsche Revolution und Wilson-Frieden: Die amerikanische und deutsche Friedensstrategie zwischen Ideologie und Machtpolitik 1918/1919.* Düsseldorf, 1972.

Selsam, J. P. *The Attempts to Form an Anglo-French Alliance: 1919–1924.* Philadelphia, 1936.

Sherwood, John M. *Georges Mandel and the Third Republic.* Stanford, Calif., 1970.

Shideler, James H. *Farm Crisis, 1921–1923.* Berkeley, 1957.

Silverlight, John. *The Victors' Dilemma: Allied Intervention in the Russian Civil War.* New York, 1970.

Simonds, Charles G. "American Participation in the Occupation of the Rhineland, 1918–1923." M.A. thesis, Stanford University, 1939.

Simonds, Frank H. *American Foreign Policy in the Post War Years.* Baltimore, 1935.

Slosson, Preston W. *The Great Crusade and After.* New York, 1930.

Smith, Clarence Jay, Jr. *The Russian Struggle for Power, 1914–1917.* New York, 1956.

Smith, Daniel M. *Aftermath of War: Bainbridge Colby and Wilsonian Diplomacy, 1920–1921.* Philadelphia, 1970.

422

Bibliography

Smuckler, Ralph H. "The Region of Isolationism." *American Political Science Review* 47 (June 1953): 386–401.

Snell, John L. "Wilson on Germany and the Fourteen Points." *Journal of Modern History* 26 (December 1954): 364–69.

———. "Wilson's Peace Program and German Socialism, January-March 1918." *Mississippi Valley Historical Review* 38 (September 1951): 187–214.

———. "Wilsonian Rhetoric Goes to War." *Historian* 14 (Spring 1952): 191–208.

Sontag, Raymond J. *A Broken World, 1919–1939.* New York, 1971.

Soule, George. *Prosperity Decade.* New York, 1947.

Spencer, Frank. "The U. S. and Germany in the Aftermath of War: I. 1918 to 1929." *International Affairs* 43 (October 1967): 693–703.

Stambrook, F. G. " 'Das Kind'—Lord D'Abernon and the Origins of the Locarno Pact." *Central European History* 2 (September 1968): 233–63.

Stenger, Wilbur. "Walther Rathenau and the Policy of Fulfillment: The Reparations Issue in German Foreign Policy, 1919–1922." Ph.D. diss., Georgetown University, 1966.

Stoessen, Alexander. " The End of the American Watch on the Rhine." *South Carolina Historical Proceedings* (1966), pp. 18–26.

Stone, Ralph A. "The Irreconcilables' Alternatives to the League of Nations." *Mid-America* 49 (July 1967): 163–73.

———. *The Irreconcilables: The Fight against the League of Nations.* (Lexington, Ky., 1970).

Strakhovsky, Leonid I. *The Origins of American Intervention in North Russia.* Princeton, N. J., 1937.

Strickland, Charles E. "American Aid to Germany, 1919 to 1921." *Wisconsin Magazine of History* 45 (Summer 1962): 256–70.

Struck, Wolf-Heino. "Die Revolution von 1918/1919 im Erbleben des Rhein-Main Gebietes," *Hessisches Jahrbuch für Landesgeschichte* 19 (1969): 368–438.

Sullivan, Mark. *Our Times: The United States, 1900–1925.* 6 vols. New York, 1927–1935.

Surface, Frank M., and Bland, Raymond L. *American Food in the World War and Reconstruction Period.* Stanford, Calif., 1931.

Taylor, A. J. P. *English History, 1914–1945.* Oxford, 1965.

———. "The War Aims of the Allies in the First World War." *In Essays Presented to Sir Lewis Namier*, edited by Richard Pares and A. J. P. Taylor. London, 1956.

——. *Politics in Wartime, and Other Essays*. New York, 1965.

——. *The Origins of the Second World War*. New York, 1961.

——. *The Trouble Makers: Dissent over Foreign Policy, 1792–1939*. Bloomington, Ind., 1958.

Thompson, John M. *Russia, Bolshevism, and the Versailles Peace*. Princeton, N. J., 1966.

Tillman, Seth P. *Anglo-American Relations at the Paris Peace Conference of 1919*. Princeton, N. J., 1961.

Tötter, Heinrich. *Warum wir den Ruhrkampf verloren: Das Versagen der deutschen Pressepropaganda im Ruhrkampf*. Cologne, 1940. (HIL)

Totten, Christine M. *Deutschland—Soll und Haben: Amerikas Deutschlandbild*. Munich, 1964.

Trafford, D. W. "A Study of the Problem of French Security in the British and French Presses, 1919–1925." Ph.D. diss., University of Indiana, 1948.

Trask, David. *The United States in the Supreme War Council: American War Aims and Inter-Allied Strategy, 1917–1918*. Middletown, Conn., 1961.

——. *Captains and Cabinets*. Columbia, Mo., 1972.

Treue, Wolfgang. *Deutsche Parteiprogramme 1861–1954*. Göttingen, 1954.

Tucker, William R. *The Attitude of the British Labour Party towards European and Collective Security Problems, 1920–1959*. Geneva, 1950.

Tulchin, Joseph S. *The Aftermath of War: World War I and U.S. Policy Toward Latin America*. New York, 1971.

Ullman, Richard H. *Anglo-Soviet Relations, 1917–1921*. 3 vols. Princeton, N. J., 1961–1972.

Van Der Slice, Austin. *International Labor, Diplomacy, and Peace, 1914–1919*. Philadelphia, 1941.

Vinson, John Chalmers. "The Drafting of the Four Power Treaty of the Washington Conference." *Journal of Modern History* 25 (March 1953): 40–47.

——. *Referendum for Isolation: Defeat of Article Ten of the League of Nations Covenant*. Athens, Ga., 1961.

——. *The Parchment Peace: The United States and the Washington Conference, 1921–1922*. Athens, Ga., 1955.

Waldman, Eric. *The Spartacist Uprising of 1919 and the Crisis of the*

Bibliography

German Socialist Movement: A Study of the Relation of Political Theory and Party Practice. Milwaukee, 1958.

Wandycz, Piotr S. *France and Her Eastern Allies, 1919–1925: French-Czechoslovak-Polish Relations from the Paris Peace Conference to Locarno.* Minneapolis, 1962.

Watt, D. C. *Personalities and Policies: Studies in the Formulation of British Foreign Policy in the Twentieth Century.* South Bend, 1965.

Wecter, Dixon. *When Johnny Comes Marching Home.* Boston, 1944.

Weill-Raynal, Etienne. *Les Réparations allemandes et la France.* 3 vols. Paris, 1947.

Welter, Barbara Ann. "The United States and Weimar Germany, 1919–1929." Ph.D. diss., University of Wisconsin, 1960.

Wentzcke, Paul. *Ruhrkampf: Einbruch und Abwehr im rheinisch-Wesfälischen Industriegebiet.* 2 vols. Berlin, 1934.

Wheeler-Bennett, J. W. *The Pipe Dream of Peace: The Story of the Collapse of Disarmament.* New York, 1935.

White, David Glen. "Einige Kapitel aus der grossen Politik zur Zeit der Ruhrbesetzung." Ph.D. diss., University of Berlin, 1939.

White, Dorothy Shipley. "Franco American Relations in 1917–1918: War Aims and Peace Prospects." Ph.D. diss., University of Pennsylvania, 1954.

White, Elizabeth B. *American Opinion of France: From Lafayette to Poincaré.* New York, 1927.

White, John A. *The Siberian Intervention.* Princeton, N. J., 1950.

Willert, Arthur. *The Road to Safety: A Study in Anglo-American Relations.* London, 1952.

Williams, William Appleman. "The Legend of Isolationism in the 1920's." *Science and Society* 18 (Winter 1954): 1–20.

Willis, F. Roy. *The French in Germany, 1945–1949.* Stanford, Calif., 1962.

Willis, Irene Cooper. *England's Holy War.* New York, 1928.

Wimer, Kurt, and Wimer, Sarah. "The Harding Administration, the League of Nations, and the Separate Peace Treaty." *The Review of Politics* 29 (January 1967): 13–24.

Winkler, Henry R. "The Emergence of a Labor Foreign Policy in Great Britain, 1918–1929." *Journal of Modern History* 28 (September 1956): 247–58.

———. *The League of Nations Movement in Great Britain, 1914–1919.* New Brunswick, N. J., 1952.

Bibliography

Wohl, Robert. *French Communism in the Making, 1914–1924*. Stanford, Calif. 1966.

Wolfers, Arnold. *Britain and France between Two Wars: Conflicting Strategies of Peace Since Versailles*. New York, 1940.

Woodward, David R. "Britain's 'Brass-Hats' and the Question of a Compromise Peace, 1916–1918." *Military Affairs* 35 (April 1971): 63–68.

Woodward, Sir Llewellyn. *Great Britain and the War of 1914–1918*. London, 1967.

Wormser, Georges. *La République de Clemenceau*. Paris, 1961.

Wright, Gordon. "Franco-Belgian Relations, 1918–1934." M.A. thesis, Stanford University, 1935.

———. *Raymond Poincaré and the French Presidency*. Stanford, Calif., 1942.

———. *France in Modern Times: 1760 to the Present*. Chicago, 1960.

Yates, Louis A. R. *United States and French Security, 1917–1921*. New York, 1957.

Zeender, John K. "The German Center Party during World War I: An Internal Study." *Catholic History Review* 62 (January 1957): 441–68.

Zimmermann, Ludwig. *Deutsche Aussenpolitik in der Ara der Weimarer Republik*. Göttingen, 1958.

Zink, Harold. *The United States in Germany, 1944–1955*. Princeton, 1957.

Zwoch, Gerhard. "Die Erfüllungs—und Verständigungspolitik der Weimarer Republik und die deutsche öffentliche Meinung." Ph.D. diss., Kiel University, 1951.

Index

Adenauer, Konrad, 285, 286
Advance General Headquarters, AEF, 39, 277
Albert, King, 298
Alcoholic beverages in Rhineland, 37, 38, 60
Allen, Gen. Henry T., 140, 141, 142, 150, 173, 174, 179, 180, 188, 198, 199, 200, 232, 233, 250, 332, 340, 345, 346, 351, 355, 356, 364; takes command of AFG, 126, 146, 312; and treaty coming into force, 136–137, 160–161, 316; and Noyes, 139, 152, 161–162, 165, 168, 169, 329, 331, 347; negotiates new zonal boundaries, 146–148; trains raw recruits, 148–149; eases restrictions, 149; position and policies of, 170–172, 226–227; reports on black horror, 181, 206, 214, 334, 347; and High Commission, 202–203, 204–210, 217–225, 232; and France, 203, 217, 256; and Robertson, 210–211, 217; and Bergdoll affair, 214, 352; and Paris conference, 217–218, 353; and Smeets case, 220–221, 240–241; and railways, 221–222, 241, and Kilmarnock, 223, 240, 355–356, 363; and Washington, 223, 241–242, 260, 353, 371; and French units, 227, 364; German appreciation of, 238, 251, 371; and Ruhr occupation, 247; makes special overture, 250–251, 368–369; withdraws from High Commission, 252, 369; biography of, 319
Allied zones of occupation, 27–29, 35, 136, 209, 213
Allies, 5, 8, 11, 17, 18, 21, 34, 39, 44, 55, 57, 69, 74, 90, 91, 96, 99, 114, 119–122, 125, 129, 138, 140, 156–160, 162, 163, 166, 167, 175, 181, 182, 184, 193, 194, 195, 198, 203, 205, 207, 208, 215, 217, 225, 255, 258, 260, 337, 341
Alsace-Lorraine, 10, 11, 12, 15, 21, 31, 55, 61–63, 291; and Fourteen Points 5; Lloyd George on, 7, 294; French occupation of, 29
Amaroc News, 49, 122, 211, 252
American delegation at Paris Peace Conference, 72–73, 82, 117, 125, 129, 134, 291
American Expeditionary Force, 38, 41, 79, 95, 260, 319; size of, 30; General Orders No. 218 of, 37; General Orders No. 225 of, 38–39; University in Beaunne, 49; departure of, 126
American Forces in Germany, 130, 131, 133, 134, 135, 141, 143, 148, 160, 170, 175, 176, 179, 180, 183, 185, 187, 189, 190, 191, 197, 199, 202, 214, 222, 223, 228, 233, 235, 238, 242, 252–253, 256, 260, 339, 340, 362; size of, 126, 128, 141, 145–146, 180, 190, 211, 227, 243, 261, 273; establishment of, 126, 146; withdrawal of, 245, 246, 247, 248, 250–251
American Legion, 181, 187, 260, 337–338
American Mission (in Paris), 124, 125, 132, 133, 151, 152, 312
American occupation. *See* Occupation of Rhineland, American
American zone of occupation, 40, 45, 112, 126, 135, 139, 150, 160, 170, 173, 183, 205, 209, 210, 215, 221, 242, 259, 260, 286; description of, 29–30; Foch's threats to seal off, 99; re-

427

Index

duced in size, 146–148, 320; French pressure to penetrate, 221, 222; French units in, 227; population of, 351

Anordnungen, 38, 46–47, 149, 281, 327

Antifraternization orders, 37, 50, 149

Armenia, 79, 130, 314

Armistice, 56–57, 70–71, 79, 93, 132, 133, 148, 205; Allied talks preceding, 8–9, 16–21, 271; discussion of, at Senlis, 14–15; negotiations with Germans on, 21–23; French concerns about, 69; third renewal of, 74; and army costs, 93, 342; remains in force for U. S., 316

Armistice Commission, German, 44, 56, 58, 89, 121

Armistice Commission, Permanent Inter-Allied, 36, 57, 285

Army costs of occupation: Lloyd George's efforts regarding, 92, 109, 119–120; French efforts to reduce, 92–94; Allied negotiations to determine, 94–95, 126, 152, 193, 195, 310, 341, 343; controversy over reimbursing U. S. for, 95, 141, 175, 192–195, 199, 221, 229, 235, 258, 341–342; American unhappiness over lack of payment for, 180, 185, 186, 195–198, 200, 233, 255, 258, 370; German complaints regarding, 207, 228; Allied-American agreement on, 370

Army of occupation, Allied, 77, 80, 92, 116, 126, 127, 134, 137. *See also* American Forces in Germany; British Army on Rhine; French Army of Rhine; Third Army, United States

Army size (of occupying forces): during Armistice occupation, 30, 41–42, 273; Allied negotiations on, peacetime, 95–96, 110, 119, 126, 145; Berlin requests information on, 158; Berlin complains about, 228. *See also* Reductions in American army of occupation

Assemblage in Rhineland, 38, 149, 159

Attitudes in American army: on Germans, 33–35, 49–51, 122, 170,

212–213, 219, 225–227, 242–243; on French, 40–43, 227, 242

Attitudes in Coblenz zone on American occupation, 33–35, 50–51, 122, 149–150, 170–171, 213, 219, 225–227, 242–243, 251

Attitudes in French army on American occupation, 40–43, 227, 238, 242, 251

Attitudes in U.S.: on occupation, 1, 7–8, 77–78, 125, 130–132, 137, 142–143, 258; on Europe, 133, 142–143, 200–201, 258, 260

Attitudes in unoccupied Germany on American occupation, 52–53, 59–60, 150, 171–172, 213–214, 227–229, 256, 362

Baker, Newton, 1, 41, 79, 318; and letter from Bliss, 10; and cable to Pershing, 15; and Congress, 126–128, 312–313; reacts to Frankfurt occupation, 140

Balfour, Earl of (Arthur James), 12, 67, 115–116; ignores French overture, 7; negotiates with Tardieu and House, 75–76, 293; and Balfour Note, 233

Bardoux, Jacques, 289

Barnes, G. N., 115, 120

Baruch, Bernard, 102, 103, 104, 107, 108, 155

Bauer, Gustav, 123

Bavaria: areas occupied in, 26; extremism in, 215; and Reichskommissar, 326

Belgian zone of occupation, 30, 112, 163, 350

Belgium, 12, 21, 23, 31, 70, 105, 193, 198, 199, 236, 247; reception of Americans in, 32; and Luxemburg, 42–43; and reparations, 192, 193, 194, 300, 341; and army costs, 193, 341; and French military alliance, 203; and retention of AFG, 224, 230, 239; memory of occupation in, 255; at Paris Peace Conference, 298–299; and Frankfurt occupation, 329

Bell, Johannes, 61, 213

Index

Benson, Admiral William S., 17
Bergdoll, Grover Cleveland, 214, 352
Berlin, Treaty of, 185, 186, 187, 190, 205, 215, 219, 226, 228, 337
Bernstorff, Count Albrecht von, 350
Bernstorff, Count Johann Heinrich von, 62, 308
"Big Four," 46, 109, 116, 120, 145
Billeting in Rhineland, 37, 46. *See also* German protests and complaints
Black horror agitation, 64–65, 177–178, 181, 182, 206, 230, 235, 258, 260, 333, 336, 358, 360. *See also* Colonial units in French army
Bliss, Tasker, 1, 15, 80, 82, 94, 106, 118, 119, 125, 126, 135, 145, 146; and military representatives, 10; and House, 16; proposes disarmament, 16, 270; suggestions of, and Lloyd George, 21; concerned about conference, 72–73, 291; delays decisions on army, 95–96; makes trip to Rhineland, 107; advises Wilson, 108; and treaty protocol, 134
Blockade of Germany, 43, 45, 46, 59, 104; and Rhenish economy, 44–45; revocation of, 125
Blockade-running, French, 100, 104, 303
Bloc National, French, 153, 162, 327
Bolshevism, 22, 33, 51, 84, 109, 296
Bonar Law, Andrew, 120, 237, 248, 367, 369
Borah, William, 180, 185, 186, 188, 195, 245, 367; and Hughes, 245–246
Boyden, Roland, 191, 193, 194, 195, 244, 248, 250, 253, 343
Brandegee, Frank, 184–185
Briand, Aristide, 6, 191, 204, 215, 216, 217–220, 266; and reparations, 182, 204, 215; resignation of, 192, 216; and sanctions, 215, 217–218
Bridgeheads, Rhine, 14, 91, 122; proposed by Foch, 11, 13; Lloyd George on, 21; German plea regarding, 22; Foch's plans for, 29, 40; Solf urges Allies to forego, 55; Tardieu on, 77; Clemenceau demands five, 81. *See also* Coblenz bridgehead; Mainz bridgehead;

Strassburg bridgehead
Britain, 70, 72, 79, 82, 105, 141, 185, 216; attitudes of public in, 6 f.; and demobilization, 278; Kerr on opinion in, 77; toughening mood in, 89; Harding's loyalty to, 182–183; and Washington Conference, 191; and army costs, 193, 195, 341, 342; and reparations, 193–194, 203–204; and AFG, 199, 224, 230, 239, 248, 327, 345; developing factions in, 210–211; and BAOR, 248, 367–368; memory of AFG in, 255; and Rhenish policy, 362. *See also* Foreign Office, British; House of Commons, British; Parliament, British
British Army on Rhine, 101–106, 242, 248, 275, 304
British cabinet, 76, 116. *See also* War cabinet, British
British delegation at Paris Peace Conference, 107, 109, 115–116, 145
British zone of occupation, 30, 48, 112, 320, 351
Brockdorff-Rantzau, Count Ulrich von, 56, 57, 61, 115, 308
Buffer state. *See* Rhenish republic

Cambon, Jules, 362
Cambon, Paul, 271–272
Campaign of 1920, American presidential, 174, 175–179, 180, 199
Cannes Conference, 191, 194, 216, 221
Castle, William R., 140, 179, 182, 244, 254, 319, 355, 364, 365
Catholic church in Rhineland, 27, 36, 55, 56
Cattoir, Fernand, 322
Cecil, Lord Robert, 73, 107, 118
Censorship: of French press, 6, 68; in Rhineland, 38, 46, 149, 170, 328
Center Party, German, 27, 54, 55, 122–123, 283
Chamber of Deputies, French, 68, 84, 87, 162, 216, 248, 327, 361
Chamberlain, Austen, 342
Chicago Tribune, 189, 352
China, foreign troops in, 108, 196, 343
Christian Science Monitor, 178, 249
Churchill, Winston, 294–295

429

Index

Index

Council of Four, 85, 90, 98, 298, 302, 304

Council of Ten, 75, 293, 302

Cox, James, 176

Crewe, Lord, 367

Cuno, Wilhelm, 237, 251, 252, 365

Curzon, George Nathaniel, Earl, later Marquess, 154, 195, 202, 295, 344, 355; on American presence, 165–166; on Frankfurt occupation, 168; at Paris Conference (1921), 218, 353

Customs, German, 115, 217, 354; Allied interference with, 156, 158, 183, 217, 239. *See also* "Hole in the West"

Customs, Rhenish: treaty provision for, 114; part of sanctions of 1921, 183, 210, 215. *See also* Economic sanctions

Czechoslovakia, 83

D'Abernon, Edgar, Viscount, 367

"Dariac" report, 361

David, Eduard, 61

Davis, John W., 118, 309

Davis, Maj. Manton, 322, 328

Davis, Norman, 107

Dawes Plan, 253, 255, 370

Day, Wallace, 100, 103, 104, 152, 301, 303, 328, 347

Daylight savings time in Rhineland, 240, 363

Declaration of June 16, 1919, Allied, 120, 128, 310, 313

Degoutte, Gen. Jean Marie, 164, 222, 242, 247, 324, 328, 355, 364

Democratic Party, German, 54, 55, 122–123, 173, 228

Democrats, American, 130, 137, 176, 187–188, 246, 249–250; newspaper press of, 197, 249

Derby, Edward Stanley, Earl of, 289

Dial, Nathaniel, 338

Dickman, Gen. Joseph T., 30, 33, 34, 35, 43, 47, 49, 110–111, 279

Disarmament, American movement for, 180, 188, 258

Disarmament of Germany. *See* Military clauses

Disciplinary action against German officials, 48, 212, 281. *See also* Expulsion of German officials

Dolan, John, 322

Dorten, Hans Adam, 110; plottings of (May 1919), 111–112, 306–307; and incident of July 1920, 206–207, 214, 215

Dresel, Ellis Loring, 132, 139, 140, 165, 169, 179, 181, 334

Duffy, Father, 33

Dulles, Allen, 175

Dulles, John Foster, 126, 158, 322

Düsseldorf, 26, 40, 110, 182, *See also* Ruhr ports

Ebert, Friedrich, 53, 54, 55, 57, 61, 166, 167, 276

Economic sanctions, 182–183, 191, 204, 209, 214, 215, 217, 218, 228, 260, 353

Economy drive, in U.S. Congress, 175, 180, 188, 258

Edge, Walter, 313

Educational and vocational training in American army, 49, 149, 212

Ehrenbreitstein, 148, 239, 251, 280–281, 320, 371

Eighth Army, French, 111, 328

Eighty-ninth Division, U.S., 30, 275

Entretien controversy (1919), 93–94

Erzberger, Matthias, 52, 121, 285; and armistice negotiations, 22–23; confers with Allied representatives, 115, 308; assassinated, 215

Esher, Reginald Brett, Viscount, 71, 290

Essen Coal Committee, 155

Evacuations: German army, 14, 22, 31; from peacetime occupation, 86, 87, 92, 255

Expulsion of German officials, 48, 251, 330. *See also* Disciplinary action against German officials

Fayolle, Marshal Emile, 306

431

Index

Fehrenbach, Konstantin, 173, 183, 203, 207, 286

Fifth Division, U. S., 30, 275

First Corps, U. S., 30

First Division, U. S., 30, 35, 128, 275, 320

Fletcher, Henry P., 174, 223, 231, 233, 242

Flint, Addison, 322

Foch, Marshal Ferdinand, 26, 44, 46, 47, 48, 51, 52, 56, 65, 66, 73, 85, 87, 94–96, 98, 102–104, 109, 111, 114, 123, 126, 133–135, 139, 141, 145–146, 149, 153, 154, 181, 208, 303, 306, 334, 355; submits armistice proposals, 11, 15–17, 20, 268; writes Clemenceau, 13; at Senlis conference, 14, 15; presents armistice terms to Germans, 21–23; directs occupying armies, 35–36, 276; quarrels with Pershing, 40–43; enthusiastic for treaty, 45; in London, 69–72, 289; circulates memo, 73, 292; campaigns for preliminary treaty, 74–75; fights Clemenceau's decisions, 89–91, 299; and Luxemburg Commission, 99–100; and Rhineland Commission, 105–107; tries to block High Commission, 118–119, 310; establishes American zone, 148; and separatism, 306, 324

Fontainebleau Memorandum, 82–83

Food Committee, Inter-Allied Military, 100, 104

Food supply, Rhenish, 44, 47, 48–49, 51, 57, 164

Foreign Ministry: German, 58, 113, 150, 153, 159, 207, 228, 323, 350, 363; French, 69, 70

Foreign Office, British, 100, 210, 294, 348, 363; developing split in, 211; and AFG, 224; and black horror, 333

Forty-second Division, U. S., 30, 275, 277

Four Power Pacific Treaty, 195, 197

Fourteen Points, 5, 9, 17, 18, 21, 33, 55, 63, 67, 69

Fourth Corps, U. S., 30, 275

Fourth Division, U. S., 30, 31, 275

France, 12, 23, 31, 70–72, 73, 79, 83, 87, 90, 93, 97, 104, 105, 107, 118, 125, 127, 128, 131, 137, 139, 141, 177, 181, 185, 187, 188; attitudes in, regarding Germany, 6; policies of, on Rhenish trade, 44–45; and army costs, 92–94, 152, 193–194, 341, 342; Clemenceau defines requirements of, 117; Wilson views opinion in, 117; Noyes distrusts motives of, 138; Wilson says "militaristic," 138–139; American attitudes toward, 142–143, 263, 319, 244, 367; shifts in mood and foreign policy of, 153, 162–163, 168–169; and German coal, 155; and black horror, 178; Harding's loyalty to, 182–183; and Washington Conference, 191, 339; and further shifts in European affairs, 191–192, 198, 203–204; and reparations, 193–194, 203–204; and Poincaré's policies, 199, 221, 224–225; and Allen, 206–210, 224, 230, 238, 369; and burgeoning crisis (1922), 236–238, 243, 247; and Ruhr occupation, 247–248, 254–255, 369; and withdrawal of AFG, 248; memory of occupation in, 255–256. *See also* Chamber of Deputies, French; Foreign Ministry, French; Senate, French

Frankfurt, 26; occupation of, 125, 139, 140, 142, 166–169, 170, 173, 178, 203, 329; evacuation of, 140, 172

Frankfurter, Felix, 108

Frelinghuysen, Joseph, 130

French Army of Rhine, 155

French-Belgian Military Accord, 203

French-British pact. *See* Guarantee treaties

French cabinet, 89–90

French delegation at Paris Peace Conference, 80, 89, 102

French economic penetration of Rhineland, 44–46, 48–49, 100, 155, 225, 237, 354. *See also* Commerce and industry, Rhenish

French proposals for peace confer-

432

Index

Index

Haniel von Haimhausen, Edgar, 238
Hanotaux, Gabriel, 162
Harbord, Gen. James, 199, 233, 234, 242
Harding, Warren G., 174, 175, 184, 185, 190, 204, 223, 224, 227, 229, 231, 232, 257–258, 260–261, 339, 340, 353, 366; and campaign of 1920, 176–179; first policies of, 181–183, 214; on American influence, 189; and Washington Conference, 190–191; and order of March 1922, 197–199, 224, 234, 344, 355; and decision of June 1922, 199–200, 358; trepidation of, 232–235, 359; and burgeoning European crisis, 244–245; and withdrawal of AFG, 247–248, 367
Hartman, Cardinal, 58
Harvey, George, 3, 218, 344, 353
Hatzfeld-Wildenburg, Prince Hermann von, 209, 238, 240, 358, 361–362; biography of, 349
Hearst, William Randolph, 186, 249
Herrick, Myron T., 223, 224, 225, 238, 242, 244, 256, 339, 355, 364
High Command, Allied, 90, 99, 105, 156
High Commission, Inter-Allied Rhineland, 98, 107, 119, 120, 126, 132, 138, 140, 141, 144, 151, 153, 156, 160–161, 170, 172, 173, 179, 199, 203, 204, 212, 255, 257, 304, 313, 326, 337, 361; takes control, 136, 175, 159; and role of Noyes, 161–162; and manipulation by French, 163–164, 167, evaluated by Germans, 170–171; and sanctions of 1921, 182–183, 218; and Allen, 204–211, 217–222, 225, 239–242; and Smeets case, 220–221, 237, 240–241; and Momm case, 239; and Ruhr occupation, 250–251; and Allen's leaving, 252; American section of, 322, 352. See also Rhineland Commission, Inter-Allied
Hitchcock, Gilbert, 138, 235, 314, 360
"Hole in the West," 155–156, 325, 354
Holt, Hamilton, 180
Hoover, Herbert, 102, 107

Houghton, Alanson S., 198, 202, 224, 238, 242, 244, 248, 356
House, Edward M., 41, 42, 67, 70–73, 80, 100, 107, 256, 270, 289, 291; and Inquiry, 5; and Armistice, 9; at pre-Armistice negotiations, 16–21, 23; Pershing's complaints to, 43; negotiates in Wilson's absence, 74–78, 294; as intermediary for Clemenceau, 81–82, 296; represents Wilson at Council of Four, 85–86; and Rhineland compromise, 87–88
House of Commons, British, 84
House of Representatives, U.S., 130, 141, 142, 188, 190, 195, 196, 197, 235
Hughes, Charles Evans, 184, 185, 190, 191, 205, 210, 218, 231, 232, 234, 235, 241, 243, 256, 260–261, 339, 340, 366, 369; rebuffs German feeler, 182–183; and army costs, 195–198, 258, 343, 344; and decision of June 1922, 199–200, 345; and burgeoning European crisis, 244–247; and AHA address, 245, 247, 253, 255; and Borah, 245–246; and warning to French, 246, 247, 253, 259; and withdrawal, 247–248, 253, 367; and Allen's overture, 250–251; thanks Allen, 371
Hunt, Col. I. L., 47, 327
Hymans, Paul, 299

Identity cards in Rhineland, 38
Imperial War Cabinet, British, 71
Independent Social Democratic Party, German, 53–54, 213
Inflation, 172, 207, 226, 235, 236, 243, 254
Inquiry, 5, 72, 77, 265
Internationalists, American, 2, 3, 177, 179, 232, 253, 263–264, 366
Irreconcilables, 125, 127, 129, 130, 137, 143, 176, 184, 246, 258, 263, 314; campaign against occupation, 184–188, 337
Isolationists, American, 2 f., 129, 177, 184, 187, 189, 232, 245, 246, 247, 249, 253, 263, 264
Italy, 71, 72, 79, 146, 235, 247

434

Index

Majority Socialists. *See* Social Democratic Party, German

Malone, Dudley Field, 178

Mangin, Gen. Charles, 25, 111, 112, 113, 305, 306, 307, 328

March, Gen. Peyton C., 234

Marriages in Rhineland, American military, 50, 131, 170, 212–213, 243, 251, 257, 321, 352

Marsal, François, 342

Marx, Wilhelm, 256

Mason, William E., 318

Max of Baden, Prince, 22

Mezes, Sidney, 77–78

Middle East, 71

Military appropriations, American, 141, 196–197, 233, 338, 366

Military clauses (of Treaty of Versailles), 74–75, 82, 87, 153, 165

Military conventions (for Rhineland), 97, 106, 107, 108, 109, 154

Military council at Versailles, Allied: proposed by Foch, 134–135, 153; proposed by Tirard, 153, 154

Military courts in Rhineland, 51, 58, 226, 242

Military government in Rhineland, 38–39, 121–213, 277, 329, 349

Military police in Rhineland, 50, 150, 213, 252

Military representatives at Versailles 106, 154, 267, 304; and first German overture, 10; and size/cost of occupying army, 92, 95–96, 145

Miller, David Hunter, 71

Millerand, Alexandre, 142, 162, 163, 167, 168, 172, 203, 316, 327

Ministry of Economics, German, 58

Momm, Dr., 239

Moratorium on German reparations, 216, 236, 243

Mordacq, Gen. Jean-Jules Henri, 19, 86

Morel, E. D., 178, 333–334

Morgan, J. P., 244

Morgenthau, Henry T., 232

Moselle River, 29, 148

Munich, 215; civil war in, 53; coup in, 84, 111

My Rhineland Journal, 251, 255, 256; reviews of, 370–371

Nation (New York), 131, 142, 335

National Assembly, German, 53, 55, 57, 58, 113

National Defense Act: of 1916, 127, 312; of 1920, 188

Nationalist Party, German, 54, 55

National Property Administration (German), 208, 209, 214

Naval terms of Armistice, 12, 271

Navigation of Rhine, French demand control of, 155, 163, 328

Negro troops, American, 64

Neutral (demilitarized) zone, 56, 62, 69, 80–83, 87, 115, 169, 287; suggested by Foch, 15; pre-Armistice alterations in, 20; negotiated with Germans, 22–23; German incursion into (1920), 166, 167; soldier-worker councils in, 275

New, Harry, 190

New Republic, 142, 249

New York Times, 1, 4, 79, 127, 131, 137, 177, 181, 187, 191, 345, 346

New York Tribune, 4, 249

New York World, 131, 142

Ninetieth Division, U.S., 30, 146, 275, 277

Noyes, Pierrepont, 97, 98, 110, 118, 126, 131, 141, 144, 148, 173, 176, 203, 205, 210, 211, 222, 257, 306, 316, 347, 371; appointed commissioner, 102–103; and Rhineland Commission, 103–105; travels to Paris, 107; writes to Wilson, 108–109; and treaty, 136, 160–161, 316; and Rhineland Agreement, 137–140, 162, 163–166, 169; preaches to State Department, 140, 169, 331; recalled, 140, 169, 317–318, 331; in 1919, 151–156; and Allen, 161–162, 329; and Frankfurt occupation, 166–168; and Robertson, 168, 330; praised by Germans, 171–172, 331–332; biography of, 302; and withdrawal of AFG, 366

Index

Obstruction in Rhineland, German, 207–208

Occupation of Rhineland, American, 52, 59, 124–125, 127, 130, 138, 142–143, 150, 175, 176, 178, 179, 180, 181, 182, 185, 186, 188, 189, 192, 197, 199, 214, 224, 225, 229, 231, 232, 233, 238, 239, 245, 246, 250, 255, 259, 261, 339, 340, 364. *See also* American Forces in Germany; American zone of occupation; Third Army, U.S.

Occupation of Rhineland, Armistice, 12, 30–31, 58, 62, 66, 98, 110, 154; proposed by Foch, 11; Clemenceau demands, 14, 19; House endorses, 20; German delegates on, 22; area of, 26; German government and, 55 f., 61

Occupation of Rhineland, peacetime, 67, 70, 77, 78, 85, 86, 88, 89, 90, 96, 97–99, 106, 109, 113, 114, 115, 116, 124, 135, 139, 153, 165, 177, 180, 204, 207, 257

Officer in Charge of Civil Affairs, 39

Officer in Charge of Civil Affairs, Third Army, 39, 47, 277, 327

Officers in charge of civil affairs, American, 47–48, 349

Ordinances of High Commission, 119, 136–137, 161, 206, 208, 219, 220, 221, 225, 239, 251, 326, 328, 354; preparation of first, 126, 151, 155, 157, 160; proclamation of first, 159

Orlando, Vittorio, 9, 71

Osborne, Lithgow, 175

Palatinate, 26, 29, 62, 111, 112, 241

Paris conference (Aug. 1921), 217–218

Paris Peace Conference, 65, 66–67, 85, 87, 91, 98–99, 109, 111, 113, 114, 126, 135, 153, 257, 259

Parliament, British, 89, 90–91, 119, 128

Passau-Ingolstadt incident, 241

Paxkonferenz, 62, 63, 286–287

Payot, Gen. Jean Charles Marie, 36, 104, 153, 154, 155, 222

Peace, separate American-German, 142, 177, 183, 184, 185, 204, 219, 229

Penrose, Boies, 176

People's Party, German, 54, 123

Pershing, Gen. John J., 15, 16, 30, 35, 38, 39, 51, 95, 96, 99, 107, 108, 112, 148, 149, 199, 217, 283, 242, 281, 306, 340, 345; at Senlis, 14, 269; and House, 17; quarrels with Foch, 40–43; and withdrawal of AEF, 41–42, 278; Erzberger's overture to, 57; on *entretien*, 94; and size of AFG, 145–146, 180

Petain, Marshal Phillipe, 13; at Senlis, 14 f.

Phillips, William, 198, 224, 231, 234, 235, 241, 245, 252, 345, 369; staff study by, 199; and withdrawal of AFG, 247

Pichon, Stephen, 80, 292

Poincaré, Raymond: and Foch, 89–90; and Tardieu, 91; writes Clemenceau, 91, 299; becomes premier, 192, 216; and aggressive policy, 221, 224–225, 233, 236, 237, 293, 361, 367; and AFG, 237, 238, 248; and Hughes, 244–247; and Allen's overture, 250; and Armistice, 269

Poland, 6, 83, 84, 203, 216, 219

Polk, Frank, 125–126, 133–135, 138, 140, 149, 151, 154, 160

Porter, Stephen, 335

Preliminary treaty with Germany, proposed, 74–75, 293

Press, Rhineland, regulations for, 38, 46, 149, 159, 219, 351

Productive pledges, French demand for, 236, 243, 251, 362

Prohibition in U.S., 212, 226, 252

Protocol affair (December 1919), 133–134, 150, 323

Prussia, 26, 29, 113; protest by government of, 153; new constitution of, 203; Diet of, 240. *See also* German government in Rhineland

Quin, Percy, 141

Radicals, French, 327

Railway Commission, Inter-Allied, 159

Index

Railways, Rhenish: French efforts to militarize, 155, 221–222, 230; strikes threatened in, 221–222, 223; proposed destruction of strategic, 225

Rapallo, Russo-German Treaty of, 216

Rathenau, Walther, 113, 215, 221, 341; and AFG, 198, 223–224, 229, 238, 356, 358; assassinated, 236

Rathenau-Loucheur Agreement, 215, 341

Rayburn, Sam, 141

Reductions in American army of occupation, 41–42, 126, 180, 190, 191, 219, 222, 227, 340, 355, 358

Reed, James, 184, 186, 188, 245, 246, 366

Regulation of Rhineland press, 38, 58–59

Reichskommissar for Occupied Regions, 114, 158, 168, 214, 220, 238, 350; French attempt to abolish office of, 208–209, 225, 230; functions of, 326

Reichstag, 173, 216, 228, 241, 286

Reichswehr, 34, 166

Reparations, 18, 68, 74, 83, 84, 90, 91, 92, 93, 98, 111, 113, 116, 117, 155, 165, 195, 203, 233, 254, 259, 261; House's compromise on, 85; Erzberger on, 115; interim committee on, 132, 152; Anglo-French agreement on, 182, 183; Hughes rebuffs German offer on, 182, 214; apportionment of, 192–194; negotiations on, 203–204, 210; German attempt to fulfill, 215–216, 218, 229, 235; burgeoning crisis regarding, 233–237, 244–245; and security, 237; Hughes plan for, 245–246

Reparations Commission, 90, 132, 155, 179, 183, 191, 192, 193, 195, 204, 216, 225, 236, 243, 244, 245, 247, 248, 299, 337, 342, 344

Repington, Charles, 210, 254

Republicans: American, 78, 127, 130, 176, 179, 184, 187, 197, 246, 249–250, 335, 370; French, 162, 203, 216, 327

Requisitions in Rhineland, 37, 46–47, 208

Rhenish republic, 7, 67, 70, 75, 76, 77, 80, 90, 111, 112, 285, 294–295

Rhineland, 23, 31, 39, 62, 66, 67, 68, 76, 77, 80–81, 91, 94, 95, 99, 103, 107, 110, 111, 123, 125, 130, 132, 137, 139, 140, 175, 177, 181, 183–184, 188, 189, 209, 210, 222, 240, 247, 334; French attitudes on, 6, 8; American-British attitudes on, 7 f.; proposed occupation of, 11; Foch's questions on, 13; Clemenceau's promise regarding, 19–20, 271–272; history and character of, 26–27; post-Armistice situation in, 44–46, 48–49; German attempts to protect, 55–59, 63–64; Clemenceau's policy on, 68–69; Americans focus on, 72–73, 291–292; French notes on, 83, 293–294; interrelationships with, 84–85; Allied agreement on, 86–89, 298; Anglo-American concern about, 100–101; modus vivendi regarding, 105–106; discussed by Americans, 108; German counterproposals regarding, 114–115; and Rhineland Agreement, 119–122, 304; French goods in, 156; French urge to control, 164; Harding's attitudes on, 181–183; as European cockpit, 199, 204; Poincaré's desire to dominate, 225

Rhineland Agreement, 119–122, 126, 128, 135, 138, 144, 153, 157, 159, 160, 172, 173, 241, 304, 310, 311, 326, 356; meetings on, 157–159; Noyes fights to preserve, 163–165; Allen fights to preserve, 232, 239

Rhineland Commission, Inter-Allied, 98, 101, 102, 126, 131, 152, 156; struggle to establish, 103–106; and future ordinances, 150–151; during autumn 1919, 154–156; Conger on, 308

Rhine pact, proposed, 243, 365

Rhine Province, 26, 27, 29, 39

Rhine River, 4, 10, 14–15, 26, 29, 30, 41, 43, 51, 52, 55, 57, 63, 64, 66, 67, 73–75, 77, 84, 93, 96, 117, 122, 124, 130, 131, 137, 144, 145, 158, 169, 172, 174, 181, 182, 186, 187, 189, 198, 213,

Index

221, 222, 224, 229, 233, 238, 247, 254, 255, 256, 292
Ribot, Alexandre, 265
Robertson, Malcolm, 167, 202, 209, 219, 322; and Noyes, 168, 330; and Allen, 210–211, 217, 353; biography of, 329, 349
Robertson, Gen. Sir William, 304
Robinson, Joseph, 366
Roehrer, Erich, 171
Rogers, Will, 257
Rolin-Jacquemyns, Baron Edouard, 151, 167, 202, 208, 209, 217, 221–222, 223, 225, 240, 251, 330; biography of, 322
Roosevelt, Franklin D., 280–281
Roosevelt, Theodore, 3
Rosenberg, Frederic von, 248
Roussellier, Amedée, 322
Ruhr ports, 182, 204, 214, 217, 228, 255
Ruhr rebellion, 166–167
Ruhr region, 26, 44, 133, 138, 139, 155, 167, 225, 239, 241, 251; French desire to occupy, 163, 164, 167, 172, 179, 316, 324; Allied threats to occupy, 183, 203, 204; Franco-Belgian occupation of, 192, 231, 232, 243, 246, 247, 248, 253, 256, 259, 260, 261, 367; rumors on occupation of, 236, 245; final evacuation of, 255
Rumors of American withdrawal from Rhine, 170, 190, 211, 219, 227, 235, 238
Russia, 74, 79, 109, 127, 142, 146, 203; critics of intervention in, 296
Ryan, Col. Rupert, 349, 369

Saar region, 5, 29, 62, 63, 67, 72, 81, 84–86, 111; mines of, 193, 194, 289, 291, 342
Sanctions, Allied. See Ruhr ports; Economic sanctions
San Remo conference, 140, 169, 172, 317
Scapa Flow, 133
Scheidemann, Philipp, 55, 57, 61, 113, 123
Schools, Rhineland, 59, 158, 219, 354
Scott, James Brown, 151
Second Division, U.S., 30, 35, 128, 275

Secret treaties, 129
Self-determination, 56, 75, 76, 84
Senate, French, 87, 90
Senate, U.S., 90, 124–125, 128, 130, 134, 136, 142, 169, 176, 181, 188, 189, 197, 296; and Treaty of Versailles, 132, 137, 144, 160, 175, 261; and Treaty of Berlin, 186–187, 190; and withdrawal, 246–247, 366
Senegalese, 65, 287
Senlis conference, 14–15, 269
Separatism, German, 27, 203, 215
Separatism, Rhenish, 27, 33, 62, 207, 242, 259, 307; French encouragement of, 57, 97, 108, 109, 111–113, 138, 159, 164, 216, 217, 219, 220–221, 228, 237, 254, 258, 291, 305, 324; coups involving, 97, 108, 111–113, 139, 238, 363; German discouragement of, 237
Service des Territoires Rhénans, 36–37
Seventh Corps, U.S., 275
Severing, Carl, 238
Seymour, Charles, 72
Siberia, 131; American intervention in, 125, 130
Silesia, 121, 217, 219; plebiscite in, 129, 191, 215; U.S. involvement in, 129–130, 313; League decision on, 216, 218
Silesian brigade, American, 126, 129, 131, 148–149, 180
Simons, Walter, 207
Smeets, Joseph, 220; case, 220–221, 225, 228, 237, 240–241
Smith, Gen. H. A., 39, 45
Smuts, Gen. Jan Christian, 115–116, 300, 309
Social Democratic Party, German, 53–55, 122–123, 173, 275, 283
Socialists, French, 327
Soldier-worker councils, German, 34, 35–36, 53, 274–275, 276
Solf, Wilhelm, 55–56, 64, 285
Sonnino, Baron Sidney, 18
Spa Conference, 172, 193, 203, 317
Spartacists, 53, 166
Springfield Republican, 142, 177
Starck, Carl von, 168, 171, 172, 205,

439

Index

207, 214, 323, 324, 330, 332; and ordinances, 159, 326; and removal
from office, 208, 209; biography of,
326
State Department, U.S., 45, 124, 127,
132, 135, 136, 138, 139, 140, 152, 165,
169, 175, 179, 193, 205, 206, 223, 224,
252, 268, 316, 352, 355, 371
Stevenson, Frances, 295
Stone, Col. David, 322, 347, 354
Strassburg bridgehead, 20, 56
Stresemann, Gustav, 254
Stuart, Sir Harold, 97, 160–161, 166,
207, 211, 304, 331; and Tirard, 103–
105; prepares draft of convention,
107–108; appointed High Commissioner, 151; and Noyes, 155, 156,
165, 329; and Rhineland Agreement, 163–164, biography of, 302–
303
Submarine warfare, German, 2, 14
Supreme Council, Allied, 159, 195,
204, 217
Supreme Economic Council (of Paris
Peace Conference), 48, 49, 103, 107–
108, 157, 303; established, 46; subcommittee of, on Germany, 101,
104, 108, 151; and Wise report, 101–
102; and compromise with Foch,
105–106
Supreme War Council, Allied, 10, 42,
92, 119, 132, 133, 134, 145, 152, 160
Suspension of German officials, Allied, 212, 351
Swem, Charles, 294
Switzerland, 27

Tardieu, André, 82, 88, 266, 362; prepares fourth French agenda, 69;
negotiates with House and Balfour,
75–76, 293–294; as member of
special committee, 77; and guarantee treaty, 80, 296–297; Wilson
warns, 86; and Poincaré, 91
Telephone and telegraph in Rhineland, 38, 47, 149, 155
Tenth Army, French, 111, 328
Third Army, U.S., 33, 34, 35, 39, 43,
44, 48, 51, 53, 59, 60, 64–65, 112, 148;
established, 30–31; Memorandum

No. 4 of, 37; attitudes of, 46, 50;
prepared for advance, 122, demo-
bilized, 146. See also Attitudes in
American army
Third Corps, U.S., 275
Third Division, U.S., 30, 128, 275, 320
Thirty-second division, U.S., 30, 32,
35, 275, 277
Thwaites, Gen. William, 106
Tilson, John, 199, 235, 345
Tirard, Paul, 37, 101, 102, 155, 160–
161, 206, 214, 358; delays Rhineland
Commission, 103–105; appointed
High Commissioner, 151; on
schools and military council, 153–
154, 323, 324; and "Hole in the
West," 156; manipulates High
Commission, 163, 164, 167; and
Allen, 206–209, 217, 219–225, 238,
239, 347; and Smeets case, 220–221;
and Ruhr occupation, 248, 250–251;
biography of, 276
Tobacco monopoly law in Rhineland, 164
Trade, foreign, American interest in,
45, 125–126, 132, 175, 188–189, 258,
338
Trade regulations, German: Allied
disregard for, 57; German demands
on, 64
Trier, 29, 39; arrival of Americans in,
34, 275
Tripartite alliance. See Guarantee
treaties

Underwood, Oscar, 132, 184, 195
United States, 82, 86, 95, 96, 97, 105,
124, 126, 127, 133, 135, 137, 138, 145,
149, 153–154, 165, 172, 179, 192, 242;
war fever in, 4; public apprehension in, 78–79; guaranteed role by
Rhineland Agreement, 121; opinion
divided in, 142–143, 319; impact of
occupation upon, 143; and Frankfurt occupation, 167–168; German
feelings about, 171–172, 230; and
black horror, 178; xenophobia in,
189; and army costs, 192–198, 341–
342, 344; response of, to European
crisis, 200–201, 235, 244–246, 346;